Meaning and Power in a Southeast Asian Realm

Meaning and Power in a Southeast Asian Realm

SHELLY ERRINGTON

Princeton University Press PRINCETON, NEW JERSEY

Copyright © 1989 by Princeton University Press

Published by Princeton University Press, 41 William Street, Princeton, New Jersey 08540

In the United Kingdom: Princeton University Press, Guildford, Surrey

This book has been composed in Linotron Galliard

Clothbound editions of Princeton University Press books
are printed on acid-free paper, and binding materials are
chosen for strength and durability. Paperbacks, although satisfactory
for personal collections, are not usually suitable for library rebinding

Printed in the United States of America by Princeton University Press
Princeton, New Jersey

Library of Congress Cataloging-in-Publication Data

Errington, Shelly, 1944-
    Meaning and power in a Southeast Asian realm / Shelly
    Errington.
        p. cm.
    Bibliography: p.
    Includes index.
    ISBN 0-691-09445-4
    1. Ethnology—Indonesia—Luwu. 2. Spatial behavior—
Indonesia—Luwu. 3. Luwu (Indonesia)—Social life and customs. I.
Title.
GN635.I65E76   1989
306'.09598'4—dc19   88-39412
                                                   CIP

For my mother, Elizabeth Baker Johnson

Contents

Acknowledgments

It was my privilege during fieldwork to live in the Palopo and Senga households of *almarhum* [the deceased] Andi Pangerang Opu Tosinilele, his wife Opu Damira, and his sister Opu Senga. Their children, niece, and household members were always helpful. Thanks are due to Andi Kaso' for good conversation and to Dr. Pangerang and Andi Nurhayati for hospitality in Ujung Pandang. Special thanks are due the oldest son of Opu Tosinilele and Opu Damira, Andi Muchlis Pangerang, known as "Andi Anthon," whose help throughout my research was invaluable. It is rare in any society to come across such gracious, well-informed, and intellectually curious people, particularly a whole family interested in how their society functioned and functions, and frank about its politics. Aside from knowledge and stimulating company, the family offered me hospitality and protection. I hope that "Opu Lele," as he was affectionately known throughout South Sulawesi, would have found this book interesting and true, and that his descendants and extended family will view it as a tribute to their *ToMatoa*, respected elder.

My hosts in Ujung Pandang for several months were Datu Hasan and Datu Batari, who also generously shared many insights and observations about their society. I studied Buginese with *almarhum* Pak La Side' Daeng Tapala, who was an exceptional intellectual. I am grateful to have been given the opportunity in 1976 to present a lecture, "Siri', Darah, dan Kekuasaan Politik didalam Kerajaan Luwu Jaman Dulu," at Hasanuddin University; among those present were Pak Mattulada, Pak Abu Hasan, Andi Zainal Abidin, and Pak Dharmawan, with whom I had interesting conversations on that and other occasions.

Many island Southeast Asian peoples reckon forebears bilaterally, and may regard collaterals in senior generations as forebears, too, facts that multiply the number of people one might legitimately count as forebears into somewhat astronomical numbers; and so such peoples are notorious, in Western commentary, for tracing themselves *to* prominent ancestors rather than *from* almost infinite possible forebears. I understand their position perfectly as I struggle with the other half of the acknowledgments, the half that acknowledges the help one had before and after fieldwork instead of during, which is harder to pinpoint because more diffuse, though no less deeply felt.

Like all students of island Southeast Asia, my debt to Clifford Geertz is more than personal. The generally high quality of scholarship on Indonesia is due in part to the long Dutch tradition of careful work on the area, which contemporary scholars can build upon; but more immediately ancestral to American anthropology is the formulation of the issues laid out in the 1950s and 1960s by Clifford Geertz. Regardless of whether or not later authors agree with his general approach or the specifics of his arguments, the interest of our work to a broader audience than area specialists, is due in part to the fact that the topics he addressed were worth developing, modifying, or refuting. My debt to Clifford Geertz's and Hildred Geertz's work on Java and Bali is also more specific: in this book I have touched upon, developed, or viewed differently many of the topics addressed in their works. Finally, I would like to thank each of them for conversation and sustained interest in this project.

Benedict Anderson's writings on cultural configurations and expressions of power, especially his classic "The Idea of Power in Javanese Society," stand more like the "parent" than a remote "ancestor" of this book. I am grateful to him for the inspiration of his always enlightening writing and for his unfailing kindness in difficult times.

David Schneider's views on kinship have been liberating for me. I am grateful to him for conversation and friendship as well as his most useful insight.

Although I wrote this book and did the fieldwork on which it is based several years after completing the Ph.D., I want to acknowledge two of my teachers in graduate school. From Victor Turner I learned social anthropology from the inside, developing an interest in "kinship" and the dynamics of social organization evident in this book's Part III. From James Siegel I learned an attitude of mind, which can be summarized briefly as the willingness not to get off the bus before you reach the end of the line, regardless of how at odds with common sense the route and end-point are.

So much for ancestors: what about siblings, cousins, and allies?

For many conversations over many years, for their generous sharing of ideas and references, and for the inspiration of their writing, I owe a great deal to James Boon, Ward Keeler, Bradd Shore, and the late and much-missed Shelly Rosaldo. For conversations lately, especially concerning Southeast Asian gender, I am grateful to Jane Atkinson. Without the lively interest, encouragement, and generosity of these people and their writings on subjects of relevance, this book would have been different and poorer. Susan McKinnon, Elizabeth Traube, and Valerio Valeri have educated me as best they could about Eastern Indonesia, and my vision of the area, as is evident in Chapter Eight, relies heavily on theirs.

Several people have read part or all of this book or earlier versions of it. Hildred Geertz gave an early draft a careful and generous reading, as did Elizabeth Coville, and Patricia Horvatich and Bradd Shore read late drafts. Jane Collier, James Peacock, and Renato Rosaldo each read the conclusions and commented usefully on them. David Schneider has ferreted out lingering biologism in Part III, or at least has attempted to do so. All have made useful comments.

Copyediting was done at various stages by Kathy Weston and Janet Robinson; both of them improved the manuscript. My copyeditor at Princeton University Press, Sherry Wert, combined non-intrusive editing with an intelligent reader's confusions and misunderstandings, which induced me to rewrite rather more than I had anticipated or wished would be necessary. The book is much the better for it.

Parts of several chapters have been published previously. I am grateful to the *Journal of Asian Studies*, the Yale University Southeast Asia Program, and *Cultural Anthropology*, respectively, for permission to reprint the following: "Embodied Sumange' in Luwu" (1983), "The Place of Regalia in Luwu" (1983), and "Incestuous Twins and the House Societies of Island Southeast Asia" (1987). (Complete bibliographical information can be found in the References.)

Fieldwork was supported by the Ford Foundation Southeast Asia Fellowship; the John D. and Catherine T. MacArthur Foundation provided support during the book's writing.

Notes on Orthography, Pronunciation, and Language

A glossary of most-used terms is provided after the text.

There is no standardized romanization of Buginese script, so various writers use their own methods. The conventions I will use for Indonesian, Buginese, and Tae are simple and few.

Five of the six vowels, *a, e, i, o,* and *u,* are pronounced as they are in Spanish or Italian (without diphthongs). The sixth, which occurs in Buginese and many local versions of Indonesian, is called *pepet* in Indonesian, written "*e,*" and pronounced like the *u* in "understand." The other *e* is often written in Buginese romanized script with an accent to differentiate it from the *pepet*; when that *e* comes at the end of the word, I have added the accent, otherwise not.

These languages do not pluralize except, in certain circumstances, through doubling. Rather than add an "*s*" to Austronesian words to make them plural, I have left them in their original forms and use either plural or singular verbs with them in English, depending on my meaning.

The word in Buginese and Tae for "human" is *tau,* pronounced "to" when joined to a modifier, such as *toraja,* "people of the interior." (The term *raja* in this case is an Austronesian word, not the Indian word *raja* meaning "ruler.") Throughout this book I have capitalized *To* and its modifier and joined them together as a single word in order to simplify recognition of the construction. Thus we have *ToLuwu,* "people of Luwu"; *ToLaing,* "other people" or "alien people" or "strangers"; *ToMatoa,* "respected elder"; etc. The exception is *toraja,* which is spelled as in Indonesian.

Buginese and Tae languages have glottal stops, often represented in romanized script by an apostrophe, e.g., *Pa'Bicara.* The same sound in Indonesian is usually represented with a final *k,* e.g., *Pak.*

I have used most of the same conventions in romanized script for Buginese and Tae as are used for Indonesian. *P, t,* and initial *k* are used but are not aspirated. *C* in Indonesian is pronounced "ch," so that *Bicara* is pronounced "bichara," and *baca-baca* is pronounced "bacha-bacha."

Many Buginese words end with the sound "ng," like *arung*, "noble" or "lord," and *daeng*, "older sibling" and also a noble status-title. In spoken Buginese, the first consonant of the next word after an *ng* ending usually doubles and the *ng* sound is dropped. The name of a famous seventeenth-century Bone ruler and warrior, then, can be written "Arung Palakka," but it can be written "Aru Palaka," which corresponds to the way it would be written in Buginese script, or even "Aruppalakka," as it is pronounced. Similarly, two middle-noble names could be written "Daeng Parenreng" and "Daeng Massiga," but are pronounced "Depparenreng" and "Demmasiga." *Ng* undergoes other transformations as well. In most cases where an *ng* is dropped in the spoken language, I have separated the spelling of the two words in the written version so that the constituent words are recognizable.

Readers familiar with Austronesian languages, especially with Indonesian, may be interested in similar constructions in Buginese and Tae. The Indonesian ke——an construction corresponds roughly to the Buginese a——eng and the Tae a——ang. In modern Indonesian, the ke——an construction can sometimes be used to make abstract nouns, whereas that is seldom if ever the case in Buginese, Tae, and the old Malay from which Indonesian is derived. Thus the Malay word *kerajaan* (from *raja*, "ruler") and the Buginese word *akkarungeng* (from *arung*, "lord" or "noble") mean not "kingship" but "kingdom," or, more accurately, "a place where a ruler occurs."

Like many Philippine languages, intransitive Buginese and Tae sentences often begin with *ma* followed by a "predicate root" preceded and/or followed by modifying particles, followed by a pronoun. Most "predicate roots," which are the bases of either verbs, adjectives, or nouns when modified by the appropriate syllables and translated into English, are virtually never used alone. Translating accurately to preserve a "part of speech" that in fact emerges only in the context of a sentence in Buginese or Tae is therefore awkward, and I have compromised somewhat in various instances. One instance is *mabusung*, the state of being afflicted by a malady that strikes people who offend the hierarchical ranking of the cosmos. *Busung*, the root, is simply not a word; *abusungeng* is the noun in Buginese, but it is seldom heard; what one hears quite often are sentences using *mabusung*, and I have usually treated the word as though it were the noun rather than an incomplete sentence. A few other instances of this sort of compromise occur in the book.

Because three languages were used in fieldwork, I have indicated which is being used when the context would otherwise be unclear with the notations "Ind.," "Bug.," or "Tae"; e.g., " 'the center' (Ind. *pusat*, Bug. *posik*)."

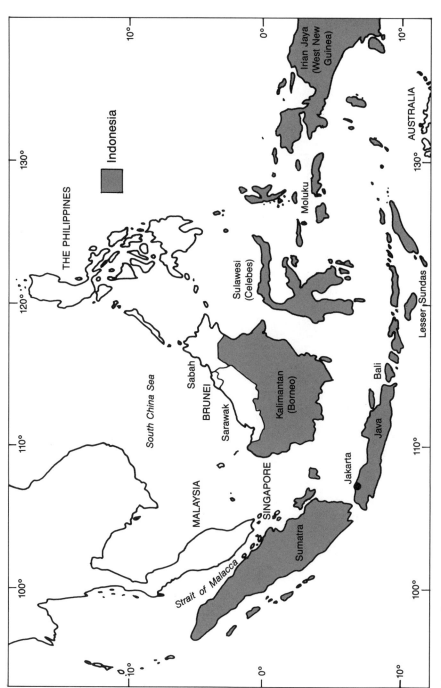

Map 1. Indonesia

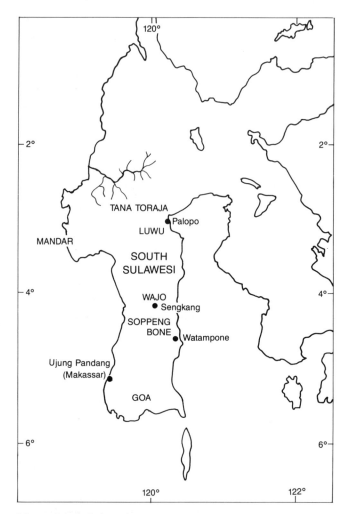

Map 2. South Sulawesi

Meaning and Power in a Southeast Asian Realm

Introduction
The Problem of Meaning
in the Study of Politics

From Hobbes's Leviathan to "the student body," the body has provided, in Western political thought, an image of the polity. A "corporation" is a legal body with "members" and a "head." A nation's "head of state," appropriately enough, lives in a "capital" city. It would seem natural enough that the head should be the part of the body used to image superiority and leadership. Yet throughout hierarchical Southeast Asia, the ruler of the polity was said to be not the head of state but its navel.

The difference between a ruler called "the navel of the world" and one called "head of the body politic" seems at first glance a trivial one—no more than a difference in figures of speech. I did not think a great deal about the significance of this difference myself until I did anthropological fieldwork in a former "Indic State" of Southeast Asia called Luwu, now incorporated into the Republic of Indonesia as a sub-district of South Sulawesi (formerly Celebes). There, under the protection and sponsorship of the former polity's chief minister, I studied the construction of the "person" and the relations between leaders and followers. I came to appreciate the fact that important figures of speech, like important words, do not travel lightly from one language to another. Imbedded in alien worlds, they are immobile. At best one can visit them, and return to tell the tale.

The tale told in this book concerns the meaning of the "center" or "navel" in the shape of political life and the way the "person" is construed and socially constituted in Luwu. Many of the facts I report and points I make will resonate with what is known about other hierarchical polities, former and current, of Southeast Asia. The polity's central city was the polity itself, as many commentators have pointed out.[1] The conduct of the ruler and the safety of the state regalia, whose presence located the realm's most central and socially highest point, were considered crucial to the prosperity and peace of the entire realm. The ruler in these polities was the fount of social

---

[1] The literature on the topic of what Geertz calls "the exemplary center" is more or less coextensive with the topic of Southeast Asian Indic States. Some of the most useful and concise statements can be found in Anderson 1972; C. Geertz 1968: 36-39; C. Gertz 1980; Moertono 1968; Schrieke 1957; and Tambiah 1976: ch. 7.

and political status, the high and concentrated location of the spiritual potency on which the fertility and prosperity of the realm and the individual person alike were thought to depend. Deeply centrist, Southeast Asian polities represented themselves to themselves as perfect, undivided, centered unities. For them, dualities of any sort implied challenge, instability, and the possibility of de-centering. Needless to say, the political center's goal was to remain central: to remain unchallenged, immobile, and eternally stable. Just as obvious as the ideal of stability was the difficulty of attaining it; before colonial powers fixed their boundaries, Southeast Asian political centers sometimes became de-centered. Not just polities but persons were (and continue to be) conceptualized there as centered entities that embody and locate cosmic energy, which, in Luwu, is attached at the navel. The centering and de-centering of realms, whether the realms we term "Indic States" or those we call merely "persons," is the process that I analyze as "political" in this book.

A basic part of my account, then, is the local concept of the "person"—how the person's anatomy, motives, and consciousness are locally construed. Some notion of the person is inevitable in any account of social life, for no social theory can avoid postulating a concept of the person, a "psychology" (broadly defined here as a conception of motivations and perceptual schemata) that is compatible with itself. The people who inhabit the worlds described by economists are aware that there are no free lunches; they continually weigh costs and benefits in order to reach their economic goals. Those who dwell in the imaginative universes of political scientists are engaged in calculating their own advantage as they pursue wealth, status, and power. Durkheimian people need to be recharged, so to speak, for social life through collective ritual activity; Lévi-Straussian people occupy themselves full-time in thinking contrastively, and when they suffer, it is less from physical pain than from unintelligibility; Geertzian people think and live in public forms, making meaning from anything that comes to hand, from cockfights to naming systems. Any writer (whether social theorist, novelist, historian . . .) who makes an effort to avoid imputing a motivational structure and taken-for-granted understandings to the people who inhabit the imaginative world she or he creates, can succeed only in making those elements implicit in the text.

Just as every social theory postulates, explicitly or implicitly, a psychology compatible with itself, so do social systems. A social system postulates, as it were, the sorts of people who will respond to its rewards and abide by its rules, and then goes about trying to create them (the process is called "socialization").

Since I cannot write about a social system without presuming a set of understandings and rhetoric of motives for the people who inhabit the world I create through writing, I have tried to make this "psychology" as near a local one as I am able. The social selves from Luwu that I write about in this book exhibit local passions and sensibilities rather than a putatively universal human nature. Their "psychology" is compatible with their own thinking about the nature of their society, their own version of social theory, which is predicated on the notion of a center, a navel of the world, towards which all peripheral matter (including humans) is oriented.

Inserting a local notion of the person (as near as I can fathom it) into my account rather than importing a putatively global one to it is imbedded in a larger argument, which has to do with the central issue of the book: how to reconcile the study of meaning with the study of "politics." Meaning, I take it, is largely embodied in local forms of activity and thought, which are intimately bound to context and to local ideas about what is real. Studies of "politics," by contrast, have tended to discount the surfaces and forms in which politics is conducted in favor of the alleged universals that political activity presumably displays—the nature of "power," for instance, or the political actor as calculating maximizer. Clifford Geertz makes this point sweepingly, if briefly, in his conclusion to *Negara: The Theater State in Nineteenth-Century Bali* (1980), where he lists several "tired commonplaces" about the nature of the state: the "great beast" views à la Hobbes's Leviathan; the "great fraud" theories, in which the state is seen as a mechanism by the elite to extract surpluses from the masses; the populist view that sees it as an expression of the spirit of the community; and the liberal or pluralist models that see politics as "an endless jockeying for marginal advantage." Different though these views of the state are, Geertz points out, they all view "political symbology from myth, insignia, and etiquette to palaces, titles, and ceremonies, [as] but the instrument of purposes concealed beneath it or towering over it" (C. Geertz 1980: 122-23).

The two views of politics that have most commonly been applied in modern times to Southeast Asia are those derived from Marx and those liberal ones derived from Utilitarianism. The work in each of these traditions has told us valuable things about the conduct of politics in Southeast Asian societies and states; and, of course, the work derived from each tradition can be argued against on various grounds. I do not want to survey or review either one here, but only to discuss briefly the postulated "person" in Utilitarian-derived theories in order to show its shortcomings for the study of meaning. (Different points could be made about the shortcomings of certain strands of Marxist thought for the study of meaning.) I use the term "Utilitarian" loosely for those schools of social science that view political actors as maximizing calculators, a stance that in the study of

Southeast Asia tends, for instance, to cast relations between "patrons" and "clients" as implicit contracts for mutual advantage, or to cast peasants as rational decision-makers calculating their benefits and losses. These studies are not "untrue," for they tell us something of value; but they are of limited use as ways to understand the meanings, hence the forms, of the actions and institutions they describe and analyze.

The postulated political actors featured in accounts of politics emanating from the liberal varieties of Anglo-American social science are preeminently rational, calculating maximizers (whether conscious of it or not) of wealth, status, and power. Calculation, maximization, rationality, and the pursuit of "real" advantage ought in theory to be separable notions, but in fact they all usually imply each other. In *The Passions and the Interests: The Political Arguments for Capitalism before Its Triumph* (1977), Albert O. Hirschman has traced the historical reasons why this is so by pointing out that the idea of being "rational" came to be merged with "calculation" in Europe in the seventeenth and eighteenth centuries; to maximize one's wealth, one must apply reason calculatingly; eventually "rationality" itself came to mean calculation of advantage, particularly "real" advantage (paradigmatically wealth, but with status and power admissable runners-up; seldom merely "symbolic" advantage).

This model of human nature and motivation is undeniably useful for certain purposes. Moreover, it is the enabling assumption of several major strands of Anglo-American social science, which without it would be, simply, a different enterprise from what it is. The study of "politics" in this tradition is especially unimaginable without it, for what is meant by a "political" analysis (as opposed to some other kind) is one that shows the processes by which some people gain or maintain advantage.

Nonetheless, those of us who study non-Western traditions often feel somewhat dubious about and even hostile to maximizing models of human nature applied to exotic social processes, and our discomfort has several sources. "Economic Man" was originally postulated as a convenient fiction in order to analyze a market *as if* people maximized, not to suggest that they actually do. "Political Man" broadened the realms to which the maximizing model could be applied by allowing the imaginary people of these worlds to seek status and power as well as wealth. Yet when an analysis attributes the motivational structure and frame of mind of Economic Man or Political Man to humans who happen not to be buying stocks and bonds in a monetized economy, the effect is to suggest that people actually think and feel in terms of advantage and utility. (Insofar as they do not, in this model, they are "irrational"—which has more or less the status of sin). And as the root metaphors derived from activities compatible with a money economy (the language of contracts, of calculated reciprocity, of saving and wasting limited resources) increasingly seep into the discourse within which Anglo-Americans describe everyday life, such a model of human motivation becomes a part of our local "common sense." Thus it is that sociological, psychological, economic, and political analyses originating in the industrial West that postulate Utilitarian models of human motivation "ring true" to Western readers, who in effect are reading about themselves. Such analyses both reflect a common-sense folk model of motivation and, by casting experience in its terms, help to constitute that model as "natural" in readers' minds and sensibilities.

If nothing else, this model of human nature impoverishes the language with which we speak of human experiences, narrowing our understandings of human motives and possibilities, domesticating the world by making it all too familiar. Moreover, to make a particular local psychology appear universal is, in Roland Barthes's useful expression, to "mythologize" it: to make what is cultural and historical appear natural and inevitable. Part of my rejection of a maximizing model to explain the motivational structure of the people in this book, and my replacement of it with something closer to their own views of themselves, is attributable simply to a wish not to mythologize Utilitarianism.

Anything can be evaluated in terms of a utility function in classic Utilitarianism, for whatever a person is maximizing can be considered his goal. It need not be wealth, or status, or power, or advantage in any commonly recognizable form. It could be risk-avoidance (rather than wealth) for a hungry peasant, or even pain for a masochist. Thus as a model of human nature, Utilitarianism is incontrovertible; nothing can contradict it: it is "true" by tautology (cf. Gellner 1965). Nonetheless, once a goal is fixed (for example, wealth), "irrationality" (failure to maximize) is possible. Therefore the postulation of "rationality" generates the specter of irrationality, its unavoidable flip side.

When a liberal post-World War II social scientist imagines only two possibilities for depicting the actors in a political or economic study, as either rational (calculating real advantage) or irrational (innocent, naive, mystical), there is an understandable tendency to attempt to dignify the objects of study by insisting that they are "rational." For instance, Samuel Popkin, a political scientist who writes on Southeast Asia (Vietnam), proposes 'a view of the peasant as a rational problem-solver, with a sense both of his own interests and of the need to bargain with others to achieve mutually acceptable outcomes. I hope to leave the reader not with pity for peasants or with a longing to recapture their presumed innocence and simplicity, but with a respect for the intelligence with which they develop practical solutions to the complex problems of resource allocation, authority, and dispute settlement that every society faces" (Popkin 1979:x). The urge to "dignify" them in this way is probably most marked when the study is of people outside the Western tradition, where to suggest that the people are not "rational" in this narrow sense can be construed, and regularly is, as an indication that the analyst views them as mystical, irrational, naive, or dis-interested. But in my view, the question of peasants' and others' rationality versus irrationality or naivety emerges due to a failure of imagination: it emerges only when rationality is given a rather narrow definition, and when only this definition of "rationality" and its opposite come to be seen as exhausting the universe of human possibilities. (For a discussion of these issues in Southeast Asian studies, see Keyes 1983; Popkin 1979; and Scott 1976.)

The sub-discipline known as "political anthropology" adopted the idea of the rational maximizer and inserted him into the social processes of ex-otic places. This move allowed anthropologists to conceptualize very alien ways of life as "political systems" and their denizens, e.g., "The African," as seekers of wealth, status, and power. The forms in which these exotic societies cast wealth, status, and power, however, may be all but unrecog-nizable—from leopard-skin capes to tasteless tubers. In the tautological version of Utilitarianism, the oddness of maximizable goals is of no con-sequence. But there is a strong tendency on the part of social scientists using the utility model to imagine not only that the only way to be rational is to calculate advantage, but that the advantages either are or should be "real" ones, that is, ones the analyst believes are worth attaining. This usu-ally unstated but strongly held assumption tends to put "symbols" in the utility model in more or less the same place that one finds "false conscious ness" in a Marxist one. A tension almost necessarily emerges in these stud-ies between the postulated rationality of the political actor and the goals he strives to achieve, which often seem "irrational," that is, merely "sym-bolic." Evans-Pritchard articulates this tension succinctly in his introduc-tion to *African Political Systems*: "The African does not see beyond the sym-bols; it might well be held that if he understood their objective meaning, they would lose the power they have over him. This power lies in their symbolic content. . . ." (Evans-Pritchard 1940: 18). "The African," it seems, believes himself to be pursuing what is real, but the goals he takes as real are actually merely symbolic; if "The African" understood "their objective meaning," their merely symbolic nature, the goals would lose their power over him. In other words, on the one hand, if the analyst insists that the people studied are pursuing "real" advantage (real to the analyst) in spite of appearances, the "symbolic" form in which that advantage is cast in the local culture has to be discounted as inconsequential; on the other hand, if the analyst admits that the symbols themselves are what political actors seek, that assertion is uncomfortably close to suggesting that the political actors are irrational mystics. The status of culture (which is constituted of symbols and values the analyst does not share) as the source of irrationality is especially clear in the literature on economic development during the 1950s and 1960s: "culture" is invoked to explain why "development" (read: "Them" becoming more like "Us," by valuing the accumulation of capital over kinship obligations, growing bank accounts over ritual display, the puritan ethic over sitting at the men's ground smoking tobacco, etc., etc., etc.) fails.

Discounting the goals the political actors imagine they are striving to attain has a long history in social-science approaches to the analysis of politics outside Euro-America. The general message of so many such studies is that maximizing activity (or whatever) is really directed towards different and more abstract goals than the political actors in question realize. The political actors *really* seek wealth, status and power, and only think they are defending their honor, seeking the blessings of the gods, etc. Or (to take an example from another tradition of analysis), peasants *really* have a common-sense view of the superior value of items of real use over mere symbols, or would anyway, if they were not deluded by the ritual language and so forth imposed upon them by a deceiving elite. (In this sort of study, one has the feeling that all the good and real things—surplus crops, obedience, and political support—travel from the bottom of the system to its top, while all the false and worthless things—symbols, ritual language, and myths—travel from the top down.) Thus the task of the analyst is to unmask the really real, which lies behind a fog of superstition, false consciousness, bad faith, psychological and material investment (depending on the analyst's own views of what is really real)—in short, *culture*. In this book I have taken seriously the goals that political actors strive to attain. Because humans make real through practice what they think is real, their ideas about these things are not either superstition or false consciousness but what becomes socially real. Only by attending to those ideas can we understand the *forms* in which they conduct their lives.

To be an analysis of "politics" in our time and language, an account of a society must address the competition for wealth, status, and power. No less than other cultural forms, wealth, status, and power are local, predicated on a metaphysics and consequently an epistemology that may be different from those of the observer. "Power," for example, in Luwu and other Southeast Asian Indic States, is basic to the polity's shape and meaning. This "power" is not the abstract relation familiar to us but cosmic energy, which could be accumulated by states and still is sought by individuals. This "power" or spiritual potency is itself invisible; people infer its presence by its signs. I have found it useful to regard the former kingdom of Luwu as a vast device, backed by (unstable) force, for restricting access to potency. Actually, since potency could not be perceived directly, it was not so much to potency as to the *signs* of potency, over which political entities had some control, that access was restricted. Among the signs of potency were wealth, status, and influence—the classic threesome of a "political" analysis; but cast in local form, they are signs of potency, not goals in themselves. An analysis of how they are attained must, if it preserves meaning, take seriously their status as signs, and must explicate the ways signs are read and acted upon in Luwu. Regarding the polity as a device for restricting access to the signs of potency allows me to take into account what people thought and think they are striving to attain, the sensibilities and habits of mind they feel obliged to cultivate in order to attain those goals as they conceptualize them and live them, and at the same time to discuss matters necessary to a "political" account, such as force, competition, and structures of inequality.

I came to these topics—the person, the meanings of politics, and their relations—not head-on from a study of political science, but via a rather arcane route: by trying to make some sense of a court text written in archaic Malay.

Interpreting a Text—Literally

Fieldwork stands as the paradigmatic "anthropological" experience, both in the popular mind and in the folklore of the discipline. If all goes as it is supposed to, the fieldworker, immersed in an alien language and set of habits, is forced to confront the Self through the Other, as Ricoeur said. Such serious self-reflection, however, was only minimally my own experience during my first fieldwork, in Papua New Guinea. Other humans can quickly come to seem familiar. Everyday life is everyday life, even in exotic New Guinea.

The radical fieldwork experience I expected came not on a coral island in the South Pacific but several years later in the library. I was reading a text in archaic Malay, written in the court of Malacca-Johor, the polity that lay on the coast of the Malay peninsula and dominated for several centuries the trade travelling through the Strait of Malacca. For my doctoral dissertation I was attempting to understand the meaning and form of one of these court texts of the genre known as *hikayat*.

A contemporary Occidental reader confronting a traditional Malay hikayat is plunged into a world as alien as that of *Beowulf* or *The Song of Roland*, perhaps more so. True, the figures in the hikayat live in a recognizable and named world, Malacca, and they act in ways that are vaguely comprehensible. But the narrative proceeds in episodic lurches, the repetition of elements is pervasive, and it is difficult to locate a temporal or even sequential causal-logical axis. Almost more disturbing, the world that is constituted within and by the text is completely without psychology: without interior motives, without the unfolding of characters.

My model and inspiration for literary analysis during the writing of the dissertation was Erich Auerbach's *Mimesis: The Representation of Reality in Western Literature* ([1946] 1953). Auerbach's method is to move between the smallest particulars of syntax and style and the largest questions about the way that time, the social world, and reality itself are constituted within each text he examines.

Using Auerbach's method of a very close reading of style in order to open onto the largest questions of meaning made me aware of an enormous epistemological chasm between myself and the Malay text. A text read with attention to style—to the surfaces of a world as presented in a text—retains its opacity and unfamiliarity for a very long time. The opposite is true of a text read for deep universals. That sort of reading makes the text seem familiar: eventually and inevitably, the reader discerns the universals sought, because the reader knows what to look for and consequently what to find. Reading for style rather than content or deep structures, I felt baffled, bored, and irritated at alien conventions for which I had no ready set of reader's presuppositions that would have allowed immediate comprehension.

Reading the hikayat made me aware of myself as a reader as nothing had before. By analogy, it made me ponder the enormous amount of equipment—intellectual, sensory, epistemological—that any audience brings to the interpretation of any event. The experience of closely reading an alien text left me with an abiding interest in unravelling the presuppositions that the observer/interpreter brings to the event, whether it be a text, an object, a dance, an utterance, an image. . . . And I came to conceive the act of interpreting as a contrastive enterprise. The gap between the experience of long-dead Malays who listened to a mellifluous and graceful hikayat being chanted and my experience with the "same" hikayat as I struggled over a tediously repetitious and generally opaque written text in private silence involved me in a dialectic of comparison between my foiled expectations and what I discovered before my eyes, between the world's reality as constituted in the text and the world's reality as I discerned it from reading the history and anthropology of the region.

I had willed my own plunge, without flotation platform or compass, into an alien mode of consciousness, and had almost drowned (or so it felt). Yet, after I had resurfaced and made it to shore, Ph.D. in hand, I was dissatisfied with my level of understanding. I had explored the hikayat as well as I could, but I knew the exploration was shallow, given the depths I had begun to fathom. I had snorkeled in the text, and a new world had been revealed. I wanted to dive deeply, taking along only the minimal equipment—sanity in one's own time and space—needed to stay alive.

Three issues stood out in my mind as points of entry into the alien consciousness I had glimpsed.

Most striking was the fact that the people depicted in the hikayat had no interior life to speak of. They were flat and reactive, more like "figures" (to use Propp's phrase) than like the "characters" who inhabit novels (cf. Bastin 1964 and Watt 1957). That the authors and audience of a seventeenth-century Malay court text did not have a nineteenth-century European novelist's view of motivation, nor a European twentieth-century view of psychological motivation, cannot surprise. But what sense *did* they make of those aspects of the self that we call "consciousness," "emotions," "interior life," "motivation," and "psychology"? How did they imagine that individual persons are constituted, emotionally, physically, and spiritually? All humans do have ideas about such matters (although only a few anthropological treatises have tried to explore them). I was unable to infer them from the written text. The most I could do was note the absence of a familiar "rhetoric of motives," to use Burke's phrase.

The second issue was that the hikayat's action was literally centered around the ruler. Like the other figures in the text, the ruler was virtually non-existent as a "personality." Yet the ruler's presence was the reference point that organized action and, in a curious sense, caused it: Action happened because of the ruler's existence, yet he did not order it. I came to think of the function of the ruler's presence in the hikayat as the element that propels action forward and makes the plot happen. In this sense, the function of the ruler's presence in the hikayat came to seem, curiously enough, like an analogue of the function of interior psychological motives in the novel (again, see Watt 1957). What we think of as "interior" motives seemed to be displaced onto or into a figure exterior to the figures of the hikayat, who themselves exhibited no interior subjective life.

Actually, the hikayat's action did not move "forward," in a temporal-causal line, but more or less in circles.[2] I had begun to make sense of the hikayat when I came to realize that it was organized spatially—around the ruler—rather than temporally. The shape of the hikayat's action begins with a ruler of the Upper World who sends his son to earth so that it will have a ruler; the son of that ruler, in turn, becomes ruler of Malacca. From there on, the hikayat consists of stories of the journeys of Hang Tuah, the ruler's high subordinate and loyal henchman, who travels far from the court, and comes back to report to the ruler of Malacca, the center of the world. Each time Hang Tuah travels to a more distant place, and each time he returns to the center. So the plot consists of widening circles and reports back rather than action that unfolds within an overarching temporal frame, which is what European readers of histories and novels have come to expect since the nineteenth century.

Approximately ten years of further investigation of island Southeast Asian symbolic forms has transformed an initial impression into a firm conviction: that spatial metaphors, both implicit and explicit, form a pervasive mode of organizing consciousness in that part of the world. These metaphors are fundamental to the symbolic forms ranging from the deictic structure of pronouns to the plots of shadow theater to the concentric shape of kinship structures. The spatial organization of political life and consciousness is the fundamental organizing principle of this book.

A third issue that stood out in my mind concerned the ontological status of language in local understanding. Words in the hikayat are potent, almost palpable in their presence and effects. I came across Foucault's sentence about the status of words in the Renaissance and it seemed a familiar thought: "Words took their place among rocks and trees. . . ." The arbitrariness of linguistic signs is the fundamental insight, indeed the enabling assumption, of modern linguistics. But most humans do not regard words and sounds as arbitrary, unglued from their referents and inconsequential in their effects. A literature has recently appeared on this very topic within the discipline of anthropology, with titles like *Dangerous Words* (Brenneis and Myer 1984) and *Deadly Words* (Favret-Saada 1980). The topic has a special tone, so to speak, in Southeast Asia, where one sometimes has the impression that some Southeast Asia symbolic forms privilege sound over what we often think of as "meaning" (cf. A. L. Becker 1979; Clifford Geertz 1973b; and James Siegel 1979).

My questions about these issues could be answered not with "causes" but with more comprehensive contexts. I could deepen these questions,

---

[2] I have written on issues of time, space, and narrative in this hikayat in my dissertation (1975b) and two articles (1975a, 1979a).

encountered in the course of unravelling a Malay text, I thought, by doing fieldwork in Southeast Asia. I was fortunate in having friends, Leonard Andaya and Barbara Watson Andaya, both historians of island Southeast Asia, who, knowing something of my interests, suggested a study of the Buginese or the Makassarese, who occupy the southwestern peninsula of the island of Sulawesi (formerly called Celebes) of Indonesia. The Buginese and Makassarese polities of South Sulawesi existed for several centuries prior to the establishment of the Republic of Indonesia, though just how long remains obscure. They were hierarchical and of a recognizably "Indic" cast, roughly comparable in size and complexity to the sultanates of the Malay peninsula. The ideas that informed the conduct of politics in these societies—the search to accumulate potency drawn from formless cosmic energy, the reverence for ancestral legacies in the form of state regalia, the sacredness of the ruler, the mandala pattern in state organization—clearly link them to the historical so-called "Indic States" of Bali, Java, and the Malay peninsula, and to scattered smaller polities elsewhere on the coast of Kalimantan (Borneo) and the islands of the southern Philippines. To a lesser but still marked degree, these notions are reminiscent of those informing the conduct of politics in the great historical states of mainland Southeast Asia, in the countries now known as Burma, Thailand, and Cambodia. Like these other hierarchical states, the Bugis-Makassarese have a very long tradition of writing in script derived from India.[3]

The area seemed promising for research on the sorts of questions I brought from textual studies: questions about space, about language, about the constitution of the person, and most important, about the place of the ruler in the constitution of the meaning of the world.

South Sulawesi and the Circumstances of Fieldwork

Sulawesi is the name given to the orchid-shaped island that lies to the east of Kalimantan (Borneo) and to the west of the Moluccas (Spice Islands) (see Map 1). The Gulf of Bone is formed by the extension of two southern peninsulas, the western and eastern; "South Sulawesi" refers to the southwestern peninsula (see Map 2).

By convention, it is said that four languages are spoken there. In fact, there are many variations and dialects, especially in the northerly part of

[3] A whole issue of *Archipel* was devoted to the Buginese and Makassarese scripts, which are closely related. Among the writings of this area is the "epic" *I La Galigo*, a document of stunning length catalogued by Rudolf Kern (1939). Introductions to aspects of *I La Galigo*, to other lontara' (manuscripts, originally written on palm-leaf), and to aspects of the literature can be found in Abidin 1974 and Pelras 1975a, 1983. Additional material concerning language and literature can be found in Abidin 1971; Hamonic 1987; and Noorduyn 1965.

the peninsula that melds with Central Sulawesi. The four primary languages are Mandar, Tae or Toraja, Makassarese, and Buginese. They are mutually unintelligible but closely related. Again by convention, the speakers of the four languages are spoken of as though they form distinct ethnic groups; again, a range of culture and social formations exists within each, especially in the more northerly, mountainous areas.

Mandar and Tae speakers live mainly in the hilly northern part of the peninsula that becomes mountainous in Tana Toraja and in Central Sulawesi. Although for the most part they cultivate wet rice, their social formations tend to be less radically hierarchical than those of the Buginese and Makassarese. Many of them are Christians. Others follow the "way of the ancestors" (*aluk to dolo*).

The Buginese and Makassarese live primarily on coasts and in the fertile interior of the peninsula. Their economy is based on long-distance trade and wet-rice agriculture. For centuries they have travelled around the South China Sea, and today settlements of Buginese and Makassarese can be found all over the archipelago. They are best known as fearless sailors and fierce fighters, and for their touchiness in defense of their honor.

Sulawesi is one of what the Dutch called "Outer Islands." (The "inner island" was Java, where Dutch economic and governmental activity was most concentrated.) Compared to Java, colonial rule in South Sulawesi was both late and superficial. Dutch presence had been felt there since the mid-seventeenth century, for the important port town of Makassar was a stopping-place between the Moluccas (the "Spice Islands") and the Strait of Malacca, through which passed virtually all trade between China and islands of the South China Sea, and points west of it. The Dutch succeeded in establishing a fortress and eventually became active in limited ways in local politics (cf. Andaya 1981), but they had little economic interest in the interior of the peninsula. It was not until early in the twentieth century that South Sulawesi, like Bali, was officially annexed by the Dutch in the final and definitive burst of expansion of their overseas empire. Although administration was "direct," local rulers were allowed to maintain their residences and many of their prerogatives. In any case, Dutch presence was relatively thin (again, compared to Java), though no less keenly felt.

Many "Indic States" existed in the Buginese- and Makassarese-speaking areas of South Sulawesi before World War II and Indonesian Independence. (I will use the term Bugis-Makassarese to refer to these peoples because, historically, their nobilities intermarried and their cosmologies are very similar.) One of the major three states was Goa, which was centered at the port city of Makassar on the peninsula's west coast and was Makassarese-speaking. Another was Bone, centered at the city of Bone on the east coast, and Buginese-speaking. The one said throughout South Sulawesi to be the oldest was Luwu, the place where Batara Guru, son of the ruler of the Upper World, and his first cousin and wife We Nyilit'timo', daughter of the ruler of the Lower World, descended to the empty Middle World to found Luwu and populate it with their many cousins, servants, and eventually descendants. Luwu was centered at Palopo, which lies at the top of the Gulf of Bone; the populace is mainly Tae-speaking, but the high nobility speak Buginese as well. Many other polities existed, among them Wajo and Soppeng, areas that are all Buginese-speaking. After some exploration, I decided to do fieldwork, beginning in late 1975, in the former polity of Luwu. During my fieldwork, I lived in the household of *almarhum* Andi Pangerang Opu Tosinilele, whose position was "Opu Pa'Bicara" or Lord Spokesperson of Akkarungeng (kingdom of) Luwu. I will return to the circumstances soon.

The history of Indonesia, and of South Sulawesi in general and Luwu in particular, has been complex and violent since 1945. In that year, the colonial subjects of the Netherlands East Indies, still in the midst of fighting the Dutch, declared independence and announced the creation of the Republic of Indonesia. Resistance to the Dutch was strong in parts of South Sulawesi, but the main fighting and victory occurred in Java. Among the fighters in Java was a contingent from South Sulawesi under the leadership of Kahar Muzakar, a man from Luwu. The establishment of the Republic of Indonesia meant, with a few exceptions of *Daerah Istimewah* (special districts) in Java and Sumatra, the abolishment of the old forms of hierarchical polities, whose self-justification was their rulers' and nobles' descent from beings of the Upper World. As Anderson (1983) has pointed out, not just the apparatus of state but the terms in which people imagine themselves to be linked are radically different between a kingdom organized around a high center through a series of personalistic ties between high and low, and the wishfully secular bureaucratic infrastructure of the nation-state. As Anderson puts it, "The great classical communities conceived of themselves as cosmically central," and their "fundamental conceptions about 'social groups' were centripetal and hierarchical," while the nation-state imagines itself as "boundary-oriented and horizontal," its sovereignty "fully, flatly, and evenly operative over each square centimetre of a legally demarcated territory" (Anderson 1983: 20, 22, 26). Such contrasts in styles of imagining the polity were far from understood by many people in South Sulawesi in 1976.

The new republic had much to contend with in the 1950s in what was called by the press "outbreaks of regionalism." One such "outbreak" was the "Kahar Muzakar Rebellion" of South Sulawesi, and for almost a decade, from the mid-1950s to the mid-1960s, the area was in a state of virtual anarchy, producing unthinkable hardships and suffering, at war both against itself and against an external enemy. Although the "Kahar Rebellion" was waged against the new national government whose capital was Jakarta, it was South Sulawesi rather than Java that suffered most from it. People fled to the main cities, all but abandoning the countryside, which was subject to destruction and looting alternately by rebel forces, Javanese troops, and every possible combination of factions within each (cf. Harvey 1974).

The rebels, who claimed to be a part of the wider Darul Islam movement of Indonesia, purposely chose to cast the fight in the public idiom of fundamentalist Islam, which seeks to cleanse Islamic worship of local syncretic practices (cf. Harvey 1974). It was clear to everyone in South Sulawesi, however, that the fight was about *siri'*. Kahar Muzakar and his followers, who had fought in Java in the war against the Dutch that led to independence, had not been honored by the new government by being made members of the regular new Indonesian army. They felt *ripakasiri'*, deeply shamed, "discarded like the skin of a langsat [small fruit] when the sweet pulp has been sucked out," as people of South Sulawesi often put it. In Bugis-Makassarese culture, siri' is what distinguishes humans from animals. The concept is deeply imbedded in notions of human difference (ranking) and spiritual potency, which implies manhood and the capacity for violence and pitiless action channelled by self-control but by no means vitiated.

After Kahar's capture and death in the mid-1960s, order was slowly restored to South Sulawesi. People moved back into the countryside and attempted to reestablish some reasonable ways of life. Foreign researchers even began to arrive in the late 1960s.

The transformation of South Sulawesi has accelerated since the change in government in Jakarta in 1965, when General Suharto replaced General Sukarno. The present government has promoted "development" in the form of capital-intensive exploitation of natural resources such as oil and timber, and encouragement of tourism on a massive scale. These developments have introduced new sources of wealth. Their unprecedented scale and the differential access to them held by various segments of South Sulawesi's population, help to construct realities different from those which were promoted and enforced by the pre-Independence polities. Of course, more is involved than a shift in the sources, scale, and accessibility of a new type of wealth. The instruments of force and persuasion used to promote and enforce ideas about what is real, what is desirable, and how people should arrange their lives accompany these vast economic changes. The meaning of the world and how one can live in it are in the process of being reshaped.

In late October 1975, I arrived in Ujung Pandang, the city formerly called Makassar and formerly the center of the pre-war polity of Goa. Many Buginese live in Ujung Pandang now, partly as a result of the Kahar disturbances, and partly because it has become a major city offering new economic opportunities. My hosts were Datu Hasan and Datu Batari, themselves children of the former rulers of two of the former polities of South Sulawesi. I studied Buginese with Pak La Side', and became aquainted with the archives of the Yayasan Kebudayaan Sulawesi Selatan (The Institute of Culture of South Sulawesi). I made an initial trip north to the city of Palopo, then moved there at the end of the year.

Palopo is located at the northern end of the Gulf of Bone, a few hundred miles from Ujung Pandang, which in 1976 meant a twelve-hour bus ride between the two (if the axle did not break and the river did not flood). The Gulf of Bone lies to its east. Rising steeply to its west are the mountains where the Toraja people live in the district now called Tana Toraja, Torajaland. Palopo, formerly the center of Akkarungeng Luwu, is now the capital of the Kabupaten (district of) Luwu. Because the old polities were not organized territorially, the present districts that are named for the polities whose centers each contains do not coincide perfectly with the effective social boundaries or extent of the former polities. Akkarungeng Luwu, for instance, had tributary entities in several areas outside what is now Kabupaten Luwu—in Tana Toraja and across the Gulf of Bone in Sulawesi's southeastern peninsula.

Luwu's linguistic/ethnic situation is mixed. The high nobility there speak and write Buginese, but the middle nobility and villagers for the most part speak Tae (the language of Tana Toraja). The people do not consider themselves to be Toraja, for the Toraja are Christians and live in the hills; yet they do not think of themselves as Buginese (ToUgi). If pressed, they will say that they are ToLuwu, "people of Luwu," and I will refer to them in that way.

I chose Luwu as a place for fieldwork in part because, coming to fieldwork with historical interests in the literature, politics, epistemology, and sensibilities fostered in the Indicized states of Southeast Asia, I sought an area in which I could see lived some of what I imagined that earlier life to be. Luwu, I was assured, was a region outside the main currents of "development." People spoke of it as "traditional," and implied or said outright that "progress" and "development" were passing it by. They said it was *masih feodal*, "still hierarchical" or "feudal." Actually, a great deal of development was in process, though it had not been completed at the time of my fieldwork. I.N.C.O., an international nickel company based in Canada, was building the social and literal machinery for extracting nickel from the red soil in the northernmost area of Kabupaten Luwu, and a road was planned from there down the coast through Palopo and on to the south (see Robinson 1986 for an account of it). Tractors were being introduced on a large scale to replace the labor of water buffaloes in plowing; our household had the first one in the district. Tourism had been increasing exponentially in Tana Toraja, the area neighboring Luwu. At the time of my fieldwork in 1976, however, these changes had barely begun, and their repercussions had not yet been much felt in the Palopo area.

Yet the peaceful scene presented by the orderly landscape belied the events that had taken place during the preceding quarter-century. The well-worked padi fields, the apparently stable hamlets with houses with disintegrating woven walls, the passion with which people regarded their "white blood" (the invisible, spiritually potent blood of nobles) and their siri' (honor/shame), all as yet nearly untouched by the efforts to "modernize" promoted by the current government in Jakarta, conspired to make it seem that Luwu was caught in a time warp. As it turned out, the time warp proved to be as much substance as illusion—not because the main currents of history had passed around Luwu, but because the region had been ravaged by them, and was trying to re-create itself in the terms it had known before World War II.

The rural areas of Luwu near the site of my fieldwork were all but abandoned during the worst of the Kahar period. Kahar himself came from a small village only a few miles from where I worked in Senga. Because Kahar had drawn many followers from this area, and because the mountainous regions near his home and in the northern part of Kabupaten Luwu were areas of retreat, the entire district was a special focus of attention in the fight. The area was unstable and very dangerous, especially for "small people." Schooling and agriculture virtually stopped, and people sent their children to Ujung Pandang to live with relatives or other protectors. They also went themselves, seeking protection and sustenance in the households of high nobles whom they had followed and served in the pre-war polity of Luwu.

Following the period of the Kahar rebellion, people moved back to Luwu. What I witnessed was a sort of hiatus in history. The old regime was over—the akkarungeng had been abolished, the former Datu Luwu had died in the mid-1960s—but the new regime of "progress and development" had barely begun. ToLuwu who had laid low during the period of anarchy had moved back to their places, built their houses, and were trying to refashion their world. The only ordered world they knew was theirs as it had existed before World War II.

Another and connected major reason I went to Palopo was to live in the household of *almarhum* Andi Pangerang Opu Tosinilele, known affectionately far and wide as "Opu Lele," who had been the Opu Pa'Bicara of Akkarungeng Luwu. This remarkable gentleman died a few months after my departure from Luwu. In Luwu, as in many parts of island Southeast Asia, it is disrespectful and prohibited to speak the name of the departed. I have therefore referred to him by his more impersonal title, "the Opu Pa'Bicara," rather than by his personal name.

In the absence of the Datu or his widow, who lived in Ujung Pandang, the Opu Pa'Bicara was the most influential and highest-status person in residence in the area. His many followers and relatives looked to the Opu Pa'Bicara and his immediate family for leadership and protection in difficult times. At the same time, the establishment of a national government meant that legal authority and governance had been removed from high nobles as such, along with their ability to use instruments of force to back their judgments. In other words, the protective aspect of being a patron in a "patron-client" relation was virtually all that was left to responsible high nobles. High nobles who felt their responsibilities to their followers were in a position to mediate in very limited ways between their followers and officials of the government, settle disputes, arrange marriages, conduct ceremonies, and distribute favors and goods. They were not in a position to enforce their decisions, nor did most of them have much influence with the officials of the nation-state. All of this, combined with the fact that the family of high nobles with whom I stayed were indeed people of the highest integrity and intelligence, meant that during my fieldwork at this juncture in history I was impressed far more with the benevolent aspects of the "patron-client" relation than with the violence and exploitation that have often struck observers at other historical moments. The authority and influence that the Opu Pa'Bicara exercised over his followers was of necessity entirely voluntary on their part. When we add to this the fact that many of the present government's policies are better in conception than in execution, we can readily imagine why the Opu Pa'Bicara was regarded with great respect and gratitude by his many followers.

The Opu Pa'Bicara had been appointed to this position in the 1930s, as a young man. His formal schooling was very limited, because his parents did not want him to go to Java to pursue further studies: he was the only son of a very high family, and the danger was considered too great. He spoke Indonesian, Buginese, and Tae fluently, read Indonesian publications voraciously, and was literate in Buginese.

His political experience and responsibility were vast. His mother was first cousin to the Datu whom he served as Opu Pa'Bicara, and his father was Opu Andeguru Anak Karung, the keeper of genealogies, the highest position in the akkarungeng with the exception of the Datu. His *kapolo*, or entourage of family-followers, was sizeable: he had more than a hundred first cousins, and many hundreds of more distant ones. In the 1930s, A. A. Cense, the Dutch government anthropologist at the time, recognized the Opu Pa'Bicara as a remarkably capable young man. Cense arranged for the Opu Pa'Bicara to assist Cense's ethnological work by taking one day a week to go to villages and collect descriptions and accounts of their customs. Thus it was that the Opu Pa'Bicara had a far more extensive knowledge than most high nobles of the akkarungeng's many peoples and customs.

The Datu Luwu and the Opu Pa'Bicara were leaders in South Sulawesi in the struggle against the Dutch. Both had been captured by the Dutch and, with their families, banished to different places. The Opu Pa'Bicara and his family were sent to the island of Biwa. On the boat trip going there, he told me, the Dutch official guard who accompanied them tried to convince Opu of the benefits of Dutch rule, of the hardships ahead for the colonized area if the Dutch were to leave, and of the consequent immorality and foolishness of the struggle against the Dutch. "Tuan [Sir]," Opu told me he answered, "if a crocodile bites a goat and tries to eat it up, we do not condemn the crocodile. That is its nature. But when the goat struggles to get free, we should not condemn the goat, either." Within the space of about a year, the revolution and the war over, both Datu Luwu and the Opu Pa'Bicara and their families returned to Luwu.

The Opu Pa'Bicara accepted no government position, such as Bupati (district head of the kabupaten), in the new Republic of Indonesia. Opu considered South Sulawesi opposition to the Dutch to be due to siri', defense of honor. About a decade later, Kahar and his followers opposed the newly formed Republic of Indonesia for the same reason—to defend their honor. Siri' must be defended exclusively for itself, uncontaminated by other interests, especially material ones; to mix the defense of siri' with the hope of material rewards of any sort is to mix one's motives and make them impure, thus dirtying the soul. As a consequence, South Sulawesians take a rather perverse (to Western eyes) pride in the fact that the Kahar rebellion, for instance, cost South Sulawesi far more suffering and loss of material wealth than it cost the new government. Their losses prove to themselves that their motives were pure defense of siri', unmixed with baser desires. Similarly, both Datu Luwu and the Opu Pa'Bicara suffered substantial material losses as a result of the war against the Dutch; but neither one accepted a position in the new Indonesian government, and therefore neither gained honor or income from the part they played in the war of independence, which helped bring about the new government. They and other ToLuwu view their lack of material gain—indeed, their loss of a kingdom—as proof of their purity of motive in opposing the Dutch.

During the post-War years, his extraordinary intelligence, his "clean soul," and the many experiences and responsibilities he had had in the course of his long career made the Opu Pa'Bicara a well-known personage among scholars from Indonesia, Europe, America, and Australia. Many had come to interview him over the course of the years. I am the only anthropologist who had the privilege of living in his household in order to participate and observe as well as simply to ask. I am sad he will not see the published results of my research on Luwu.

The Opu Pa'Bicara and his wife, Opu Damira, stayed in a stucco house in Palopo that sheltered a large number of household members, including two of their daughters, Andi Eda and Andi Tenri. I chose to live, however, with the Opu Pa'Bicara's older sister, Opu Senga, in the village of Senga in the countryside south of Palopo. It was an easy ride from Senga to Palopo by *bemo*, the small bus-vans that traverse rural areas throughout Indonesia, and I made the trip every few weeks in order to talk to the Opu Pa'Bicara or attend an event in Palopo.

The house in which I lived in Senga was a magnificent traditional structure on stilts, consisting of two joined buildings (typical of high noble houses). Opu Senga, like many very high-status ladies, had never married. She was keeper of the sacred texts (*lontara'*), and she spent many of her days reading and copying them. Other household members included Andi Minneng, Opu Senga's niece by a deceased full sister, and Andi Anton, Opu Senga's nephew, the Opu Pa'Bicara's oldest son by Opu Damira. Opu DaMuchlis, a high lady and close cousin of Opu Senga's, lived there as well, as did a collection of other family members who took care of the kitchen and household management.

It will be clear that the view of the culture that I acquired was largely a view from the top, and the vast majority of those in the middle and on the bottom that I worked with were very respectful of the old order of things, especially of the Opu Pa'Bicara and his immediate family. Unlike some other high nobles of South Sulawesi, the Opu had come through a variety of upheavals unscathed. Because he had been a leader on the side of the struggle against the Dutch that turned out to be the right side, the winning side, he was a nationalist, not a collaborator. Because he had refused to accept any material gain from the new national government, he was viewed as not trying to use his birth and former position to exploit new circumstances; his soul remained "clean." Because he was a very observant Muslim—he prayed five times a day, kept the fast, had made the haj to Mecca, and attended to other observances—he was regarded by all as a staunch and clean-souled Muslim, even though he was not a member of any fundamentalist Islamic sect or political group. During the Kahar Rebellion, he had refused to aid or abet Kahar, who was in fact a member of his extended kapolo; but he of course welcomed back into his realm of influence all those who had followed Kahar. Moreover, he continued to maintain the benevolent aspects of the "patron" side of the "patron-client" relationship: his Palopo house was filled with children of his family-followers, sent by their parents in more rural areas to be fed and housed by Opu while they attended school, and he continued to settle siri' disputes, arrange marriages, and so forth.

Luwu was indeed, therefore, masih feodal (still hierarchical) in a sense that few other districts of South Sulawesi were. The difference was not the awe with which spiritual potency continues to be regarded, or the desirability of marrying people of "white blood," or the importance of defending one's siri', which are much the same throughout South Sulawesi. The difference was that Luwu contained a relatively intact hierarchical social organization with the Opu Pa'Bicara at its top. As I have pointed out, this was due to special circumstances, primarily the fact that the Opu Pa'Bicara's purity of soul had not been discredited before, during, or after Independence, and because the area had been emptied for about ten years during the Kahar Rebellion and people had not gone through the experience of "development"—many had never had schooling, and the governmental infrastructure was still somewhat thin. During my fieldwork in Luwu and in the circles in which I moved, villagers looked to a remembered past rather than an imagined future for patterns of how to live.

I had long been interested in the culture of the courts of Southeast Asian states, particularly in how nobles understood and regarded issues of instrumentality and self-interest, and how loyalty and the bonds between leaders and followers were conceptualized and acted out in practice. Living in the household of a former court minister, surrounded by myriads of followers who continued to look to him for guidance, presented an extraordinary opportunity to study politics and the meaning of politics at the level of the "person." At the same time, it was my conviction that a study of higher-status and lower-status sub-cultures within a hierarchical society should be mutually illuminating.

I decided to live in the village of Senga, rather than in Palopo with the Opu Pa'Bicara's immediate household, in order to broaden the range of my informants and to see more of village life. In order to converse with the people of Senga, however, I had to learn to speak Tae. Although many village men speak Indonesian, and a number who are well-travelled speak Buginese as well, few women and older people speak either language. I conducted fieldwork sometimes in Indonesian and sometimes in Tae. I had to abandon the serious study of Buginese begun in Ujung Pandang. I did enough linguistic comparison to understand how Buginese works as a language and to perceive some of the regular transformations between Tae and Buginese. Because the Buginese script is only partially phonetic, a reader must know the language well in order to read the script. I learned the script enough to understand how it worked, but I was far too slow to make use of it except for painstakingly deciphering sentences to enhance my understanding of how the language works.

I had come to fieldwork with an interest in discovering something about South Sulawesian conceptions of space, language, and the person, and about the bearing such notions had on the conduct of politics. I found myself in ideal circumstances for studying the rhetoric of social relations between leaders and followers, a subject that could not fail to bear not only on the issues I had planned to investigate, but also on two topics about which there is a large literature concerning Southeast Asian hierarchical polities: indigenous ideas about the nature of power, and notions about the "exemplary center."

Style and Scope

The organization and style of what we write carries no less a burden of meaning than do the social organizations and styles of thought we write about. It is not by accident that I have outlined in some detail the circumstances of my fieldwork and named the cast of characters who will feature prominently in my account. For one thing, disguising the names of either persons or places would be pointless. The days in anthropology are gone when either the writer or the people who are written about can preserve their anonymity. In not too many years, ToLuwu will be reading English and assessing this book; no disguise would conceal identities from them. But even more to the point, ToLuwu would be offended at the idea of disguise: they are proud to be who they are, proud of their history, and they look forward to seeing a book about their way of life.

Nonetheless, any anthropologist has struggled with the delicate balance required in ethnography between tact and accuracy. Sometimes the anthropologist has been privy to information that no one wants to have bruited about. This is particularly so when it comes to people's status and their siri'. I have not provided extended case studies of siri' disputes, although I have some stories of high drama, many abstract examples, and many casual anecdotes, because the principals would recognize themselves or be recognized. This is a deficiency in the book, because a Victor Turnerian "social drama" is a wonderfully dramatic and convincing way to present and to understand the minutiae of political microprocesses. But in Luwu, a person must choose between being an ally or an enemy in siri', and for the sake of posterity and in gratitude for the many secrets about status and siri' disputes to which I was privy, revealed to me purely for the sake of my understanding (for the Opu Pa'Bicara and his immediate family understood disinterested observation, although the rest of the populace did not), I prefer to choose to be among their kapolo rather than to become a ToLaing (family/ally rather than alien enemy). To avoid sensitive cases (which were most of them), I occasionally use myself as an example, refer to the characters very vaguely, or use hypothetical and abstract examples.

The decision not to disguise the circumstances of my fieldwork is related to another stylistic decision. I very much believe in accuracy (trying to get things right), but not in the idea of "objectivity"—the notion that there can be an encompassing overview that incorporates (or ignores) all points of view, regardless of the interests, concerns, and passions of the observer or those observed or the historical moment in which observer and observed meet. In American social science, a stance that strives for "objectivity" often translates stylistically into anonymous personal pronouns and bland writing. This book, by contrast, is an extended essay, a rumination whose method is contrastive. Sometimes the "I" that appears in it is that of the epistemologist, the Occidental mind and sensibility reflecting upon a metaphysics, a common sense, and an interpretive construction that is alien to it. It is an essay about Us meeting Them, the Occident meeting the Orient, a historical consciousness reflecting on an ahistorical one—or whatever analogous contrastive pairs a reader cares to discern.

The other "I" that appears in the text is that of the narrating ethnographer. I make no effort to conceal that I was in Luwu at a particular time in its history, stayed with particular people, conversed with some categories of people more than others. The narrator's "I" appears in the text at points when it seems important to make those circumstances clear. In other words, the "I" enters at times for the sake of modesty: it disclaims objectivity for the sake of accuracy.

In its conscious reflexivity, in its acknowledgment of named informants, in its having an argument, and especially in its search for a form appropriate to its meaning, this essay belongs to the modern (but not quite postmodern, I daresay) era of anthropology. Although part of its aim is to subvert certain standard ethnographic categories of analysis, nonetheless, the book also shares much with ethnographies of the old style. Specialized works (which this is not) devoted solely to ritual language, funeral practices, or curing rites, make sense as ethnographic accounts only when the general outlines of a particular society are known. In that case, the ethnographer can draw on earlier studies and take for granted the cultural, social, and historical background against which the events the ethnographer describes take place. But like the older style of ethnography, this work attempts to lay out some of the most pervasive organizing themes that the ethnographer has perceived and experienced in another culture in order to paint a vision of that society's life in broad strokes.

The book is divided into three parts. The task of Part I, "A Geography of Signs," is to lay out the ontology and metaphysics of the realities of centers as they are constituted and lived in everyday life. Chapters One, Two, and Three, on the person, the house (which bridges person and polity), and the polity respectively describe a world in which these items are conceptualized and socially constituted as material organized around a central, vital point. "Reading Movement" ends Part I with a comment on the danger of movement and how it was read in a society that conceived of itself as a perfectly formed center.

The politics of such states were constituted around a center, but that very fact meant that they were predicated on a paradox, a contradiction that was ultimately unresolvable. From one angle, the political life of the state was deeply centrist: the fount of status was the ruler at the "navel of the world." Political "advancement" moved the contender higher in the hierarchy and closer to the center, which were the same thing. The desire for status, of which the ruler was the source and fount, can therefore be considered a centripetal impulse in these states, holding together in some semblance of a polity people and groupings that were widely dispersed geographically and that sometimes had little to gain materially by becoming vassals of the polity's center.

Yet the same impulse to attain status, viewed from another angle, was a centrifugal or de-centering force in the state's political life. In theory, there is no place for people who are equal in status in hierarchical systems such as these. Forms of demeanor, address, and speech are predicated on the assumption that one of the parties is higher, the other lower; it is almost impossible, in these systems, to speak without locating oneself socially with respect to the other person. Two people may be close in status, but there are no true equals. Inevitably, the closer two people are in status, the more obscure is the difference between them, and the more uncertain it is which of the two should defer to the other. As a result, their relations take on the character of a contest. The continual testing and contesting for social place informs virtually all interactions between people with any pretensions to dignity in these societies, albeit sometimes unconsciously. The competition between peers shapes much of the meaning of political life.

In Part II, "Centrifugal Tendencies," we leave a stable ontology and turn to the shape and meaning of the sensibilities, the selves who are always under duress because they are always threatened by a challenging Other. The subject of this part is the competition between peers, and it includes two chapters. Chapter Four, "Vulnerable Places," is so named because everyone's social place is vulnerable to attack; thus every person, like every ruler, could be de-centered by the realm's internal division and, in their view, by internal divisions of the sort we call psychological. In that chapter I explicate the shape and meaning of etiquette, and expound on the psychology of *siri'*, a word that could be translated as "honor" or as "shame." Chapter Five, "The Contest for Place," discusses the problem confronting a polity dedicated to maintaining a vertical hierarchy when at every level of society it contains contesting status-peers whose constant competition tends to inflate the value of signs of status.

Part III, "Centripetal Structures," examines the obverse side of the coin of status competition: the alliances between high and low, and the structures that keep the categories apart. The social worlds of hierarchical societies (and of most stratified ones, for that matter) are arranged in such a way as to disadvantage the disadvantaged and enhance the enhanced. The focus of these chapters is white blood, which stands as an ultimate goal in political striving. Chapter Six, "The Potency of Names," concerns the practice and logic of naming systems, for a person's name is believed to reflect that person's degree of white blood. Nobles record their forebears' names in genealogies and, partly as a consequence, have a considerably greater scope of known relatives than do teknonymous commoners. In a society that assumes that followers are kinspeople, the remembering and forgetting of forebears and their descendants have serious and immediate political implications. Chapter Seven, "Forgetting Genealogies," addresses that issue as well by exploring how genealogies are kept by people of different levels and the implications for their respective amounts of political influence. A third chapter in Part III, "Centripetal Marriage" (Chapter Eight), discusses the centripetal tendencies of endogamous marriage in Luwu, clarifying these structures both by comparing them with similar systems in more level societies of the area and by contrasting them with the "asymmetric alliance" marriage systems practiced in Eastern Indonesia.

The book ends with three conclusions. The first, "Local Conclusion," called "Transcending Politics," looks back to Luwu and this text. It de-

scribes a social epistemology predicated on a center that—if it succeeds—
ceases to exist. So, like the plots of Javanese shadow-puppet theater, the
plot of the book moves from centering (Part I) to de-centering (Part II) to
re-centering (Part III) and then, in that first conclusion, the re-established
and victorious center disappears. The second, "Comparative Conclusion:
The Political Geographies of Potency," looks out from the configurations
of potency in centered hiearchical insular Southeast Asian polities to view
them comparatively within the context of other, more egalitarian and/or
more ideologically dualistic insular Southeast Asian and Oceanic societies.
The third, "General Conclusion: Empowered Signs," suggests a general
way of conceptualizing political processes that melds aesthetics with the
pursuit of advantage without being obsessed by the exclusive reality of
either. In the Epilogue, I make a few comments about present and future
transformations in the meanings of social life in South Sulawesi.

A final word is in order about the phrase "a Southeast Asian Realm" in
the book's title. I had begun fieldwork with an interest more in Southeast
Asian Indic States than I had in the wider Malayo-Polynesian cultural setting within which these societies exist, but the most fervent contextualists
(among whom I count myself) cannot help but be gripped by a rage for
comparison when delving into this part of the world. Everything in Indonesia, and beyond it in the Malayo-Polynesian and mainland Southeast
Asian worlds of which it is a part, seems to be a transformation of everything else, sometimes even more so than it seems to be itself: it is no accident that structuralism was invented about Indonesia. Since several kinds
of world overlap in South Sulawesi, it is sometimes enlightening to point
to other transformations of the patterns found in Luwu.

First, the hierarchical polities of island Southeast Asia (those of South
Sulawesi, Bali, Java, the Malay peninsula, and scattered others) are cousins
to Polynesian chiefdoms. The people speak languages of the same family
(Austronesian, also called Malayo-Polynesian), and, as Hocart recognized
early and others are increasingly realizing, their political formations are
transformations of each other. As James Boon has commented, if Bali had
been approached by Europeans by way of Polynesia rather than by way of
India, it would have rightly seemed "Western Polynesia" rather than the
"East Indies" (Boon 1977).

Yet these hierarchical polities of island Southeast Asia *were* approached
via India, by Indians, many centuries ago, and like the great historical kingdoms on Southeast Asia's mainland, they were influenced by some Indian
ideas. The extent and significance of the influence is currently a matter of
considerable dispute (cf. Wolters 1982), but that historical contact occurred
and that the hierarchical "Indicized" polities of mainland Southeast Asia

and island Southeast Asia bear a family resemblance to each other is not. The second set of patterns of which Luwu can be considered a part, then, is the one formed by the Indic States of both mainland and island Southeast Asia.

Unlike the "mountain people," "hill tribes," or their own peasantry, the courts of Indic States entered history, in several senses. They had writing, genealogies, and calendrical systems, and a sense of the past as very long indeed. Occidental commentators, finding inscriptions on stone and in palm-leaf manuscripts, have for Indic States the archival documents so necessary to the historian's craft. So these former states entered "history" both by creating documents that make their past accessible and by being written about by historians.

The peasants and so-called "hill tribes" of island Southeast Asia had a different fate. Peoples of this humbler sort—the slaves and commoners at the base of a state hierarchy, or peasants living in the immediate vicinity of the court centers and subject to their rule; the mountain horticulturalists in tributary but only occasional contact with court centers; the hunter-gatherers "upstream" who traded forest products with the centers "downstream"; and the remote bands high in the mountains or deep in the tropical rain forest, living so far from the centers that they had no contact with them—for the most part left no inscriptions or texts (love-magic scratched on bark using Indian-derived scripts notwithstanding). And so, through an accident in several senses historical, such peoples entered the discourse of anthropology rather than of history.

The division of labor and the consequent disjunction within the organization of knowledge has been far from absolute. Yet for the most part, anthropologists have done fieldwork among hill people, in peasant villages, and with lower-status people in the court centers. With notable exceptions, anthropologists have stayed away from high nobility and court texts. For their part, historians tend to have little notion, for instance, of the striking similarities between the hierarchical polities of island Southeast Asia and those of Polynesia, or of the deep similarities in kinship terms and marriage strategies between court and neighboring hill, similarities that, when explicated, can illuminate the political processes of each.

In this book I have sought to begin to correct the vision of the Indic State as a different sort of entity from a hill tribe in island Southeast Asia. The marriage patterns of Iban of Sarawak (Borneo) can illuminate, by contrast or comparison, those of Luwu with which they share more features than not; patterns of competition among the Ilongot hill-people of the Philippines can be similarly illuminating. I make extended comparisons in only a few chapters (Five, Eight, and the second Conclusion), but the comparative cast of mind informing this work is, I hope, unmistakable. I have drawn freely from the literatures on these three "realms"—the Indic States of Southeast Asia, Oceania and Eastern Indonesia, and other societies in island Southeast Asia—wherever it seemed appropriate. Thus the "realm" in the book's title is meant to have a double meaning: the realm for which there was a ruler, and the realm of Southeast Asia and beyond.

Part I
A Geography of Signs

In discussions of political life and of health practices in Luwu, certain words kept recurring. One of the most reiterated was the term *pusat* in Indonesian (Bug. *posik*), a word that refers not only to the human navel but to all sorts of vital centers.

"But why *pusat*," I asked in the middle of a discussion in which the word was prominent. "Why not just *tengah* [middle]? What's the difference?"

Clearly, I needed a language lesson, and to that end my "sibling" Andi Anthon put three objects in a row on the table. Pointing to the one in the middle, he informed me that it was the *tengah* of the other two. Now he took two more objects and put one on each of the remaining two sides, so that the central object was surrounded on four sides rather than two.

"Now," he said, "you could say that it is the *pusat*. But really," he continued thoughtfully, "there should be something above and below it, too."

I brought the matter up later with the Opu Pa'Bicara, Andi Anthon's father. "We read nowadays," Opu said, "about three dimensions [Ind. *tiga dimensi*]. In the old days there were seven dimensions—four sides, above and below, and the Datu [ruler] in the *pusat*." Thus he described the shape of a world whose various directions were unified and focused on a central point.

In traditional accounts, the center of the akkarungeng was the center of the world itself, the place where Batara Guru, a spirit from the Upper World, descended to the Middle World with his myriad followers and retainers to become the first Datu of Luwu. The center of the world was defined by the Datu, by the objects brought down to earth from the Upper World (*arajang* in Buginese, usually referred to as "regalia" or "ornaments" in English), and by their place of residence.

Polities smaller than the akkarungeng also have centers. The type of polity/social organization that I was able to observe was the kapolo, a grouping that consists of an inner high core of closely related high-status leaders together with its follower-relatives. A *polo* is a break or section—for instance, a section of bamboo. Thus a kapolo is an entity, a distinct "piece" of a larger polity. Like other social entities, each kapolo has a center, its high inner core.

If the central point of the akkarungeng was its datu, the central point of individual people is similarly said to be the pusat, which is marked or located by the human navel. Each person has a center, and guarding it, especially the *sumange'* or life energy attached at it, is a matter of constant concern. Houses, too, have "center posts" (Tae *pinposik*) that run through their approximate geographic centers. The house has its own sumange', too: the spirit that hovers at the center post, called the *Ampo Banua* (Tae, roughly "owner of the house").

In this first Part, I will explore some of the ways that the person, the house, and the polity were socially constituted as centered entities, an exploration that will also require an explication of the metaphysics underlying that social constitution.

Chapter One
The Person

In an illuminating and now classic explication of traditional Javanese political thought, Benedict Anderson has argued that the "idea of power in Javanese culture" contrasts at almost every point with the ideas about secular political power that have been prominent in Occidental political thought since the seventeenth century. In Java, he points out,

> Power exists, independent of its possible users. It is not a theoretical postulate but an existential reality. Power is that intangible, mysterious, and divine energy which animates the universe. . . . In Javanese traditional thinking there is no sharp division between organic and inorganic matter, for everything is sustained by the same invisible power. This conception of the entire cosmos being suffused by a formless, constantly creative energy provides the basic link between the "animism" of the Javanese villages and the high metaphysical pantheism of the urban centers. (1972: 7)

The idea that a cosmic energy suffuses and animates the world is an extremely common one in island Southeast Asia. Among the Bugis-Makassarese of South Sulawesi, the term given to this energy is *sumange'*.

My aim here is to begin to unravel the cultural logic informing everyday life, in which the existence of sumange' (named or not) has the status of "tacit knowledge" (in Polanyi's phrase) rather than, or more importantly than, explicitly stated "belief." That is, I am interested in the basic assumptions that structure people's perceptions and orient and underlie their actions. Such notions are relevant to what they think it is to be a person.

Some notable efforts have been made to socialize "the person," to claim that people are not only organic-biological entities or mental-psychological ones, but also public and socioculturally constituted artifacts. In an effort to rescue thought from the realm of the private and make it available to anthropological investigation, Clifford Geertz has written that "human thought is consummately social: social in its origins, social in its functions, social in its forms, social in its applications. At base, thinking is a public activity" whose forms are available for study in the "traffic of significant symbols" (1973c: 360). In a parallel rescue operation on the other half of the Cartesian person, Mary Douglas has insisted that social concerns are inscribed on the body (1966). We might then say, that, like thinking, embodying is a public activity, and that the body's constitution and meaning are publicly construed in locally particular ways.

The First Seven Days

Having brought forth progeny into the world, humans make efforts to turn their infants not into abstract humans exhibiting a universal "human nature," but into humans as they conceptualize humans to be. A revealing place to study the formation of the "person," then, is in the practices surrounding birth. The dangers to which an infant and its parents are subject, and the ways in which the child is protected and treated, can be unravelled to reveal how the person is thought to be formed.

People in Luwu occasionally call on the services of practitioners called *sando'* (Ind. *dukun*), who have different specialties: types of sicknesses, birth, building a new house, and others. I had thought of the sando' associated with birth as a sort of midwife, but after I attended several births and birth ceremonies and had a number of conversations, I discovered that the sando' is seldom called until after the birth has already taken place. During labor itself, I was told, the mother remains conscious and in a squatting position, assisted, if at all, by a female relative or neighbor. The greatest danger to a mother is thought to be not the act of giving birth but the possibility that the placenta will remain inside her, a rotting lump (as they put it), after the baby has emerged. The greatest danger to the baby is not being born but, rather, having its umbilical cord cut. So for the health of both, every effort is made to keep the baby and placenta together and attached, so that the two are born together. After giving birth the mother takes it easy for a while, sitting, standing, or walking around, but she remains in a torso-upright position rather than takes a nap, for, as in most parts of Indonesia, putting the body in a horizontal position except for sleeping is considered unconducive to health.

The placenta is said to be the baby's "older sibling"; the two newly born siblings, still joined by the umbilical cord, are placed in a prepared spot to await the arrival of the sando'. The sando' has the job of preparing the baby for the shock of having its umbilical cord cut. After the cord is cut, the placenta is buried. The baby remains in a state of great vulnerability for a minimum of seven days. During that period, the baby and mother must not leave the house, a place of protection. During that time, water for cooking and bathing is brought into the house by a relative or neighbor. The infant is considered especially vulnerable on its third night, the *bongi sapa'* (Tae; *bongi* means "night," *sapa'* means "prohibited" or "tabu"). On that night (and, if the parents can afford it, on subsequent uneven nights, the fifth, seventh, etc., before the mother descends from the house), parents, neighbors and relatives *maroja*, which is to say, they stay awake all night inside the house, snacking and playing dominoes, in order to guard the infant with their alert consciousness. By the end of seven days, the baby's umbilical cord stump will have fallen off, and a ceremony is performed with the sando' in which the mother descends from the house to bathe outside. (Roughly, the higher the status of the parents, the longer the mother and the infant should remain inside the house for their protection. High noble women stay inside, I was told, forty days after giving birth.) The Buginese house is on stilts above the ground. Descending from it marks a transition from safe interior protected space to dangerous exterior open space. During this seven-day ceremony (or longer for higher-status parents), the baby is introduced ritually to the dangerous world outside the house. Attended by a sando', the mother bathes outside for the first time since giving birth. High nobles, I was told, also ceremonialized the first time the baby's foot touched the ground—theirs was a very protected life, but the sensibilities evident in such a ceremony were similar to those I saw among commoners in Senga, simply taken to an extreme.

The following account of the first of the ceremonies sketched above is taken from fieldnotes. The fieldnotes appear as indented quotations; comments and elaboration appear in brackets in regular text. I have translated several words into English here, and have made the prose slightly more readable.

GIVING BIRTH

> At 12:30 or so Sahari came to tell me that a baby was born at Padang. We arrived at the house at one o'clock. The baby had apparently been born about an hour earlier. The sando', Indo'Musu, had not yet arrived. The baby, its umbilical cord and placenta still attached, was on a tray in the bedroom, loosely wrapped in a sarong.

[The sando' said that a special place should be made for the newborn to rest as a sign that it is awaited and welcomed. She attributed one baby's constant fussiness to the fact that minimal preparations had been made for its arrival. One family, for instance, laid the infant on a stack of seven new sarongs. Each day after birth they removed one sarong until the seventh-day ceremony, thus marking the infant's continued health and growth while dismantling and using the sign of its being awaited. Another family prepared a special area and surrounded it with a *boco'*, the name for a cloth that surrounds a resting-place, whether it be a mosquito net enshrining a bed or a fabric curtain covering the contents of a shrine. Needless to say, such preparations would be much more elaborate for the arrival of a high noble infant.]

> I went back to the front part of the house and chatted with the father until the sando' arrived. She immediately went back to the baby, but it was decided to bring it out on its tray to the front part of the house where there was more light so I could see the proceedings better and photograph it. The father said he has had a different sando' for each of his children. The sando' ordered hot water, and she squeezed green leaves [*daung cuppa-cuppa*] into it. She then touched the baby's head, hands, navel, and feet with the leaves, squeezing green juice out. Then she took the umbilical cord [*lolo*] and touched it to the placenta [*erung*] and to the baby's navel, then knotted the cord itself into a kind of loop. They sent a small child to get the bamboo knife [*bila'*] and some turmeric root. Yellow thread was brought on a plate. More hot water was added to the bowl, and the sando' put into it the bamboo knife, an old copper coin, and the turmeric roots (they were uncut, so it did not affect the water's color). Into this water she dipped a white cloth and then touched it to the baby's forehead, mouth, and chest, saying spells [*baca-baca*] while doing so; she did that twice. She then baca-baca some shallots and cut them up into a small jar of coconut oil. She sharpened the bamboo knife. She then pressed the umbilical cord against the baby's penis, and then tied the yellow thread around the umbilical cord. The baby's grandparent, its mother's father, came over to cut the umbilical cord. He took a root of turmeric and put it under the point on the cord that he wanted to cut, bracing the cord, and then cut it with the bamboo knife.

[A bamboo knife rather than a metal one is used, as ToLuwu feel that it will cause less of a shock. Usually the sando' cuts the umbilical cord, but she had delivered this baby's cousin the day before. For second cousins too, I was told, she could not have cut it; three days after the first birth, it would have been all right.]

> Now he took the slightly bloody end of the cut cord which was attached to the placenta and touched it to the baby's mouth. They said it was to prevent the child from being *matesse'* [cheeky/insolent] to its parents. Now they prepared the placenta, the baby's "older sibling." They put it into an empty shell of the bila fruit, along with some rice, some fishbones, some daung cuppa-cuppa, a bit of the Koran [a scrap of paper with Arabic letters], and daung pallang.

[The placenta is being prepared for burial. It is put into a container, along with various other items, and later will be carried out of the house in a sling, just like a baby, by the father. Often the placenta is placed in a coconut shell; in this case, the container is the hard shell of a fruit whose skin is flexible until the pulp is removed, when it dries to a stiff, lightweight container. With the placenta were placed a number of items. Daung cuppa-cuppa, a type of green leaf, is generally said to prevent stomach sickness. Daung pallang is often used in ceremonies because *jin pakkoni*, a type of spirit that likes to lick up blood, are afraid of the leaf. The fishbones, several people said, are to prevent choking on fishbones. These and the rice and the Quran are standard items in such ceremonies, though things may be added or deleted. Some families insisted that a needle (for "*konsentrasi*," spiritual concentration) should be added, and others included turmeric in the package.]

> Now that its umbilical cord was cut and the baby was separated from its after-birth, the sando' proceeded to oil the baby with the coconut oil that had the shallot dropped into it with spells. She stroked the baby thoroughly on the back and chest, each palm, its feet, legs and forehead, occasionally leaning over and whispering into its ear, saying spells. The infant was really greased up, and it was stretched and its fingers and hands pulled back, so that, they said, it would be "flexible" rather than "stiff and awkward."

[The sando' was indeed making the baby flexible, but she was also protecting its most vulnerable spots, called its *leso-leso*, places where bad things might enter it. She protects the baby by baca-baca into its ears and oiling the leso-leso with oil into which she had whispered spells. Leso-leso areas include behind the ears, at the palms of the hands and feet, in the armpits, behind the knees, and at the backbone. The balls of the fingers and under the fingernails are also places to be protected. The fontanel is an especially dangerous spot, so it is seldom washed, and often leaves are placed on it as an added barrier. Leso-leso, it appears to me, are places where the smooth surface of the skin breaks, as in a joint, or where there are naturally soft spots.]

> After being oiled, the baby was splashed with the water that had the turmeric, copper coin, and so forth in it, then dried off and given to the ToPattarima, the "person who receives it." In this case it was the baby's first cousin, a fourteen-year-old girl.

[So far as I can tell, the ToPattarima should be family, but not the parents or grandparents. It appears most often to be a parent's sibling or the baby's cousin, i.e., collaterals. Perhaps this indicates that the baby is welcomed by a supporting collection of relatives larger than its immediate family.]

> The baby was dressed now by its mother's mother in white infant clothes, purchased at the market, and sprinkled with baby powder by its father, and put on a tray and on the bed. The attention of the sando' now turned to the mother, while the father stayed in the front part of the house. The sando' and the mother went to the back of the house, the kitchen, and I accompanied them to watch. The mother lay down and the sando' massaged her stomach and pulled and stretched her arms, rather the way she had done to the baby while oiling it, and she baca-baca all the while. The mother then got up into a squatting position [*ma'cudengkeng*, a comfortable and customary posture] and the sando' dipped some water on the mother's forehead while baca-baca, then on her hair. She massaged the mother's back a little bit. The mother washed herself off a little, and they lit a *dapo-dapo* and put dry leaves and some dried rice stalks in it so that it produced smoke.

[A dapo-dapo is a small clay container for burning coals, used in many ceremonies. Onto the burning coals people place palm sugar, rice stalks, or leaves with particular associations; the rising smoke is often fragrant.]

> The mother stood over it, straddling it, so that the smoke rose between her legs. This they said was so that the blood wouldn't clot into a ball, but instead would flow out and her stomach wouldn't hurt. When this was almost over, I left the kitchen for the front room, where the father was preparing to announce the baby's presence to the world with the [Islamic] Call To Prayer. He put a big pair of scissors under his left arm, and, holding the baby and facing west, sang the call to prayer. [The point of the scissors was to have some iron; a knife would be good too, or a keris if they had had one.] After that, the baby was taken back and put onto the bed.
>
> Now the placenta was to be buried. It had been put into the bila-fruit shell along with various items and was now wrapped in a banana leaf, then covered with an old cloth and tied into a bundle. The baby's maternal grandmother arranged a piece of cloth around its father's neck in the manner of a *slendeng* [a sling-arrangement in which women carry their babies]. The placenta package was placed into the slendeng and the father carried it that way down the stairs and out of the house, over to the nearby tree where a hole for it had already been dug by the baby's mother's father. The father returned to the house immediately. The grandfather finished burying it.

[In this area, burying the placenta under a tree near the house is the most common practice, but it can also be sent out to sea or hung from a tree. If you hang it from a tree, the father told me, you have to make sure it is very well-wrapped so it doesn't smell bad.]

> I had been told that it was customary to bonk a coconut several times on the floor near the newborn's head in order to get it used to loud noises, sort of immunizing it to prevent *aseddingeng* [sudden loss of sumange']. I was disappointed that they hadn't done that, and asked the sando' about it. She said that these days babies hear a lot of loud noises, like radios, so you don't need to bother with making a special point to introduce them to it, the way you used to.

THE THIRD NIGHT

Before the mother descends from the house, the child is considered to be very vulnerable, especially on its third night, the *bongi sapa'*. It is protected on that dangerous night by being surrounded by adults who maroja (stay awake all night). Parents who can afford it make the night of maroja into a somewhat festive occasion, inviting neighbors in and serving *lappa'-lappa'*; the men stay up all night playing a type of domino game. Lappa'-lappa' are long thin leaf-packages of sticky rice steamed in coconut milk, considered auspicious. For this occasion they must be cooked and eaten inside the house. The local imam (Islamic religious leader) may or may not be called in to say a prayer over the lappa'-lappa'. Even if the parents are too poor to do anything else, they stay awake all night, usually joined by a few close neighbors or kinspeople. The third night is the crucial one, but people maroja on all uneven nights before the mother leaves the house if they have the funds to provide snacks and the energy to stay awake. If the mother leaves the house on the seventh day, people maroja on the third and (if they can afford it) fifth days; if she leaves the house on the ninth day, people maroja on the third, fifth and seventh days; and if she leaves the house on the eleventh day, people maroja on the third, fifth, seventh, and ninth days.

THE SEVENTH DAY

After the dangerous nights when people maroja, the next marked point in a baby's life is the seventh (or ninth, or eleventh, or, for a high noble, fortieth) day. At that point, the mother descends from the house for the first time since giving birth, accompanied by a sando', to bathe. And the baby, first washed inside the house with water brought from the outside, may be further introduced to the outside world by being carried down from the house and walked around it three or seven times.

The following account, again slightly modified, is taken from my field-notes of September 3, 1976.

> This morning we went to the house of the child who was born a week ago. The household I went to yesterday asked for a name for the baby, so I gave them "Betty," which will become Betti. Sahari asked for a name for her niece, so I gave her Linda.

[People ask their respected elders to give names to their children, or the respected elders will bestow names as a favor and to express a link. The names are chosen so as to reveal a relationship between the giver and receiver, so I had to consult with my immediate family to choose names that sounded appealing to their ears but that were distinctive enough to be clearly foreign, and therefore clearly from me.].

> . . . Back to today's events. The mother here is called "Indo'Tuo," mother of the living. Several of her children died, so they gave her the name "living" to prevent further deaths. The mother, the sando' Indo'Musu, and I descended from the house to go to the family's well for the mother's bath. Indo'Musu brought a plate with money, egg, and betel nut and two leaves. I neglected to find out what kind they were. The money was brought back into the house after the bath. Anyway, at the top of the house stairs, Indo'Musu baca-baca, which I hadn't noticed at yesterday's ceremony. At the well they drew water and the sando' baca-baca into it, and splashed most of it over the mother's head and back. The mother had brought a couple of pieces of soiled clothes with her—thought she'd do a little washing while she was at it. After she'd bathed and washed, we went back into

the house, taking the remains of the baca-baca'd water, but leaving the plate of things by the well.

[The plate held an offering to the spirits. Anyone other than household members who finds the offerings may use them, and it is considered lucky to do so. The egg used must be fresh and edible, and it should be a chicken egg (rather than the more common and cheaper duck egg), because it tastes better and is more special, better for use in ceremonies.]

Inside the house, the baby was washed with this well water, to which they added turmeric, a copper coin, and *kemiri* nuts. Then it was rubbed with oil. N. Z. said it was especially necessary to protect it behind the ears and at the palms and underarms and other leso-leso. She said the fontanel was the place where it was likely to *tama angin* [Ind. *masok angin*, "to be entered by air," which generally contains spirits], so it shouldn't be washed but should be covered up. After the baby was washed and oiled, it was dried and given to its mother, and I took their picture. The people who came were the husband, his first cousin, and her husband. Back in the kitchen, everyone was working on spices and chopping because they are going to *hakekat* [an Islamic ceremony] the child. A goat was bought yesterday and they killed five chickens. Allung's father, who is an imam, came to do the job. Then we went to the little room behind, where the mother and baby were to be given lappa'-lappa' [the long thin packet of sticky rice]. The sando' burned palm sugar in the dapo-dapo [charcoal container], then put her hand over the smoke and touched it to the baby's head and the mother's head and over both breasts and chest. Then she took the whole dapo-dapo in her hand and moved it counterclockwise in the air above the mother and child, then ditto over the lappa'-lappa'. Cool water was brought in a glass, and a fingerbowl of water. The sando' looked through the lappa'-lappa', chose one and unwrapped it, then took a bit of palm sugar and grated coconut from a plate beside her and put them on the end of the stick of rice. She touched it to the baby's lips, then put it into the mother's mouth. The mother ate a bite. That seemed to conclude matters, so I went to the back to see kitchen activity. The names of the people there were. . . .

[Lappa'-lappa' literally means "released," "let go," "untied." It is often served at ceremonies that mark the end of a prohibition. The food served also has meaning. Rice, some form of coconut, and palm sugar are often used in combination in ceremonies. Their association indicates fullness and plenty: the necessary (rice, the basis of life, the word for which [*anre*] also means "food in general") is supplemented with the sweetness of sugar and the fatness of coconut.]

In two of the seventh-day ceremonies I attended, the baby was further introduced to the outside world. After being bathed in the manner described above, it was carefully wrapped, then carried to each room in the house, where the bearer circled the room. This procedure apparently introduced it to the house and to movement. It was then taken down the house steps and around the house, three times in one case, seven in the other, apparently to introduce it to the world outside the safe confines of the house. In the old days, I was told, the toddler's first step upon the ground outside the house was ceremonialized, particularly if the parents were wealthy or of high status.

This marks the end of the period of greatest danger to mother and infant.

EXPLANATIONS OF DANGER

Why is the third night dangerous, and why does the worst period of danger end after seven days? Like many other cultures in the Malay Archipelago, Luwu had an elaborate calendrical system from which auspicious and inauspicious days for various activities could be determined. The baby's third-night danger, the importance of uneven days, and so on, are undoubtedly related to this system, though most people do not know exactly how.

But when I asked people why the baby is in danger for its first seven days, they always answered that the baby is in danger until its umbilical-cord stump has fallen off. Mary Douglas (1966) has used the phrase "medical materialism" for explanations of ritual practices that relate them to health rather than to categories of thought. There is a sense in which this standard answer, that the baby is in danger for seven days because its umbilical-cord stump has not fallen off, is a sort of indigenous medical materialism. After all, the stump usually falls off before seven days have passed, and besides, some people wait nine or eleven days before ceremonializing the end of the greatest danger, and the corresponding ceremony for a high noble did not take place until forty days had passed. So something besides the stump falling off must be going on, something clearly related in some way to their calendrical system.

But indigenous medical materialism, as contrasted with the kind originating from a notion of biology alien to the practices discussed, is certainly enlightening. After hearing this answer a number of times, I inquired further about just why the stump's continued attachment should keep the child in a state of danger. The gist of the answers was that until the stump falls off, the baby's navel is not yet sealed over; the baby's sumange' will fly away; there is still a hole at its navel. Sumange' is thought to be attached at the navel, and it is clear that its attachment to an infant is tenuous and unstable, all the more so when the body has a hole right at the point of attachment.

The shrivelled stump is wrapped by the mother in a cloth and stored, usually in a small container with her other children's cord stumps. It becomes a talisman for the growing child and is sometimes used in curing practices if the child becomes sick.

Ritual Substances

Certain substances commonly make an appearance in practices that are intended to cure sickness or ward off harm. These could be called "ritual substances" (not an indigenous category) as a shorthand way of indicating that they are considered to be in some degree effective. I think it is true to say that almost anything could be used as a ritual substance in Luwu, because sumange', the invisible animating energy that makes items effective and potent, is in everything, though to different degrees. Nonetheless, some items are viewed as having special qualities, appropriately directed to particular purposes: pallang leaves ward off blood-licking jin; other leaves have names like "cool" or "safe"; the hardness of iron associates it with invulnerability; yellow, the color of turmeric, is auspicious. A selection from such items is usually put into a container of cool water, which, when bespelled, can be used for cure or prevention. So, for instance, mother and infant are bathed in bespelled water during the infant's first seven days of life. Similarly, bespelled water is splashed on red spots or running sores, common childhood afflictions, in an effort to heal the child. Hot feverish people drink bespelled water to cool themselves. And household members who stay behind will try to protect the sumange' and therefore the safety of a household member who has left on a journey by placing a bowl of bespelled water in his or her sleeping place.

I had carefully recorded the items used in curing rites and had carefully quizzed people about, for example, why *pallang* leaves are effective, because I had been assuming that they were treating maladies or "diseases" as they saw and categorized them with an indigenous "pharmacology." The scheme of treatment that I was imagining them to have obviously was analogous to the Occidental medical treatment I was familiar with from my own experience: it assumes that different diseases have different aetiologies, that people catch those diseases by being invaded by different categories of microbe, and that the diseases are then cured by the application of disease-specific pharmacological items. Hence my care in recording what I took to be the analogue of those items.

But after observing a number of these practices and recording the same inventory of items, give or take a few, for virtually all occasions of prevention and cure, I began to wonder whether I had understood what, in fact, was going on. My suspicion that leaves and pieces of iron were considered useful additions in a cure but were not, after all, the crux of the matter was confirmed when a gnarled old gentleman, who was not generally regarded as a sando' or curer, came over to the house to treat a feverish household member. He did this by baca-baca into cool water with no added ingredients and having the patient drink it. He remarked by-the-by that, although *other* people used a lot of stuff in their water, *he* didn't bother with all that.

Prompted by that comment to ask other sorts of questions, I found that, indeed, the cure, as it were, is inside the curer: the curer's "clean soul" effects the patient's cure, rather than some technique divorced from the curer's person. The curer's powers are augmented by his or her knowledge (*paddissengeng*), which consists of spells. Paddissengeng of whatever sort is stored in the chest. How is the curer's effectiveness conveyed to the patient? Whispering the spells brings them out of the chest and into the breath, through which they can be conveyed into the patient through the ears. So the birth-sando' will baca-baca directly into an infant's ears, protecting the infant by "filling" it. Similarly, people preparing a corpse for burial will baca-baca into its ears, helping to augment the last shreds of sumange' that cling to it. Ears are the apertures that can receive whispered sounds directly.

Spells can be applied in other ways as well, commonly by being whispered into water. Thus substantialized, they can be applied to bodies or ingested. The water must not only be cool to the touch when used, but it must never have been boiled. Coolness is associated with self-control and therefore with health, while hotness is associated with loss of control, hence vulnerability. Substantialized in cool water, baca-baca can be applied to measled skin surfaces, or poured over a mother taking her first bath outside the house after having given birth, or ingested to cool a fever. In short, it is not the leaves and turmeric and fragments of iron that cure, although they may contribute their own potencies; nor is the water itself curative. Water is simply a vehicle, a substantializer of the potency conveyed into the fluid through the breath of the curer.

There is, however, a hierarchy of ritual substances, as revealed to me first in the old man's boast that he did not bother to use the stuff (like leaves and turmeric) that lots of people did. He was asserting that his own potency was such that it did not need material aids to effect a cure. He drew it out of his body on exhaled whispers, conveyed it into water, and in that form the patient ingested it.

The hierarchy of ritual substances is predicated on the fact, assumed in South Sulawesi and many other parts of Indonesia, that the visible world is animated by invisible potency. The one realm, invisible and potent, is *pammasareng* (Ind. *alam ghaib*). Beings and powers in it are potent and invisible, *malinrung*; its coarse and visible aspect is *talle'*, tangible or perceptible. Sumange' is malinrung: it cannot be seen, heard, touched, tasted, or smelled. So is *kabusungang* (Tae; in Bug. *abusungeng*) being struck by misfortune for having offended the hierarchical structure of the cosmos (by being disrespectful to a high noble, for instance). As one old peasant lady in Senga said to me, *iato disanga kabusungang, tae'namabusa, tae'na mahido, tae'na malotong, tae'na mararang, tae'na makunyit* ("what they call *kabusungang*, it's not white, it's not green, it's not black, it's not red, it's not yellow"). The meaning of her concrete response was clear enough to her: kabusungang is invisible; it cannot be perceived directly. The invisible world of potency must be inferred by its effects, which are talle' (evidence, material traces), not malinrung (intangible). Thus the world is present to ToLuwu as a system of signs, which they constantly "read" and heed to guard their health and welfare.

To "read" or "utter" is *baca*. Any sign or inscription can be "read." A person's inner feelings can be "read" by others if he or she does not maintain an inscrutably neutral demeanor; hence high nobles tell their children, "don't let people read you!" which means that the children should eventually learn to control their inner emotions (and thus the external expression of those emotions on their faces and in their body stances), so that people will be unable to interpret or assess those feelings and will be unable to utter, to talk or gossip about, their assessments of the high nobles' feelings. A written text, of course, can be read, which means uttered or recited. Spells are baca-baca, texts stored in the chest and uttered in whispers. ToLuwu, in sum, constantly monitor other people, the world around them, and their own bodies, in order to remain or become cognizant of the tracings sumange' makes through its waxing and waning in particular locations, and to some degree to outguess its path.

Thus the world presents itself as a system, or at least a collection of signs. These signs are classically "indexical," to use C. S. Peirce's well-known classification: they are direct expressions of their referent, intrinsic to it, in the way smoke is a sign of fire, steam a sign of water, dark clouds a sign of rain. These signs are signs of potency, providing dilute but direct readings of it. In this sensibility, the world, whose status is a set of signs rather than the ultimate referent, stands as something like a reflection or shadow of cosmic potency. This theme is well developed in commentary on Javanese *wayang kulit*, shadow-theater with puppets made of leather, performed behind a white translucent screen and in front of a source of light, so that the puppets' shadows are cast upon the screen. It is worth noting, though, that other sorts of Javanese *wayang* ("shadow") theater—*wayang golek, wayang* using rod-puppets; and *wayang wong*, which is performed by humans—do not use puppets that cast a shadow. *Wayang* (Jav.) is cognate with *bayangan* (Ind.), a word meaning not just shadow but also reflection, as in a pond or mirror. The point is that everything tangible to humans, everything perceptible, is a sign (though some are more important than others); *bayangan* could well be translated "indexical sign," for that, after all, is what a shadow or a reflection is.

This metaphysic and ontology, like all others, imply a common sense. For ToLuwu it is common sense that, if something must crudely assert itself in order to bring about effects—with loud shouts or weapons—it is obviously lacking in potency; otherwise it would not have to rely on such talle' methods to bring about results. And since that which is most potent is also imperceptible, intangibility becomes a sign of potency. People also have a strong feeling that when the intangible-potent becomes tangible, it loses some potency in the process. The more talle' its vehicle, it would seem, the more is lost.

In this common sense, whispers make sense as a ritual medium and have a higher status, as it were, than shouts do. Thus the Datu, an embodied spirit, was supposed to say almost nothing at all; the ruler's presence itself was thought to bring about effects in the world, without effort or intention on the Datu's part. This sensibility informs everyday conversation, as well. In the Occident, we tend to emphasize a point by saying it more loudly. Important people in Luwu say important things in very soft voices, while around them their followers and visiting anthropologists strain for the aural equivalent of a glimpse of this all-but-inaudible pronouncement. And a high noble who raises his or her voice in anger not only demonstrates a failure to bring about effects silently, which would have been a demonstration of potency, but loses some potency, as well.

Barely audible sound, conveyed by invisible breath, can transfer potency from one place to another, from the curer who stores it in his or her chest and clean soul to the patient who is in need of it. Water is another substance whose properties make it an appropriate medium for invisible potency: transparent and tasteless, it is only a step away from being intangible. Another commonly used ritual substance is smoke: fragrant and barely visible, it rises and disappears. From the point of view of ToLuwu, however, it is not so much that the smoke is the vehicle to convey prayers upwards; rather, smoke is the talle' aspect of the rising malinrung prayers. Sound is not so much the vehicle of potency as its talle' aspect. In other words, these evanescent substances are signs, delicate signs, "indexical" signs that allow humans to read the world and make inferences about potency's paths through their lives.

In addition to their obvious properties, smoke and water travel directionally—a fact that, given the notion of the cosmos in Luwu, makes them especially appropriate ritual substances for communication with spirits. As in many cultures in island Southeast Asia, the cosmos in Luwu has three layers: the *boting langi'*, the peak of the sky, the Upper World of spirits; the *peretiwi*, the Middle World of humans (Luwu itself); and the *toddang toja*, the deepest point below the sea, the Lower World of spirits. Smoke rises, carrying whispered prayers to the spirits of the upper world. Streams and irrigation ditches for rice flow downward, eventually running into the sea, so offerings to the spirits of the lower world are sent by moving water.

Ritual substances straddling tangibility and intangibility are read as signs of potency's movement. But potency does not need even an evanescent sign to be present: smoke, after all, is a sign of potency, not its cause, vehicle, or medium. Thus potent effects may be brought about using no material medium or vehicle at all. Such is the case in the practice called maroja, in which the awake state of its parents and other people protects the new baby during its dangerous third night of life.

The Protection of Consciousness

A sick person, an infant, or one who has suffered "shock" can be guarded and aided without the use of any physical substances at all. People do this by gathering around the weak person to maroja. The root of this word is *roja*. In its transitive form, roja means to guard or care for something specific. In its intransitive or stative form, *maroja*, it means to be in a state of being on guard, to be alert, to be conscious. In this it parallels the meaning of its Indonesian cognate, *jaga*. *Menjaga*, the transitive form, means to look after something specific; *berjaga*, the intransitive form, means to stay conscious and aware.

Before I attended a third-night evening of maroja, I tried to elicit accounts of what goes on during them. People kept answering, "We maroja." I knew that to "maroja" is, basically, to stay awake. That did not seem to me to constitute a sufficient answer. "But what do you actually *do*?" I kept asking, because I was certain that what I thought of as a ritual must surely take place. As it turned out, of course, what they *do* is maroja, which to them (unlike to me) was something active and effective in itself.

People maroja in shifts, all day and all night, for the first forty days of the life of an infant of extremely high rank, such as the child of the ruler or of high nobles with large followings. In such a case, the mother's ritual bath takes place after forty days rather than after the seven or nine or eleven that commoners and lower nobles usually wait. Similarly, a high-status

person who becomes very weakened and sick is constantly surrounded by
at least a couple of followers, dependents, or other close members of the
household. The duty of such people is simply to stay with them in shifts,
day and night, so that the weak one is always surrounded by people awake
and alert.

Since the state of maroja is a way of guarding and aiding weak people,
it is used, not surprisingly, for cure as well as for prevention, and it is practiced to help sumange' reestablish itself in a person who has been rudely
surprised. People maroja for me one night when I suffered a nasty shock.
I had been reading late at night by the light of an unstable oil lamp that
suddenly overturned. The house was made of wood and grasses, and
nearby was a mosquito net. I grabbed the lamp and its spilling, burning oil
and threw it out the window in a wise panic, calling to my sleeping cousins.
Cursing myself for allowing so close a call and for the severe pain in my
scorched hand, and definitely feeling *majiong-jiong pinawangku* (my feel-
ing-tone had sunk very low, indeed), I prepared myself mentally for the
pain and loneliness of the night to come, anticipating that I would distract
myself by reading one of the books I had brought for afternoon rest hour.
Is this the time to face *The Brothers Karamazov* or *Raffles' History of Java*? I
wondered disconsolately.

Meanwhile my cousins and aunts had assembled and placed mats on the
floor so we would all be together, and they had brought me the basin of
water that I requested for soaking my hand. I was not, of course, to be
allowed to stay alone in a state of dismay after an unpleasant and disorient-
ing event. We all lay on our mats, seven or eight people. Opu Senga, keeper
of sacred texts, read to us in measured tones from the epic *I La Galigo*. The
epic describes the founding of the kingdom of Luwu by Batara Guru, its
first ruler, and the adventures of his twin opposite-sex grandchildren, Sawerigading and Tenri Abeng, and of Sawerigading's son La Galigo. All of
us drifted to sleep, permeated and protected by the gentle sounds made by
a person of calm and pure soul reading the sacred text.

Reading a sacred text in order to calm and protect household occupants
after one of its members has suffered a rude shock was a vivid but small
example of the larger function of the Opu Senga. (As an unmarried high
noble, her title would usually have been "Andi," followed by a name that
itself indicated high rank. But she was called "Opu," a title usually reserved
for married high nobles, because she was a member of the high inner core
of their extended kapolo, or family/following, who was posted, as it were,
in Senga.) Although within the extended family/following who lived in her
household, Opu Senga's rank by birth was matched by that of her niece
and nephew through different full siblings, she was preeminent, partly by

virtue of age. Further, as the unmarried female of the high inner core, she was herself a sacred object and guardian of the family's honor. She had assumed the function, common among older, unmarried, high-ranking women in South Sulawesi, of guardian of the family's sacred texts and genealogies, and she read them and recopied them and wrote notes on events for herself in Buginese script. Finally, she was the person who held the title *Opu* (lord of) *Senga*. One of the duties encumbent upon the holder of such a title is to cultivate a calm soul and pure intentions, not to become angry overtly or even in the heart ("liver," they say), and to exert a positive calming and purifying influence on others. Just as she protected the sumange' of household members that night when she read to us from the ancient text, so too, people felt, her presence would protect the larger realm, the people and crops that constituted Senga. Her spiritually potent presence was both inherited and attained, people believed. Her rank by birth was very high, so some of her potency was attributable to the nearly pure white blood she embodied, a heritage from her spirit ancestors. In addition, she cultivated a calm, judicious, and pure inner state.

From the point of view of villagers, it is far more important for a leader to be tactful and firm, to settle disputes, and (best of all) to prevent fights from happening than for a leader to, say, encourage the introduction of a new strain of rice (in the current era). But in order to be an effective leader in this sense, a person must not be subject to capture by factions, and must be calm, dispassionate, and not easily excitable. One of the ways that those characteristics can be achieved, people feel, is through meditation. Not surprisingly, it is a common practice throughout South Sulawesi for people in positions of leadership and responsibility to meditate.[1]

People of high rank with large followings commonly meditate, in the sense of putting aside a particular time during which the practitioner reviews and cleanses his or her thoughts and intentions. But the most feared and respected high-ranking leaders do not meditate at particular times (aside from praying five times a day, because they are Muslim, and the prayer is considered a short purification procedure). They are said not to need set time for meditation, for they are always conscious, always aware. Some evidence of their constant awareness includes their perfect self-control, never showing anger or distress; the fact that they anticipate trouble and thus prevent its occurrence, which takes constant alertness; and the

[1] Formerly, only people with inherited high rank and large followings held such positions of leadership, but now lower nobles and commoners have been elected or appointed as headmen or mayors or district officers, and they often take up the practice of meditating. Frequently a village officer lets it be known that he should not be disturbed between the hours of such-and-such, a fact that in itself increases his prestige, whether the meditation seems to have an effect on his behavior or not.

fact that they are never caught off-guard, and are always calm and composed.

By remaining constantly aware, such high-ranking spiritually potent people in effect maroja constantly, occupying a state of awareness that protects their followers as well as guards and increases their own potency. Just as its parents' awareness on the infant's third night protects it in its weak and vulnerable state, so too the constant awareness of high-ranking people is felt to protect their dependents and followers, who are intrinsically weaker and more vulnerable. They are more vulnerable because their own awareness is not so highly developed and constant, and because their concentration of sumange' is not so great—for higher-ranking people are, by definition, more potent nodes or centers and collectors of sumange'.

Being born of high "place" means being born with a considerable degree of "white blood," the intrinsically potent but invisible blood of unseen spirits. (ToLuwu speak of it in Indonesian as "white blood," *darah putih*; in Buginese, a person with white blood is said to *maddara takku'*, to have "cactus blood." If it were visible, it would be white, like cactus sap; but in fact it is invisible, malinrung.) So there is a presumption that, all else being equal, people born of high place are more potent than those born of low. And yet it is well known that high nobles, though born with a potential for achieving great spiritual self-control and social potency, require careful rearing and constant self-examination to purify and cleanse their motives, if they are to fulfill that potential. At the same time, people born of low status whose souls are pure may receive a gift of potency from God, called *were'* or *bere'* (from the root meaning "gift") and may become great leaders. (I need hardly add that such leaders tend to emerge in periods of chaos, when the nobility by birth are not entirely in control of the political/spiritual situation. But the presumption that the lowly may have "cleaner," "purer" souls than the high, and that they may consequently have special gifts and rise meteorically, is part of people's everyday awareness and common sense.) The social hierarchy predicated on such a rationale, is, obviously, sacred rather than legal, and fragile rather than fixed.

One reason for this fragility, not only in the grand plots of the historical fates of states, but in the smaller fates of individual lives, is the fact that sumange' can be gained and lost. The sumange' attached at a person's navel can be gathered in and more tightly attached, or it can be loosened, dispersed, or almost entirely lost.

Losing and Gaining Sumange'

From its most dense concentration at its point of attachment to the navel, sumange' spreads out, thinning in widening circles, not contained or bounded by the skin or body, but becoming increasingly thin with distance from the vital center. The hazardous state of tiny infants and weakened sick people means that their sumange' is loosely or unstably attached to their torsos. Sumange' can leave that point of attachment suddenly, rendering the trunk relatively inanimate. This, as I have mentioned, is called aseddingeng. What may not be entirely obvious is that aseddingeng is only an extreme and sudden case of sumange' loss, which happens gradually and continually in the course of simply living.

Humans are constantly shedding sumange'. It drops from us like feathers from a molting bird; it radiates from us like light from a glowing bulb. We lose it by being in the world, for we continually and inevitably shed pieces of ourselves: body wastes, such as feces, urine, menstrual blood, hair and fingernail clippings, sweat; and less gross and tangible aspects of ourselves, such as shadows thrown on a wall, footprints in the dirt, warmth on a seat where we were sitting, the sounds we make when speaking. Our clothes and possessions, through long association with our sumange', become (like our talle' bodies) pervaded with our sumange'.

Each of these leavings has characteristic fates and dangers. ToLuwu consider human excrement to be extremely repellent, and yet (they say, with horrible fascination) there is a type of human werewolf, called a *pakkoni*, who goes out at night and *eats human excrement as if it were sokko!* (*Sokko* is cooked glutinous rice, an especially delicious treat served for breakfast at feasts.) This activity, disgusting in itself, also functions as a type of black magic, because the people whose excrement is consumed become sick. Jin pakkoni, invisible nonhuman creatures, are attracted to blood and lick it up. So, men in battle quickly cover their their open wounds, I was told, so as not to make a bloody puddle attractive to jin pakkoni. And women, who use pads of fabric to collect their menstrual blood, are careful to wash the pads in flowing water—a stream or irrigation ditch is ideal—so that no attractive bloody puddle is made that would draw jin pakkoni to it. Less messy and repellent leavings may be used by other people to work black magic: hair, fingernails, pieces of clothing, photographs, footprints.

Clearly, the more intimately an item is connected with a person, the more that person's sumange' pervades it, hence the more potent and effective the leaving, when used by another person for good or ill. So a person who wants to work black magic will seek, say, an old rather than a new shirt belonging to the proposed victim. Black magic is worked by attacking a person's sumange' whose perceptible aspect (the talle' fragment it imbues) has become separated from the person's central concentration of it, the navel and the torso. But the sumange' is continuous. People's blood, for instance, remains a part of them even if it is no longer confined within their torsos. They say that when a jin pakkoni eats their blood, they feel a sharp pain in the stomach, as though lemon juice has been squeezed into an open cut.

Simply because shedding bits of oneself is inevitable in the course of living, a person who moves around from place to place disperses sumange', leaving it scattered in those places rather than densely and tightly concentrated in one location. Dutch sources on South Sulawesi mention a ceremony called *pakurrusumange'* that is performed for rulers who have suffered shock (apparently aseddingeng). I witnessed it several times in Luwu, but not for aseddingeng: it was performed as a matter of course when high-ranking visitors came to our house. I puzzled about the word for some time: *sumange'* obviously forms part of the word, and *pa* is the causative prefix, but what about *kurru'*? Then one day I heard a lady of the household calling to her chickens to feed them: "Kurru', kurru', kurru'," she gently cooed. When I wondered if that kurru' had anything in common with the one in pakurrusumange', I was told that, of course, they were the same: pakurrusumange' is performed to coax back sumange' that is dispersed.

Not just high-ranking people but also ordinary ones shed and scatter their sumage' in the course of ordinary living and moving around, but this low-level shedding by ordinary people is not considered of such cosmic import that a pakurrusumange' ceremony need be performed for them in the usual course of (say) their moving from one village to another. If an ordinary person sustains a great shock, however, his or her sumange' may loosen or leave; and so if shock has been sustained, a ceremony to call back sumange' may be performed for villagers, as well. I never witnessed it, but if, say, a child falls off the steps (said my informant, a young woman whose baby sister had done just that) and its parents feel it is somewhat disoriented, they call a sando', who comes to the house with a small fishnet. The parents and child go into the house, while the sando' circles the house making scooping motions with the net and cooing "kurru', kurru' sumange' " three or five times. Then the sando' calls up: "Is it there yet?" and the parents call down: "It's here!" Thus it is coaxed back. One morning I was doing something that struck an old lady of the household as quite inappropriate for someone of my status. She came over and gently stroked my arm, murmuring "kurru', kurru'," not only expressing her sympathy but aiding me, calling back my sumange', which I was dispersing by my willful disregard of my status. (When I returned to Senga in 1986, villagers flocked to the house with baskets of rice to perform the pakurrusumange' ceremony for me. They had heard that I had been in many lands before arriving in Luwu, that my journey was hard, and concluded that my sumange' was probably scattered about and needed re-centering. I heartily agreed, and gratefully received their ministrations.)

Perhaps it is not surprising that the state of bodily stillness provides an image of unity and concentration highly appropriate to rulers. The image of the cosmically still ruler is most familiar from its depiction in Javanese shadow-theater, in which the ruler, barely moving, whispers orders that have enormous effects and repercussions for the realm and the play's plot. At an everyday level, I found that people often resort to staying still as a way to protect themselves and stay out of danger or trouble. People do not move around much or make large gestures during the periods of transition in the day (dawn, noon, dusk, midnight), which are considered dangerous. Similarly, a bride and groom should not move around much for a period before their wedding, a day and night for the groom, at least a week for the bride (and longer for high nobles). In this case, it is not the cycle of the day, but they themselves who are undergoing a transition, and caution is called for.

Then again, the same sensibility informs potency magic. Once a delegation from our household, accompanied by kapolo from the surrounding village, went to a fairly distant wedding. One of the men in our party was known as a fearless warrior, and his duty was to guard us from harm. When we arrived after the dusty journey, all of us except this man trooped off to the river for a cooling bath. On inquiry, it was explained that his not bathing was a part of his invulnerability magic. When humans bathe, we lose part of our selves: some hairs always come out when we wash our heads, and, if nothing else, the *boring* is washed away. (Boring [Ind. *daki*] is the name for the dirt in pores that can be worked up by rubbing the inside of one's elbow on a hot and humid day.) On another occasion, the driver of a small passenger vehicle was describing to me his daily precautions, how he paid attention to omens from his own body (e.g., a twitching eye) and to omens on the road. He said also that some days you know that *nothing* will happen to you: "Everything is in place, not a hair will fall off." It struck me when he said it as an odd way to describe a feeling of security and well-being. Only later did I come to realize that he was enunciating an image of unity and concentration rather than of diffusion and lack of focus.

Physical stillness clearly does provide both an image and a practice of unity that implicitly and explicitly contrast with those of dispersal and loss. But a deeper stillness comes with a state of awareness and concentration, visibly indicated by composure and often by physical stillness. High nobles especially, whose duty it is to remain aware, dislike intensely the feeling of disorientation. Dizziness and drunkenness are, to them, particularly unpleasant feelings and, with seasickness, are called by the same name in both

Indonesian and Buginese. The point is the unpleasant condition one finds oneself in, not what external condition caused it (whether alcohol or rough seas is irrelevant). To be unaware, unprepared, taken by surprise is to be "swept away like a banana trunk in a swift current," a vivid image of utter lack of control over circumstances and oneself.

A state of awareness has several names, the most important of which is *paringngerreng* (Bug.). Paringngerreng is the noun form of the root that means "to remember" or "to be conscious of" when made transitive (obviously cognate to Indonesian *ingat*). Paringngerreng means something like "consciousness," "memory," and "awareness." In infants and toddlers, paringngerreng is clearly not yet developed, while in severely sick people it is simply not "strong," as evidenced by the fact that such people may be faint, suffer dizzy spells, or feel nauseated. Paringngerreng names a state of awareness, and there is thus some semantic overlap with our terms consciousness/alertness/awareness, even though the presumed sources and consequences of this state are quite different from the ones that we imagine.

Paringngerreng is, obviously, not the same thing as sumange'. Yet sumange', it will begin to be clear, is deeply associated with conscious awareness. Varying degrees of lack of consciousness are explained by lack of sumange'. For instance, it is said that sumange' has flown if a person faints. A sleeping person is also unconscious, and coherent dreams are explained as the experiences of the sleeper's wandering sumange'. The unpleasant disorientation following a shock is viewed as cause-and-effect and as evidence that sumange' has loosened or left. Lesser losses are experienced when people are distracted. One high noble said that a burst of uncontrollable laughter, like a burst of visible anger, makes you feel as if you have holes in you; he obviously experienced the lack of control implied in such outbursts as vulnerability. Another high noble said that outright laughter makes you feel "loose." Again, the implied opposite is "concentrated," which is a state of dense fullness and safety.

None of these conditions is as severe or as dangerous as the total loss implied by radical shock, aseddingeng, but they are nonetheless lapses from perfect concentrated awareness, and they are seen as an index of the fact that the person's sumange' has loosened its tight, densely full attachment. Lack of awareness means that one can be taken by surprise: it makes one vulnerable. That can happen, for instance, if a person concentrates too much on a fascinating conversation, is absorbed in eating, loses him/herself in guffawing, or stares abstractly into space.

The poles of what might be called "consciousness" or "states of awareness," then, are a relaxed distraction on the one hand and a concentrated, aware focus on the other. Just as Javanese speech levels range from *ngoko* (low/intimate speech) to *krāmā* (high/formal speech), so too states of awareness range in Luwu from loose distraction to focused concentration.

It is true that ToLuwu value the condition of extreme and constant awareness, considering it to be attainable only by a few particularly strong and pure people, usually those born with high rank. Lesser and less constant states of focus are attainable by everyone, and are regarded as necessary for health and self-protection. Yet however necessary and good focus is, everyone enjoys relaxing distractedly. Chortling over jokes, weeping unconstrainedly, eating in the kitchen with close kin with all the outer doors and windows closed, cuddling and playing with infants and toddlers: this is the stuff of delicious unawareness, possible within a protecting presence when no ToLaing are about. ToLaing are "other people," non-family, with whom one must be on guard. The condition of relaxed distraction makes a person open and vulnerable, and is therefore a dangerous state to be in when outside the house or in the presence of ToLaing. But inside one's own house or, even better, inside the house and in the presence of a respected elder with no ToLaing present, people enjoy relaxing distractedly.

There is, then, not so much a time to relax as a place to relax. The navel or center point of the house is the attachment point of the sumange' of the house, which apparently encompasses the lesser sumange' of its occupants. Within that protected realm, the occupants can relax, eat, or go to sleep. The center point of the kapolo is the inner core of high-ranking, same-status people, whose dense concentration of sumange' protects the kapolo members who are within it. People say that they feel cool and calm within their Opu's presence. Those realms are clearly safe places.

At a certain distance from the navel—the ill-defined border, if you will—the potency of the center is insufficient. Less potent navel-centers, obviously, have smaller realms. Outside that realm of protecting influence, at the thinning peripheries of the navel's potency, lies danger. When people talk about the journey from Palopo to Ujung Pandang, they do not mean between cities but between the safe house they leave in Palopo and the safe house they arrive at in Ujung Pandang. Between safe spots, one must be on guard.

Most common people, simply in the course of living, must make daily transitions from safe spaces to dangerous ones. As people will tell you, the real danger does not lie in the unprotected outside space but in being unprepared for it: "If you concentrate, you'll be all right! Nothing can harm you!" One man enjoyed telling me repeatedly about how he rode around South Sulawesi on his motorcycle during internal disorder (the Kahar period, from the mid-1950s to mid-1960s). He knew that nothing would happen to him because he "trusted God." (He was asserting that he was so potent and so pure that he would remain safe.) It will be apparent, though, that making transitions requires preparation so as not be caught unaware and subjected to the possibility of shock. To that end, people say spells and *pabaloi to paringngerreng* (Tae; in Bug., *pakasingi paringngerrang*; "adjust or make right one's conscious awareness") when leaving the house.

By now it will be clear that the great danger to being healthy/safe (*salamat*) is the loss of sumange', either sudden or slow. One becomes or stays salamat by guarding sumange' from loss or even by acquiring more. This clarifies why prevention and cure are the same thing. Certain changes of state are ceremonialized in Luwu: being born, dying, getting married, changing residence, and having body flesh pierced or cut (as in ear piercing or circumcision). The deep purpose of these ceremonies is to prevent shock before it happens. Ceremonies or rituals[2] for people who are sick or shocked have, as their deep purpose, the correction or mitigation of varying degrees of shock that has already taken place. Some practices, like pakurrusumange', have the same name when used for either prevention or cure.

Weak people must be treated with great gentleness to prevent them from experiencing shocks, even minor ones: they should not eat peppery-hot foods, become upset or angry, hear other people in a state of anger, move around unnecessarily, or leave the protecting realm of the house. Healthy people, especially during dangerous transitions, take due precautions—it would be arrogant not to—but they do not have to be coddled.

Nonetheless, the precautions taken by healthy people are less extreme forms of the curative practices performed by or on weak people, involving such things as not leaving the protective safety of the house, keeping physical movement to a minimum, neither becoming angry nor subjecting oneself to other people's anger, and in general avoiding disturbing circumstances, activities, and foods. In fact, I think it is fair to say that the notion of good health in Luwu is precisely the ability to withstand (and even seek out) trying circumstances—circumstances that would shock, panic, disorient, or discourage lesser souls—and to survive or best them.

Ranking and Danger

It seems self-evident to people in Luwu that different items in the world are capable of supporting concentrations of sumange' in differing degrees. In the realm of social relations, this means that people can be ranked. The

---

[2] The generic name in Luwu is simply *gau*, "what is done."

highest person in Luwu, the being who supported the greatest concentration of sumange', was not said to be a person (*tau*) but a spirit (*dewata*). Tau are people, creatures who are tangible and who have needs and desires that tie them to the world. Dewata are intangible invisible spirits. The Datu (ruler, the highest person) was thus said to be a *dewata mallino* (a spirit [*dewata*] in-the-state-of [*ma-*] the world [*lino*]). As a pure malinrung spirit who was nonetheless in palpable talle' form, the Datu was a miraculous living contradiction. We can think of the ruler as a location: the navel of the world, whose sumange' was the guardian of the realm.

Every image or analogy used to describe one sort of thing in terms of another more familiar one has its disadvantages and inaccuracies, because the matters in question are not identical. Still, it is important not to think of "space" in Luwu as an empty expanse occupied by containers filled with sumange'. A somewhat more helpful image is a field of energy. The energy exists everywhere in the field, but it is unevenly distributed: in some places it is quite thin; in others, densely concentrated. The energy is continuous—there are no boundaries and no empty spaces, but only thinner and thicker concentrations. The energy in this field is distributed not only unevenly, but unstably. It is continually moving, waxing and waning from particular locations. Its flux is usually, though not always, gradual. In addition to currents of energy, numerous visible objects occupy this field. One of the differences between the objects and the currents of energy is that the objects are discrete: they have boundaries and surfaces. Thus houses have walls, and humans have skin. But if we could see the energy, or if we were in the habit of thinking of the world in this way, we would understand that the boundaries or surfaces of these objects are the least important things about them. The objects provide locations and nodal points at which the energy collects, though in differing degrees of concentration.

I have mentioned that people's bodies and clothing absorb their sumange', and can therefore be used by other people for black magic. The examples I have given would make it appear that the process of absorption of sumange' is one-sided—that clothes absorb the person's sumange' but not vice-versa. But other habits show that the process is mutual. There is a feeling that any two items—for instance, a man and his motorcycle—must be suited if they are not to have harmful effects on each other. One man bought a new motorcycle and very soon had an accident. He had it repaired but soon had another accident. He concluded that he and the motorcycle did not mutually suit each other, so he sold it and bought another. The term he used was Indonesian, *cokcok* ("to mutually mesh or fit one another"). Sometimes a name is given to a child, who turns out to be sickly; the name is changed, on the assumption that the name and child do not cokcok. Sometimes all the inhabitants of a house fall sick; if all else fails, people sometimes change houses, on the assumption that they and the house have ceased to cokcok. Husband and wife, similarly, must discover after their wedding that they cokcok, if they are to remain married.

Implicit in the notion of cokcok, at least as used in South Sulawesi, is the feeling that two items, originally distinct, must become one if they are to remain long and comfortably associated. The Buginese term for the process by which two become one is *si-temmak-temmak*. *Temmak* is "to swallow or gulp," while *si-* indicates reciprocity. In demonstrating to me what the term meant, my informant put the corner of a cloth napkin into a bowl of water, and we watched the water slowly move into the napkin. The napkin and water si-temmak-temmak.

It is because sumange' is mutually absorbed that people can augment their own potency by acquiring potent objects. A widespread practice among Buginese-Makassarese men is to carry a dagger, usually strapped to the back near waist level and covered by a garment. A casual reading of this practice would call it the heritage of a warrior people carried into the modern age, but it can be read more fully. Talismans are often put in small silver containers and strung around the waist, a position close to the vital navel-center. Further, daggers are made of iron, considered the hardest substance. Just as a fragment of an iron pot may be put into a bowl of cool water, contributing strength by its hardness/potency, so, too, iron daggers placed near the vulnerable but crucial mid-torso area can contribute their strength to the hardness-potency of the men wearing them. High-ranking men who own them wear a small and a large keris, the distinctive iron sword associated throughout the Malay world with potency. The potency/hardness associated with the keris is explicitly phallic.

People wear daggers and other talismans, they say, so that they will be salamat—safe, healthy, and, most of all, invulnerable to penetration. The protection these things offer is like, they say, "an umbrella before it rains"—you take it with you, just in case. The dominant image of safety among the Bugis-Makassarese is being impenetrable, though, as I have pointed out, they consider themselves safe if there is dense potency at the navel rather than external walls or barriers. The literally impenetrable quality thought to be conveyed by effective talismans was expressed in an anecdote I was told about a high noble who went to a dentist. The dentist was a rather distant lower-ranking kinsman of the high noble, hence aware of the latter's status and deferential towards him. Unfortunately, the patient's treatment required a tube to be put down his throat. The dentist tried twice to insert the tube, but simply was unable to, and gave up apologetically. (Since to touch a high noble's head is a serious offense in normal circumstances, one can imagine the deferential dentist's hesitation not only to touch his ToMatoa's head but to pierce into it with a tube.) The high noble suddenly understood the problem: it was his invulnerability that prevented the tube's penetration. He then rose and removed the string of talismans from his waist, which had been hidden by his garments. The dentist was then able to insert the tube. A similar intuition, I suspect, prompts men to remove their weapons before they eat, laying them on the table; it seems illogical and counter-intuitive to open themselves and ingest something while wearing something that specifically makes them invulnerable to penetration.

The fact that sumange' is unevenly distributed among people means that the bodily leavings of high-ranking people can automatically become talismans for people of lesser rank. Followers may come from quite distant regions to ask for fingernail clippings from their high Opu, which they will then put in a silver vial and wear around their waists. In court literature throughout the Malay world, one often comes across passages in which the ruler, as a special beneficence, rewards a favored follower by bestowing upon him one of the ruler's own robes. In such accounts the ruler apparently is giving away potent fragments of himself.

It should be clear that fragments of the high noble, usable as talismans, are precisely the sorts of leavings that can also be used for black magic. I inquired whether it was not therefore dangerous for people to give away their sumange' in such form. The theoretical danger was readily admitted, but of course one would give such fragments only to one's allies, kinsmen who are also followers, and only they would dare to ask for them. A To-Laing who sought such leavings would clearly have intent to harm.

An implication of this way of understanding is that the higher one's rank, the fewer people there are whose leavings can augment one's potency. A very high noble, for instance, would be honored by the bestowed fragment of the ruler, but by that of few others. They seldom use talismans of the sort that lower people do, because they know that they are themselves living, breathing, walking talismans, whose presence protects those within their realm. Because much of curing consists of conveying potency from one location that has it to spare to another that is sorely in need of it, the impotence of almost everyone relative to the ruler meant that if the ruler fell sick, the means available for a cure were extremely limited.

Lower-ranking people, by definition, usually have lesser concentrations of potency, but they are certainly not without it. They may be brave soldiers, effective curers, fertile parents, or knowledgeable about religious matters. Their fragments may be requested for special purposes by their friends and neighbors. So, for instance, a childless couple will ask for an old shirt from a man who has fathered numerous children. It will be worn or stored by the childless couple, in hopes of strengthening their own fertility.

People want to augment their own potency, and to that end they seek potent items, which they wear around their waists or keep in their houses. Following instructions from voices in dreams that tell them where to dig, they often are successful in finding fragments of ancient pottery, and sometimes old daggers or pieces of iron, considered to be ancestral leavings. If a dagger is valued, the more so is a keris. (Few people, however, ever own or hold a keris. With rare exceptions, kerises are not in circulation, since traditionally they were never discarded or sold.) People will also try to augment their potency through meditation (seldom practiced by commoners) or through training in invulnerability magic, by finding a *guru* (teacher) to instruct them in the appropriate spells and practices.

Until now, I have emphasized the beneficent aspects of sumange': it animates, it protects and encompasses, it imbues with consciousness and fertility. But sumange' is not anthropomorphized in Luwu. It is neither benevolent nor evil, and it has no intention. It is potency and effectiveness, so it is dangerous as well as desirable.

Because it is hazardous to approach pure potency, people who have any wisdom do not embark lightly on schemes to augment their own potency in sudden or huge degrees. As the Opu Pa'Bicara put it, a baby chick will choke on a whole grain of corn. In other words, people can swallow only what they are capable of assimilating, else they harm themselves. Perhaps the most common explanation of madness is that the afflicted person was seeking powers beyond his or her capacity, or tried to acquire them too fast. That was also the explanation given of why a woman who lived not far from our house had turned into a pakkoni (the werewolf figure who eats human wastes in the still of the night). When it becomes known that a particular place is *makerre'* (Ind. *keramat*; also *sakti*) or charged with potency, people go out of their way to avoid it. People who are highly potent, most obviously the ruler and very high nobles, are similarly dangerous. Like the danger that inheres in makerre' spots in the terrain, the potent stinging energy of rulers and high nobles exists quite apart from their intention. They, too, are said to be makerre', and must be treated with delicacy, deference, and care.

When I began to understand that people or places that are makerre' are repositories or attachment points of dense concentrations of sumange', knowing that all humans have sumange' attached at their navels, I inquired as to why all people are not said to be makerre', since the difference is one of degree rather than of kind. Understanding my logic, people thought about the question carefully and answered like this: it is like the difference between warm ashes and a bright burning fire. It is true that both of them are warm, but the difference is so great between them that we call only one of them "fire."

High nobles who are clearly effective and potent are said to be makerre', and their capacity to command is called *moso*. Moso is also the sting of a snake bite. People who lack moso have these characteristics: they nag and reprimand their inferiors; they become visibly annoyed at small things; they speak carelessly and often; if things don't go as they wish, they easily panic or seem at a loss. A person who wants to retain moso will then do none of those things, which disperse it.

As people listed for me the ways that moso could be lost, I was struck by how universally applicable, how psychologically true, the rules were: they surely apply to anyone in authority who wants to remain so. That the interpretive scheme that produced them is not a psychologized one became clear, however, on another occasion when I inquired casually about the way that high nobles' food is served on ceremonial occasions, and in a less exacting way at home. At ceremonies, nobles' food is served on elevated platters that look rather like cake-stands. Sometimes a high-noble woman eats sitting in the kitchen with lower household members, in which case she will eat on two stacked plates as a casual substitute for a plate-stand; when eating at the table, high nobles do not bother stacking dishes, for the table itself is elevated enough. But when Opu Datu, the widow of the last Datu of Luwu, came to visit us, her tea was served in a cup resting upon two saucers and a paper doily. Why all these layers? I asked. The layers of dishes, it was explained, are to prevent a noble's moso from draining away.

The danger that high nobles pose to people beneath them is divorced from either their intentions or the political force that they command. Even if they lose their moso, even if they are poor, even if they go mad, they are not to be trifled with, for, as people say, "even a dried-up chili pepper is hot." The danger increases with the discrepancy in the potency of the two people. A lower person who has direct inappropriate contact with forces too potent for his or her own potency will become afflicted with malady or misfortune. Such a state of affliction is called *kabusungeng* (Tae *abusun-geng-ngé*; Bug., the verbal or adjectival form is *mabusung*, and it appears in much Western literature as if that were a noun, a practice I will continue). So, for instance, a person who looked directly at the ruler, especially into his eyes, would suffer mabusung; so would a person who failed to get off a horse or close an umbrella when passing in front of a high noble's house.

The suffering caused by inappropriate contact with people and things lower is called not mabusung but *kasalla'*. One village woman who became very annoyed by a cat that used to steal fish from her house cut off its head in a fit of rage; she subsequently went mad, and this was said to be from kasalla'. A book and some papers dropped to the floor from a table where I was in the habit of writing. Typing, I ignored them, and when I rose I did not bother to pick them up but stepped over them. Fortunately, only one close friend was with me, because my friend was scandalized: I would be kasalla' if I behaved so, stepping on or over things whose place is not under my feet.

The same sensibility, I think, informs the way people place things in piles or hang them on the hooks that are often on bedposts. Shoes are placed on the floor at the foot of the bed, never at the head, and when a pile of clothing is made, sarongs must be placed under blouses, never the reverse. This sensibility, if that is the right word, feels that everything should be in its place, and "place" (*onro*) is defined as a spatial relationship to things above and below. Appropriate action consists of respecting that place.

One respects things and people more potent than oneself by handling them delicately and circumspectly, knowing that they are more potent whether or not they intend to be. One respects things and people less potent than oneself by treating them according to their rank, neither humiliating them by stepping on them (unless they are the ground, or the floor, or shoes, for that is their place) nor trying to elevate them to a place that they cannot sustain without danger to themselves. Benevolence and wisdom do not feed whole grains of corn to baby chicks.

Chapter Two
Microcosm/Macrocosm

The human body is the talle' (tangible) aspect of sumange' (intangible potency) gathered or centered at its navel. The body is talle', but then, so is everything else in this world that is encountered through the senses. Everything tangible has the ontological status of being a sign, visible evidence that can be read by those who are alert to its meaning. A shorthand and abstract way to put this is to say that virtually everything perceptible stands, to use Peirce's well-known term, as an indexical sign; e.g., smoke is an indexical sign of fire, dark clouds are indexical signs of rain. But To-Luwu do not regard only (what we call) "natural" phenomena as (what we call) "indexical" signs, because they do not distinguish a sharp break between natural and conventional, or at least, the breaks and permeations of the two do not occur for them where they do for us. The akkarungeng was not a human invention, and its laws and rules were not regarded as merely human conventions. It reflected and provided evidence of the structure of the cosmos. Thus names in Luwu are indexical signs of birth, bodily gestures are indexical signs of inner spiritual state, house decorations are indexical signs of status, and so forth. This fact, the non-conventionality of signs—so alien to the sensibilities of Euro-Americans, for whom most signs are unglued from their referents and meanings (that is what we mean, in a nutshell, by "secular")—constructed the politics, the psychology, and the epistemology of Akkarungeng Luwu. As an epistemology, a mode of knowing, it means that people are very close readers of the world and of other people's bodies, for nothing talle' (perceptible) is without meaning beyond itself.

In the course of fieldwork in Luwu, I became increasingly struck by the importance of location as a perceptible sign of rank and/or spiritual power. Rank is conceptualized as a location, a "place" (onro) in the social order. To "be aware of one's place" (*naisseng onrona*) is to exhibit siri' (honor, dignity, and the capacity for shame) and to show that one is fully human. Onro, a term used to mean both physical and social location, derives its sense within the particular notions of the constitution of space that To-Luwu hold. As the Opu Pa'Bicara phrased it, they had not "three dimensions" but seven: up, down, right, left, front, back, and the ruler in the center. It is striking to me that the seven points he mentioned can almost be assimilated to "three dimensions." Up-down describes the axis of height, right-left the axis of width, and back-front the axis of depth; or, in statistics, rows, columns, and layers. But it is no accident that the term "three dimensions" describes the shape of a homogeneous and empty box, while Opu's seven points describe a full center with its visible periphery.

Opu's "seven dimensions" would probably make perfect sense to peoples in other hierarchical centrist island Southeast Asian states, where "order" was symbolized and in large measure constituted by differential ranking. Historically, the distinctions between people who were "higher" and "lower," and "near the center" and "far from the center," revealed in a variety of media, were powerfully comprehensible ways of organizing and playing out social and political life.

The Balinese, for instance, are a rather extreme example of a people whose orientation is spatial. Balinese villages, compounds, houses, and beds are arranged in such a way that it immediately becomes apparent, visually and experientially, which direction "north" is. The word used in the south of Bali and commonly translated into English as "north" (*kaja*) is the word that in the north of Bali could be translated as "south." The term refers not to an absolute geography of north-south-east-west, but rather is the direction "toward the mountain"; the opposite direction, *kelod*, is "toward the sea." The mountain in question is Gunung Agung, at whose top dwell the gods. Balinese dwellings are arranged in such a way that the highest, most sacred structure, the ancestral shrine, occupies the compound's kaja corner; the cooking space and beyond it, the area for urinating and keeping the pigs, lies in the kelod corner. The human body and its consciousness, no less than architecture and village planning, map themselves onto the same directional schema: "up," the head, the front, and the right side of the body are kaja, while "down," the feet, the back, and the left side of the body are kelod. The Balinese sense of disorientation and nausea, *paling*, refers to the alarming feeling of "not knowing where kaja is." The high and central Gunung Agung, in short, is the reference point Balinese use to make sense of and experience the landscape, both human and natural. It fixes the landscape's center. The human landscape, in turn, is littered with smaller centers, whose rank and potency are seen as derived from the gods who inhabit the top of Gunung Agung. Those are the palaces of the rulers, each of which, before Indonesian Independence, defined the central and high points in their respective realms.

As in Bali, though not as extremely and in somewhat different ways, much of what is socially important in Luwu is cast in spatial terms—literal, metaphorical, and linguistic. In Luwu, as in the historical polities of Java,

Bali, and Siam, "high" rank required literal high and central placement on ceremonial occasions. Even on non-ceremonial occasions, the dimensions of right-left, back-front, high-low and inner-outer are enacted in the medium of bodily gesture and arrangement in space. Thus etiquette in the courts of these historical polities featured low-ranking people virtually crawling in the presence of very high-ranking people, with downcast eyes and bowed heads, not daring to approach closer than the feet of the ruler. Even now, to be polite, one must keep one's head lower than the head of the higher-ranking person in whose presence one finds oneself. Even casual visitors to Southeast Asian areas influenced by the etiquette of courts are struck by the polite way in which people stoop if they need, say, to rise from a sitting position and cross closely in front of one, their knees and back bent, their right arm extended, their heads and eyes bowed, murmuring softly "tabe—tabe—tabe" or "monggo—monggo—monggo" (pardon—pardon—pardon). I was amused to note in a tourist brochure about South Sulawesi, written in both Indonesian and English, a caution warning that Buginese are likely to stab you if you point your foot at them. The warning is a little overdrawn, but captures the sensibility.

The most salient directions for nobles were "up" and "inner" or "towards the center." The two directions were effectively the same for nobles, in that socially "higher" persons were by definition closer to the center defined by the ruler's presence.

The importance of spatial location generally in Luwu, and the fact that a "place" or location derived its meaning with respect to an implicit center, I came to understand, had to do with the fact that sumange' becomes accumulated at particular locations. Those locations, in turn, become the visible embodiment, the tangible expression, of the potency centered at them. Virtually any location can be imbued with potency, but some locations are more potent than others, and some are intrinsically able to accumulate more potency than others. Two significant locations for potency are humans and the houses they dwell in. These places or locations, one human, one not, can be read by the signs they shed.

Architecture: Directions in Houses

At first glance, it is more than a little difficult to imagine that a Luwu house could have any meaning beyond rather rudimentary shelter. Indonesia is a country of spectacular structures; one thinks only of the multitiered roofs on Balinese temples, or the jutting prows of the Toraja granaries and houses, festooned with pigs' jaws and carabao horns on the support post, or the carvings and sweeping roofs of Minangkabau structures. In comparison with these, Luwu houses look plain and utilitarian, suggesting nothing more than the convenience of a roof over one's head.

The only striking feature of these houses is that they are uniformly built on stilt-like supports. Throughout island Southeast Asia, people who place their dwellings in the shallow waters just off the coast build houses elevated on posts. Virtually identical houses can be seen in South Sulawesi, the southern Philippines, and parts of the coast of the Malay peninsula. In shallow waters, the elevation posts have the useful function of preventing the living space from becoming wet during changes in tide or rough seas. Yet South Sulawesians build houses on this model inland as well, even in the dry interior. On dry land, in fact, the floor's elevation can actually be a hazard. Floors in these houses are made of roughly fitted slats, and the space below the house easily accommodates a person standing upright. It was a common practice in the coastal world between the Malay peninsula and the southern Philippines for enemies of a household to sneak under the house at night and stab upward through the floor slats with their long knives, killing or wounding those who slept on mats on the floor.

Because houses are elevated, entering them requires ascending the front stairs. A ToLaing ("other person" or "stranger") is by definition a "guest" rather than kapolo ("family," "follower," or "entourage member"), and will always enter the house by the front stairs. Guests find themselves in what is clearly a "front" room. Many houses now have a few chairs, a low coffee table, and perhaps a cabinet where the householders store pieces of porcelain, often ancient and broken, dug up by men on quests prompted by their dreams; perhaps the children's dry, withered umbilical cords, carefully wrapped and tucked in a drawer; and other items that should be guarded well, such as a copy of the Quran, or notations of one's genealogy. A bed or two might also be in the front room. There a guest will be served tea and a sweet: either white cookies or, to show special deference and respect, crisp batter-covered just-fried bananas. If you are a guest, you will not penetrate further into the house. This was made perfectly explicit in several houses in Senga in which I noted little hand-lettered signs in Indonesian hanging above the door leading to the back room: "BATAS TAMU," "off-limits to guests." When the household hosts a ceremony to which more guests are invited than can be accommodated in the front room, a temporary wide platform is built for them. It is attached to the front of the house and covered with an awning.

Kapolo and household intimates, by contrast, go freely into the back room. A person who is a ToMatoa (respected elder) of the household, even though he or she does not reside there, will enter through the front entrance (as befits his or her dignity), but, like household members and other intimates (like the householder's siblings, or even first cousins who are also close friends), a ToMatoa has free run of the house. If a ToMatoa wishes to go into the back area, household members feel flattered and touched that the ToMatoa is showing such interest in their everyday life.

I experienced this often, incidentally, during my first month or two of fieldwork. If I had made the rounds of introducing myself to community leaders alone, I would have automatically been a ToLaing, a rather bizarre alien who would have been served tea and cookies and treated with some doubt and extremely formal politeness, which is the same as social distance. Fortunately, introductions were arranged by Opu Senga, or Andi Minneng, or Andi Anthon, and initially I went always with one of the latter two or with another high-status household member. Their presence effectively gave me a stamp of approval and asserted that I was indeed kapolo, not ToLaing, that I could be trusted and cooperated with. The high nobles explained to their kapolo-members (the householders we visited) the intention of my research in pretty speeches that made sense to the kapolo members—that I was filled with admiration for the ancient customs of Luwu, that I came to Luwu to learn from Opu Lele, that I was going to write a book that would introduce Luwu to the people of America, that I was especially interested in their ceremonies and births and how they cure people of illness, that nothing should be regarded as so ordinary that I would not be interested in it, because the customs in America are very different and I had much to learn. After all this was established, and many questions and polite responses exchanged, and tea and fried bananas consumed, I would occasionally express an interest in seeing the rest of the house. Surprised and rather shocked, the householders would look inquiringly to Andi Anthon, or whoever was in company. "It's all right," he would assure them. "She really is kapolo!" Then some flurry followed as the back room was readied, and amidst many soft apologies ("*Kotoro'!*" "It's dirty!") and reassurances to the contrary on my part, I would proceed to the back room to meet the rest of the family, the children and perhaps visiting nieces and nephews or an old parent, inquire after their well-being and the children's ages, make more small talk, and leave. Thereafter, I could enter those houses' interiors and others without such formality and brouhaha.

The back part of the house is the cooking area, divided from the front by an interior wall and curtained door. A wealthier family's back area may contain several beds or even a table, but minimally it has an elevated area made of wood and filled with sand and rocks on which fires are made and food cooked. In this room, family and intimates gather to chat and eat, and women cook and prepare food. Many houses have a hole in the floor of this area, over which both men and women squat to urinate. These holes are used especially at night or in periods of transition during the day (dawn, high noon, and twilight), when people tend to be loath to leave the ritual safety of the house. Some households separate the actual fire-bed and dish-storage area from the communal family room by placing it even further behind, at a lower elevation than the rest of the house; sometimes one steps down into it, and sometimes one traverses a short bridge connecting the two. In any case, a small and inconspicuous stairway leads from the house's back area to the ground. Household members leave by this door when they go to work in the field, or to defecate, or to take out refuse.

The house's internal division between front space for "guests" and a back one for intimates is itself organized like (and for) the interactions of everyday life, in which perhaps the most salient social division that people experience is the distinction between ToLaing and kapolo, between rivals/enemies/peers/guests and allies/intimates/superiors/inferiors/"family." The realm of kapolo is the realm of intimates, of people who cook and eat together, and who often prefer to marry each other rather than strangers. It consists of a person's superiors and inferiors to whom he or she can trace a relation and considers to be allies. A kapolo, actually, consists of a person's loyal supporters, who are within this cultural logic bound to be that person's inferiors, if only slightly so. Thus, even though people throughout South Sulawesi translate the term "kapolo" as *keluarga* in Indonesian, or "pamili" ("family") in their pronunciation of English, the term is not used reciprocally, as "family" is in English. If I am in my second cousin's family, so is he in mine; but while I may be in the Opu Pa'Bicara's kapolo, he most definitely is not in mine. A better gloss than "family" would be, then, something like "entourage," with the note that the entourage members can trace relation to their ToMatoa, who is always higher than themselves in status. Thus the household members we visited for introductions were in the Opu Pa'Bicara's kapolo, not the reverse. A ToMatoa can enter his/her kapolo member's back room because the ToMatoa is, in effect, the "owner" of the house. (An "owner" is a person who protects the thing or people he "owns" and if necessary will use force to do so.[1])

[1] ToLuwu will say that they "own" people, or that a ceremony is "owned" by someone, or that the ruler was the "owner" of all the land. (The root of the word is *pu*, the same root found in *Opu, Ampo, Puang*, etc.; the "verb" is *punna*; an owner is *punnana*.) The meaning of "ownership" in Luwu is nicely described by Kiefer, writing about the Tausug of the southern Philippines. He points out that "when a Tausug says he owns something (for example when he says that he owns a group of Samal), he is mainly stressing that he will use his own personal power to protect it against transgression; one owns something if one is ultimately responsible for its protection. . . . Hence, when a Tausug headman says that he owns a group of Samals, he is not referring to them as slaves, but rather stressing a certain form of authority over them" (Kiefer 1972: 23).

Commoners theoretically are all of the same status, in contrast to nobles, who measure degrees of high and low status in terms of degrees of white blood, which only they, by definition, possess. When I went to the houses of commoners before ceremonial occasions, they often said to me, gesturing to the women and men making preparations for the event, "These are all kapolo! No one else! No one is paid!" In short, commoners refer to all their helping relatives as kapolo; they will reciprocate that help, however, when those relatives themselves have a ceremony. The realm of kapolo for a commoner is also rather small, since, due to the way that genealogies are kept (a subject explained at length in Part III), the lower a person's status, the fewer people to whom he knows himself to be related. Age is the only formal difference in "status," if that is the appropriate term here, among, say, a set of siblings, or between a senior and a junior generation. Of course, commoners differ in standing due to wealth and accomplishments, but these are not enough to attract a permanent entourage of allies of the sort that a noble's kapolo forms, and in any case the naming, genealogy, and marriage systems operate in such a way as virtually to preclude the formation of large enduring bodies of allies around lower people, as I show in Part III. The realm referred to as its kapolo by the high core of high nobles who lead it, by contrast, may involve hundreds of people, whose descendants themselves become the loyal inferiors of the high core's same-status descendants. (I use the term "high core" rather than a single leader for the sake of clarity and accuracy; it will be particularly apt later in the book when I explicate the activities of the high core.)[2]

A high core's kapolo members come to work at its house, preparing for the ceremonies that the core "owns." High nobles do, of course, have obligations to their followers, but they do not do physical work or help their followers prepare for ceremonies; the exchange is asymmetrical. As in smaller ceremonies belonging to lower people, the "guests" at a high-noble core's ceremony consist of the core's rival-peers, each accompanied by an entourage of kapolo members.

The kapolo, then, is the realm of safety and mutual aid, of intimacy, and of relaxation. Among nobles, it is also the realm of marriage, because in Luwu, the higher in status people are, as a general rule, the closer they

[2] The kapolo I studied was sometimes called "kapolona Opu Lele," "Opu Lele's kapolo," as if the group had a single leader; but to reproduce itself and carry out its duties, a kapolo must have at its center not just a male leader but a high core of status-peers who act in concert. The more exalted the high core and the more extended its kapolo, the greater the range of the statuses of the people who follow it. The high core of the kapolo I studied consisted of the Opu Pa'Bicara, his same-status wife and first cousin Opu Damira, his older full sister Opu Senga, his same-status children (five of them, but Andi Anthon was most prominent in my research), and his same-status niece Andi Minneng.

prefer to marry. (First cousins are the closest allowed, a subject explored in Chapter Eight.) Because the kapolo consists of loyal supporting inferiors, it is the high core's ally in the core's contest for status conducted against its rival-peers. For their part, kapolo members feel safe with their high core, because their status with respect to one another is guaranteed and controlled by the leader, to whom they defer as their acknowledged superior. In short, the kapolo is a safe realm precisely because it is internally ranked. Within it, everyone should "recognize his/her place [*naisseng onrona*]" and not offer challenges to superiors or insults to inferiors.

ToLaing, as their name suggests, are "Other People," non-allies, non-kapolo. As it happens, they are not just a residual category, not just non-kapolo, but anti-kapolo. ToLaing may be total strangers, in which case they are unaware of one's status. Structurally, however, ToLaing are peers, or nearly so, with respect to status, and they need not be strangers. Two middle-level nobles who are unrelated or distantly related and acknowledge a common ToMatoa can both be counted as their ToMatoa's allies. When the ToMatoa is present, or in a context defined by the ToMatoa's presence, such as work in a ceremony that the ToMatoa owns, these middle-level nobles are able to work together for the prestige of their ToMatoa, and to respect each others' status as defined and controlled by their ToMatoa. But their connection to each other is through their ToMatoa; it has no independent existence. By themselves, in the village, they operate in an implicit rivalry, each suspicious (with good reason) that his status-peer wishes to encroach upon his dignity and prerogatives.

Structurally, then, the category of "kapolo" continually shifts its personnel. In contexts in which status-peers metaphorically look up towards the center of the kapolo to which they belong, they can act solidarily, in their capacity as the peripheral aspects of the central core. But in contexts in which they look to the side and see their peers, each other, each becomes his own center and must defend his "place" (onro), his dignity. These status-peers become ToLaing to each other, and must remain on guard, suspicious and watchful of every gesture that may show disrespect: "Makare-tutuko aké deng ToLaing!" (Tae, "Watch out if there are ToLaing!")

It is therefore always rather tiring to confront ToLaing. When ToLaing enter one's house, they enter as "guests," remaining in the front room, prevented from penetrating further into the house. The redundant but emphatic signs "BATAS TAMU" say it all: contact with ToLaing should be circumscribed in place and limited in time, their presence should be announced and their departure certain.

Incidentally, it would be a mistake to equate "front guest area" and "back family area" to "public" and "private" spaces. Both are social spaces, and in that sense both are "public," although the term makes sense only in opposition to "private." Individual autonomy is not given spatial expression in the house's layout in the way that the bedroom came to give spatial expression to a sense of individual and autonomous selves in nineteenth-century Europe.

Because houses are built on three levels, high and low are also significant aspects of the house. The highest level, called the *rekeang*, consists of the space under the roof. (There is no ceiling. Rafters and the underside of the roof are visible from below.) People formerly stored two precious items there: unhulled rice, which is associated with the rice spirit and treated with respect throughout island Southeast Asia (see Pelras 1974 on rice in South Sulawesi); and *mana'*, the objects inherited from ancestors (this corresponds to the Indonesian *pusaka*). High nobles stored, albeit temporarily, a third precious item: their unmarried daughters remained in the rekeang on special platforms during ceremonies, out of sight of the males from rival kapolo. In brief, this area was reserved for storage of items having intimate connection to spirits of the Upper World.

I use the past tense in describing the rekeang's contents because practices have begun to change. Some people continue to keep mana' in the rekeang, but often it is placed at the top of a high cupboard instead. The problem of rice is more distressing to ToLuwu. Rice used to be harvested in stalks, which were bound together in surprisingly heavy bundles and carried home on women's heads or balanced on each end of a pole slung over men's shoulders. At the house, these bundles were carried inside and then thrown up into the rekeang, where they were placed in a bin. Now, however, some ToLuwu have begun to plant and harvest new high-yield strains of rice, whose grains shatter and fall easily from the end of the stalk when ripe. As a result, the grains must be separated from the stalks in the fields and carried home in wrapped bundles or tin pots. Those containers cannot be easily tossed from someone inside the house to someone in the rekeang to be placed in a rice bin. Now the growers of rice put it loose in a covered bin under the house or inside it, near the cooking place. Several people expressed some unease about this displacement of rice from its rightful spot.

Below the house is the ground (or sea), the *sullu'* (Tae; in Bug. *riawa bola*). Miscellaneous refuse tends to gather there, especially below the cooking area of the floor, since dirty dishwater and food waste are dropped through the floor slats. Dogs and ducks and chickens live on the ground, often congregating under the cooking area to scavenge scraps. People keep their motorcycles and bicycles there, and Senga's first tractor, purchased by the family, was parked under Opu Senga's residence. Small children may play there to get out of the sun.

Humans live in the middle level, the house "itself" (Tae *kale banua*; Bug. *ale bola*), whose interior structure I have already partly described. This tripartite division in architectural space parallels the tripartite division of the cosmos: the Upper World, associated with the potent and revered ancestral spirits; the Middle World, where humans live; and the Lower World, associated with the sea. The coastal peoples who live in houses of this type simply drop garbage through the slats to be washed away by the water. For them, the metaphorical association between the Lower World and the region below the house is also literal.

Another possible directional division in the house, one that in my experience was virtually unrealized, is between right and left. In houses of some Indonesian societies, notably those of Eastern Indonesia, right and left (often corresponding to men's and women's spaces) are prominent divisions (cf. such classic accounts as Cunningham 1964). In my experience, right and left are not given great prominence in the house in Luwu, though in an article on the Buginese house, Pelras (1975) writes that the contrast was once more marked than it is now. Still, there presumably never was the radical distinction commonly found in Eastern Indonesia. In those societies, the dualism of house spaces parallels and confirms the dualisms endemic to that area in every medium—the oppositions between wife-giving and wife-taking houses, the parallel pairs of phrases in ritual language, the cosmic importance of binary distinctions between earth and heaven, night and day, male and female, right and left, and so on. Saussurians inspired by the notion that meaning lies in distinctions have for good reason been attracted to analyzing that area of the world, which provides abundant evidence that the human mind (or anyway, those local minds) thinks through contrasts (cf. Fox 1980; Lévi-Strauss 1962, 1969; some articles in Needham 1973; and Traube 1986).

But the hierarchical centrist polities of island Southeast Asia, the "Indic States," were ideologically opposed, as it were, to dualism at the center. They represented themselves to themselves as mountains, umbrellas, or banyan trees, or as mandalas (a central point surrounded on four sides). Speaking of followers and their patrons, they say *de'naulle ripassareng— batu mata malotongngé, batu mata maputié* ("indivisible, inseparable, cannot be torn apart—the eye's black, the eye's white"). The unmistakable purport of all these images is a stable, concentric, undivisible unity. In these centrist states, dualism at the center could have meant only instability. Thus the icon of dualism in these centrist states was not the stability of eternally paired complementary opposites, like right and left or heaven and earth, as it tends to be in Eastern Indonesia. Excepting Thailand (still formally a monarchy), the Indic States as political entities have been replaced or absorbed by secular nation states. Yet within such societies the sensibility persists that abhors permanent dualisms. Historically as well as now, the icon of dualism in these societies, the remnants of centrist states, was not and is not the complementary dualism of Eastern Indonesia but irreconcilable dualism: the contest between closely-matched peers, one of whom must vanquish the other and re-establish a hegemonic center. In contests between two peers in these centrist societies, everything is at stake; one emerges victorious, the other utterly vanquished. Thus the contest is "deep play," as Geertz (1973a) has called it, in these Southeast Asian societies with centrist aspirations. For these reasons, it seems to me, a strict division between right and left in the house would be alien to the sensibilities of Luwu, although some mild acknowledgment of the distinction was made. (I will soon make further comments on the right-left distinction in the human body, and deal with the contest as a symbolic form in Chapter Five.)

I turn now to the center, the seventh of the Opu Pa'Bicara's "seven dimensions." Like people, houses have navels—the center post (pinposik) around which the rest of the structure is built. The building of houses is supervised by an expert in houses, a Pandei Banua. His expertise is not primarily technological, though he does supervise construction. His expertise lies in the spells and procedures by which a house is built. The house's construction is attended at every point by spells; its building is a ritual event, no less than is a human birth. So too is its occupancy, which is ceremonialized as much as a wedding or circumcision. To change residences involves moving from one location to another, and must be conducted with care.

After the proposed site for the house is determined, the Pandei Banua ritually clears the area of spirits. Then a hole is dug, in which he places certain bespelled objects, followed by a post that will run from the ground through the space below the house and through the living level, halting at the space below the roof (the rekeang). In short, it intersects the bottom two levels of the house but stops short of the highest one. This post is the house's center. The center post of the ruler's house (I was told but did not observe) intersected all three levels.

Like people and houses, Bugis-Makassarese pinisi (a type of boat) have ritually constructed "navels," at which offerings to the spirits are placed. Even the shavings of wood that accrue from making the "navel-hole" of the ship are treated as an umbilical cord, wrapped and preserved and hung on the mast (as a parent sometimes hangs the infant's wrapped umbilical cord on the center post of the house). This item is used for protection when the boat is in danger, just as a child's umbilical cord may be used. (On the symbolic aspects of pinisi-building, see Pelly 1977.)

A spirit, called the Ampo Banua (Tae, "lord or owner of the house"), lives hovering at the center post. Or perhaps it would be better to say that the post is the spirit's point of attachment to the house. The Ampo Banua is offered food once a week, on Thursday nights, and on ceremonial occasions. (A tray of food is placed by the navel post and left for a while. Spirits, being insubstantial, consume smells.) Every few years, a house-purifying ceremony should be done for it.

What is the Ampo Banua? When pressed for a translation into Indonesian, people said that it was a type of dewata, a spirit. Observing that its presence protected the household's inhabitants, and that people tried to keep it from straying afar by attending to it, I wondered aloud whether it was not the sumange' of the house. People were quite aghast at the obviousness of it all. It was so clear that no one had thought to tell me so explicitly.

Etiquette: Directions in Bodies

Like houses, human bodies are entities within space, palpable and visible, the talle' aspect of the sumange' gathered at their centers. ToLuwu, especially those of higher rank, tend to be conscious of themselves—of their stance, demeanor, gestures, styles of speech, physical locations, and movements in space—as shedders of signs that will be read by others.

At the same time, they view the relation between inner state and outer indication as a continuum; actions at one end have an effect on the other. Thus outer gesture reveals inner state, but inner state can be calmed and purified by restraining outer gesture. The two poles are reciprocal and mutually influencing. (In this respect their views are extremely similar to those of the Central Javanese; see Geertz 1960 and Keeler 1987.) As a consequence, the gestures, movements, and so on made by human bodies are taken literally, not with ironic distance.

Some anecdotes involving Westerners will illustrate this literalness. Several years ago I visited Java and met a Westerner who was studying Javanese. She had learned a fair bit of krāmā, the highest speech level, by speaking with her Javanese teacher. Krama is used when speaking to superiors or to people with whom one wishes to maintain a respectful distance. She wanted now to learn to speak ngoko, the lowest level of speech, which is used when speaking to intimates and inferiors. But her teacher, while certainly willing to speak *ngoko* to her, was too discomfitted by the prospect of her speaking ngoko to him, and rejected it. Most Westerners, certainly most Americans, would think his discomfort ridiculous, or that he was foolishly obsessed with his own status. After all (we might think), their lessons were private, and no one would know what level they used to speak to each other; and it would not matter anyway because language is not real but mere arbitrary signs—how could he take it so seriously? And, even if he took it seriously, surely the occasion of lessons allows or requires ironic distance, a suspension of disbelief, a circumstance in which no one could blame teacher and student for playing an "as if" game for the sake of conveying expertise. But a language lesson in Java, it turned out, was not a hiatus from real life; it was real life, like everything else. On the same trip to Java, I visited an anthropologist and his distinguished old *gamelan* (percussion-music ensemble) teacher. I wanted to take photographs of the instruments of the entire gamelan, including the old gentleman sitting there on the floor. The ideal picture could have been obtained by standing on a chair at the edge of the room, but, my friend informed me, this was out of the question; to be so high above his seated teacher would be highly rude and shocking. The best I could do was to photograph what I could from the edge of the room, semi-standing but bent over to indicate respect. Again, taking photographs does not allow a suspension of "etiquette," the rules and sensibilities regulating one's safe conduct in the cosmos.

Because inner and outer form a continuum (the latter being merely a diluted expression of the former), this way of construing the analogue of psychology, although it has its paradoxes, does not imply the deception and the schizoid relation to one's "true" self found in, say, the view of human nature revealed in books like "Dress for Success," or even in the way Erving Goffman writes about interaction. In Goffman's works, a homunculus seems to dwell behind the mask, manipulating the exterior to influence others, promote itself, or even simply to be polite. In our folk psychology, between inner subjectivity and outer form lies a radical break, a disconnection that can be disguised, but not overcome, by self-conscious and instrumental manipulation. Construing the "self" as an inner subjectivity inevitably cut off from its exterior manifestation of body, yet at the same time insisting that it should express itself directly, with "sincerity and authenticity" (see Lionel Trilling [1972]), forms for us an insuperable paradox.

In Luwu, inner state and bodily manifestation have an intrinsic connection. So, for instance, although in English we may speak of a "well-balanced personality," we have no expectation that that fortunate person will have good posture; but in Luwu, as in Java and Bali, balance or centeredness is taken literally. To slouch is not exactly immoral, but it is a failing that reveals a lack of inner composure. The body's gestures, the location in space of its parts, and its placement in space have meaning in Luwu.

Head and feet mark the extremes of high and low in the body. Feet are the lowest part of the body, and must be hidden, or at least not pointed. In hierarchical centrist Southeast Asia, men sit cross-legged on formal occasions, their feet tucked out of sight. Women sit in a variety of positions in different Southeast Asian societies, but on formal occasions the soles of their feet are always out of view, tucked under the fabric of their sarongs. To expose the sole of the foot to someone in these societies or to make the feet prominent is an insult. Once, when I was in Ujung Pandang, recovering from an illness in the house of an American there, two very high-status ladies from other former kingdoms paid me a social call. The American man of the house came out to the living room while the ladies and I were chatting and drinking the inevitable tea, and he began conversing casually. He rested one foot on the coffee table, crossed his arms and loomed there above us while talking. I was shocked and humiliated: What sort of people would the ladies think were my friends? They must have been appalled but in good noble fashion kept their composure, no doubt having had confirmed what they already knew, that Westerners are, after all, arrogant, disorderly, and completely without manners or finer sensibilites. Since feet are the lowest part of the body, to step on or over something whose place is not beneath the feet is to commit a cosmic error; the offender may suffer either kasalla' (if the offended is below the offender in status), or mabusung, if the offended is above. Throughout island Southeast Asia, people remove their shoes as gesture of respect when entering another's house.

The head is the emblem of a person's social "place." To approach a person's head or face too closely is to risk offending; to touch it is a grave insult. I suspect that children become aware very early in life of the sacredness of their heads. I did not observe it in Sulawesi (for one thing, I never saw adults teasing children), but Margaret Mead describes the fury of tiny children, beside themselves with rage, when their mothers teased them by placing their younger siblings above their heads (Mead 1942). Especially on ceremonial public occasions, high-ranking people are placed centrally, which is symbolically the highest place. (If everyone is sitting on mats on the floor, the higher people do not need a platform; their prominent central placement is equivalent to height.) People approaching them deferentially lower their heads and eyes and stoop, squatting while approaching them. Obviously, the greater the difference in status, the greater the obeisance made by the person approaching. On one occasion, for instance, several members of the high core of the Opu Pa'Bicara's family visited a rather remote area of Luwu for a ceremonial occasion, and a couple of old ladies, old family retainers (themselves not of noble blood), rushed to greet their ToMatoa (who were sitting in chairs), sitting at their feet and hugging their legs with joy. When people are closer in status, by contrast, they straighten up after the initial greeting. Thus when Opu Datu, the widow of the last ruler of Luwu, visited Luwu, or if we visited her residence in Ujung Pandang, members of the Opu Pa'Bicara's immediate high-core family greeted her deferentially, but not excessively so. If she was sitting, they approached upright until within a few feet of her, then with bent knee and head, and downcast eyes, they extended their arms with palms together. Those in the generation below hers would drop until their heads were a good head or so below hers, and look fully down. Those in her own generation would drop briefly so that their heads are below hers, but receive her reciprocal greeting while looking at her. For her part, she would touch the other person's hands with hers in a reciprocal gesture and urge them to get up and sit around her. They then would do so, sitting upright, but of course not guiding the conversation and always deferring to her. The lower-ranking people of her household, by contrast (many of them nobles, but middle-ranking ones), would serve tea to this assemblage of august persons by bringing in the tray and then dropping to their knees in front of Opu Datu, as though the tray were an offering, and placing it on the coffee table, then, still squatting, would exit backwards for several yards, rising and turning only at the door.

Memory and thinking are located in the chest, not the head or brain. Being the highest part, the head is emblematic of a person's status, and must be guarded on that account. I suspect its elevated value is purely locational: if humans had been constructed such that an elbow were the uppermost extremity, the elbow would in South Sulawesi be the emblem of status. Yet the head has another attribute that distinguishes it: our sensory capacities—hearing, taste, smell, and sight—are concentrated there. The apertures located there, although not our only ones, constitute a concentration of the means by which we communicate with the world and through which the world penetrates us. I use the term "penetrated" deliberately, for the notion of being penetrated by the hostile outside world of spirits and enemies figures large in images of sickness and health among the Buginese, as among some other island Southeast Asians. The head, then, as the part of the body at once the most vulnerable and the most high, is a precious hazard to its owner.

Between high and low lies the torso. Most human functions are thought to take place there. Knowledge in the form of spells (paddissengeng) is stored in the chest, as I have already described, and is brought up from the chest and conveyed to another medium through the whispered breath. To think or imagine [*manawa-nawa*] is an activity that takes place in the chest. Strong emotions are associated linguistically with areas deeper in the abdomen—stomach, guts, and liver.

Since the human body's front contains its receptive organs, probably in no human society is it polite to turn one's back on someone; to present one's back to someone cuts them off literally as well as metaphorically. In Luwu, the front of the body is its presentational side, presented humbly, with head bowed if the occasion requires it, to superiors. Or it can be presented directly and confrontationally, level-eyed, to enemies and rival-peers.

What resemblance more perfect than that between our two hands! And yet what striking inequality there is! wrote Hertz in 1909. Actually, the poles of right and left are the least different of the three directional pairs of distinctions offered by the human body, and consequently they can be made to speak to either symmetry or asymmetry. The distinction suppressed speaks of symmetry, as in Japanese etiquette, where using either right or left hand to give or receive is equally polite, for a symmetrical body stance signifies respect. Or right and left can be highly distinguished but made into an icon of near peerdom, in which one has a slight advantage over the other but they stand as a dyadic pair, uncollapsable; Eastern Indonesian societies seem to take this approach, using the right-left distinction in the house to speak to the paired opposites of male and female, as well as to other nearly parallel but distinct members of pairs. In Luwu and other centrist hierarchical former states of Southeast Asia, right and left are highly distinguished and right is clearly dominant, equated symbolically with high and front. One gives and receives with the right hand. In a gesture of special respect, the right hand is extended, the left hand touches the right elbow, the head is slightly bowed and the torso slightly stooped. This stance has been adopted in modern times for shaking hands, a gesture previously unknown, upon being introduced to people of great bureaucratic superiority. And the right hand is used to touch and deal with the upper half of the body (including, of course, eating), while the left is used to deal with the lower half of one's body.

Every society conscripts its members' bodies, making them into instruments to express its notions of order and of what it is to be human. The radical hierarchization of body parts in centrist hierarchical Southeast Asian societies reflects and helps to constitute social order; it is one way to make the body into a social instrument in a hierarchical society. If right and left hands, head and feet, and so forth are marked as distinctive from each other and differentially valued, they can be made to speak to a social order by reflecting, and in turn enforcing, its main coordinates. By embodying order, the body itself makes order public and open to inspection; it becomes an ambulatory lesson in visible order. But it also enmeshes people in social life as public beings rather than as private islands. One cannot speak some languages (like Javanese or Thai) without placing oneself as higher or lower than the interlocutor, which means that to utter a sentence locks the speaker into becoming an instrument of a particular form of social life. By the same token, because gesture is fraught with meaning, one cannot interact in these societies without placing oneself higher or lower than the person with whom one is interacting, and with similar effect. To speak and to be in another's presence forces one to participate in a particular version of order. In these circumstances, one can succeed as a social being, or one can fail, but there is no neutral space in which to be only "oneself," sincere and authentic. The American I mentioned who put his foot on the coffee table in the presence of high nobles was not read as an individual with his own idiosyncratic gestures, but as arrogant and ill-mannered. In such a society, there are only socially adept persons or social failures; self-referential autonomy is not an option.

Inner and Outer: The Collapse of Directions

To the unpracticed eye all Luwu houses, with the exception of the most magnificent, look about the same. But in fact every decoration elaborates status. A ladder leading to the front porch is a sign of lower status than is a stairway; a stairway covered with a flat slanting roof is higher-status; a stairway covered with a pointed slanting roof even higher; a stairway covered with a pointed slanting roof and a landing partway up is higher yet. Another visible indication of the occupant's status is the number of *tipe-tipe* the house has. Tipe-tipe are flap-like structures that are visible at the house's front. Three is the maximum in Luwu, suitable only for rulers. In Bone, a Buginese area to the south, the maximum was seven. (Some people in Luwu pointed this out to me as being typical of the excesses of parvenus.)

Large size in itself does not indicate higher status, merely wealth. Higher status is indicated instead by elaboration of spaces and of decoration. The household of very high nobles where I lived is by far the most elaborate in the area. It consists of two structures, side by side, one set further back than the other from the road that they both face; the two are joined by an elevated walkway at their backs. The larger structure functions as the "front" of the house. Three tipe-tipe and an elaborate covered stairway with two landings precede the outer front porch. Inside, the porch is spacious and high, suitable as a place for village girls to practice ceremonial dancing (promoted and revived in this era by the Council of Arts) or for large numbers of men to sit, cross-legged and in a circle, for occasional small ceremonies (such as the one we had in order to initiate the new tractor). Needless to say, "guests" enter by the front stairway.

The other structure functions as the "back" of the house. Lower and set back from the road, it too has a covered stairway facing the road, but the stairway's roof is not peaked, and it has no landings. The seller of silk sarongs from Wajo travelling through Luwu, the fish merchant making his daily rounds, women coming to visit Opu Senga to seek her advice, and other such people come and go from this structure's front. Its front porch, which is screened from view from the road, is used as an informal space for negotiations, chatting, weaving small baskets, crocheting, delousing hair on a lazy afternoon, and the like. Behind the front porch is a sleeping area, where Opu Senga and her close female associates sleep. Behind that is the cooking area, from which a tiny inconspicuous ladder leads to the ground and out to the fields behind. The two structures are connected, as I mentioned, by an elevated walkway, which itself has a rather rickety stairway leading to the ground. Household members go from one structure to another via this walkway, and often use its stairs when they descend to go out to the fields.

The inner structure of all houses in Luwu is the same, for all have pinposik, center posts. From commoner's shanty to high noble's palace, the logic and aesthetic are the same. The differences lie in the degree of elaboration of layers around a common central core. The same can be said, I think, of the Luwu view of humans. Commoners and nobles, as well as men and women, are in a profound sense the same sorts of beings in Luwu. Each has a navel, each has sumange' centered there, and consequently birth and curing ceremonies of both are based on the same principles.

People do claim to see a radical break between commoners and nobles, but in fact the transition is gradual (as I will elaborate in Chapter Three and Part III), and the reality of a break is belied by the fact that the ceremonies of the lowest people, their fears of sumange' loss and efforts to bring it back, parallel those of nobles. Lower people's ceremonies can be viewed as diluted or impoverished versions of noble practices, or noble ones can be regarded as overblown and elaborate versions of peasants'. (Historically, I imagine it went both ways.) But they clearly are related to the sorts of "anatomy" and constitution that humans in general are regarded as having.

In Chapters Four and Six I will discuss in some detail the sorts of social "armor," the layers of elaboration around the central core, that protect nobles from penetration by ToLaing. Here I will mention only that, like nobles' houses, the cores of their social persons are elaborated by protective layers composed of several media. An entourage accompanies them whenever they leave the safety of their houses. In the old days, this entourage consisted of bodyguards who actually protected them from danger. Now it is a sense of appropriateness that prevents a high person from wandering about unaccompanied. It is especially horrid for them to contemplate travelling long distances alone, particularly women, unaccompanied by family and allies.[3] The only really appropriate occasion on which to travel alone is when one (usually a man) journeys alone to seek a guru for invulnerability spells, or to the mountains or forests to meditate. I did not witness or hear about people going to the mountains to *bertapa* (meditate ascetically), as Javanese are said to do, but I did hear much about men seeking gurus to strengthen their bravery, skill, and invulnerability. The necessity for a bodyguard lingers as a sensibility; high-status people simply do not go about alone. High nobles are also protected by their potent names and titles, as well as the polite form of "you" used to address them. (Buginese, Makassarese, and Tae do not have speech levels like Javanese, but it is remarkable how much can be done along the same lines with body stance, polite and intimate forms of "you," and titles.) These respectful linguistic forms acknowledge the utterer's deference to the person addressed; they protect the higher person from the penetrating shock of challenge. Architecturally, the protective medium consists of multiple and elaborated layers of rooms and decoration constituting noble dwellings. These similarly prevent an easy penetration into the house's core by outside beings.

Although such high-noble houses are certainly more elaborate than others, their logic and aesthetic are precisely the same. The sameness in house logic parallels a sameness in the way the person is thought to be constituted: whether high or low, humans have centers that locate the sumange' that animates them. The difference in their persons, like the difference in their houses, consists of an elaboration around a common core.

In *The Religion of Java* (1960), Clifford Geertz diagrams Javanese speech

---

[3] Needless to say, my solo journey from distant America, landing almost unannounced in the midst of Senga, needed some explaining. Why would I leave my family and friends and the comforts of rich America to put myself at the mercy of ToLaing? True, I was wise enough to put myself under the protection of Opu, people agreed, but it was still bizarre. After some discussion in the household, Opu DaMuchlis suggested that I was seeking spiritual power, and that this journey was to purify my soul—rather like going out to the forest to meditate alone, she implied. I was grateful for that interpretation rather than other ones that might well have been proffered.

by representing the person as dot, surrounded by concentric circles. The higher the speech levels used when the person is spoken to, the larger the number of concentric lines around the dot. (He writes that respectful speech surrounds the person like a wall or barrier, but, paradoxically, it is a wall created by someone else.) This diagram would make sense to people in Luwu, because they use an image very similar to it. Followers of a high noble, discussing their loyalty and unity with him, say that they and their ToMatoa, like the dark pupil-iris and the white of an eye,

de'naulle' ripassareng
batu mata maltongngé
na batu mata maputié

inseparable—
the dark of an eye,
the white of an eye.

Concentric circles image hierarchy, as much centrist as vertical, and their social grouping, which, hierarchically fused, becomes a single social body.

In the image of the pupil and white of an eye, the pupil is the highest noble or core of nobles, which is at the same time the most "inner" aspect of the social grouping. The innermost/deepest place in the hierarchical polities of island Southeast Asia was the most central place, the place defined by the ruler. The residences that defined the centers of the many hierarchical centrist polities of central Java, Bali, and South Sulawesi were called or associated with the "inside" or "inner." In Central Java, the ruler's palace was the Dalem, the "inside." In Bali, the inner core of the royal lineages, the Puri Gede, was often referred to as the Dalem, while the secondary royal houses were called *jero*, a word that also means "inside" or "within." The term is also often incorporated into noble titles. Commoners, by contrast, were called "outer people," people of the periphery, *jaba*. (On Bali, see Geertz and Geertz 1975, and C. Geertz 1980: 58.) In Luwu, the premises of the center, including the palace, was *ilaleng bata* ("within the walls"; *laleng* is a cognate of *dalem*), and members of the court were *ToMarilaleng*, "people located inside."

The diagrams of speech levels drawn by Geertz for Java are intended to represent also the distinction between the inner life, *batin*, and the outer manifestations or layers of visible behavior, *lahir*. The two are continuous and are defined relationally. That is, the outer layerings that accrue to the inner point are seen as manifestations of it, in lesser and lesser degrees of intensity the further away from the central core. But they are continuous with it: inner and outer are degrees on the same scale; "inner" and "outer" mean simply "closer to the center" and "further from the center." No radical break is posited between what we call inner subjective life and outer objective or material world, or between mind/body or private/public. These outer layerings are less the machinery haunted by an inner ghost than they are the leavings, the evidencings, the rearrangements of the visible world that occur when potency is located at the center, rather like iron filings leaning toward a hidden magnet. Like the conventions of respectful speech and gesture and the entourage of bodyguards that surround a potent navel-center in the political realm, the physical structure of the high-noble house forms an elaboration around its potent protecting spirit at the center.

No one consciously constructed houses to seem like people, or vice versa. Thus it would be misleading to say that houses and human bodies, with their many aesthetic and logical parallels (their microcosm-macrocosm relation, if you will), are replicas of each other or have an iconic relation of similarity to each other; their similarity lies deeper. They exhibit parallels because they both exist in a particular version of the shape of space whose directional structure they cannot *not* exemplify. Because a center must have a periphery to be known as a center, six points are generated around it; so house and body reveal similar directional logic. Moreover, although the six peripheral points consist of three opposing pairs of directions, these oppositional pairs at the periphery are not the crux of the matter, digital-contrastive Saussure-derived theories of meaning to the contrary. The meaning of the house and the body lies in the collapse of the directions each reveals, at the center that is their source.

The Full Center

In Chapter One I described some of the spatial dimensions of birth ceremonies. The infant is born within the safe confines of the house. Its mother remains within this safe space until the ceremony in which she "descends from the house" and bathes outside, attended by a midwife. The new baby's descent is marked ritually at the same time. It "descends from the house" in someone's arms and is walked around it several times. The point seems to be to introduce the infant, in a cautious and brief way, to the dangerous outside. All this is more elaborate in the case of a high noble. I was told that the high-noble new mother stays inside for forty days, and that the high-noble baby's first footstep onto the ground was also ceremonialized.

The fact that the house is elevated on posts means that "descending" and "ascending" are clearly marked activities, brief periods of transition between the safer space inside the house and the dangerous space outside it.

Daily, people enact in miniature the concern with transitions between safe and dangerous space that ceremonies for the new mother and the newborn mark on a larger scale. Before they leave the house, if they are meticulous about their health, people *pabaloi to paringngerreng* (Tae, "make good/correct consciousness/awareness"). To do this, they say a prayer surrendering themselves to the care of God while they are in the dangerous outside. On entering the house, they pause for a moment at the top of the stairs to shake off clinging jin, and leave their shoes. They thus leave the outside, outside. They do not introduce it into the inside. (It stands to reason that, other than the navel-post, the stairway or ladder is the house part whose construction and attendant spells are considered most crucial when it is being built.)

A major spatial transition occurs when people move from one house to another. These transitions also are marked by ceremony. "Ascending a new house" is a ceremony celebrated throughout South Sulawesi. It should be regarded as a life-crisis ceremony, for its rationale is similar: the sumange' of the house and the sumange' of its new occupants must be brought together ritually so that they can mesh or mutually accommodate (Bug. *si-ura'-ura'*; Ind. *cokcok*) rather than shock each other.

The house, then, is treated as a place of relative safety. Descending from it and entering it are daily marked by minor acts that dissociate inside from outside, while major descents and ascents are ceremonialized. One could argue that the ritual distinction made between "inside" and "outside" is merely a "symbolic expression" of the material and functional fact that the house offers physical protection from the elements and from enemies. The house does offer some protection from sun and rain, but no warmth to counter the cold dampness and winds during heavy monsoons; and it positively invites insects, which not only crawl freely within the house but, in season, nest there, producing thin streams of falling sawdust bored out from rafters, and the occasional plop of egg sacs falling onto one's fieldnotes. The occasional huge beetle buzzes heavily by, and sometimes centipedes hide behind and under things. (Unlike all other insects, centipedes are promptly killed.) I mentioned before that the slats of which the floor is composed were, in former times, the place where enemies stabbed their long knives upwards into sleeping bodies on mats.

The house, in short, is anything but hermetically sealed against the natural elements or enemies' weapons. Its surfaces are full of holes in contact with the outside, more like permeable membranes than like barriers. Nasty creatures, both human and not, can easily penetrate into it, and often do. A particularly dangerous one enters through the triangular opening at the front of the house, made by the peak of the roof. An especially virulent type of black magic comes through that hole, making a distinct PING! sound as it enters. Sometimes when people are certain that an enemy is out to get them, they try not to sleep at night, since unawareness and a prone position will make them more vulnerable. Various other spirits come in through holes in the roof, like the *popo'*, a flying creature whose cry is like that of a distant duck. It enters through the roof and eats out people's stomachs if they are weak, sick, and unaware.

It would seem that the house's relative safety is compromised by its permeability. It can be invaded through its open unguarded apertures, and in this respect, too, houses and humans resemble each other.

In Chapter One I mentioned that soon after birth, infants are rubbed with oil and bathed with water that have been bespelled. Special care is taken to rub these substances on the infant's leso-leso, the soft spots (like fontanel and temples) and the creases made where the planes of skin surfaces meet, such as the insides of the elbows, the backs of the knees, under the fingernails, or the middle of the palm of a cupped hand. Leso-leso are vulnerable spots, entry points for invasions from outside the body. If creases and soft spots are vulnerable, actual holes are more so. These holes are the orifices of the human body, considered to be obvious entrees into it.

One of the meanings of these holes in local theories of illness appears to be derived from the Indic notion, which we in the West inherit from the same source, that there are five senses, each of which is located at an orifice or skin surface. In this conception, humans are linked to the world through our five senses. The senses allow us to be aware of aspects of the world, and with our organs of sense we act on the desires that are prompted by the world's invasion. For instance, hunger may be prompted by the smell and sight of food. Responding to an urge to eat, one opens one's mouth and ingests. But a person who has withdrawn from the sight, smell, and presence of food is neither prompted to appetite nor able to act on such an urge. That person has withdrawn from the world's distractions. If one allows oneself to be aware of the world through one's senses and allows oneself to be goaded into desiring it, one will find oneself in a never-ending engagement with it. Desires will prompt other desires, and the world will never satisfy. As the Opu Pa'Bicara put it, trying to quench desires by pursuing their fulfillment is like trying to quench thirst by drinking sea water: the more you drink, the thirstier you become. The solution to this is to cease to thirst.

One mode of withdrawal from the world is through meditation. The point of meditation is to achieve a state of internal oneness, a state of being perfectly undisturbed: no doubts, anxieties, appetites, or needs. The language is instructive. To meditate is *makkamala'* (Ind. *bertapa*); its purpose is to achieve oneness (*asseweng riallata'alah*, "oneness with God [Allah]"). Concentration is *appaseweng* (*mappasewa* is the stative verb). The root of these words is *sewe*, "one." The word *sewe* appears as *sewe-sewe*, "all of God's creation"; the doubling of the word "one" indicates the two aspects of creation, that which is intangible and that which is tangible (the malinrung and the talle'). The desire for oneness with God, and therefore with the universe itself which is God's creation, is expressed as a deep longing in this saying: *Narekko uddani' ni ata ripuanna, naéuddanit'na puangng e riattanana, ripapasangini samp, apuangeng naripalinkajo.* It is more poetic in Buginese, but it translates something like this: "If a servant is in a state of intense longing for his master, and his master longs intensely for his servant, the servant will be wrapped in his master's clothing."

Achieving this unity requires sacrifice or offering, called the *pinanrakka'*. Virtually all rituals, however small, require a pinanrakka', which is cast off to be carried to Guru RiSelleng, the spirit ruler of the sea or underworld. A few betel nuts and an egg, for instance, are put at the edge of a nearby stream when a woman goes for her first bath after giving birth, as I mentioned in Chapter One; all wedding ceremonies, likewise, have a small pinanrakka'; and I was told that long ago on certain great state ceremonial occasions low slaves were tossed overboard as pinanrakka'. These pinanrakka' embody—are the visible, tangible, talle' aspect of—that which must be tossed off in order to achieve oneness. One very good informant told me that he thought that in meditation, the pinanrakka' is what English-speakers call the "self"—all desire that individuates. That is what must be sacrificed if one is to succeed in meditation.

To practice meditation, most people must retreat to a quiet place where they will not be disturbed. For some, this is their bed. There they draw the *boco'*, a fabric covering that may be of mosquito netting or cloth. They then dissociate themselves from the world by closing their apertures. Closing the apertures forms a physical barrier to interacting with the world, and can be a first step in meditation.

While people who practice meditation are respected, the ones most "feared" (regarded with respect and awe) are the very few who are known to be extremely potent, who never show anger, yet who also never meditate. These few people, rather than withdrawing from the world in order to control their desires, walk freely in it. Such persons are conscious of their impulses as well as of the world's pleasures, and thus have not excised or blocked their awareness. Yet they remain steady, "unmoved" by their impulses, as evidenced by the fact that they do not act on them. This is a very high state of consciousness indeed, a sort of unceasing and ambulatory meditation, the highest and most admired form of asceticism. The deep and secret truth of this form of knowledge is that the world's temptations are nought but one's own desires, which exist as temptations only if one is tempted.

A practitioner who construes the relation between his self (almost all serious practitioners of meditation who also have political responsibilities are men) and the world in the way I have sketched above may come to feel that the world really is an aspect of himself, with the corollary that he is responsible for everything that happens in the world, and that he can control his surroundings by controlling his own impulses and awareness. This capacity is precisely what was attributed to the ruler in Southeast Asia's Indic States (see, e.g., Schrieke 1957: Part II, for Java); or, as Soedjatmoko put it, "A central concept in the Javanese traditional view of life is the direct relationship between the state of a person's inner self and his capacity to control the environment" (quoted in Anderson 1972: 13). The pitfall of this way of understanding the world is that it can lead to delusions of grandeur or to a feeling of frustrated impotence if the practitioner fails to succeed in controlling circumstances that are (in fact) beyond his control. In society as it was and to some extent is constructed, however, as I will explicate in Chapter Four, the self-control of leaders was indeed a factor in their ability to control their followers.

In any case, the account I have just sketched offers a rather abstract understanding of the notions that at some level underlie the attitudes toward meditation held by those who meditate or who know something about it. I have just condensed into several short paragraphs what was whispered to me in fragments, or expounded in a private place as though it were a secret. Some of those who spoke thus were people who have thought long and deeply about potency and the soul's purity. One man had read in Indonesian magazines about "yoga," and saw a similarity to what he had read. In the above version, these South Sulawesi practices seem to be derived from Indic notions.

The version that anyone from pedicab drivers to high nobles can tell you, however, is not necessarily or even probably Indic in derivation. This version concerns itself with invulnerability and with the possibility of being penetrated. I think it is fair to say that South Sulawesians generally view the human body or "trunk" (*watang*) as a location under siege. Its skin and physical clothing and weapons offer some protection and some barriers to penetration from the outside; yet we humans are soft, vulnerable, and replete with invadable apertures. The everyday, commonsensical view that ToLuwu have of, say, eating, is that it opens one to invasion.

Throughout South Sulawesi, people protect themselves during eating by first closing all the windows and doors. They eat upright and in a formal position, not lolling about or slouching—not that they are much given to slouching, in any case. A man who is wearing a knife tucked into his belt at the back removes the weapon before he eats, placing it by the side of his plate. As mentioned in the last chapter, I think that it seems counterintuitive to people to ingest while wearing a talisman whose purpose is to aid their impenetrability.

The feeling of formality and the need to be closed off from dangerous interaction (which is to say, any interaction at all) is characteristic, it seems to me, of eating habits in several societies in island Southeast Asia. One lady commented to me that Europeans eat in a way that is "disorderly." Further inquiry revealed that she saw that Europeans talk and then eat, then talk, then eat, then help themselves to more. It is impossible to tell whether they have finished or not! By contrast, Indonesians generally eat what is on their plate quickly and in silence, especially on ceremonial occasions, then drink a glass of water to signal the end. Only then do people chat and sometimes relax. Margaret Mead tells of the horror that the Balinese felt when she told them about public restaurants; the thought of eating in public was repugnant to them. Now Bali is filled with little roadside stands selling food, and snack vendors surround public performances of dance and drama. Yet still at night performances in Bali, where everyone is eating on the street, one sometimes sees an old man crouching by a wall, facing it while eating the rice he has just bought at a street stall. In South Sulawesi, people do not make quite such a thing of it, at least now. But for nobles, at least, eating is not a casual matter, to be undertaken in public. And people insist upon sitting when eating or drinking (to drink standing up, even for a swig of water on a hot day, is "disorderly"). A person who nibbles snacks and smokes while strolling along the street is regarded as both rude and foolish.

One day a group of women was telling me about the dangers of the outside: the black magic, the malicious jin, the possible encounters with disrespectful ToLaing, and so on. Suddenly concerned that they were alarming me by alerting me to dangers I had not known to exist, they hastened to reassure me: "but if your concentration is strong [*paringerrengta kuwat*]," they said, "there is nothing to worry about, nothing at all! Don't worry! You'll be safe!"

At that point I asked them about mad people. (The mad are not confined to insane asylums. They are either cared for in the houses of those who are wealthy and high status, or they become wandering mendicants.) I pointed out that mad people are likely to be wandering around during periods of the day's transition; yet they never seem to come to harm on that account. Surely, I said, they are not "concentrating" and "aware." How to account for their safety?

They had not considered the question before, but after thinking about it, they offered this suggestion. Mad people, they said, are completely unaware of dangers. As a result, they are *malebu* (Ind. *bulat*). Malebu means "round," "complete," "perfect," "unbroken." Undistracted by the fears afflicting the sane, it seems, mad people are ungoaded and undivided, at one with themselves, and consequently safe.

Their answer, admittedly ad hoc and invented on the spur of the moment, nonetheless resonates with other thinking about the body and the person in South Sulawesi and in the wider Malay world. A reading of accounts that touch on health routines and village curing rites leaves one with the impression that it is common in Indonesia and Malaysia to associate images of unity, fullness, and wholeness with health and potency; and images of internal conflict, loss, dispersion, and penetration with sickness and dangers to vitality.

So, for instance, it is widely thought in this area that it is dangerous to stare vacantly into space (Ind. *termenung-menung*), as this lapse in alertness renders one empty and vulnerable to entry by spirits. Interestingly enough, the Tae word *takkajenna'* means both "to stare vacantly" and "to be amazed or surprised." In either case, one is not calm and concentrated. "Fullness" can be an image of health and potency, "emptiness" of weakness, vulnerability, and distraction. In central Java, a potent person is a *wong isi*, literally "full person" (see Keeler 1987). In South Sulawesi, similarly, a *tau malise'* is a "full person" (full of paddissengeng, spells stored in the chest, and full of potency generally). Millar summarizes succinctly the distinction between a tau malise' and a *tau massissi lalo*.

> People who have well-developed self-defense capabilities are known as *tau malise'* (literally, "persons densely filled up"). By virtue of *akal* [reason] and self-discipline, the *bateng* [interiority] of a *tau malise'* . . . is impervious to the intrusions of malevolent supernatural spirits and resistant to the dispersion of *bateng* heat, which inevitably afflicts undisciplined people. Tau malise' can summon great physical strength in dangerous situations and also inspire the fear and admiration of their consociates. In contrast to a *tau malise'* is a *tau massissi lalo* (literally, "person who it runs out of," even through a skin of scales), a person who is not "densely filled up." *Tau massissi lalo* are people who have few defenses . . . whether against natural or supernatural dangers. (Millar 1983: 479)

It is as though the person is leaking vitality, unable to anchor and stabilize it within the body.

In this part of the world, people quite commonly conceptualize potential harm to their persons as penetrations of objects, words, or strangers from the outside; or as a breaking-up, shattering, or dispersion of what was formerly seamless and whole. The shamanic practices of the Wana, shifting cultivators of the mountainous interior of Sulawesi, restore patients' health by fetching back their various dispersed parts, which have been stolen by spirits or lost (Atkinson 1989); sickness is imaged as dispersion, loss, and penetration by alien objects and spirits. The Malays of Malaysia fear sickness by penetration, and the oral orifice seems to be viewed as especially vulnerable (cf. Provencher 1979, which suggests a psychoanalytic interpretation). Poisoned food is for them an especially prominent fear. Provencher adds elsewhere that, although Chinese patients come to Malay curers, Malays shun Chinese curers. That is partly because the Chinese are known to practice acupuncture, and "poisoned needles" feature in the Malay beliefs as sickness-causing items. I would suggest further that acupuncture, which requires many tiny punctures of the body, is too alien for a Malay sensibility to countenance.

The link of fullness, potency, and inviolability at the political level of the center is nicely expressed by Elizabeth Traube, writing about the Mambai of Timor in Eastern Indonesia. Like most Eastern Indonesians, the Timorese structure much of their ritual and social life as dyadic pairs; they were neither Indicized nor politically centralized. But again like most Eastern Indonesians, they postulate a primal unity that existed before it split itself into the world of paired oppositions in which the Mambai live. The dyadic and relatively unhierarchical Mambai are nearly as preoccupied with the unity of the center as were centrist hierarchical Indic states, although they work this out in very different ways. In myth and through their Ritual Lord, the Mambai express a number of themes common throughout island Southeast Asia. The Ritual Lord of Mambai is said to be *tema* and *benu*, "whole" and "full." *Tema*, Traube tells us, "refers to an object that has not been penetrated in any way, something from which no part has been removed or extracted. . . . *Benu* . . . signifies a quantity that can be reduced, but not decomposed into parts. . . . Wholeness and fullness, in these contexts, connote a kind of closure, a turning inward, an imperviousness to external influences" (1977: 133).

One might argue that the fear of penetration and concern with wholeness is merely panhuman common sense, predictable from our common anatomy. After all, we humans do not have exoskeletons, as crabs or lobsters do. The fact that we have endoskeletons means that our vulnerable flesh is exposed to the world, and our bipedal stance exacerbates our vulnerability by exposing the soft underbelly. It should not be surprising, then, if many cultures image "danger" as intrusive elements from the outside into the body—whether they are conceptualized as germs or as evil spirits.

Yet different cultures conceptualize body boundaries to be in different places, and the body's defenses to be various, and they preoccupy themselves with different aspects of the body's vulnerability. Penetration from the outside might preoccupy one culture; the growth and spread of uncontrolled matter in the hidden interior of the body might preoccupy another. What strikes me in particular as culturally specific to Luwu and some other island Southeast Asian cultures is the way their people think about their source of protection against the external penetrating elements. The emphasis is not on wall-like barriers thrown up against the outside, but on internal centeredness and "fullness"; not on the borders or the boundaries of the "self" but on its center. These people therefore attend to their centers, especially to the center's alert consciousness and undivided unity with respect to itself, in order to protect what surrounds it. This "center" can be the navel-centers of individuals, guarding their own health. At the time of the akkarungeng, it was the center of the polity, embodied in the ruler.

I was first prompted to investigate the parallels between humans and houses by the observation that people in Ujung Pandang closed the windows before eating and the men removed their knives from their hiding places at their belts and placed them on the table; and in Senga and Palopo, it seemed to me, people felt markedly more relaxed inside the house, and with the windows closed for meals or naps, than outside it. As I phrased it to myself then, the house's walls seemed to form a second skin around them. Initially I saw the house as a sort of larger body encompassing the bodies of its occupants. Implicit in my thinking then was the idea that people attain protection by erecting barriers: thick fortress walls (like German castles) protect from enemies; well-insulated roofs keep out sun and rain; screens discourage insects; and solid walls keep out wind. But that sort of thinking, I found out, is backwards. Village houses in Luwu offer few material barriers to enemies, the elements, or fauna. At best, I have concluded, a person's skin or house's walls (which are indeed rather like skin, a flimsy permeable barrier full of apertures) provide a barrier that prevents ToLaing from penetrating visually into the interior. It is the vital center—the navel and the sumange' gathered there—that protects the health and well being of the inhabitants within its realm of influence.

The Presiding Spirit of the Realm

Just as the Ampo Banua is the protecting sumange' of the occupants of a house, the ruler was the protecting, presiding, and central spirit of the realm. The plot thickens if we explore the etymologies, even anecdotally, of *Ampo* and *Banua*. *Ampo* has the same root, in Buginese, as *Opu*, the highest title in Luwu with the exception of *Datu* ("ruler"). *Ampo* and *Opu*, like other similar terms in Eastern Indonesia and throughout the Pacific, are "cognates of a single Austronesian term meaning 'trunk,' 'base,' 'root,' or 'origin,' " as Fox (1980a: 14) has pointed out.[4] *Banua* (a Tae word; the Buginese word for house is *bola*) has different associations, which, along with its cognates in other Austronesian languages, seem mainly to cluster around notions of a land and location.[5] Expanding the meanings of these clusters of cognates with the cultural practices and beliefs surrounding them suggests that words with the root *pu/fu* connote an original unitary source from which other things are derived. Such words are associated with ancestors, with high rank, with invisible potency, with owning and protecting. Words with the root *banua/vanua* often imply land and people who are of the earth rather than the sky. If so, the Datu, a spirit of the Upper World who descended to the earth to rule and protect it, could really be called the "ampo banua," the presiding spirit of the realm.

Rulers, who were descendants of the cosmic sources of their polities, were urged to cultivate internal unity with respect to themselves, as evidenced by an undistracted stance, control over their anger, and the like. The ruler's spiritual/bodily state translated into the well-being of the realm or caused it disaster. Many palm-leaf manuscripts were devoted to advising the ruler concerning appropriate conduct and disposition, forming an analogue of post-seventeenth-century European political theory. Internal dissension between two royal siblings, or between prominent members of the court, were considered potential disasters.

People would read political signs of discord in the state as they now continue to read each other's body language: a laxness in the periphery—a

---

[4] *Opu* is used in Luwu; in Java, we have *Ampo*, a noble title; in northern Sulawesi, *empung* means "ancestor." These words have the root *pu*. In Buginese, *pu* is the root of such words as *punna*, to own and protect; *Puang*, the noble title used instead of Opu in Buginese areas to the south of Luwu; *apongeng*, which is a source or origin point, applied to either rivers or genealogies; and *rapu*, a Tae word used in Luwu to indicate a cluster of people with a close common ancestral source. Close by in central Sulawesi, for the Wana (who are without nobility), *pu'u* is a source or point of origin.

In Eastern Indonesia, the mother's brother is the "source of life," and cognate terms describing the relationship to him occur throughout, summarized by Fox near the passage I have just quoted. He continues, "Such cognate terms ('epu,' 'pu,' 'hu,' 'fu,' 'uf') give a definite botanic cast to affiliation and alliance relationships" (1980: 14) because, in Eastern Indonesia, the descendants of a "trunk" are compared to branches, leaves, and "tips" of a tree (see, for instance, Fox 1971b and Traube 1986). In Chapter Eight I explore these botanic terms further.

[5] In modern Indonesian, *banua* means "continent"; in old Javanese, it was a district. In eastern Borneo, *banua* refers to commoners as well as to dwellings and planted areas, while, interestingly enough, *samangat* there means "headman" and other "aristocrats" who are descended from spirits (King 1978). An Austronesian word, *banua* crops up further afield in the Pacific, as in Vanuatu, the new name of the former colony called New Hebrides.

court of bickering and uncontrollable nobles, a rebellious tributary state—
signalled a lack of control at the center, its vulnerability to attack. In a
theory of the state like this, in which unity's source is from the central top
and any discord is a sign of the center's weakness and internal lack of control, a show of opposition or dissension could be as damaging as an enemy's capacity to inflict substantive damage. Indeed, there would be very
little if any difference between the "symbolic" and the "substantive" in such
a case. The political solution was to quash the show of dissension as soon
as possible, before it escalated and became impossible to control. A "loyal
opposition" would have been an unthinkable contradiction in terms in this
sort of system. Unity at the center and throughout the realm was considered the key to prosperity, health, fertility, and peace.

In historical accounts of the Indic States of Southeast Asia, the central
city and especially the ruler's palace are commonly said to be a microcosm
of the cosmos. The center *was* the polity, and the ruler was the center of
the central city.[6] The political realm consisted of the population that served
the center and was oriented around it as the rest of the body is oriented
towards its navel, or rather, towards the potency lodged there.

Once more it is worth pointing out that the different levels of "centers"
in Luwu and in the Akkarungeng Luwu do not and did not stand as iconic
representations of each other. Rather, each realm (body, house, polity) is
a field, a realm of a different size, in which similar forces work themselves
out. Smaller fields or realms did not replicate larger ones in any mechanical
way. The smaller centers of the realm were partial, incomplete, derivative.
Their "incomplete" nature was symbolized overtly in house structure. In
only one dwelling, the ruler's palace, did the center post span all three layers—sea, land, and sky; lower, middle, and upper. It was as though there
was only one complete person in the realm, and that one was the ruler.

The entire political realm stood as the "king's body," the material embodiment of and supporting material "trunk" (watang) of the energies
whose most concentrated location was the ruler and the regalia. Yet no
Southeast Asian Indic State represented itself as a human body; nothing
remotely on the lines of Hobbes's Leviathan ever graced a Southeast Asian
court text, and none called the ruler the "head" of state. Heads in Luwu
are not powerful, but they are emblematic of status. Heads are precious,
but a hazard to the "trunks" that support them. Because they are vulnerable
to insult if approached too closely, heads must be protected. Rulers were
not "heads" of state, but, like heads, they were their highest points, and

---

[6] A useful collection of diagrams and summary of sources on this point can be found in
Tambiah 1976: ch. 7.

they share some of the same hazards and needs of heads. The political center, located and locatable by the presence of the ruler, the royal residence, and the state regalia, was the state's highest and most inner central place, at once its most vulnerable to insult and attack and the most powerful in its intrinsic potency. Navels or centers, not heads, are the locations of power and effectiveness in these societies. Thus the ruler was the navel of the world.

The people of these historical polities represented themselves to themselves using icons that imaged high centers with extensive peripheries. Their icons were mountains, like Bali's Gunung Agung or Java's Mount Meru, or mountain representatives, like the multiple rooflets on Balinese temples called *meru*. Or they used the shade-producing, encompassing banyan tree, which, once stably grown, drops roots from the top, revealing that the source of life is from above rather than below. Or they used umbrellas, a sign of royalty throughout centrist hierarchical Southeast Asia. In Luwu, the ruler's representative carried a red umbrella when he was sent out to settle disputes and quell disorder. As a footnote on radial images in Luwu, it is worth noting that the nobles of the center (in contrast to the local nobles, important in their own areas but of lower status when they came to the central palace) were called the *rombena kamumu'*. *Kamumu'* is the color purple, the wearing of which was restricted to high nobles when the akkarungeng existed; *rombena* is fringe. Rombena kamumu', the high nobles of the most central court, stood as purple fringe on the royal umbrella.

These radial self-representations of the polity not only have high points and central ones. They also image unity—and the one was the ruler. They gave palpable form to what was experienced by at least the central nobility of these societies as deep truths about the shape of the world they inhabited.

Chapter Three
The Polity

A division of the polity into three ranked categories was common in hierarchical Southeast Asian Indic States, a visible demarcation of gross differences in the degrees of potency embodied in the people of each category. In Luwu, the three gross divisions were the *ToMalebbi'* (literally the "big" or "better" people, including the ruler and the nobles of the center); the *ToSama* (the level or same people, who included the regional nobles with posts outside the center as well as the non-noble "freemen," as they are often called in commentary on other Southeast Asian polities); and the *ata* (the so-called "slaves").

At the time of my fieldwork, needless to say, none of the three categories existed officially. The Dutch had made an effort in the late nineteenth century to eliminate the worst practices of the capture of people and their subsequent selling as slaves, especially as labor for European plantations; and soon after they seized direct administrative power in the peninsula in the first decade of the twentieth century, some tried to eliminate the legal existence even of "family" or "inner" slaves, the personal servants and retainers of Bugis-Makassarese, although that issue was much more politically difficult (cf. Bigalke 1983; Sutherland 1983). The Dutch continued in any case to sanction a dual division of society into nobles and commoners, for, although their rule was direct, they continued to allow many of the prerogatives and signs of nobility. With Indonesian Independence, all people are to be considered as equal citizens rather than as persons of different inborn spiritual potential. As may be imagined, however, people's ancestry was and continues to be a matter for gossip and of relevance for marriage alliances. The tripartite division of society, or at least a dual one, although unofficial and without sanctions, continues to be relevant to social action.

The value of white blood, the importance of siri', the importance of good marriages with people of high degrees of white blood, and so forth are still matters of great concern and interest to ToLuwu, as they are to people throughout South Sulawesi, even though such matters have no official place in the Republic of Indonesia; they are maintained in Luwu as elsewhere by practice and desire rather than by regulation backed by force, as they were in the akkarungeng. Luwu was widely regarded as a backwater at the time of my fieldwork there, *masih feodal* (Ind., "still feudal" or "still hierarchical"), passed over by history, not because it was unique in the peninsula in the high value its people put on siri' and white blood, but because Luwu had the living remnants of a social hierarchy from the ak-karungeng that commanded considerable unofficial loyalty, obedience, and belief. One contributing factor, as I mentioned in the Introduction, was that the ruler of Luwu and the Opu Pa'Bicara had been leaders of the South Sulawesi opposition to the Dutch (not collaborators) and support-ers of the new Republic, although neither had accepted positions in the new government, thus maintaining their "clean souls" by showing that their opposition and subsequent support were not based on self-interest. The Opu Pa'Bicara and the regime he represented, then, had come out of the turmoil unscathed, indeed heroically, which was not the case for all high nobility of South Sulawesi. Moreover, thoughout the Kahar period, the Opu Pa'Bicara had protected and shielded his followers and continued to exert a beneficent presence. The Opu Pa'Bicara was, therefore, still the leader of a large kapolo and still respected throughout the peninsula. In the absence of the ruler or his widow, the Opu Pa'Bicara was the undisputed high noble presence of the area. When I visited it, Luwu seemed to be, and for much of its population still was, a hierarchy, albeit a hierarchy without a top because the ruler was gone and the legal force that sustained the hierarchy was abolished. Because I went to Luwu with some historical knowledge of the operations and meanings of the social hierarchies of In-dic States, my experience there, in a partial hierarchy with no top that op-erated within the interstices and unofficial contexts of the Republic, none-theless clarified some things that had been obscure to me concerning rank and marriage in Indic States. In the following, then, I use the past tense to speculate about the situation as it was during the time of the akkarungeng prior to Independence, and the present tense for the ethnographic present of fieldwork, except when it is clear from context that the past tense refers to my fieldwork.

Power and Place

Western and Western-trained commentators frequently diagram the social divisions of the Indic State as a pyramid consisting of three layers: nobles, freemen or commoners, and slaves. Such a diagram strikes me as mislead-ing on two major counts. First, it emphasizes horizontal breaks between the categories, as though these societies consisted of solidary classes in op-position to each other. Second, a pyramid connotes the fixity of stone, the eternity of the ages. In fact, the ties were far more vertical: high and low were (and are) allies, while peers in place were and still tend to be rivals. The continual competition between rival-peers, as I detail in Part II, guaranteed that any ranking of persons was fragile and that centers were always vulnerable to being knocked off-center and replaced with a victorious rival. Centrist hierarchical Southeast Asian states certainly liked to imagine themselves to be as stable and immovable as sacred mountains, but maintaining the center in fact required continual alertness and effort.

If we must depict the akkarungeng as having a shape, better to think of it not as a pyramid but as a circle with a high point—an umbrella, a mountain, or a banyan tree, as Southeast Asians did themselves. Or we could borrow an image from Anderson (1972), who likens the shape of a (Javanese) kingdom to a cone of light cast from the ruler. Social ranking in Akkarungeng Luwu, viewed from the top, could be seen as an infinitely gradual dispersion or diminution of the white blood lodged in its purest form in the Datu or ruler, whose presence defined the polity's center.[1] Like light cast from a single source, white blood in Akkarungeng Luwu can be thought of as a gradual diminution from its pure source, the Datu and the Datu's dewata (spirit) ancestors, which fades finally to darkness at the vague perimeter.

"ToMalebbi," "ToSama," and "ata" named the three gross divisions of people in the akkarungeng, but each was highly differentiated internally. Nobles of the center, the rombena kamumu' or "purple fringe," were differentiated by degrees of white blood and the titles that accrued to them. The highest rank and blood was the Datu. Surrounding him were the keeper of genealogies (Opu Andeguru Anak Karung) and his main four ministers (Opu Pantunru, Opu Pa'Bicara, Opu Balairante, and Opu ToMarilaleng), and below that other rombena kamumu' nobles who resided in the center; these, in turn, were subdivided into a number of named ranks. ToSama were divided into two main types: the higher was the ToDeceng or "good" people, who were the "regional nobility" (the *arung palili* or *aruppalili*), some of whom had titles and duties assigned by the ruler; the lower was the *jemma lappa'*, who were, as one noble put it, "like a level field," undifferentiated by degree of white blood—but while they might be level from a noble's point of view, we can be sure that they differentiated themselves internally. (They may well have ranked themselves by the amount of bridewealth given for women in marriage, as Cha-

---

[1] Because a person's degree of white blood is inherited (more or less equally) from both parents, full siblings share the same social place. They are differentiated among themselves by relative age, and younger ones are supposed to defer to older ones, while older ones are supposed to protect younger ones; but those outside and inferior in place should treat them all with equal deference, for their degree of white blood is the same.

bot [1950] 1960 shows was the case for Makassarese commoners prior to Indonesian Independence; I have no data on this issue as I did not concentrate my study on this category of people.) Ata, the so-called "slaves," were also internally differentiated. The four main types were the *ata mana'* (those who were inherited), the *ata mariale-ale* (the "interior" ones, close attenders to the owner's social center); the *ata rieli* (those who were bought); and the lowest of all, slaves owned by slaves, the *ata tai manu'*, literally the "chicken-shit slaves."

While I have written as though I were laying out a clear hierarchy of places, the hierarchy was considerably more confusing and inconsistent, probably especially among the class of ata. Sutherland (1983) points out that an important problem in Southeast Asia generally was control of labor, and the ways of controlling people were numerous. That is one of the several reasons it is difficult to define or discuss "slavery" as if it were a single issue or phenomenon.[2]

It is my impression that within any given polity, the hierarchical ranking of noble categories and titles was somewhat clearer than the ranking for people at the lower reaches of society, but even there, the grosser the divisions, the clearer the ranking. The status of individual titles and title-holders was considerably more obscure. Pelras (1971) summarizes the ranked divisions in several Buginese polities according to several Dutch writers publishing before Independence as well as according to his own informants' memories, and they reveal an inconsistent ranking of named divisions both from polity to polity and within particular polities. As Pelras puts it,

> One could then present the contributions of other informants, or establish comparisons with other areas of South Sulawesi. . . . Such work would be necessary if one wished to establish a synthesis. But is such a project justified? Because that would be to presume that a coherent ideal system actually exists, of which each informant has provided merely a distorted image. Yet nothing is less certain. (Pelras 1971: 191, my translation)

[2] As Sutherland puts it, "There was an almost infinite variety in the actual conditions of people within the same formal category of 'slave.' There were occasional examples of wealthy men being slave-holders in their own right, though slaves themselves, but also of wretched starving beings of virtual non-human status. Domestic slaves could indeed be 'members of the family,' or abused and exploited; 'outside slaves' could differ very little from independent peasants, or work as sharecroppers, but they might also be used in the intensive cultivation of specific crops, such as pepper, rice, coffee or copra. In extreme cases, slavery merged with debt-bondage, but also with the ordinary subject status of 'free' men. Its character shifted according to internal and external pressures, and theory was often far from practice. For these reasons, it should be remembered that slavery was just one form of bound labour, and could be located on various parts of the continuum of 'controlled people' " (Sutherland 1983: 280).

Which subdivisions and titles were higher and which lower was inconsistent from polity to polity in South Sulawesi, and it is not difficult to imagine a rather Polynesian political process of title-competition in which the status of a title may rise or fall over a period of generations depending on the political prowess and status of the people who are able to acquire it, or "capture" it, as Polynesianists tend to word it. What *was* consistent was a gross ranking into three major categories of status, and an infinitely expandable number of social places from top to bottom, each of those titles or places requiring their title-holders to defend their social places in order to maintain them.

The gradual diminution of the potency of places can and should be read as a diminution in rank, yet that is not the full story. It is also a diminution of autonomy. The ruler was the only wholly autonomous complete "person" in the realm, for he or she was the dependent of no one, but rather the guarantor of other people's places. Everyone else was to some degree dependent and therefore partial, until finally the lowest of low slaves "owned," and therefore commanded, no one, not even his own body or time, which was in the service of his superior. (This way of conceiving of slavery, as degrees of dependence rather than as degrees of oppression—which is not to say that it did not involve both—was very common in Southeast Asia; cf. Reid 1983.) As a consequence, slavery, like nobility, was relative—except for the ruler and lowest of low slaves, whose positions were in theory absolute. This means that titles and modes of reference can be misleading. Opu Damira, the wife of the Opu Pa'Bicara, told me that when asked who she was, she would say "ata Luwu," a slave of [the ruler of] Luwu. The ruler then would say, "These are my kapolo," my family-following. In the right circumstances, there is nothing humiliating in a high noble saying she is an "ata Luwu," for it means she is the loyal dependent of the ruler; it does not designate an absolute social class. Similarly, commoners in the village may call a noble who lives locally "Opu" or "Daeng" (another high-status title, lower than Opu). To the villager, he or she is noble, a person to respect. But that same noble in the presence of a member of the rombena kamumu', the nobles of the most central center, becomes virtually a nobody. He or she is prohibited from being addressed by a respectful title. A large frog in a small puddle looks large; the same frog in a lake becomes one of many, their relative sizes of negligible interest.

Since white blood is invisible, a person's true place (onro) in the hierarchy is actually invisible, but it can be read and judged by its visible attributes: by the person's stance, demeanor, and self-control; by the way the person is treated by people of importance of undisputed high place; by the extent of the person's entourage and its deferential attention; by the status-title and name the person has; by the honors and titles once bestowed by the ruler. Indeed, before Indonesian Independence, virtually everything spoke to this issue: the number of plates used to serve a person on ceremonial occasions; the colors and ornaments the person was allowed to wear; the elaboration of certain key elements of decoration on the person's house. Very little was not made to speak to the issue of place.

One of the most crucial attributes of a potent center was a large following, an observation made to me late one night during the preparations for a wedding ceremony to which our Senga household had sent a delegation. That night, a noble man was expounding to me on the subject of his loyalty to his ToMatoa, the high noble Opu whose kapolo the man was in. He asserted that he would die gladly for Opu, because Opu always protected and cared for him, he said, sheltering him when he was in trouble and always guarding his siri'. The man illustrated his points with touching anecdotes and by quoting poems about siri' and loyalty and death. Suddenly something occurred to him and he said, "But you know, Opu needs us, too!" Opu's blood, his place, would be no different, he said, whether he had a kapolo or not. But, he said, we make *visible* who Opu is. He went on to compare Opu to the ruler of the Upper World, Patoto-é, before Luwu was founded. On the advice of his ministers, Patoto-é was considering sending his son, Batara Guru, to become the first ruler of Luwu. At that time the Middle World was empty. Before agreeing with his ministers, Patoto-é consulted with his wife. She urged him to adopt the plan. "For," his wife said, "when humans are in trouble they will beg help and pity. And when they have good fortune, they will praise Patoto-é's benevolence. Thus Patoto-é's greatness will be *visible*."

I must first make clear that far from all high nobles are born into the high-core leadership of an extensive kapolo; even those who are may not have the character traits necessary to maintain it. Being born with many followers ready-made, as it were, is the result of the wise and numerous marriages made by one's great-grandfather and his male siblings, grandfather and his siblings, and father. I explain this in far greater detail in Chapter Eight, but the point can be illustrated by the fact that the Opu Pa'Bicara was born with more than a hundred first cousins of lower place than himself, the progeny of the progeny of his grandfather's marriages to tens of women lower than himself. Then again, even a person born into the high core of a large kapolo may be half crazy, or unreliable, or have little of the self-control and judgment necessary to settle disputes among a touchy people. Lower nobles will not submit their siri' grievances to someone higher if they think the higher one will take sides against them, will talk about them disadvantageously, and so forth. A Buginese saying goes, "Life I offer up, and breath—but not my siri'." In other words, "I am willing to die for my lord, but he may not abuse my dignity." The nobility of many high nobles consists of nothing more than their status-title and belief in their degree of white blood, unconfirmed by wealth or followers. These feckless nobles, even if high by birth, are at a tremendous disadvantage in political and social life. Inferiors accord them the minimal deference allowable on formal occasions, and their status peers will constantly act toward them in a way that borders on discourtesy, knowing that without a loyal band of henchmen they cannot easily seek revenge or demand apology.

A large kapolo formed the substance and source of influence as well as its sign, in several ways. Followers were the people who listened to their leader, who did his bidding, who defended his honor against encroachment from rivals, whose disputes he settled and marriages he arranged, who fought in his battles against rival-peers. To have "influence" and "power" in Western terms, in short, one needs someone to influence, and that was the kapolo. Kapolo members were also a source of wealth. High nobles with large kapolos necessarily had extensive land to be worked or other sources of wealth, such as plantings of coconut palms, shrimp-growing areas, or nowadays, plantings of clove trees. A kapolo was not and is not a fiefdom, and high nobles with large kapolo have far more kapolo members than tenant-farmers; but clearly a high core needed wealth to survive politically. It needed wealth because this system was redistributive. Wealth was used to put on ceremonies, which were crucial as a sign of place; and wealth was needed to support followers in need and feed those who lived in the household doing its work. In most human societies, it is more prestigious to distribute wealth than to receive it, and Luwu was and is no exception. But of course the produce itself was distributed, not the rights to the produce or the land.

Besides a large following, another crucial sign of high place was a title bestowed by the ruler. The ruler, as all commentators on Southeast Asian states have pointed out, was the fount of status in several senses. For one thing, the ruler physically reproduced (usually) his own high place as well as lesser degrees of it in his children, each of whose status depended partly on the mother's status and family influence.[3] For another, the ruler distributed marks or signs of legitimacy and favor in the form of titles, posts,

[3] Rulers often had tens of wives, of a variety of statuses; typically only one was of his own status, the consort and presumed mother of the future ruler. But there was no rule of primogeniture, and the relative statuses of royal wives were not always clear, nor were rules of succession linked to status clear or enforceable. Hence murderous royal half-brothers competing with each other for kingship were a feature endemic to Southeast Asian politics.

letters of appointment, robes, and swords, for example. These marks of honor and titles, unlike the status-titles like "Opu" or "Andi" or "Daeng," which are part of a person's name, were in effect appointments to office and could carry with them responsibilities. "Opu Pa'Bicara" was one such title; three others were main ministerial posts in the akkarungeng's court, and there were many lesser ones. The presumption was that these titles, like a large following, confirmed, exhibited, and recorded, rather than bureaucratically created, the recipients' high place—which in theory already existed, inherited with the degree of purity of white blood.

Confirmation by the ruler, however, was extremely important. Nobles in such systems continually had to assert their places within the socio-political ranking by demonstrating the attributes and eliciting the deference appropriate to the ranks they claimed. There is a way in which the high are at the mercy of the low in these systems, for deference must be shown if a person's claim to high place is to be believed. The very presence of a person of high rank and great spiritual potency (which ought to coincide) is supposed to evoke deference. If it consistently does not, the presumption tends to be that the person does not possess as high a degree of white blood as claimed or—what is almost the same—that the person's self-control, hence control over others, is deficient and inappropriate to the rank or degree that person was born with. A person whose own self-control is weak is judged incapable of leading inferiors or demanding their deference.

Thus much of the conduct of social life, from etiquette to skirmishes and, formerly, wars between the polities, is impelled and given form by the necessity of demonstrating the place one claims to have and then insuring that others show proper deference to that place. Thus a title received directly from the ruler, who was the ultimate and (in times of peace) unquestioned source of social place, was an especially unassailable and prestigious demonstration of place.

To capture a high title, particularly one that carried with it responsibilities, a noble almost certainly needed a large following. For one thing, the ruler would be foolish to pass over a noble of broad influence (large following) when distributing honors, titles, and posts. That influential noble, if disgruntled, could cause trouble. For another, only an influential noble, once given a post of command, would have sufficient numbers of people at his disposal to carry out his orders. One of the basic political forces of the ranked polities of the archipelago stretching from the Malay peninsula to the sultanates of the southern Philippines was precisely the need to make the polity's titles and honors (whose fount was the ruler) relatively congruent with political influence (whose basis was the people who followed the potential title-holder).

Followers looked to their high-noble leader (and in 1976 still did) to settle disputes among themselves and to protect and shelter their lives and their siri' from the omnipresent challenges of their rival-peers. Following Lucien Hanks (1962, 1975, 1977), but extending his use of the term, I call this grouping of followers the "entourage."

The Polity as Entourage

James Boon has written that space in Bali is of two types, sacred and de-monic. He writes that temple spaces "and the relations among them are fixed; groups that attend to the religious needs of spaces are flexible" (Boon 1977: 113). This attractive and telling way of describing groupings implies a world in which certain stable, sacred points exist. Around them form collections of humans, which (their composition slowly and con-stantly changing) serve and attend those sacred points. The temple spaces that Boon describes for Bali are, of course, spatially fixed. The sacred points or places I will describe in Luwu society are able to move around: they are human places attended by service groupings or entourages.

The entourage is the paradigmatic type of social grouping found in Southeast Asian societies with internal ranking. This type of social group-ing has been given various names by observers. In his early (1960) discus-sion of social organization in Southeast Asia, G. P. Murdock called them "occasional kin groups." The occasions that called forth these "kin groups" were great ceremonies, at which all the followers, dependents, and kin of the grouping's high core came to work for it. At other times, Murdock writes, the "kin groups" were invisible. James Siegel, writing about Acheh, calls them "a body of retainers who were the real source of [the leader's] power." Without these followers, he points out, the leader "was powerless to enforce his prerogatives" (1969: 10, 30). Like J. M. Gullick (1958) describ-ing nineteenth-century Malay sultanates, Irving Goldman (1970) calls Pol-ynesian groupings "status-lineages." In his work on Thailand, Hanks terms the leader's immediate retinue an "entourage" and the wider circle of peo-ple on whom he can count—the entourages of his entourage-members, and so on down the line—his "circle" (Hanks 1962, 1975, 1977). Though they exist in warfare on a temporary and rather ad hoc basis, the same sorts of alliances are apparent in Thomas Kiefer's very clear description of the fighting groupings among the Southern Filipino Tausug (Kiefer 1972). Analyses of contemporary political behavior in the Philippines suggest a similar configuration there. In this literature the groupings are usually called "patrons and clients," and the ties that bind the patrons and clients are seen as pseudo-contracts based on utilitarian impulses (Kaut 1961;

Lande 1977; Scott 1977). Writing about Java, Benedict Anderson (1972) is concerned with ideas of power and only incidentally with the shapes of groupings; but the same configuration is easily discerned in his cultural account. In his overview of the area's history, O. W. Wolters (1979, 1982) suggests that "men of prowess" and their followers have since time immemorial formed the basis of social groupings throughout Southeast Asia. In short, regardless of the names given this sort of social grouping or organization, regardless of whether the writers ignore or explicate the place of kinship in it, and regardless of whether the commentators are radical culturalists, social-structural anthropologists, or network-utilitarian political scientists, certain features of this method of organizing society begin to emerge from a reading of the literature.

The leader's place, by definition, is higher than the followers'. In those internally ranked polities with courts and rulers, that higher place may be inherited; in the post-Independence politics of the Philippines and Indonesia, the higher status may be achieved through the distribution of favors and privileges. Moreover, these groupings are known by their leaders and often exist only as long as the leaders do or can control them. Every leader, it would seem, tries to expand his entourage by increasing the number of his social/economic dependents. A powerful impulse, in this way of organizing social relations, is to convert wealth into followers. (This tendency has been noted and decried by development economists in the 1950s and 1960s who, operating with a notion of the meaning of wealth entirely different from that of the people they studied, preferred that capital produce capital rather than followers or rituals.) In usual circumstances, expansion or contraction of the entourage happens at the edges of the grouping; that is, the people who come and go are those least strongly or most recently attached to the leader, rather than those at the relatively stable core. The grouping is, as Hanks puts it, "well-knit at the center but has a tattered and shedding fringe" (1969: 208). At the same time, these social borders may be fuzzy as well as permeable, and a person may belong to the fringes of two centers and be forced or induced to pay deference to both. Nonetheless, the focus of attention is on the center, not the periphery. The extent of the periphery is often thought to reflect the activities, status, or state of spiritual potency of the center.

Social ties between the leaders and followers in these groupings have been called "personalistic" or "dyadic," by which is meant that a follower's loyalty is to a particular leader rather than to a group as such, whose composition, in any case, may be changing. As a corollary, the grouping may collapse if the leader dies or ceases to be effective: it is not a corporation or enduring "structure" that lasts beyond the lives of its members. (Thus,

Lande [1977] contrasts "dyadic politics," which are based on personalistic ties of favor between two people, with "group politics," which are based on members' common interests, defined impersonally.) Loyalty in "dyadic" groupings is to a person rather than to an abstract idea. Thus when factions form in Burmese towns, they form around people, not political platforms (Spiro 1968). And if voting is introduced into a society so organized, people vote for a particular leader (their own) rather than for a platform.

The members of the grouping face toward the center rather than toward each other. Characteristically, the most enduring and solid relations are between leaders and followers rather than among followers. To put it another way, there was no incipient class struggle in traditional societies. That is not to say that there was no oppression. But there is almost no way to conceptualize, let alone act on, horizontal ties in such a society. In those languages in which differential rank is highly developed, such as Javanese and Thai, even to speak is impossible prior to mutual status-assessment by the interlocutors. I have pointed out previously that to speak or gesture in these societies already embroils one in the collusion known as social life. Between peers, there is competition; between higher and lower persons, alliances.

Most of the analyses cited above concern groupings smaller than those polities which had or have rulers and courts and are designated "states." But one could imagine (and Hanks has done so) this type of polity as the vast entourage or "circle" of its ruler. The inner core of this entourage-polity consists of its high nobles who have the highest titles and offices, and are intermarried with the ruler's closest kin. (Indeed, such marriages have been going on for generations; the nobles therefore are the ruler's closest kin, and they are married to each other.) These high nobles, in turn, are leaders of their own entourages, which may themselves be quite vast. Each high-noble core tries to expand its own entourage, thereby putting itself in competition with every other high-noble core for followers. Within the entourage or following of each high-noble core are lower-noble cores, which have their own supporters.

In such a way a large polity could be constructed, arranged in a pattern of entourages whose size, power, and control of human and material resources (which tend to overlap) decline with increasing distance from the ruler at the center of it all. Each smaller entourage would be similar in principle and in organization to the larger entourage encompassing it, but would be a lesser, paler, weaker version of it.

In general outline, this pattern characterizes what I studied as the ka-polo, which would have been only one of many in the Akkarungeng Luwu.

The levels of clusters in the kapolo were not the perfect replications of each other that are so neatly outlined in Hanks's useful model of Thai politics, for the differences between levels were not merely differences in scale. The dynamics and shape of the groupings at each level are rather different within kapolo, because the politics of marriage and leadership vary at each level. (See Chapters Seven and Eight for more on kinship and the structure of the entourage.) I assume the same was true of the internal organization of the akkarungeng.

The highest, most encompassing level of entourage was the akkarungeng itself. Its limits or boundaries were not territorial, as I will show in the next section, but were defined rather by the extent of the court center's influence in mobilizing people for ceremonies and work. Below the ruler were a number of very high nobles, some of whom had large followings of nobles lower than themselves, and on that account were politically powerful. These are the groupings called kapolo, and they are known by their leader's name: "Kapolona Opu X" is "Opu X's Kapolo."

Because of the way that kinship and marriage are organized in Luwu, there are very few exceedingly high nobles, but numerous middle and lower nobles. These latter form the bulk of the followers, the members of a noble kapolo, and they may consist of hundreds, sometimes thousands, of people. Smaller groupings within kapolo are called *rapu* in Luwu (but not in the Bone and Goa areas). A rapu is a cluster of trunks growing from a single stem—people use the word to describe the root-clumps of banana and coconut trees. If the high-noble core of the kapolo is wise in ways of arranging marriages and settling disputes, the rapu are never able to solidify around a lesser central core that might break off from the higher core or become a challenge to it. The tendency for rapu to become smaller replicas of the larger kapolo exists, however. Rapu, like kapolo, are led by their highest and most eminent member, and are known by that leader's status-title and name: "Rapuna Daeng D" is "Daeng D's rapu." (Daeng is a status-title.) The extended circle of very influential high nobles includes not only a large kapolo made up of numerous rapu, but also many dependents and commoners with no claims to white blood. (Only nobles, however, are said to belong to kapolo.)

At first glance, the term "entourage" sounds too mobile, impermanent, and based on personal bonds to be applied to a polity as solid and stable as the kind connoted by the terms "kingdom" and "state." But of course the social/political organization of Southeast Asian states was also characterized by the tensions and tendencies to impermanence: the central ruler was constantly in danger of being de-centered by his close high-noble relatives (among others), who were sometimes able to challenge successfully the ruler's hegemony of influence. In times of great anarchy or war, the physical center of the state was challenged by parvenus with large warrior-followings who came out of the forests and displaced the center, sometimes then physically relocating the state's center in another place, which then became the new center. At the level of thought, such tensions and displacements are easily accommodated. The "men of prowess," to use O. W. Wolters's phrase, were thought to have special potencies or merits; but these are intrinsically unstable, and may disperse or be lost. Challenges to their leader can be interpreted by followers as evidence that his potency is waning.

Particularly in the post–World War II era, those tendencies to instability at the center are less clearly visible at the state level than they are in the smaller versions of entourages that are the pervasive form of social organization in hierarchical Southeast Asia. These tensions were to some extent controlled and masked in times of peace by the use of sacred heirlooms or "regalia." Like the notion of office, something that stands outside the particular person who holds it and continues to exist whether the office is occupied or not, regalia are external to the person who captures or holds them, and they continue to exist even if their holder disappears. But to make this argument it is necessary first to point out the irrelevance of territory in the definition of a "kingdom's" geography.

Territory

It is by now fairly well accepted in the study of Southeast Asian history that political centers were more concerned with control of people than of territory.[4] Territorial boundaries, especially, were a matter of some indifference, a fact nicely illustrated in an incident retold by Clifford Geertz (1980: 25) in order to make a point about Bali; conveniently for my purposes, it happens to be about South Sulawesi:

> V. E. Korn relates an anecdote concerning south Celebes, where political arrangements approximated those of Bali, which makes this point with the grave irony of traditional wit. The Dutch, who wanted, for the usual administrative reasons, to get the boundary between two petty princedoms straight for once and for all, called in the princes concerned and asked them where indeed the borders lay. Both agreed that the border of princedom A lay at the farthest point from which a man could still see the swamps, and border of princedom B lay at the farthest point from which a man could still see the sea. Had they, then, never fought over the land between, from which one could see neither swamp nor sea?

[4] On the importance of the control of people over territory in Java, see Anderson 1972 and C. Geertz 1980; in mainland Southeast Asia, see Tambiah 1976 and Rabibhadana 1969.

"Mijnheer," one of the old princes replied, "we had much better reasons to fight with one another than these shabby hills."

The fact that a polity was not defined by or confined to the piece of territory upon which it perched was misunderstood to their disadvantage by Europeans in the sixteenth and seventeenth centuries. The Portuguese planned to monopolize the control of spice trade to Europe. Not unreasonably, they expected to do it by capturing Malacca, the port city sultanate that had hegemony over the Strait of Malacca, through which virtually all trade from China and the lands around the South China Sea had to pass: "Whoever is lord of Malacca has his hand on the throat of Venice," Tomé Pires wrote in 1512 (quoted in Wheatley 1961: 313). In 1511 the Portuguese captured Malacca—as though it were an eastern Rome that, once taken as a piece of territory, was indeed taken. But the ruler of Malacca escaped with a number of his nobles and dependents and, a little further down the coast, established Johor. Johor *was* Malacca, for the polity had been located not on a rather inconsequential piece of land but around the ruler. By capturing territory and establishing themselves on the Strait, the Portuguese and Dutch in those two centuries succeeded only in destroying the hegemony of any single power over the Strait, not in gaining it for themselves (Andaya 1975a).

To claim that territory did not constitute or define traditional Southeast Asian polities is not to say that the production of wealth was of no concern to the elite of these polities—quite the contrary. A leader of any sort, from the ruler on down, required wealth both to support his myriad dependents and hangers-on, whose presence provided evidence of his greatness, and also as evidence of his greatness in itself. It is worth noting that in the Malay peninsula, *orang kaya*, literally "rich person," meant a person of noble birth; a parallel use in South Sulawesi is *ToSugi*, literally a rich person, one of the degrees of nobility. In other words, wealth was necessary, but, as these people tended to see it, wealth followed greatness rather than the reverse; moreover, wealth was used not to reproduce itself—that is, capital was not used to create more capital—but to attract and maintain followers.

It is probably true of any hierarchical or stratified society that those who have, get. Wealth was pursued in order to attract people, but at the same time, control of people was the key to economic success, whether a polity's wealth was based on trade or on agriculture. In the "coastal" polities, such as Malacca, whose economies were based on trade, control of territory could be incidental: Malacca was so small and barren that it had to import rice. But its hegemony over the Strait of Malacca depended on sea-people (*orang laut*) and on the mobile sailor-warriors who patrolled the water and forced all traffic to stop there. Attracting and keeping them in the service of the ruler, the center of the polity, was crucial to its survival. Similarly, in mainland or "interior" polities where wealth derived mainly from the cultivation of rice, there was historically a chronic shortage of people to work the land, which, after all, could produce only if worked. People—farmers and followers—produced wealth by making the land productive.[5]

The wealth produced by trade or agriculture was used largely to support followers and to hold ceremonies. To these ceremonies of the center, lower/smaller centers came as workers and tribute-payers; representatives of a center's rival-peers attended as guests. If the center that "owned" the ceremony was itself encompassed within a larger center's entourage, then a representative of the superior center might also attend, as a token and gesture of benevolent esteem.

Holding a ceremony was a political act in several senses. A ceremony exhibited and exhibits its owner's centrality. Mobilizing followers to come to a ceremony as workers and contributors of food and tribute required and requires considerable influence over them, influence that had to be established and maintained in non-ceremonial times. One of the effects of a ceremonial display, then, was and is to exhibit the owner's vast influence over countless followers. By exhibiting its influence, a center exhibited and exhibits its centrality and greatness (the same thing) to its own followers (who wish to be attached to the most potent center possible), to its rival-peers (with whom it is in competition), and to its superiors (whom it may be challenging). Like the competitions through ceremonies of Big Men in New Guinea, of which they are more than a little reminiscent, the ceremonies of Southeast Asian states are appropriately understood both as demonstrations and as tests of their owner's place: demonstrations, for the reasons outlined above; tests, because the extent of the worker-following, of the audience, and of the places of the guests who come as rival-peers, could never entirely be known in advance.

Indeed, the nightmare that haunted Southeast Asian "men of prowess," from the grandest ruler of a hierarchical state to the humblest elder trying to settle a dispute among a few ragged hamlets in the depths of the tropical forest, is that they might try to get together an audience, which would exhibit their authority, and no one would come. An audience was critical in these systems as both witness and substance of power. To have the followers and the wealth, and to be capable of mobilizing them for spectacular ceremonies, constituted in large part what "power" was about. What I

[5] The distinction between "coastal" and "interior" polities is, of course, a classic one. A particularly clear explication of the fragility of "coastal" polities, in relation to the "coastal" polity of Srivijaya, can be found in O. W. Wolters's *The Fall of Srivijaya in Malay History* (1970). For a study of the orang laut, or sea-people, see Sopher 1965.

have sketched above were the political circumstances, pervasive throughout Southeast Asia, that led Clifford Geertz (1980: 13) to state of Bali that "power served pomp, not pomp power." Periodic exhibitions of one's centrality were necessary to maintain it and to become more central, and the medium of exhibition was the ceremony.

State ceremonies are no longer performed: cleaning the royal regalia, for instance, or announcing a new ruler cannot be state ceremonies in the absence of an akkarungeng. Nonetheless, numerous events continue to be ceremonialized: weddings, post-burial death ceremonies, "ascending a new house," and an infant's completion of seven (or, in the case of high nobles, forty) days of life. These ceremonies still provide the occasions for which the host's inferiors come to work and cook, while rival-peers and their inferiors come as "guests." People of all statuses "own" such ceremonies, but the grandeur of each differs with the status, wealth, and influence (number of worker-followers) of the host. Needless to say, the tone of these ceremonies must be somewhat different from what it was formerly. In 1976, nobles in Luwu and throughout South Sulawesi continued to have influence, but they no longer had the right, as they did prior to the establishment of the nation-state of Indonesia, and especially prior to the advent of Dutch colonial rule at the turn of this century, to enforce that influence if clusters of followers (navel-centers smaller than themselves) failed to attend their ceremonies as workers or bearers of tribute.

What could be called the sacred/ritual part of such ceremonies is determined beforehand by astrological experts, and must be performed regardless of whether any guests or followers show up. Often the ritual is over in a trice, sometimes performed where no one can see it. As Clifford Geertz remarked of Balinese rituals, the "central events were bracketed on the one side by a long crescendo of gettings ready and on the other by a dying fall of finishings-up" (1980: 117). But it is in the extensive preparation and cleaning up that social relations are reaffirmed and made visible—as Victor Turner remarked, ritual is condensed social structure.

Regardless of their ultimate sacred/ritual purpose, and regardless of whether the event that occasions them is a wedding or moving into a new house, the social organization of ceremonies is the same. A time (determined astrologically for the most important ones) is set for the ritually effective moment. This becomes the ritual center, around which everything else is organized. Word of the event then spreads or is sent. The extended following or supporters of the center who "owns" the ceremony begin preparing to come to the household or area where the ceremony will be held.

If the core host is very small—a commoner husband-wife pair of no great wealth, for instance—it will be helped by a few close relatives and neighbors. The help of peers will be reciprocated in the future. Such ceremonies are not extensive in size, duration, or display of wealth. Lower nobles are helped by their economic dependents, business employees, and commoners with whom they have traditional ties, as well as their close relatives (especially those who are younger or of slightly lower status). The help of inferiors will not be reciprocated in kind.

If the owner/center is a core of high nobles with a large kapolo and extensive material resources, the ceremony can be of considerable size and duration. Preparations for one of the high-noble weddings that I witnessed in Luwu (the largest that I happened to attend, but preceded and followed in other years by much bigger ones) involved hundreds of people and lasted weeks. A useful measure of size is the amount of rice consumed. At this relatively small wedding of a very high noble, three tons of raw hulled rice were used. Weddings put on by ex-Datu and other very high nobles can involve thousands of people and go on for months. It would be difficult to calculate the amount of wealth expended in such a ceremony.

One of the most important measures of the place and influence of the "owner" of a ceremony is the sheer number of people who arrive to work preparing for it. They contribute to its success first of all by their presence, which itself demonstrates that they are the center's followers. They also contribute to its success by cooking to feed themselves and "guests" (the host's rival-peers), and by preparing for the ritual part of the ceremony. Further, they bring contributions of food with them: a few liters of rice, some jugs of coconut-oil, a branch of bananas, a string of coconuts, a few chickens, a basket of eggs.

If the center is a high-noble core of a large kapolo, the followers arrive in clusters (their rapu) from disparate parts of the district of Luwu and further-flung areas where the high-noble core has influence. Each rapu has a leader of each sex. These leaders guide their juniors in work and behavior, and mediate with higher-status clusters should there be squabbles. Members of the cluster work at particular tasks, but a few people always leave their cluster to chat and work with their friends and relatives in other clusters/work-groups. A core of stalwarts and the leader stay with the task, which was assigned from above, making sure it is done, day after day.

The tasks, like everything else, are organized by prestige, and of course by sex, since men do the heavier work. The lowest-place people who appear at a ceremony are visiting mendicants and the insane, who habitually wander from one ceremony or large household to another, doing heavy work under direction, and contributing to the general festivities by allowing themselves to be teased. Men do the heaviest dirty work requiring brute strength, like hauling water, cutting wood, taking care of fires, and slaughtering large animals (goats and carabao). Somewhat higher in prestige is the heavy work involved in bringing in raw foods and doing the first step of preparation, such as cutting up hunks of buffalo meat, removing the outer husks of coconuts, and splitting the nuts, tasks again performed by men. Next—and here we reach the category of cooking and food preparation, which women do—is grating coconut meat, scaling and de-gutting fish, washing dishes, tending the large vats of boiling water for dishwashing, and looking after the steaming cauldrons of rice. And so it goes: preparing delicate vegetable dishes is higher in prestige, and certainly less messy, than cutting up meat and chilis and squeezing coconut pulp to extract the milk for curry; making expensive delicate small white cookies inside the household kitchen is higher in prestige than plucking chickens at the fringes of the outdoor cooking area. During the days approaching the ceremony itself, the highest ladies of the household spend much of their time attending to guests (who drop by for tea and cookies and sometimes meals). When no guests are present who require their attention, these ladies may sit in the inner kitchen, where their inferiors report to them concerning any problems or siri' offenses among the workers that may need their consideration. From the kitchen they can supervise the entire food preparation, look in on the perpetual cookie industry, and occasionally do some of the most delicate jobs, such as cutting up cucumbers or making fluted crust edges on minuscule pastry snacks.

This bustle of activity requires constant supervision and coordination, all organized and directed ultimately by the highest ladies of the household. The logistics of feeding hundreds of people daily as well as preparing for guests is work enough, but the social circumstances are potentially tense as well. Rapu members in the kapolo of a high center work in its ceremony because they are related to the high core, not because they are related to members of other rapu who also happen to be there. Each rapu is likely to be quite ignorant, in fact, of its kin relationships with all but the very closest of other rapu, and those relations are not the most important ones to them.[6] Even more salient is the fact that many attending rapu are structurally peers in status. As peers, they are in competition with each other for the favor of their shared center, and quick to blame each other and promote themselves if anything goes wrong or right.

[6] The ways genealogies are kept and marriages arranged virtually guarantee an automatic and selective forgetting and skewing of relationships, such that a lower-noble rapu might well know that it stands as fifth cousin of the high inner core while at the same time be ignorant that it stands as second cousin to a rapu whose status is near its own. I discuss this subject more fully in Part III.

Whenever people of similar social place come together in South Sulawesi, there is some possibility of tension, which easily erupts into harsh words or worse. The cooks and other workers who are near-peers to each other could easily spend their time bickering and squabbling and accusing each other of subverting completion of their respective tasks. Such small skirmishes can delay or entirely sabotage the production of food, clean dishes, cookies, and so on, which must be sent in a steady stream to the front of the house for guests—the judging ToLaing—waiting to be served.

The ceremonies owned by a center demonstrate to its rivals the extent of its influence. The people who come as "guests" are ToLaing, "other people," the host's rival-peers, accompanied by assorted followers of their own. ToLaing are people whose siri' is in opposition to one's own. They are the audience, guests, and rivals rolled into one, and they will reciprocate later by putting on ceremonies that demonstrate precisely how extensive their own followings are. They attend their rivals' ceremonies on guard, observant of any slight show of negligence that could be interpreted as a lack of respect. Any lapse in service or orderliness is an affront to their dignity (siri'), about which they will fume silently: "Does the ceremony's owner think I am no one, no one at all, that I can be treated just any way at all?" If an affronted guest feels sufficiently offended and sufficiently potent (with enough prestige and followers) to make good his claim, he or she might demand a ceremony of apology from the host. This is to be avoided, for obvious reasons: no one wants a showdown, but everyone wants to get away with as little deference to rivals as can safely be exhibited.

A guest served poorly or inappropriately—with an excessive delay, or in the wrong order of precedence, or with discourtesy, or with the wrong number of plates (the number signifies rank), or anything else at which the guest chooses to take offense—at worst may be angry and demand an apology (which, if not forthcoming, could erupt into war in the days of the akkarungeng), and at best will be contemptuous, noting with satisfaction that his host rival-core has little control over its following and that the host core is vulnerable. If a host apologized for poor service in advance on the grounds that the kitchen staff was bickering and disorderly—such an action is impossible, I insert it only for a hypothetical example—he would be admitting publicly that he had little influence on his followers, who go their own way, ignoring their leader. In fact, my notes show exactly that tension and inchoate accusation are a constant feature of these ceremonies. But a successful center has the wherewithal to squelch problems before they begin, or very quickly, so they do not get out of hand. My notes and interviews reveal a virtual cybernetic system of command and feedback of information about food arriving, the scheduling of its preparation, and the tensions and annoyances between individuals and rapu that must be smoothed over or settled by people higher than the involved parties.

The ideal ceremony happens without a hitch, without the ghost of a squabble in the kitchen or an offended guest on the veranda. If achieving that ideal is all but impossible, still, the appearance of perfect, smooth order sometimes *is* achieved. When things go well, the hosts say it happened *otomatis* ("automatically"), as though without any human effort. The effort and the administrative finesse involved cannot, in fact, be anything but enormous. Still, the illusion of effortlessness increases with the capability of the central administration (the host core). Such smoothness and good cheer are rightly regarded as a measure of the quality of the high core's influence. The presence of the high core is itself supposed to evoke peace, devotion, and willing acquiescence (*macanning ati*, literally "sweet livers") as a sign of its spiritual power.

Ceremonies demonstrate the host center's place but also test it. The extent of a center's following is made visible on these occasions, and there is little it can do to control the size. Occasionally, a host is disappointed and embarrassed when fewer people show up to work than had been hoped for or counted on. In my experience, these are nobles whose place by birth is high enough but whose followers are few; and lower nobles who have well-paying jobs in the present government or the military, but have little traditional following. Conversely, it is really impossible for the respected high core of a large kapolo to host a tiny ceremony. Hearing that a ceremony is in the offing, the kapolo members arrive at their leader's household and put up sleeping platforms. To turn them away would puzzle and crush them. It is unthinkable.

The high core of a kapolo surrounds its dwelling with the dwellings of close and loyal followers by inviting them to live nearby. But it would be a pathetic leader indeed whose followers were confined to people in the immediate vicinity. High nobles throughout South Sulawesi feel pride in having far-flung followers. One high-status Bugis lady of the south said to me, laughing merrily, that her ancestry made her like *gado-gado*. Gado-gado is a Javanese salad made of different kinds of cooked vegetables, and the point she was making in such a charming and light-handed way was that she was a "mixture" because her ancestors came from all over South Sulawesi. Since villagers tend to marry close to home (unless they are sailors, say, and marry on different islands), people with ancestors all over South Sulawesi are generally people whose ancestors' marriages were arranged by high nobles in various polities, who in this way made political alliances and ensured that they and their children married people with the proper degree of white blood, since appropriate candidates of the correct sex and age were sometimes unavailable in a single kingdom. To have family throughout the whole of South Sulawesi, this Bugis lady was implying, meant that she would be acknowledged as a high noble and treated deferentially wherever she went. High nobles with kapolo everywhere can always travel in safety and be received appropriately, even in distant areas where they do not reside. The high noble's world then consists of relatively more kapolo (deferring inferiors) and relatively fewer ToLaing (competitive peers, and ignorant inferiors who are unaware of one's status and slow to acknowledge it).

There can be no expectation, then, that the high central core of a kapolo controls either the territory or the populations that lie between its own central dwelling and those of the dispersed "islands" of its followers. The kapolo is not territorially localized (it is not a fief).

Though on a vaster scale, the organization of ceremonies of the center of the Akkarungeng Luwu was the same as those of kapolo. At these ceremonies, the extent of the akkarungeng was demonstrated and tested, and thus made visible. An akkarungeng was a center that claimed deference and sometimes tribute from smaller navel-centers and their attached service-groupings. These smaller groupings included the akkarungeng's own high nobles and their extended followings. High nobles stood as the navel-centers of their own kapolo. They in turn constituted the periphery-following of their own center, the ruler. Their lesser centrality was encompassed by the larger one. Other smaller/lower centers similarly encompassed by the akkarungeng's center included so-called "tributary states," such as peripheral villages or distant polities in the adjacent mountains. And the realm included smaller groupings of linguistic minorities and people of diverse economic-ecological adaptations (people who in the present era would probably be called "ethnic groups"), such as the Bajau or sea-people, who live on the fringes of the coast and at sea.

In Luwu, as was typical of hierarchical Southeast Asia, the largest center claimed deference and tribute from these smaller centers/groupings, but their internal administrations and customs were matters of indifference to it. As long as these smaller centers did not make war on each other or challenge the primary center, what went on within them was a matter of little concern to their superior. What was not a matter of indifference—indeed, virtually the only thing required of smaller centers—was that they acknowledge themselves to be lower/smaller (not rivals) by deferentially attending the larger center's ceremonies.

On these ceremonial occasions, smaller/lower centers (nobles with big entourages, dependent ethnic groups, tributary states and villages) showed deference by moving toward the more encompassing center, bearing gifts and tribute. Sometimes these tokens were of material value: one Toraja polity from the mountainous area near Luwu was required to bring as its offering buffalo horns filled with gold dust, panned from mountain streams. Sometimes they were not: a Bajau group living in the Gulf of Bone near Luwu's center was required to bring a coil of rope.

Gifts can be thought of as "tribute," but it would be misleading and misreading to imagine that their primary purpose was to augment the largest center's coffers, although in some cases they no doubt did so. These gifts were not primarily loot, but rather materialized tokens of deference, just as people materialized deference in their bodies by the act of travelling towards the center and, once there, used deferential speech and posture.

There was no presumption that the Datu Luwu controlled all territory lying between Luwu and its most geographically distant tributary grouping. Of course, any social-political navel-center of any importance (such as a ruler or high noble) surrounds its dwelling, insofar as it can, with loyal followers and their dwellings. As a result, territory and human following coincide at the very navel-center of the polity. But to imagine that an akkarungeng coincides with a piece of territory would be to be deceived by an optical illusion, present only at the center. As the old prince said to Korn, "We have much better reasons to fight with one another than these shabby hills." Those "much better things" have to do with deference and with the control of the people whose deference makes visible one's own status.

The Fragility of Leadership

A kapolo is known by its male leader: Kapolo na Opu X, "Opu X's kapolo." When Opu X dies and one of his same-place sons or nephews, called Opu Y, becomes its leader, the kapolo becomes known as "Kapolo na Opu Y." When the leader dies, his title and name cease to be attached to a particular social grouping. The grouping's continuity is not based on identity with a name. Nor is it based on loyalty to a legal office. The people at the top and center of a kapolo are not appointed, nor is there a particular point at which a person is inaugurated to or steps down from leadership. At the top and center, what for convenience's sake I have called the high core of the kapolo, is a collection of people who share a single social place. For a moment we can think of the core of the high core as a set of full siblings, who, as full siblings, share the same degree of white blood. They also share the same title (Andi if unmarried, Opu if married), regardless of sex or relative age.

From among these siblings gradually emerges a man who is especially capable. If, as he becomes older, he continues to act with intelligence, dignity, and compassion for the followers, he will, in his middle age, be referred to by them more and more often as their ToMatoa. I translate the term "ToMatoa" as "Respected Elder," but it means literally "Old Person" (person in-the-state-of old). It is a term that can be used by anyone of any social class to refer to someone senior to themselves, whether by generation or by status: it could be used to refer to one's own parents, grandparents, great-aunts and great-uncles, as well as to the leader of the kapolo to which one belongs. Its use implies not only seniority but also that the ToMatoa has a benevolent and protecting attitude toward the speaker. So it is a term of respect, not the name of an office. It is not even the name for a single person, a "leader" at the top-center of the kapolo, since people can refer to the preeminent man's same-status wife, full siblings, and same-status first cousins in the same way. This preeminence—what we might want to call the leadership of the kapolo—is "achieved." But it is just as true to say that it is achievable only by people who are of a certain degree of white blood.

It is sociologically accurate as well as compatible with ToLuwu's thinking to say that the high core forms a single social persona. Within the center, the ideal is to act and feel in unity, as a single entity, with respect to followers and to the outside, to ToLaing. Bickering within the high core is considered a disaster. The high core can act as one because the people who form it are internally differentiated by seniority and, to some extent, by sex. (This solidarity due to internal differentiation can be thought of as the "organic solidarity" of Durkheim, or the "hierarchical solidarity" of Sahlins [1983], which is a special case of organic solidarity.) The wife defers to the husband, who is also usually older than she is; younger siblings defer to older siblings; younger cousins defer to older cousins. Married sisters and their husbands (who should be of high status but come from a distant polity, or have no following themselves) defer to the brother who is the preeminent ToMatoa. These people are not differentiated by blood, however: they share the same place, the same degree of white blood.

Only people of high place, a high degree of white blood, can become leaders of kapolo, because no Buginese or Makassarese will knowingly, by choice, and in ordinary circumstances, defer to a person of the same, lower, or unknown place. To do so would debase one's place, both in one's own estimation and, almost worse, in that of onlookers, who would then act as though one's place were lower. After such a public lapse, it would be all but impossible to recover one's siri', and to enforce one's place in social interactions.

To defer to a person whose place is lower than one's own is to lose one's siri'. To fail to guard and defend one's siri' is to be a coward. People say, "It is far better to die with siri' than to live without it," and "To die for siri' is to die a death of palm sugar and coconut cream," that is, a rich, sweet death—the only one, in fact, felt to be worth dying for at all. Because siri' is so important, people will (except in extraordinary circumstances) allow themselves to be led only by those of a very high inherited place, who have exceptional qualities of spiritual potency.

Extraordinary circumstances do, of course, occur. During the Kahar Muzakar anarchy in South Sulawesi (from the mid-1950s to the mid-1960s; cf. Harvey 1974), Kahar was a leader of great personal influence, although he was a very low noble. People considered his personal potency to be exceptional: following him incurred no shame. Southeast Asian history is littered with analogous occurrences. Potency, then, can wax and wane. Being born a noble is no guarantee of having the qualities to be a proper noble. Being born low does not necessarily mean that one lacks the capacity to be great. In ordinary circumstances, however, the social world is arranged in such a way as to prevent the emergence of some extraordinary leader of low birth. It is no accident that these potent men of prowess emerge from the forest in times of war and disruption rather than in ordinary times.

The loyalty of the kapolo members, then, is not to an office, but to the potency that the leader or core of leaders embodies, regarded (in ordinary times) as correlated highly with their degree of white blood. This notion of the basis of authority is a radically non-legal one: neither high "place" nor the authority it engenders can be legislated by the ruler, or by anyone else.

When I was in South Sulawesi, a Buginese scholar in Ujung Pandang, who was educated by the Dutch and who had many egalitarian ideas, suggested to me that the marriage of Princess Anne of Great Britain to a commoner had made it clear to the world, even to Bugis-Makassarese, that it is perfectly all right for nobility and commoners to marry, even when the woman is higher than the man. Yet there is a fundamental and critical difference in the way that status is or can be determined in the societies he was implicitly comparing. A commoner in Great Britain can be made into nobility by an act of the Queen, and, for that matter, titles can be bought: the title is not thought to inhere in bodily substances that cannot be altered. Similarly, in the legal-bureaucratic polities of the West, authority follows a person's appointment to office. A person can become powerful upon being appointed to what is called a "position of power." In the Akkarungeng Luwu, by contrast, the ruler gave high titles and posts to people of high place with large followings, and who by that account commanded wide influence and respect. The high titles and posts were confirmations and emblems of place, attributes of place, rather than the basis of place.

The non-legal basis of authority in traditional South Sulawesi understandings of the world and of "governance" becomes apparent in the difficulties encountered by officials in the present government, the Republic of Indonesia. In the present government, of course, it often happens that a person of low place, relative to the level of the office, is appointed. In such cases, one of two things tends to occur. A local village official, whose inherited place is well known, is in the extremely unenviable position of continually offending the siri' of other villagers who do not enjoy being ordered around by someone whose place is the same as or lower than their own. Since Bugis-Makassarese have a well-earned reputation throughout Indonesia for killing people who offend their siri', "governing" at the local level becomes all but impossible without continual mediation by people who are of higher place than the parties in conflict, but who are outside the official governmental structure. If the office and the official in question are distant from the village, however, the official's ancestry is likely to be somewhat unclear to the villagers. In that case, rumors spread to the effect that the official's ancestry is really quite elevated, but it was obscured over generations due to circumstances of various sorts. These rumors arise naturally as people try to explain to themselves the very puzzling fact that an obscure person of no particular virtue has attained such eminence.

If authority was not lodged in an office in the politics of the akkarung-eng, is it then correct to say, as a number of political scientists and anthropologists do, that in Southeast Asia bonds between followers and leaders are "dyadic" and "personal"? Attachments in Luwu are indeed to persons rather than to offices, yet the notion of "person" implied thereby is curiously impersonal. Kapolo members defer to a place rather than to the transitory idiosyncrasies of what we call a "person." On the other hand, place happens to be embodied in a person, or, more accurately, in several persons who are indisputably of the same degree of white blood. The "place" to which kapolo members are loyal is the center of the kapolo.

The sacred points or places that Boon describes in Bali are temple places served by human groupings whose composition slowly but constantly fluctuates. The chance of those temple places disappearing is slight, for while demonic space can be converted ritually into sacred space, the reverse is uncommon. But the sacred points or places in Luwu that I am describing here, similarly attended by service groupings, are embodied in mortal humans, not carved stone, and thus are imminently in danger of disappearing. If these places are to endure past the lives of the mortal people who embody them, they must be reproduced in another generation of mortals, and yet another. Clearly, marriage and reproduction in Luwu was a political act as well as a duty. For what is marriage but the union of two places, whose issue will be another place, held by that entity we call a person?

As long as the high inner place at the kapolo's center manages to perpetuate itself, the current kapolo members and their children will be able to continue serving that place without losing their kapolo; in that case we could say that "the kapolo endures over generations" (has temporal continuity). But if the high inner core of the kapolo fails to perpetuate itself, then the kapolo with no center will slowly disintegrate, as followers and their children seek other high-place nobles to protect them. To echo James Boon once more: spaces are fixed; only the groupings that serve them are in flux. But if the spaces/places of Luwu, which ought to be fixed, nonetheless disappear, then the serving group has nothing to which it can attach itself. The kapolo members will disperse, joining the fringes of those groupings which serve other high places.

The people who comprised an akkarungeng were supposed to serve and care for the high place embodied by the Datu. By serving and caring for the potency located in their ruler, the service grouping enjoyed its benefits: fertile families, abundant crops, health, prosperity. Insofar as the akkarungeng served the high place embodied by the Datu, its temporal-social continuity was as fragile as an entourage, and as subject to disintegration. Understandably, one of the ruler's chief obligations to his service grouping was to perpetuate that high place by marrying a spouse of the same level of blood; failing to do so would subject the service grouping to infertility, disease, and chaos.

What was needed to ensure that the kapolo or the akkarungeng continued, even if the mortal high place that each served failed to perpetuate itself, was a "place-holder" that was not subject to death and therefore had no need to reproduce itself in order to continue over generations. If there were no arajang, it would have been necessary to invent them.

Arajang as Placeholders

I have pointed out that the central place of a kapolo is not so much "occupied," as one occupies an office that can be assumed or relinquished in a legal-bureaucratic system, as it is embodied, in the persons who constitute its center. That is because "place" is constituted by a bodily substance—"white blood." White blood is supported, it is embodied, by a material location—a person's body or "trunk" (*watang* or *batang*).[7]

---

[7] The word is the same one used for the trunk of a tree, but it is made reflexive when

The "trunk" is also a material support that allows sumange' to be located in a visible and palpable place in the world, a human body. Sumange' is in everything or pervades everything, not only humans, but rocks, trees, houses, and artifacts. Like bodies, these objects offer visible supports or collection-nodes that support sumange' in different degrees or concentrations. The being in Luwu who supported the greatest, most extensive sumange' was the Datu. The Datu was said to be a substantialized spirit, a *dewata mallino* (literally, "a spirit in the state of the world"). The material support substantialized and embodied in the Datu was most immediately his own "trunk," which was, of course, unapproachably potent (makerre'; Ind. *sakti* or *karamat*). The Datu's extended body, the extended material support for the sumange' located at the center consisting of ruler/residence/regalia, was the entire entourage-following called the akkarungeng.

Through long association with its material "trunk," impalpable sumange' pervades its material support. Thus the fingernails and hairclippings of high nobles, which are imbued with their sumange', can become talismans for lower people; similarly, a ruler's robes, imbued with his potency, could be given to his high underlings as gestures of beneficence; and the leavings of a ruler's plate could be eaten by lower people as a kind of strengthener.

From its most dense concentration at the navel, sumange' spreads or flows or disperses, thinning out in widening circles, not bound by the skin or body or trunk. But by its visible attributes, the trunk-support gives evidence of the degree or concentration of potency attached at its navel. A person's attributes—demeanor, fate, place, fortune—are visible evidence of the sumange' located within. The extent and prosperity of an akkarungeng were the visible traces, for instance, of the sumange' of the Datu. The extent and loyalty of a kapolo are the visible evidence of the sumange' of a high noble. (As the follower said, "We make *visible* who Opu is.") Lower-place people, by definition, have lesser degrees, amounts, or concentrations of sumange', but their attributes also make visible their degree of potency. They may be brave soldiers, or effective curers, or fertile parents, or be very knowledgeable about religious matters. Their "effectiveness," like that of higher people, pervades their clothing and ornaments, their hair and fingernails. Understandably, these precious fragments are not discarded when a person dies; his or her descendants keep them as talismans, although they may forget the name of the potent ancestor who produced them. Similarly, people keep the pieces of broken china, old iron pots, knives and so forth

---

speaking of a person: *watang* (trunk) + *ale* (reflexive pronoun) become *watang-aleku* (my own body); *watang-alemu* (your own body); *watang-alena* (his/her own body).

that they have dug up, guided by voices in dreams. The ancestor who produced the leavings is anonymous, so the relation of the artifact's owner to the ancestor is impersonal. But people connect themselves to the ancestors by cherishing these potent fragments as talismans, tapping ancestral potency through caring for the objects. Kept and passed on through generations, these leavings are called *mana'*, roughly, "inherited potent items." Every family, noble or not, has mana'.

The mana' kept by low nobles often consist of objects dug up from the ground, whose source is anonymous, just as it is for commoners; but they sometimes have objects given to them by their high Opu as well, which are then added to the store of mana' they pass to their children. In a few generations, its source will likely become anonymous, too.

Very high nobles store mana' in their houses and treat it with great respect. Their collections of mana' are likely to include *lontara'* (manuscripts, formerly written on palm-leaves), keris, and often brass pots, porcelain, gold ornaments, flags, and sometimes skulls, teeth, or hair. High nobles preserve and revere their ancestral mana'. At the same time, they are aware that both they and their ancestors are producers of mana' for lower people, and that their own leavings—a silk sarong, their book of daily jottings—may be added to the store of mana' when they die. They need not fetishize the mana' as lower people fetishize talismans, because they are its producers. (The term "fetish," of course, is not theirs, but the word is appropriate because the idea is similar, though not in the Freudian sense.) Their "grip" or "handle" or deep connection to their ancestors is immaterial: they are intrinsically connected through their white blood, inherited from the ancestors, and connected in insubstantial and therefore more potent and pure ways through meditation and awareness of their ancestors.

The akkarungeng itself possessed mana', leavings of past rulers, called *arajang*. Arajang are called "ornaments" or "regalia" in writings in English about South Sulawesi. Indeed, a collection of sacred objects inherited from the ancestors was an omnipresent feature of Southeast Asian states. (In Javanese and in Indonesian the term is *pusaka*.) The importance of such collections in the political life of South Sulawesi cannot be overestimated. Near the end of his *Conceptions of State and Kingship in Southeast Asia*, Robert Heine-Geldern (1956: 10) writes,

> Any account of the conceptions of state and kingship in Southeast Asia would be incomplete without at least mentioning the great importance of the regalia. Some of these . . . have cosmological meaning. . . . Other regalia are thought to be possessed of magic forces, such as the royal sword of Cambodia. . . . This magical character of the regalia is even more stressed in the Malay Peninsula and in Indonesia. It culminates in the curious conception prevalent among the Bugis

and Makassarese of Celebes, according to which it is really the regalia which reign, the prince governing the state only in their name.

The central arajang located the densest concentration of cosmic potency in the polity. The arajang had their own special caretakers in South Sulawesi, the *bissu*, transvestites who were both male and female and whose upkeep was provided by the court. (No bissu remain in Luwu, but see Hamonic [1975, 1987] for an account of a group of bissu in Pare-Pare, on the peninsula's west coast.) Chabot's information about the rationale for this institution, obtained from the Makassarese assistant to the government linguist for South Sulawesi in 1948, is as follows:

> According to the description of the ritual, performed at the inauguration of the new head of the bissu (Puang Matoa), one of them leads the new head to the ornament of Segeri, a plow, and at this point he makes an announcement the significance of which the assistant reproduced as follows: "It is neither known of the person who is here brought to the sacred object and who touches it, nor of the object, who is the man and who is the woman. If the sacred object is a man, then this person is a woman, and vice versa." (Chabot [1950] 1960: 209)

Like so many potent entities in island Southeast Asia, arajang, though "living" with spirits or energy, were considered sexually undifferentiated or ambiguous. Beings that are sexually ambiguous, I think, are considered potent not so much because they combine or conflate the duality of sexes but because they are as yet pre-difference, they embody an unbroken unity.

Although I was aware before I went to Luwu of the importance of regalia and the existence of the caretaking bissu in the pre-Independence polities of the area, what had not been clear to me was that some "royal" arajang were located in the regions outside the center. These regional arajang differ from mana' because they were considered lesser aspects or pieces of Arajang Luwu, the central regalia. The arajang were "placeholders" for the titles and responsibilities the ruler could bestow. The officiants called *pabbate'-bate* were of two sorts. *Bate'-bate' rilaleng pare'* [or *ware'*] (laleng means "inner" or "inside") were the titles and duties of the "inside," of the central court, reserved for the rombena kamumu' (nobility of the center). When a person was made, say, the Opu ToMarilaleng, he became the temporary owner of the arajang of that office. It was part of the central arajang, of course, and was cared for by the bissu; but when a state ceremony occurred, the office-holder had the right to wear the regalia, making visible to all who he was. There were also bate'-bate' risaliweng pare' (*saliweng* is "outside"), those "outside" the center, in the regions or *palili*; these were held by the *arung lili*, the local or regional nobility. Some nobles were both arung lili—for they had lesser-noble forebears of the regions, and strong followings there—and rombena kamumu'. These nobles were in the strongest of all political positions in the akkarungeng, neither cut off from the highest prestige of the center by lack of connections in the court (as some arung lili were, with myriad relatives in the boondocks but no influence at court), nor cut off from influence, wealth, and power by lack of regional followers and loyal henchmen (as some rombena kamumu' were, with high titles but no followers). The main regions in Luwu were Bua', Ponrang, and Baebunta. Below these were lesser areas or regions, including areas in what are now Tana Toraja, Central Sulawesi, and even on the other side of the Gulf of Bone. Bua', Ponrang, and Baebunta are now subdistricts with defined territorial boundaries within Kabupaten Luwu, because the Dutch used the names for administrative districts, as has the government of Indonesia. But clearly the Arajang Bua' were not located in Bua' but themselves located the center of Bua', a serving group of people surrounding its arajang. In the same way, the people of Luwu were the serving group that surrounded and served the Datu and Arajung Luwu.

Arajang were important throughout South Sulawesi. Leonard Andaya, working from Buginese and Dutch documents and writing of the historical southern Buginese state of Bone, tells us that local inherited objects there were called the *gaukang*:

> The gaukang was usually an oddly shaped stone, an old flag, a plow, or a sword which was considered to have magical properties because of its unusual physical appearance, or because of the mysterious circumstances in which it was discovered. It acted as a social integrator and a unifying element in the community, around which a power centre could form. In order to provide for the needs of the gaukang, rice fields, forests, fish-ponds and slaves were dedicated to its upkeep and the upkeep of its finder. Such great importance was attached to the gaukang that whoever discovered it was acknowledged as head of the community. . . .
>
> In Bone there is no sense of the rulers being the "sacred lodestone" around which the community evolves as in the Malay world, for this is the place of the gaukang. The ruler could be deposed at any time but the gaukang and the rest of the regalia (arajang) would continue to be accorded the highest veneration in the community. A ruler without the arajang had no authority to rule whatsoever, whereas the arajang retained its power by virtue of its being considered the representative of the gods on earth. (1975b: 118, 120)

Andaya worked from Buginese written sources, which ignore political processes. I myself find it hard to believe that "whoever discovered it was acknowledged as head of the community," although I can well believe that finding an extraordinary object believed to be makerre' (Ind. *keramat*) and taking possession of it could increase the prestige of an already prominent and respected man. I also find it hard to believe that "a ruler without the arajang had no authority to rule whatsoever," because belief in white blood and its importance in generating the leavings that become arajang or mana' is strong all over South Sulawesi, not just Luwu. And I further find it hard to believe that anyone with other than a reasonably high degree of white blood (and the connections that come with it) would be able to capture arajang and claim authority, except possibly in times of quite extreme chaos. At the same time, my work in an era of enforced peace and with high nobles gives me a different perspective (the nobles') from the perspective of villagers on this subject. It is certainly true that villagers revere their local arajang and the leftovers of ritual paraphernalia that some individuals have been able to retain and protect from removal for storage in a museum in Ujung Pandang, where these potent objects would no longer be served by or protect their devotees. In general, my several discussions with villagers on this and related subjects confirm the view Andaya proposes.

First, arajang endured over generations, protecting the realm that served it. Its presence, as well as the presence of its high-noble caretakers, helped the rice to grow and the people to be fertile and healthy; and should an epidemic strike, the arajang would be carried in a ceremonial circumambulation of the afflicted area.[8] The high noble who shared the local navel-residence with the local arajang, by contrast, was mortal. At most, he (or she, as sometimes happened) would last until the end of his life; very possibly, he would eventually be appointed by the ruler to a still higher post inside the court. During the period when the high noble was the lord of, say, Bua', he would have been given the title Opu Ma'dikka Bua' by the ruler. Were he to die or be appointed to a higher place, the title was transferred to someone else, who became the next Opu Ma'dikka Bua'. To villagers it must have seemed, quite correctly, that particular nobles came and went but that the local arajang endured, a constant presence that linked them to the ancestors.

There is another sense in which I suspect that arajang might have seemed more lasting, more permanent, and more important than particular high nobles, and that is in the constancy of their benevolent presence. In theory, high nobles and arajang both exerted a benevolent presence over their serving grouping, for both high nobles and arajang were the material supports that located ancestral potency and made it available to lesser humans in the world. Both were like enormous talismans that protected not just individuals, who wear small talismans around their waists, but entire villages or, in the case of the Datu, the akkarungeng itself. There is a great tendency in

---

[8] Bone's regalia now reside in its museum. It is worth noting that in the early 1970s, when an epidemic swept Bone, its people insisted that the regalia be removed from the museum and circumambulate the area, as had been done before Independence (Andaya, personal communication, 1983).

this sort of political system to try to make nobles into exclusively ritual objects. High nobles, and especially the Datu, were living, breathing talismans, ritual objects, just like the arajang. But unlike the Datu, who by the logic of the system could easily be encouraged to adopt a posture of total quiescence, ministers and appointees to the title-and-arajang positions of the akkarungeng were obliged to act. The lower in the system the noble caretaker was, the more he or she actually had to do: settle disputes, arrange marriages, calm crowds, make certain that corvée was carried out in the "rice fields, forests, fish-ponds, and slaves" given for the upkeep of the arajang and of the noble core that lived with it. That is to say, the high nobles who were given charge of local arajang some distance from the center did not become exclusively ritual objects for the people under their protection. Their characters must have made some difference to the people, even to the commoners who had little contact with them, and certainly to the lower nobles whose disputes they settled. The noble appointee might not be influential enough to settle disputes and prevent the outbreak of violence; or he might be especially exploitative in exacting the corvée that was required for the upkeep of himself and the arajang; or he could be negligent or capricious in any number of ways.

Arajang, then, located stable geographical centers. Like Bali's sacred mountain, Gunung Agung, these regalia defined the socio-geographical landscape's shape, for "geography" had no meaningful shape outside its connection with that center. Thus the epic of the Bugis-Makassarese, *I La Galigo*, can be read as both genealogy and cartography. In it, Batara Guru descends from the Upper World to the Middle World, bringing with him three keris, and myriads of lesser-place relatives, dependents, and servers. The three keris, whose names are La Bungawaru, La Baranak, and La Karurung, were to become the main items in the Arajang Luwu. (Other items, leavings of later rulers, were added and became part of the Arajang Luwu in later generations.) Forty of the people Batara Guru brings along are his (lesser-place) first cousins, whom he sends to surrounding mountains and islands to become their rulers. The places where they are sent are named, but no others are named, as though the others, having no relation to Datu Luwu, have no existence or are of no significance, which is the same thing. In this way, various locations/polities are given a place on the map, as it were, gaining at once a geographical and a conceptual existence through their relation to the center of Luwu.

In accord with what I take to be a general South Sulawesi view of things, I have come to think of the regalia as the stable, fixed, enduring point that centered the akkarungeng. The ruler himself in these centrist hierarchical states was considered a fixed point, of course, and the symbolism surround-ing him emphasizes his extreme restraint and physical impotence (com-bined with great spiritual potency). Datu Luwu, for instance, was said to be "bound and blindfolded," that is, a being whose every physical need was taken care of so that he need not lift a finger; indeed, he was actively pre-vented from lifting a finger. And he was virtually reduced to silence, be-cause it was said that anything he said, happened. The Opu Pa'Bicara com-mented to me that, as a result, the ruler had to be restrained from saying anything that would not happen or could not be made to happen. The ruler had to express his wishes, even the simplest, through indirect speech, allusions, and hints, which alert ministers could interpret. It will be clear that in political systems such as these, strong ministers may well be able to make the ruler into a passive and nearly lifeless symbol, whose existence is crucial (their own power depends upon there being a ruler), but whose political presence is negligible. Island Southeast Asian history is certainly full of chief ministers who become the, as we say, power behind the throne. Dominated by strong ministers, the ruler could himself become as politi-cally passive as the arajang, with as much to say about governance as the arajang did. The ruler *was* a type of arajang, for his clothing, teeth, and so forth could join the store of valuables that formed the arajang. The ruler was the current living aspect of arajang, the arajang quite literally being the leavings of dead rulers. Indeed, arajang were continually being augmented. Rulers left jewelry or other items in the akkarungeng's store of arajang, and the Opu Ma'dika Bua', for example, left items to augment the arajang Bua'.

At base, potency is one, an invisible and impalpable unity. The paradox of potency is that to *do* anything it requires a periphery, which makes two. Some societies of Polynesia and Eastern Indonesia make the duality of power explicit in their political structure. Samoa, for instance (cf. Shore 1976, 1981, 1982), splits authority between Sitting Chiefs and Talking Chiefs. The former provide the dignified, stable, and passive aspect of power, while the latter form the active, mobile, and somewhat lower-pres-tige aspect of power. Similarly, many Eastern Indonesian societies have two ritual lords, often called something like "Mother" and "Father" (both positions usually held by men); the former is the sedentary, dignified, silent aspect of power, while the latter is the active, mobile orator (cf., e.g., Traube 1986). Although the active half is always slightly lower in prestige than the fixed half throughout the Pacific, some societies institutionalize the duality, thereby giving the two nearly equal weight.

Hierarchical centrist Indic States, whose ideology was perfect unity, suppressed the intrinsic duality of potency. Or rather, the active aspect of potency was disvalued, seen as a visible crude aspect of unseen potency rather than a nearly equal partner. Viewed in this way, a ruler, being both mortal and mobile, stood as a more talle' aspect of the arajang, standing to it as a kind of mouthpiece, in contrast to the arajang's perfectly stable silence. In this sense, the ruler stood to the regalia as the state's spokesman, in Luwu called the Opu Pa'Bicara, stood to the ruler.

All of this is to say that arajang were placeholders. Their presence located centers and sub-centers in geographical space, and held the places of which the akkarungeng consisted, providing continuity over time. We can think of the internally ranked arajang of a particular akkarungeng as a sort of analogue to a "structure" of government, a set of positions or public offices that endure over time whether occupied by private selves or not. There is no distinction in Luwu between "public" and "private," in the English sense of the terms; but to pursue the analogy anyway, the analogue of "public" mana' would be the ancestral leavings to which the Datu controlled access. Only those mana' were called arajang.

In summary, "society" in Luwu was internally ranked, and within that ranking, "person" and "place" were conflated because people embodied their rank-places (their degree of white blood, the concentration of their sumange'). Yet there was another set of places, the positions of which the akkarungeng as a governing structure consisted. Such positions or places, like those of society, located varying degrees of sumange'/potency, hence were ranked internally. But unlike society's places, which were held by people's mortal trunks, the places of the akkarungeng were embodied and substantialized in objects that, being the leavings of the dead, could not die, hence could continue as stable places through generations. Their potency did not wax and wane as humans' did, and they did not have to marry and reproduce in order for their presence to span generations. Arajang held the places and made them visible by giving them a physical support, as a human body gives physical support to its place or rank. But as the leavings of dead ancestors, they were more effective and enduring than any living person.

Comment on Part I
Reading Movement

In the socio-political geography sketched so far, everything apprehensible by the senses—everything that can be seen, or heard, or touched, or smelled, or tasted—is, to a greater or lesser degree, a physical support or location for sumange'. In this ontology, the basic distinction is not constituted by a set of animate and inanimate items, hierarchized by degrees of consciousness and movement into human, animal, vegetable, and mineral, like the scheme articulated by Aristotle and modified and promulgated by Linnaeus and Darwin. The fundamental distinction in Luwu, as in many parts of Southeast Asia, is constituted by the contrast between pure potency, which is imperceptible in itself, and pure material, which is perceptible but lifeless and impotent. The infusion of the former into the latter, in differing degrees or proportions of each, gives shape to a social geography in which that which is most potent and imperceptible constitutes the center of the polity and the highest point in its system of rank. Pure potency is malinrung, impalpable, disappearing. A cluster of terms to characterize malinrung in South Sulawesi would be something like this: invisible, refined, unmoving or still, near the gods, close to the center, effective without the use of force, unmaterialized.

The most malinrung beings are the dewata or spirits of the Upper World, lead by Patoto-é ("the creator"—there are other names, as well). The dewata are entirely insubstantial and potent. Sumange', similarly, is malinrung, as is, so far as I understand it, "white blood."

Insofar as that which is malinrung becomes embodied or materialized, its potency is slightly diminished. People do not discuss this as if it were a philosophical question, but it is my feeling that a South Sulawesi sensibility could not countenance something extremely material, solid, and actively powerful—like a steam shovel, say—as something that is extremely spiritually potent: for one thing, the way it works is mechanically powerful, and can be explained in a straightforward way in physical terms—nothing from the spirit world need be invoked to explain its power; second, it is read as the talle' aspect of potency, and something so overwhelmingly physical is obviously more talle' than malinrung. By contrast, smoke, fragrance, clear water, and sounds, which straddle the perceptible and imperceptible, can easily be read as the talle' aspect of invisible potency.

Luwu's first ruler, Batara Guru, was originally a dewata of the Upper World who agreed to descend into the Middle World and rule it, thus becoming materialized, visible, palpable, embodied. He was known as the Dewata Mallino, dewata in-the-state-of-the-world, a living contradiction, pure potency that is nonetheless tangible. But in becoming tangible, Batara Guru lost some of his potency: he and the subsequent rulers of Luwu (who were, in any case, Batara Guru's potency transferred to other "trunks") were not quite as potent as their close dewata relatives of the Upper World. But compared with all others who are visible, the mere presence of a Dewata Mallino was extraordinarily effective. Rulers had only to say something—and that, very softly and through allusions—and it came about. Though embodied in a visible trunk, the ruler as a social fact was all but invisible: he was unapproachable to all but the closest and highest people, and he was surrounded by guards and paraphernalia on those occasions when he left his residence. Within the residence, to gaze directly at his face invited mabusung as well as punishment meted out by humans: invisibility by fiat.

This royal being, the most absent in terms of embodied manifestation, was also the most present by virtue of his effects. Because pure potency cannot be perceived directly, its presence is known by its effects, which take place in the material world.

People cannot see sumange', cannot see white blood. But since that which is invisible is also potent, its presence can be discerned by its effects and its attributes. When a rock is dropped into a still pond, the rock is out of sight, but the ripples it makes can be seen, in widening circles of lessening energy, and an observer can infer that a rock made them. What people can perceive, they perceive as outer signs, visible evidence, of that which is in itself imperceptible.

The perceivable world, then, is not ignored or discounted in Luwu, but attended to very closely, for it forms a system of signs that can be read. People are trained from infancy in an extraordinary sensitivity to gesture and stance. The conduct of social life requires a continual assessment and judgment of surrounding events and people, a continual "reading" of natural occurrences and of other people's behavior, stance, attributes, circumstances, and life-happenings.

There is a sense in which the states that people seek to read in the events and other people that they observe are "inner" states. "A central conception of the Javanese traditional view," which on this matter is precisely like that of the Bugis-Makassarese, "is the direct relationship between the state of a person's inner self and his capacity to control the environment," writes Soedjatmoko (quoted in Anderson 1972: 17). Everyone, regardless of social place, thinks that attaining some degree of awareness and remaining alert is necessary if one is to be human. Infants are said to "not yet be aware" and to "not yet recognize/embody meaning" (Bug. *de'pa gaga paringnger- renna*; *de'pa naisseng bettuang*). They are not yet fully human. That said, however, it is clear that the pressure to attain inner composure is much greater for those who are responsible for assuring that events turn out well, such as high nobles with vast followings. This was all the more true, during the period when there was an akkarungeng, for those nobles who were in positions whose duties included peace-keeping and mobilizing people. Certainly the extremities of ascetic practice and the burden of constant awareness and continual cleansing of one's impulses, held to be necessary to achieve deep inner composure, were considered in 1976 beyond the capacity of most people, and inappropriate for their aspirations. (This strong feeling of social place contrasts radically with Central Java, where it seems that almost everyone who is not a reformist Muslim would like to cultivate his or her individual *kebatinan* or interior state of potency. See Keeler 1987.) Lower nobles, members of an entourage, felt in 1976 that their high-noble leader's duty was to guard them through such practices, while they, in turn, guarded the well-being of the kapolo's high inner core in cruder, more physical ways (as bodyguards and farmers, for instance).

This ontology of the self engenders an epistemology with political implications. When we in the post-Cartesian, post-Freudian Occident speak of an "inner state," we usually mean the private subjective realm of an individual, congruent in some way with "mind" and "emotions," which is contrasted implicitly with an outer, objective, shared realm called the world. In much of Southeast Asia, between the "inner" and the "outer" lies not a break but a continuity. The difference between *batin* and *lahir* in Central Java, or between *loob* and *labas* in the Philippines, is more like the difference between focused and unfocused, or between concentrated and dispersed, or between the still center of a rock dropped in a pond and its surrounding concentric ripples of water, than it is like the qualitative and unbridgeable gap between mind and body or between subjective and objective. Each person has a most inner self, a navel with sumange', an animating and non-material center. Like the still center of the concentric ripples, it is imperceptible except by its effects.

The innermost core of "inner" in Akkarungeng Luwu was not located within an individual but at the center of the world: the ruler and regalia. The trusted inner core of people who accompanied the ruler were called "inner people" (*ToMarilaleng*), people who are "close" (*macawe*) rather than "far" (*mabela*). *Laleng* means "inside" or "inner," but it also means "profound" (as of arcane knowledge and wisdom) and "deep" (as of seas). The idea is not so much one of vertical depth as it is of unlimitedness and ungraspableness. Its meaning associates it with that which is malinrung.

The entire range of things that can be observed—people, their actions, objects—can be coded as being "more inner" or "less inner." So, although virtually everything in the tangible world is or could be read as signs of potency, at least two items are needed to take a reading. The less inner of the pair can be identified as such by the fact that it is more visible, less refined, more mobile, further from the gods, further from the navel, more materialized, and requires force to be effective.

Like all rulers of the Southeast Asian kingdoms that were influenced by Indian cosmology, the ruler of Akkarungeng Luwu had four ministers who were usually high nobles. They were less near the center of the world than the ruler, less inner and less potent. The white blood of high nobles is not quite as pure as that of the ruler, making them lesser dewata than the ruler, further from the gods. They were indeed more visible than the ruler, for they occasionally showed themselves outside the central palace, albeit surrounded by bodyguards. The ministers were obviously less effective, for they moved around more, which in the nature of things disperses sumange' and loosens concentration.

Lower nobles, in turn, were visibly less close to the navel than higher ones. They habitually spoke louder and with less forethought than the high nobles who lead kapolo; their blood was less white, making them ipso facto further from the dewata and more substantialized. They supplied the bodyguards and fighters in the wars and skirmishes that continually took place in the akkarungeng. In that capacity, they relied in part (though never entirely) on physical force to bring about desired results.[1] And so it could continue: commoners were similarly more materialized than lower nobles, and slaves more so than commoners. But in none of this is there a sharp break between "inner" and less so, since the less inner is less focused, more dispersed, less concentrated, less dense, more manifest, more materialized. Within this system of signs that we are pleased to call the world, stillness and movement have a special meaning.

In the grammar of spatial arrangement sketched in Part I, I pointed out that a person's location in space—-whether higher or lower, nearer the cen-

---

[1] As in other parts of island Southeast Asia, however, no action is completely physical or secular, even if it depends on material instruments such as guns and swords. The Javanese, for instance, took gamelan ensembles to battles (Schrieke 1957: 131); and the southern Filipino Tausug do not waste bullets on target practice, since they think their talismans and their inner state have greater effect on their aim and their safety than mere instrumental practice (Kiefer 1972: 75ff.).

ter or further from it—provided both an image of social order and a vocabulary for expressing a person's social place within it. The spatial arrangement of people on ceremonial occasions, the regulations that are analogues of law, the sensibilities informing the analogue of etiquette—all had the explicit and overt purpose of keeping everyone in their proper place with respect to everyone else, in a system of places whose lynchpin was the center of the world. In times of peace, the ruler, residence, regalia, and their surrounding court constituted the immobile point, the fixed center around which the polity oriented itself. Thus order was imaged as static ranked places. Within this symbolic grammar of symbolic spaces, movement—literal, in space or metaphorical, in time—was fraught with meaning.

A person could be read as more inner, as higher in status, as being a place nearer the center, in part by that person's degree and kind of movement. Briefly put, the center is still, its periphery active. Any center (and every person is one, for every person has a navel-point where sumange' is attached) shows itself to be more important, more potent, than any other given center, in part by being more still than the other. Having dissociated themselves through ascetic practices from goading emotions, people of high and central places are supposed to be even and calm, though alert and concentrated, in their most inner beings. (The image of the ruler as a being metaphorically "bound and blindfolded" provided the most extreme exemplar of stillness.) Such people should be prepared for any situation, never "carried away, like a banana-tree trunk swept away by a strong current," a vivid image not only of movement, but worse, of complete lack of control over either one's inner state or the surrounding world (control of the world is thought to follow from control of one's inner state). In the medium of demeanor and etiquette, the directly visible manifestations of a person's more inner state, people of high and central places are supposed to move and speak with composure.

Larger patterns of movement, no less than individual deportment, are read as evidence of place. In the medium of ceremonial life, high people stay where they are, while lower ones come to them. Since relative stillness is an indication of relative place, we can assess, as people of Luwu do, a person's relative place by observing their manner and occasions of movement. One could say that, roughly, the higher the individual's place, the more seldom the individual moves; the larger the number of attendants when the individual does move; and the larger the number of people who move towards the central place that the individual's presence defines. On holidays like the end of Ramadan, people visit the houses of their To-Matoa, their parents or grandparents or the high inner core of the kapolo they belong to. The ToMatoa, however, are obliged to visit only people whose place is above their own. In like manner, at the time of the akkarungeng, the ruler sat still at the top, receiving deference that was brought to him in the form of people's deferential bodies.

A ruler in his akkarungeng and a pedicab driver now represent two extremes of social place constituted as well as exemplified in their respective patterns of movement. A pedicab driver moves at unpredictable times of the day and night, in random patterns and times that could not be known beforehand, moving rather than moved, accompanying rather than accompanied, moving instrumentally for pay, unshielded. A ruler, by contrast, left his residence on ceremonial occasions that were astrologically determined: his ceremonial movements were occasioned by the patterns of the cosmos. No less important, he ended up where he began, which is the next thing to having not moved at all. When the ruler moved, his moving enacted and gave visible form to the centrality of his place. There was an explosion of symbols: quantities of people accompanied him, so many that it was (as one man put it) "dark, back and front," all arranged in orderly fashion according to their place, the ruler carried on a platform shaded with a sacred cloth, preceded by a magical mask and protected and surrounded by armed men, the paraphernalia of state, sacred panoplies, multiple tiers of umbrellas, the whole accompanied by clanging cymbals. It was clear that when the ruler moved something important was happening.

Movement and change, whether spiritual or physical, disturbs order. Order is perfectly stationary, perfectly immobile, perfectly potent. The royal regalia were more sacred, more potent than the ruler: they were more unmoving than the ruler, had no appetites to disturb their calm, and were closer to the dead/potent ancestors.

In Part I, I have sketched the socio-cosmic constitution of centers in Luwu, which, ideally, should be immobile. We turn now to disturbance and life, which are much the same thing, and to the processes that could be deemed "political."

Part II
Centrifugal Tendencies

The intent of Part I was to show that the center of whatever political level is in question—the individual's own spiritual center at the navel, the protecting spirit of the house, the leader of the kapolo, the Datu and arajang whose presence defines the center of the largest realm—has a spiritual and metaphysical *raison d'etre*. In the view of ToLuwu, striving to attain centeredness is ultimately moral as well as practical and beneficial, for to be close to the center is to be close to the ancestral potency that brings peace, fertility, safety, and effectiveness to the world.

At the social level, centering and "order" in Luwu means an orderly arrangement of people in their appropriate social places. Given that meaning of social order, we could say that ceremonies simultaneously exemplify and test social order. Order is most intense when and because the Other challenges. As a consequence, both order and the potential for challenges to it occur simultaneously. Order and disruption are thus each other's flip sides. Social order and what threatens it occur together in ceremonies because each is the result of the same impulse: the desire to become higher and closer to the center. One aspect of this desire could be called a "centripetal" urge, an impulse that kept people of the polity looking toward the center for the fulfillment of their political ambitions. The obverse of the same desire could be called "centrifugal," however, for that very desire put people into competition with their status-peers, resulting in the endless rounds of challenge and counter-challenge that could ultimately de-center a realm. Those are the processes we label "political."

Yet in sociological terms, the impulse to achieve closeness to the center or to become more central oneself translates easily into a desire for status. Clifford Geertz has remarked that in Bali, "status and the compulsions surrounding it animated most of the emotions and nearly all of the acts which, when we find their like in our own society, we call political. To understand the negara [Balinese polity] is to locate those emotions and construe those acts; to elaborate a poetics of power, not a mechanics" (1980: 123). In Parts II and III, as I turn to the political life of Luwu, I have ignored what could be called the mechanics of economic power: land-tenure and rents, and the devices by which the rich maintained themselves as such. I have concentrated instead on the poetics of power, which in societies such as these implicates the emotions and acts and the institutional arrangements and devices by which people constitute themselves within a hierarchy and try to maintain their places within it.

In Part II I turn to an analysis of the competition between status-peers, a competition whose centrifugal consequences continually disturbed and disturb the geometry of social order. The geometry of ideal social order, in which there is one center surrounded by tiers of obedient and loyal followers, could be displayed only if people stayed in their places. Most of the time people did not stay peacefully in their social places. Places in Luwu are not legal-bureaucratic places in which people can rest, as though appointed to a sinecure. People must continually assert and embody their places in order to retain them. The constitution in Luwu of a mountain-shaped society requires its members to run at full speed merely in order not to lose ground.

In a hierarchical society like Luwu, people were in theory arranged in a range of social places, falling away from the ruler in degrees of diminishing purity. Inevitably, some people were very close to each other in status: each was approximately the same distance away from the ruler. I call such people "status-peers" rather than "status-equals" because, following Dumont, it seems clear that such a society provides no ideological space for "equals." This point is basic to my analysis and is therefore worth expanding.

Dumont (1965, 1970, 1971) suggests that hierarchical societies do not tend to have well-developed notions of persons as separate, autonomous, and equal. (He distinguishes, of course, between "hierarchical" societies and those that are merely "stratified," that is, class societies, legal bureaucracies, and the like.) "Equals" are people who are separate and who therefore can interact as autonomous beings. Equals can interact peaceably without having to choose between deferring or dominating. Relations between "equals" need not be structured as a contest, since it is not necessary for either to absorb the other into his or her social body.

In Luwu, people do not imagine that they are autonomous or that their identities are self-referential, as the ideology of equalitarianism and utilitarianism suggests. In Luwu, and in other societies that exhibit sacred hierarchy in Dumont's sense (in which the higher ritually encompass the lower), the most prominent political characteristic of social relations is that they are cast in terms of high and low. In such societies, each person stands socially between people who are higher than themselves and people who are lower than themselves. These are the relations that I term "vertical": between elder and younger; superior and inferior (measured by white blood in South Sulawesi, by different attributes in other Southeast Asian societies); protector and dependent; commanding and deferring; more and less powerful; central and peripheral. "Vertical" relations are among the most stable in these societies, and they are in a sense the paradigmatic model for all social relations. Everyone is enmeshed in "vertical" relations. Stable social groupings can be formed between those who are juniors and seniors to each other, for each person in such a relation can "know their place."

The logic of a hierarchical system does not admit the possibility of exact peers in status. Yet people who are close in status are effectively status-peers. Neither is willing to admit the superiority of the other. As a result, their relation is unstable and inconclusive, characterized by competition and opposition rather than by unity and solidarity. It approaches a contest in its structure and meaning.

A major preoccupation of near-peers is to try to determine and assert which of them is higher. It can be no accident that the contest between closely matched opponents is one of the most pervasive structures of narrative symbolic expressive forms in the hierarchical societies of island Southeast Asia. The contest between near-peers, told as a narrative (in rituals, in shadow-puppet theater, in retold adventures, in cautionary tales, in recounted conversations), is itself a self-representation, a way that these societies have of telling themselves what life is like. These contest narratives are the obverse of the same societies' self-representations as mountains and immovable centers. The wishfully immovable center, challenged by a near-peer, becomes embroiled in a contest; the contest, lived or recounted, emplots lived action or forms the structure of the narrative; the old center or the new one, newly triumphant, becomes the new immovable center—immovable, at least, until another peer challenges.

Parts II and III are devoted to explicating some of the political consequences of the fact that people's relations with each other are either "lateral," between near-peers, or "vertical," between higher and lower. These two sets of relations cannot be dissociated, since everyone is enmeshed in both, and the social meaning of each is constituted by the fact that it is not the other. Part II, "Centrifugal Tendencies," concentrates on lateral relations; Part III, "Centripetal Structures," on vertical ones.

Part II consists of Chapters Four and Five. Chapter Four, called "Vulnerable Places" in order to emphasize the fact that a person's social place is always vulnerable to challenge from ToLaing, concerns political microprocesses, the ethos of personal interaction and the analogue of psychology in a world dominated by the need to exhibit siri', status-honor. Given that siri' is the most important attitudinal stance humans can exhibit, the subject of Chapter Five, "The Contest for Place," examines some of the consequences for the shape and meaning of the polity, and suggests that the "state" was a system of signs of differential status enforced by power at the top.

Chapter Four
Vulnerable Places

When I first arrived in South Sulawesi, I stayed in Ujung Pandang, in the household of very high nobles from a Bugis former kingdom to the south of Luwu. The following excerpt from my fieldnotes describes my initial puzzlement:

> I thought I should practice doing fieldwork as well as doing language so I decided to find out who lives around us. To get the lay of the land, I asked one of the noble cousins of the household to come with me. We got to the first house and I said, "Who lives there?" "Kapolo," she said, pleased. At the next one I said, "And who lives here?" "Kapolo," she said again. And again for the third house. I was beginning to feel that this was not specific enough. No names, no relationships—what happened to kinship, anyway? At the fourth house and my fourth question she stopped, lowered her voice, and all but whispered, as though it were a scandal, "ToLaing."

Eventually I came to the conviction that if ordinary Buginese were to write an indigenous social science—an effort to describe accurately what the world is like—they would begin with the great divide between kapolo and ToLaing, relatives and strangers, "us" and "them." They would not necessarily begin with central points surrounded by peripheries, as I have in this book, for that is not where most people live; it is not their *habitus*, as Bourdieu would put it. Only those at the very top of a Southeast Asian hierarchy stand outside and above the contest for place. (Those were the circumstances of the Opu Pa'Bicara and his immediate high core of relatives at the time I did fieldwork; hence he, and I looking over his shoulder, could speak about the former akkarungeng as a whole and from the top, for it was in the past, and his social place was unchallenged and unchallengeable partly because it was past.) Historically, of course, even rulers lived in a *habitus* of opposition: there were always other rulers in other kingdoms who could challenge them. But rulers were in a better position than most to eradicate opposition, and throughout Southeast Asia they imaged themselves as unchallenged and unchallengeable. Not so for ordinary humans, who lived in a dualistic world of allies and enemies rather than in the center of a wishfully and sometimes actually hegemonic center. Historically, the social place that any given person held was constantly threatened by status-peers. Status-peers vie with each other for a superior social place.

At the time I did fieldwork, society in Luwu was no longer officially and legally a hierarchy, not only because everyone was officially a citizen equal to all others, but also because it lacked a ruler and regalia, a peak to act as the ceiling of competition and the guarantor of the stability of a hierarchy of places. Nonetheless, people acted as though there was a social hierarchy whose local summit was the high core of which the Opu Pa'Bicara was the most prominent member. In a hierarchy of the Southeast Asian sort, people's social places were and are constantly threatened by status-peers, who vie with each other for a superior place. In the lived social hierarchy I witnessed during fieldwork, status-peers in the presumed hierarchy continued to compete with each other for "place." (High place in the current era can lead to no honors from a non-existent ruler in a non-existent polity, of course, but it can lead to respectable or better marriages with people of similar or higher white blood than one's own. But to look at the competition as though it has a specific goal or utility is a little irrelevant: siri', defense of "place," honor, is where people "live" attitudinally and emotionally.) Awareness of the threatening existence of ToLaing continues to inform all social life. In no trivial sense, even conversations are contests. No less so is the analogue of etiquette, which is better understood as status negotiation than as politesse.

As I remarked before, the contest is an exceedingly common way of casting experience in hierarchical Southeast Asia, whether the medium is a ritual drama, a cockfight, a shadow-puppet play, or the retelling of an encounter that happened yesterday: all are usually plotted as a struggle between two closely matched opponents. It is, simply, a rhetorical form that was and is widely experienced as compelling. Everyone in Akkarungeng Luwu had status-peers. Even the ruler, looking across to peers in other polities, saw other rulers, whose expansionist tendencies were a continual threat to his own. Currently, a high noble with a kapolo sees other high nobles with kapolo. Any and all centers have expansionist tendencies, which continually pose a threat to their peers.

A person involved in a contest looks up or down for allies. Looking up, he hopes to find a powerful protector who will view the challenge to the lower person as a challenge to himself and will bring to bear all his prestige and influence (and warrior-followers, if necessary) to move toward a satisfactory settlement. That higher person is the navel-center to whom the lower one is oriented as a peripheral server. Looking down, a person hopes to find many inferiors who offer up loyalty, support, and obedience. Those inferiors are the loyal followers who are oriented to this person as their navel-center.

When peers are in opposition, then, the contest is not between individuals. When rulers contested each other when there were akkarungeng, we would term the contest "war." When high nobles contested their peers when there were akkarungeng, we might label the contest anything from "vying for prestige" to "internal turmoil" or "civil war," depending on the level of violence and its success in de-centering the centers in the levels above it. Now, when a low noble jostles for position with his peers, the social body of followers whom he involves may be quite small. In that case, the contest might be labeled "a tense conversation," "a boasting challenge," or "a village dispute involving a siri' killing," again depending on the violence level and the number of people involved.

The point, the logic, and the dynamics of lateral opposition were and are similar, regardless of level. One continues to be judged by one's rivals: who one challenges oneself, and by whom one is challenged. At a deep level, there is no other way to know who one is.

This lived social theory, like more bookish ones, implies a psychology: an ethos, a social stance, and a way of thinking about the constitution and worth of persons. In Luwu and in South Sulawesi generally, the stance that underlies both opposition to peers and the ability to fuse into a hierarchical unity is called siri'. There are people who share one's siri': they protect and guard it. Those who do not share one's siri' attack it. And so the world is divided into two sorts of people: "us" and "them"; those who protect one's siri' and those who attack it; kapolo and ToLaing.

Siri' and Ripakasiri'

Perhaps the main criterion of who counts as kapolo rather than as ToLaing is the bond of siri' within a kapolo:

> I was talking to Andi M. about siri'. He said that you are one siri' [Tae *mamesa siri'*, in the state of being one siri'] with your family, against ToLaing. I asked him for some examples. He said suppose I owe some money to a ToLaing and I have to repay it, and the date for repaying it is approaching but I don't have it, then I go to my rich uncle and I tell him about it. My uncle will give me the money (or lend it). That is because we are one siri', and he would be embarrassed just like me if I didn't repay it. I said, suppose your uncle refused you the money once you asked for it? He said in that case, he would feel ripakasiri' by his uncle.

(The term he used, *mamesa siri'* [in Tae] or *maseddi' siri'* [in Bugis] means "in a state of one siri'." [*Mesa* and *seddi'* mean "one."] The term *ripakasiri'* means "to be caused siri'," to be offended.)

The term siri' is, so far as I know, unique to South Sulawesi, but variations on the themes of shame, embarrassment, performance, solidarity, and respect that the term points to appear throughout the island Southeast Asian world. To have siri' (to be *malu* in Indonesian, or to have *isin* in Central Java, or *lek* in Bali, or *hiya'* in Tagalog-speaking Luzon) is a good thing: it marks a person as a social being. Perhaps like all words, but especially like words that stand at the juncture of emotions, processes, reactions, contexts, and understandings, *siri'* cannot be satisfactorily translated. Conventionally rendered, it would be something like "dignity" or "honor" or "shame"—not that the meaning of any of those words is entirely transparent even in English. The Javanese term *isin* is also often rendered "shame." But the most illuminating translation of *isin* I have encountered is Ward Keeler's (1987: 66): "vulnerability to interaction." Part of the meaning of siri' could also be given as "vulnerability to interaction," because a person who has siri' is sensitive to, hence vulnerable to, other people.

When you apply it to yourself, the word indicates that you felt embarrassed or inadequate to the situation. For instance, if you tell a joke and nobody laughs, you feel siri'. Or you might feel siri' if you find yourself in a situation in which you do not know how to behave, as in the presence of a high-status person when you can't handle speech levels; or, as we might say, when you are at a dinner party and you don't know which fork to use, but everyone is judging you on your suave performance. So, when a small child, meeting a gigantic pale stranger from far away for the first time, clings and hides behind his mother's sarong, the mother says, *"Masiri-i,"* "He's [in a state of feeling] siri'," with some pride that the child is not so brazen as to approach an important stranger without hesitation.

I think that this capacity to feel embarrassment, respect, and social humbleness is precisely what Keeler meant in translating *isin* as "vulnerable to interaction." It marks a person as social, as human, in part because it means that that person is responsive to social expectations and cues, rather than wild, controllable only by force:

> AA observed that Westerners don't have siri', and for that reason they don't understand anything but policing and brute force. Shocked, I said that, quite the contrary, we have inner controls, our *hati kecil* [an Indonesian term that means, more or less, "conscience"]. It is true, I admitted, that when our hati kecil does not *jadi* [Ind., "to happen," "to jell," "to operate"], we have a problem. That's when we have to use police and armies and such, because our cosmos doesn't take care of itself, unlike theirs. I pointed out that when they do something *salah* ["mistaken," "out of place"], they suffer mabusung or kasalla'. But our cosmos doesn't *do* anything, so we have to have police.

Siri' is not an inner control in the same way we imagine conscience to be, but it does represent the capacity and sensibility required to adjust one's behavior to a situation without force or the threat of force.

Children are not born with siri'; they have to be instilled with it. In Luwu, as in many parts of Indonesia, people are horrified at the thought of hitting their children and seldom do. When asked why they consider it bad, they explain that if a child is continually hit, especially near the face, the child will grow up lacking in siri'. When pressed further about what connection those things have, they explicate what to them appears obvious. For one thing, the child becomes used to obeying only in response to force. A person with siri', by contrast, knows when and whom to obey without being forced. For another, a habitually abused child will grow up into the sort of person who expects abuse, and will not react appropriately if insulted or threatened. Such a person will be a coward and will not insist on the respect that is due him or her.

And so it is not surprising that various inadequacies and deficiencies in the siri' of other ethnic groups is both explained and emblematized by their (alleged) habit of striking their children. In actual fact, from the bands of hunting-gathering Semai of the Malay interior to the hyper-refined Javanese of the court in Yogyakarta, parents of this archipelago are appalled by the notion of using force to discipline their children. What precisely horrifies them about it differs from society to society, along with the views that each has about how proper social beings are constituted. Nonetheless, explaining alien people's inadequacies by their alleged child abuse is as widespread in the Malay world as the practice of not hitting one's own.

Again, throughout the archipelago, to be said to be deficient in siri' (or whatever: *de'gaga siri'na* [Bug.]; *kurang perasaan malu* [Ind.]; *ora nduwe isin* [Jav.]; *sing nawang lek* [Bal.]; *walang hiya'* [Tag.]) is to be found inadequately human. And so in Luwu they say,

> Siri'-e mitu tariase tau
> Narekko de'ni sirita, tanianik tau
> Rupa tau mani asengna

> Only with siri' are we called human
> If we have no siri', we are not human
> That's called: human in form only

and

> Naia tau de é siri'na
> de it rilainna olokolo-é

> The person who is without siri'
> is no different from an animal

Siri', in short, is a quality that all humans should have. But to be made siri' by someone else (ripakasiri') is something else again.

The word's construction reveals that it is siri' turned back on oneself: ripakasiri', "to be caused to have siri'." Again, this construction is found elsewhere in the archipelago: *dipermalukan* in Malay, *di gau-é isin* in Javanese, *napahiya'* in Tagalog. ToLaing differ from kapolo precisely because they do not have one's siri' as their own. As a consequence, one must be suspicious of them, for they wish to be insulting and denigrating if they find the slightest opportunity to do so with impunity. "Makaretutuko aké deng ToLaing!" ("Be on your guard if there are ToLaing!" [Tae])

Ripakasiri'

All social relations are conceptualized in terms of shared siri'. There is a presumption that people from the same "source"—siblings, their juniors, and lower-status kin who trace relations to the same forebear—should be of one siri'. In this way, "kinship" can be, to some degree, mapped onto and meshed with siri'. But kinspeople can become ToLaing to each other by offending one another. Conversely, people who are initially ToLaing to each other can, through association and habit, become joined in siri'. People in Luwu are very clear that it is intense and prolonged association, *assiwolongpolongeng*, that joins people in siri'. One farmer in Senga said:

> You feel *maseddi' siri'* ["in a state of one siri'"] with your kapolo, but it's also because of association [assiwolongpolongeng]. For instance, the wood merchant who lives with Daeng P's brother has to behave well, for his deeds are the deeds of Daeng P's brother.

When people are thrown together into association, they either develop a single siri' or else they become enemies. Consider my discussion of siri' with a sailor on a trip he made back to Luwu:

> You really feel siri' when you are away. If you are in Luwu, you may know of someone, but you do not go around together. But when you meet in a distant country, you feel that as ToLuwu you are mamesa' siri'.
>   I asked what it meant to "feel siri'" when he was far away. What did it mean for his behavior? He said that you are surrounded by ToLaing, they are looking at you, and they will judge Luwu and your ToMatoa by your behavior.
>   I asked what it meant to be one siri' with other men from Luwu, whom he had not known before. He said that the guys from South Sulawesi always stick together in fights, so people from other *suku-bangsa* [ethnic groups] are afraid of them. Many suku-bangsa don't have siri', so each person is alone. They don't have a chance against the guys from South Sulawesi.

It is my strong impression that being "one siri'" is a constant potential rather than a constant state. The feeling is activated, sometimes in a very ad hoc manner, by a challenge from the Other. Far away from home, always surrounded by ToLaing, the sailor has a heightened awareness of the oneness of his siri' with his ToMatoa and with people of Luwu.

The Other that prompts people to join together in siri' is not fixed: it is whoever challenges. The people with whom one unites in siri' are also not fixed: they can be whoever joins one against the offending Other. The following incident from fieldnotes illustrates these observations:

This morning about 10 a.m. there was a noise of strong voices. Opu D. and Tante P. and I went to the front porch to see what was happening, and AA drifted in from the neighbor's to the scene of action, which was right in front of our house on the main road. There was a *bemo* [a small passenger van] and D's younger sibling N. N was shouting. I saw him gesticulate at the driver and say something about mud and water, and he made more gestures. I saw AA come up, take his hand, and turn him away, and then AA spoke a few words to the driver. The driver immediately went over to N, right hand extended and left hand on right elbow [a deferential gesture]. The driver grasped N's hand and touched his forehead with it. He *minta maaf* [asked forgiveness] and N accepted it. Then the driver got into his bemo and drove off, and AA and N discussed it some more, and then N laughed. Then N came over to me and said in Indonesian, "*Minta maaf, kena air*," [Ind., "I apologize, I was struck by water"], and then he left and the crowd dispersed.

Report of AA a few minutes later was that N was going along on his motorcycle with his child in front and his wife in back. Seeing an oncoming bemo, he flashed his lights to show that there were puddles and the bemo should slow down. But the bemo just barrelled on through, splashing the child. N put his child and wife over to the side and halted the bemo and began yelling at the driver. A small group assembled. He hit the driver through the window and then, because the guy was sort of leaning down, put his foot in or near the driver's face, and said, "*Kau tidak melawan?*" [Ind., "You're not going to fight?"] and the driver said no. And so, N said later, he couldn't fight him because it would be like fighting a woman. N was still very hot when AA came up, whereupon the driver started making excuses, like he didn't see him and didn't know there was water and so on. AA immediately saw the danger and said, "*Kau tidak merasa salah?*" [Ind., "You don't feel at fault?"]. "*Saya merasa salah*" [Ind., "I feel at fault"], answered the driver. "*Kalua begitu, minta maaf*" [Ind., "If it's like that, ask forgiveness"]. So that's what the driver immediately did. Then the driver asked, could he be considered free to go? and was given permission by AA and N. Then N had to ask forgiveness from AA (really from Opu) because he had caused a commotion right in front of the house, and from me, because I am AA's and AM's sibling.

AA says that the siri' that N felt was for everyone—the whole populace was ripakasiri' by the driver's behavior. If the driver had been local, people would have considered it a matter between N and his immediate rapu; but since the driver was a Bugis from the south, everyone got together because they were all in it together. The paradox was that N was guarding Opu's siri' (because Opu guards theirs), but he did it by making a fuss in front of the house, which is strictly an offense to Opu's siri'. So he had to ask forgiveness from the house's high residents.

AA said that of course if the driver had been foolish enough to fight, he would have been killed easily, because everyone would have entered the fray to strike him. I asked if that wasn't unfair, a mob attacking one person. He said no, not at all, quite the contrary, everyone would feel siri' not to enter in, because when one person is guarding our siri', how shameful not to help. Just like Kahar [the rebellion against Java, the civil war of the 1950s]—when Kahar was ripakasiri' by the government, he was fighting to defend the siri' of all people of South Sulawesi, many felt, and so lots of people felt it would be shameful not to join him.

The boundaries between those fused in siri' and those opposed in siri' also shift with the actions of individuals. As mentioned, a person who begins as a complete stranger, by definition a ToLaing, can become, through assiwolongpolongeng, of one siri' with a group of people who are of one siri'. In this process, people of distinct siri' become one (si-temmak-temmak). I myself experienced this process of losing my status as a ToLaing and becoming maseddi siri' with the people I stayed with. This process is not equivalent to "establishing rapport" or "being accepted" in any sense immediately comprehensible to Occidental humanism. A person cannot live in a household and remain a ToLaing because it would be intolerable for the household.

How would one act as a ToLaing in someone else's household? One would behave as though one's actions reflected only on oneself, not on the household members. When Americans living temporarily in Javanese households do this, they often feel quite righteous, because they conceptualize the worth of the "self" (theirs specifically) as located in its autonomy and exercise of individual freedom. But people in Java and South Sulawesi do not care much for individual freedom (they translate it into Indonesian as *kebebasan*, being untied and unconnected), and they have only a slight conception of equality and democracy. They have a strong notion, however, of what neighbors will say. And they have a strong notion of how people with siri'—that is, people who properly speaking are humans rather than just wild animals—behave. Autonomy characterizes the way animals act—they do not think about how their actions reflect on their ancestors, and they apparently have no siri', for they are not vulnerable to the feelings and wishes of others. As one lady remarked to me while feeding her chickens, chickens are just the opposite of humans: when they are young, they follow their elder, but when they are adults, each goes its own way. "Not so for us humans! The more you are an adult, the more you stick with your kapolo!" she said.

People who are not bound by siri' are opposed in siri'. There is no neutral ground, and there are no alternatives. At the same time, the boundaries between "us" and "them," between people fused and people opposed in siri', constantly shift with context and with individuals' behavior. So, for instance, two followers of the same ToMatoa are joined in siri' when the ToMatoa holds a ceremony and the followers work in it. (Even that is an optical illusion, of course. They are joined in support of the ToMatoa's siri', not of each others'. If in certain contexts they work together, it is because they both follow the same high-noble core.) But if the followers are in the village and the ToMatoa is not present, they regard each other as ToLaing. They say to their children, "Makaretutuko ake deng ToLaing!" "Watch yourself if there are ToLaing!" And they mean, precisely, fellow villagers and fellow members of the same high noble's kapolo.

The reverse process, in which people who should be of one siri' offend each other and become ToLaing to each other, is also a constant potential and common event. In those instances, for example when two brothers *pakasiri'* each other (cause each other to have siri'), they become ToLaing' to each other until and unless someone higher than both and trusted by both (a ToMatoa, whether the elder of a kapolo or a respected older relative) is able to settle the matter in a way that saves face for both. Of course, sometimes a reconciliation is impossible. To put it another way, a person is as likely to be ripakasiri' by someone with whom he or she is acquainted as by a stranger—perhaps more likely.

In such circumstances, the ToMatoa is critical in preventing bloodshed, because it is an offense for his followers to fight in his presence. Here is a story, retold from my fieldnotes, illustrating the function of the high-status ToMatoa, the Opu Pa'Bicara. I retell the story in its entirety, changing the name of the murdered man and leaving out the name of the killer, so as not to pakasiri' their kin. Those who are named and alive acted honorably. The story was told to me by Andi Anthon and by Pak Yusof, who is in the kapolo of the Opu Pa'Bicara and whose house is right next door to the Opu Pa'Bicara's. We were discussing madness and people's reactions to it.

There was a second cousin of Opu's [a follower] about three years back. He was making a nuisance of himself, taking people's cars and demanding money and such. People said he was *sinting-sinting* [Ind., "mildly crazy," "highly eccentric"]. One night he appeared at Pak Yusof's in a chauffeured car, carrying all his weapons with him. "That uncle showed lack of respect, for sure," AA interjected.

The man entered Pak Yusof's house and said, "I don't regret it—only, for my wife and children," and he gave all his weapons to Pak Yusof. Meanwhile Pak Yusof had gotten out his own weapons, because the man looked dangerous and was known to be slightly crazy. When the weapons were surrendered, Pak Yusof put them in a room and locked the door.

The man opened his shirt and said repeatedly, "Hot, hot, fan, fan," and Pak Yusof fanned him. The man was weeping and burning with heat and said, "Call Opu." AA, from the adjacent house, had seen the man approaching, and had gone to report it to his father, the Opu. He had then taken off his sarong and shirt, and wearing only shorts [for maximum mobility] had returned to the scene prepared to fight. Yusof said to him, "Quick, go get Opu." And the man called to AA, "Come here, my child, go call Opu." AA saw that the man no longer had weapons, so he went back to get Opu.

Opu arrived and very slowly [so as not to make any sudden movements] approached the man and Pak Yusof. Like an unruly monster [Ind. *raksasa*] the man jumped onto Opu, weeping and embracing him, and kept saying "Lieutenant Ismail, Lieutenant Ismail." Opu said that they would fix it, or something like that, not recognizing that the man had already killed Lieutenant Ismail.

They went out to the car, and the driver revealed that the Lieutenant was already dead, something of a rude shock, his head blown off with a gun.

Pak Yusof loaded the man in the car and took him to the jail or the police station or something. The armed soldiers there all ran away from this man who had no weapons, because they thought he was invulnerable [Ind. *kebal*]. So Pak Yusof said to the man, "You will stay here, won't you," and the man said yes.

Then Pak Yusof went back to the house to ask AA to go with him to Bua', where the man's wife and children were. (AA interjected that only later did he realize what his function was to be.) As they approached Bua', there was a lot of shouting, because that is where Ismail had been killed. All of Ismail's family were there, and they yelled "Halt!" to the car, because this was a matter of siri'. The madman was a closer relative of Opu's than of the others, but Ismail was in Opu's kapolo too. So the car was stopped and Ismail's relatives said, "Who goes there?" goes there?"

"Yusof."

"Who else?"

"Andi Anthon."

"Get out." So they got out and the car was searched. The dead man's relatives thought the killer might be in the car, protected by his relatives. The two had to stand in front of the headlight beams and it was scary, but Pak Yusof was calm and AA followed (he interjected). "If the talk was just a little off, it would have been fatal," Pak Yusof commented.

"Listen," Pak Yusof said when the car had been searched. "This is my family too, and if the government doesn't take care of it, then we will all together fight to the death! Because this is siri'!"

These words calmed them a bit, but they were weeping with frustration because they wanted an enemy, and Pak Yusof was not one. They wanted to go to the madman's house, about two kilometers away, and pull it down, probably killing his wife and children who were in it.

"If you want to get the wife and children," Pak Yusof told them, "that will enter the siri' of the kapolo of Andi Anthon. And if you want to get his kapolo, you might as well start with him, as he is right here. And if you want to attack him, I will fight right now by his side." Helpless again, they wept in frustration.

So Pak Yusof remained there as a sort of hostage and AA took the car and went to the house of the man. The wife and children had shut it up and barricaded it as much as they could. They said, "Who is there?" He answered, "Andi Anthon." So they opened a window. He got them out and into the car, and they went back and picked up Pak Yusof, and then they sped off into town.

In this story Pak Yusof presents himself, with Andi Anthon's collaboration, as a powerful and calm man who is used to dealing with siri' and violence and who can command even madmen, who will obey. Pak Yusof was the main narrator, with Andi Anthon, whose status was higher but whose generation was junior, interjecting and nodding "yes" at crucial points. It was told for my benefit in order to illustrate several points about siri'. Pak Yusof and Andi Anthon present Yusof as powerful, experienced, and commanding, but also as wise enough not to try to handle this tense and potentially explosive situation by himself. He makes a point of showing that he brought along Andi Anthon, the son of the ToMatoa whom all parties acknowledged, whose presence effectively guaranteed Pak Yusof's own safety and that of the madman's immediate family. To fight in their ToMatoa's presence (or in the presence of his son, the same thing) would have offended the ToMatoa. In the days of the akkarungeng, when there was fighting, the Datu sent a delegate with a red umbrella, symbol of the Datu. At its appearance all fighting had to stop. I was told a number of stories about fighting and about the sudden appearance of a high noble or a red umbrella, obliging the warring parties to cease and desist. In such cases, the narrative continues, "They wept! They had no place for their siri'!" Grown men are not supposed to cry, except in one circumstance: when their siri' is offended, but the situation prevents showing themselves ready to die in its defense.

A person who dies because of his siri' *maté rigollai, maté risantangé*, "dies a death of palm sugar and coconut cream." Dying for siri' is the sweetest death, the only death worth dying for. To be killed or to die for any other reason is foolish and a waste.

There is a sense in which the whole system of etiquette, or better, manners and mores, is about submission (politeness), attack (rudeness), and defense against attack. It is a side of social life for which a cockfight can provide an image and teach a moral.

The Cockfight as a Moral Tale

Cockfighting, an activity popular throughout the Malay archipelago for many centuries, is now banned in South Sulawesi. Knowing, though, that cockfighting is a cultural system, I inquired, though not too vigorously, about it. My fieldnotes include this discussion of cockfighting with the Opu Pa'Bicara and his son Andi Anthon:

> I told Andi Anthon something about cockfights in Bali, what I had garnered from C.G.'s article, and he was amazed to hear that the Balinese have cockfights but then don't themselves break into fights. He said that cockfights were allowed only in front of the palace, because people could be controlled there. Other places, they were likely to get into fights. AA said that he thought that one thing you learn in a cockfight is to control yourself, and that is a very important lesson. He gave me the "refined" word for it, the stative verb *maperreng* and the noun

form *aperre-perreng*, and provided this saying: *"Narekko nacau perrekik padata urane, nacau waranitokik."* This means, "If we are defeated in our steadiness as males, our bravery is defeated too." But he said that the main point of cockfighting is a training in manhood. Cocks cannot live together without determining who is best! Further, if one is defeated it says "kraak!" and doesn't complain again, doesn't hit the opponent in the back or anything.

[On another occasion] the Opu Pa'Bicara said that a man who was a real stud in the old days was called a *pakkawacampa*, a man who cockfights. What you did in cockfights epitomized how you dealt with siri'—how you treated your opponent, how you dealt with nobles, how you reacted to winning and losing. People can forget themselves if their cock is defeated.

Cockfights apparently taught several moral lessons. Most striking, perhaps, is that cocks, like men, cannot live together without settling who is best. Equally striking a lesson is that the defeated cock defers to its superior, accepts its fate, and does not fight back, the implication being that human beings ought to do likewise.[1]

Most people who live outside South Sulawesi, and many Buginese and Makassarese themselves, tend to identify siri' (especially in the modern age in cities, where people are not certain who, if anyone, deserves their deference) only as a readiness to fight at the slightest opportunity. A middle-aged middle-ranking noble remarked:

Nowadays everything is chaotic because there are so few respected ToMatoa. So the young people in the cities think siri' is all about being brave and ready to fight. In the old days, you had to have siri'. If you did, you were sure to be brave. Now people think you have to be brave, and call that "siri'."

This man's view is that siri' is coming to signify merely a willingness to fight and the impulse to demand deference, not the willingness to defer to a superior. But the two are aspects of the same thing, and old-style nobles take as much pride in the one as in the other:

When Andi K. [a noble son of the Opu Pa'Bicara] was here and we were talking about siri', he told this story about himself. It was quite a few years ago, when Andi K. lived in Jakarta. He and his friends were high bureaucrats and hobnobbed with ministers often. They were at the airport. Word suddenly came that the ruler of Bone [an important South Sulawesi former kingdom] was at the airport. Andi K. said to his friends, who were Javanese, "Hey, don't laugh at me." And he went to the ruler and made a *sembahyang* [a deferential gesture] that showed great respect. The ruler allowed him to carry his bags. He had zillions of them, and they were really heavy! We all laughed heartily at the incident. [What we found so funny was the double incongruity of a high noble weighed down with bags like a porter; and a modern educated bureaucrat dropping everything

[1] I am told by someone who has seen many cockfights that this last is untrue: a defeated cock is likely to rise up from a state of near death to get in its last peck. The assertion that defeated cocks remain so is apparently a bit of wishful thinking concerning ToLaing, whom one wishes to be so utterly defeated that they cannot make a comeback.

to defer to an embodiment of the old regime.] Then they all explained, with great pride, that if Andi K. had not acted like that, he would have felt that he had no siri'. He would have felt that his feeling of being human had disappeared, because siri' is what differentiates humans from animals.

Siri' is about attack and defense, but it is also about holding steady (*apperrengeng*). The conversation about the cockfight highlights the importance of steadiness, of holding one's own in the skirmishes for status that compose everyday life. I turn now to the strategies and tactics used in etiquette, but will return at the chapter's end to siri' as the capacity to hold steady due to the fact that one is aware of one's place.

Siri' and the Contest for Place

What counts as attack and as injury or (as ToLuwu put it) penetration? Let us take the point of view of the attacker, and speak as though the attacker intended to penetrate and injure. Obviously, piercing soft body flesh with bullets or knives counts as penetration and attack, a type of injury that is far from uncommon in South Sulawesi. The newspaper in Ujung Pandang, its capital city, reports a killing due to siri' almost weekly. (Although no killing due to siri' occurred in the villages I frequented during fieldwork, I did observe a number of very tense incidents involving siri' whose natural end, if uninterrupted, would have been death of one or both parties.) Even to expose a weapon in another's presence counts as an attack. And so it is, as they say, "not polite" to expose a weapon in the presence of a superior. "Not polite" means "not deferential"; "not deferential" means "attacking."

Words can also be weapons. The clearest form of words used as attacking missiles is the insult. The clearest form of insult is to cast aspersions on another person's ancestry, to state or imply that the person's origins were low. Even to hint such an insult raises the level of tension in an interaction to a very marked degree. It puts everyone on guard.

To pronounce the personal name of a person can count as a hostile act, for it places him as inferior to oneself. To speak the name of someone clearly inferior—a child whose status is similar to one's own, or an adult whose status is decidedly inferior to one's own—is acceptable and, in many circumstances, appropriate. But to utter the name of a peer or a senior (by either status or generation) constitutes a challenge.

Body stance is another potential weapon. The "polite" parts of the body, used for deferential interaction, are the head, the right hand, and the front. And so one can insult by turning one's back, or by exposing the sole of one's foot, or by using one's left hand in dealing with another person. Or an attacker could approach another's head too closely, stand tall directly in front of someone who is sitting, or step directly in front of the person without bending. Those are very extreme forms of insult, however, and are seldom used. A more subtle and more common way of indicating lack of deference, a testing form of attack, is for the attacker simply to spread out casually, stretching or spreading his knees (when sitting in a chair), looking straight at the opponent with chin tilted up and shoulders thrown back and open, or getting up abruptly without asking permission. From this description it can be inferred that the most deferential body stance, the one used by inferiors with very high-status people on formal occasions, requires that the elbows and knees be kept close to the body, the head slightly bowed, the eyes lowered, the shoulders stooped, the soles of the feet hidden.

If the body speaks a language in Luwu, it is public and social, not private and idiosyncratic. The meaning of body language in Luwu is very different from the sort described in books on the subject that are available in the United States on supermarket bookracks. Those volumes instruct the reader that a person's fears and self-doubts will be discernible from the position of the knees, the hunch of the back, and so on. To "read" the body in America is to read an interior psyche with a unique history expressing itself in the medium of the body.

Body language in Luwu, by contrast, is entirely public in its code, a code instilled in children as etiquette and displayed in ceremony as social form. It is also public in its interpretation. Because one is trained from childhood to read the body stances of other people and to control and minutely adjust one's own, "reading" body language is far from a subversive or shrewdly insightful act. Finally and most profoundly, it is public in the sense that one's body stance does not express one's interiority, whether unconscious or intentional. Rather, it registers the status of the person to whom it is oriented. And so it is that one can aggress against another person by adjusting one's body, in major or minor ways, so as to register degrees of attitude ranging from deference to contempt.

Another weapon available to an attacker is penetration by insight. A person can be "read," as ToLuwu put it; that is, personal inclinations, desires, impulses, and reactions can be revealed unintentionally to an observer, who pays careful attention to the person's face and body stance. The fact that the body is a public system of signs that can be read locks the observer and the observed into an intensely reciprocal system of communication. The attentive observer is hyper-aware of minute inflections of facial expression, voice, and body stance, which may reveal reactions the observed wishes to conceal. The observed tries to maintain self-control over every gesture and to remain completely impassive and without affect, especially in situations of duress.

Needless to say, the higher one's status, the higher the stakes. A high ToMatoa is studied carefully by his followers, who take their cues for their own reactions from the reactions of their leader. The ToMatoa must not allow himself to reveal even slight annoyance at something that he does not want his followers to be furious about, for the ToMatoa's slightest reaction will be many times magnified by his faithful bodyguard. Thus if a high leader allows himself impulsively to express an emotion, the result may be bloodshed. The public expression by leaders of personal emotion attains, in this system of signs, the status of an irresponsible self-indulgence. A person who habitually indulged himself in that way would not be able to become a ToMatoa in the first place. He would be (correctly) viewed as impulsive and erratic, and therefore as a danger to his followers rather than their protector.

A corollary assumption holds that the need to make wishes verbally explicit reveals a leader to be ineffective and impotent. It shows that other people are paying the leader so little attention that he or she must resort to overt commands and rebukes, which are analogous to force and therefore bear an inverse relation to the exercise of authority. Incidentally, this is one thing that makes it very difficult for women, who are the primary caretakers of children, to attain much spiritual potency. For example, Opu Senga, the Opu Pa'Bicara's older sister, was known for her "clean soul" and calm demeanor. Once I was discussing Opu Senga's faultless reputation with the wife of a high administrative official posted to Luwu, a lady who, being *moderen* and *maju* (modern and progressive), was far from awed by the alleged virtues of the *ancien regime*. She expressed the very reasonable opinion, one that was in fact shared by ToLuwu, that few women could achieve the Opu Senga's calm state, because most of them have children. Children, as yet not fully trained in "reading," are impossible to control without being given explicit directions. Whatever moso (sting of authority) that a woman might have developed dissolves as she fusses about and instructs a recalcitrant child. It is not accidental that women of the very highest status do not take care of little children. The Opu Pa'Bicara's wife, for instance, had many administrative duties concerning the kapolo: she settled disputes among the women, administered the cooking activities for ceremonies, and so on. Members of the household (lower relatives) had cared for her five children's physical needs when they were younger.

Since it is clear that people in Luwu recognize that they are shedders of signs that will be interpreted by others, and that they therefore must control the signs they shed, it is worth comparing briefly the sorts of "selves" that ToLuwu constitute for themselves with the sort of "self" that Erving Goffman postulates in *The Presentation of Self in Everyday Life* (1959) and other works. Like ToLuwu, Goffman's postulated persons are aware that they are shedding signs—"presenting the self" for public scrutiny and appraisal. But Goffman's characters are inhabited by a sort of homunculus that manipulates their exteriors. The consciousness of an interior identity that is different from an exterior presented self pervades Goffman's work. Thus his postulated social actors appear always somewhat schizoid (their manipulating inner self seems different from the manipulated visible shell), and always somewhat fraudulent. ToLuwu are somewhat aware of an analogous possibility, but only marginally. In general, their view is that outward visible behavior is a direct, albeit diluted, expression of interior state; because they imagine a continuity between inner and outer rather than a gap, the schizoid break between interior experience and outward behavior does not usually arise. They are aware that utter fraud can take place—a lower person going to another district and passing himself off as higher—but in general they think that it would be too difficult to act as though one had a clean soul—showing patience, refraining from anger, and the like—if one did not.

Regardless of status, everyone is subject to penetration/attack within the set of understandings I have just outlined, though the stakes are higher for higher people and they work more at keeping themselves steady. (Indeed, the mark or sign of lower people is their alleged inability to control themselves.) The purpose of an "attack" on another's siri', the injury sought, is to challenge the other person to defend his social place, in the hope of dislodging him from it and putting him in a lower place, thus elevating the attacker's place with respect to the attacked. To stay steadily in one's place in spite of continual attacks is considered both moral and brave. It is no coincidence that one of the very highest-status names that can be given to a high noble translates as something like "cannot be dislodged." The understandings within which contests for place happen are shared by all. But the appropriate response to a challenge differs, depending on a person's place.

ToMatoa have the reputation of being impassive, slow to anger, judicious, and calmer than their followers. When I asked how I could recognize a person of high status, I was continually told things like "they never become angry," "a full stem of rice bows over low," and "they walk with eyes cast down, looking neither right nor left." A person with a truly "clean soul" does not go around looking for a fight. High nobles with large followings strike both ToLuwu and visiting anthropologists as calm and controlled, and this is, in their view, the way it should be.

One old village gentleman, discoursing on siri', commented on the even-tempered steadiness of his ToMatoa, contrasting it with the hot-tempered adamance he himself shared with other lower nobles. "It's like this," he said. "It's as if I have one rupiah, and Opu has a thousand rupiahs. I have to be very very careful how I spend mine, because it's all I have. That's why I have to be on guard if I think someone else wants it. But Opu! He has so much, he doesn't have to worry!"

The implication here is that Opu has siri' to spare, and can afford to be generous. Though a striking metaphor, it is nonetheless not the way high nobles see it. They feel that they are more rather than less vulnerable to insult relative to lower people. Since their places are so high, very slight and minor lacks of deference directed toward them constitute insult. The same behavior directed toward a person of lower place would be appropriate and acceptable. As a consequence, very high nobles must be extremely aware of everything that happens or is about to happen, reacting immediately to disrespect so as to quell it before it escalates. Better still, their high status and the potency of their presence should be so overwhelming that no one dares or wishes to do anything that would constitute disrespect.

Most of what can be interpreted as insult is not a legal matter in any sense. Whether or not a bit of behavior is to count as an insult depends on whether one of the affected parties chooses to see it as such. Whether a party sees it as such in turn depends on the status he or she in effect claims by insisting on a particular interpretation of that behavior. The less obvious the difference in status between two people, the more obscure to both of them which is higher, and consequently the more like a contest their interaction will be. When the difference in status between two people is greater, the difference and the direction of the difference is clearer to both of them, and consequently there will be less tendency for their interaction to take on the character of a contest.

A consequence of all this is that, viewed sociologically, competition exists between status-peers, while alliances form between high and low. But no status is immune to attack: people of every status have status-peers, as well as inferiors who may well challenge and test them. Since everyone has peers, everyone is, on some occasions, engaged in defending their place against those peers. No one has siri' to waste, contrary to what the old gentleman told me.

People of different statuses and followings do, however, exhibit different habitual attitudinal stances, as the same man noted. One of the several reasons for this observed difference is, I think, quite simply that high nobles with many followers are literally better shielded from attack. A high noble with followers has bodyguards who accompany their leader on occasions when the high noble is a guest at the ceremonies of rivals. These body-guards shield their leader not only from physical attack, which is unlikely, but also from slights to the high noble's status communicated through in-sufficient deference shown in seating or service. The point of having a bodyguard is to demonstrate potency and a large following such that the host does not dare to treat one with anything but appropriate deference. Members of a bodyguard defend their leader's siri', their leader's place. Be-cause bodyguards are extremely adamant and quick to react at the slightest presumed slight, they must be calmed by their leader. The wise leader will caution care and coolness rather than hot and dangerous outbursts, until a determination has been made as to whether an insult really occurred and, if so, whether the host is ready to make a public ceremonial apology. In this way leaders of large followings acquire the reputation for calm cool-ness, a sign of high status and potency.

High nobles who have few followers are not so fortunate. Those high nobles are relatively unshielded by others and tend to be correspondingly more anxious, more adamant, and quicker to react defensively about how they are treated. They are notorious for making nuisances of themselves by overreacting to slights. My own observation was that they "overreact" only in the sense that a high noble should not be so touchy (he or she should be calm), but not that they are imagining slights that did not happen. The host, knowing that one of his guests is of high status but has few followers, may well be careless in seating and serving him. The slighted noble, seeing his status-peer who is the ToMatoa of a large bodyguard treated better than himself, becomes miffed, because the ToMatoa's deferential treatment by the host makes a visible statement that the ToMatoa is more important and higher than his slighted status-peer. The slighted noble reacts hotly, thereby depleting his moso and confirming everyone's view that he is un-suitable to be a ToMatoa and is not really as high as the ToMatoa. Being a high noble without followers is a hard life.[2]

The women who attend a ceremony go with their associated men, sep-arating into the women's section only when the whole group of men and women has arrived. The women do not, of course, carry weapons—that is the function of their associated men. But the group's internal organization is just like the men's: it consists of a high leader and a following who pro-tects her and whom she keeps in calm order by mediating their disputes

[2] Another type of high noble with no following of his own may nonetheless be accom-panied and protected in ceremonies. A hypothetical case would be a high noble named Opu T., brought from another district in order to marry a high-noble woman, part of the high-noble core of a large kapolo. Opu T. is sufficiently high to marry the woman, but, having no independent following, is no threat to his wife's brothers. Such a man would go to ceremonies as an honored member of the navel-core of the kapolo, protected by its bodyguard.

and cautioning them if they act incorrectly. The leader of the women's group is usually the sister or wife of the men's ToMatoa. Her follower-grouping, too, looks out for slights; she, too, has a reputation for calm coolness. If a truly serious insult occurs, dealing with it is handed over to the men, for their function is to be, as a whole, the bodyguard of the women. The groupings form guarding peripheries to the navel-centers their leaders define.

Lower nobles may be in the groupings that shield higher nobles. Or they may go to a ceremony in groups that are loosely associated with the high noble, even if they do not actually form the high noble's immediate body-guard. It not uncommonly happens that lower nobles, hearing that their ToMatoa is going to be at a wedding in village X, go to the wedding in a group, announcing loudly that they are the people of Opu Such-and-Such, who has yet to show up. They may well have no idea who is getting married. When Opu Such-and-Such does show up, he will be pleased that his extended following has put in an appearance to support him. For their part, they are proud to attend the ceremonies where their ToMatoa is an honored guest, and will recount in the future the fact that they are faithful and valued followers of that esteemed and potent Opu, and that never has a ceremony gone by where they were not there to serve and protect him, for their ancestors have been allied with his ancestors since time immemorial, and so on.

Commoners, traditionally, were involved in nobles' ceremonies mainly in service capacities, not as guests. Now that commoners may have bureaucratic posts in the government or may be rather wealthy as business people, they not uncommonly attend nobles' ceremonies as guests. Since commoners almost inevitably do not have follower-kin to act as an entourage, this may lead to some embarrassment: no one wants to go unshielded as a guest to a ceremony. Bureaucrats bring their office workers with them as an entourage, but this tactic works best only for high bureaucrats. After all, the office workers may be in the entourage of some higher noble to whom they owe a more important allegiance.

Entourages, in short, shield their leaders from both weapons and slights. Everyone strives to make an appearance at potentially tense occasions either with or in an entourage. No one goes alone if there is any way to avoid it.

Bodyguards are not the only shielding periphery that can prevent penetration of a human center. The system of titles and names, which I will explicate at greater length in Chapter Six, forms a complex shield against the insult of being addressed by one's personal name. Commoners practice teknonymy, a naming system by which a person is addressed as the father, mother, or grandparent of someone. In that way, the name of the junior-generation child is uttered, but not that of the more senior-generation parent or grandparent. Childless people are given teknonyms based on their siblings' children or grandchildren. Nobles have status-titles by which they are addressed. A person who utters aloud the name of a noble of much higher status will be struck with mabusung. An effect of these practices is that nobles' names are densely shielded by a bodyguard of titles that prevent their names from being used as weapons by being uttered aloud.

A final shield, already mentioned, is the cultivation of flatness of affect and the appearance of no affect. Nobles council their children: "Ajak nabacako tau!" (Bug., "Don't let people read you!"). Reading, of course, is usually not a private activity and is never an entirely silent one. The term *baca* might therefore be translated as "utter," "pronounce," or "recite" as well as "read." The gist of this warning is: do not expose yourself such that people can gossip about you!

It may come as no surprise that, from the lowest pedicab driver to the highest noble, Bugis-Makassarese are preoccupied with being salamat. *Salamat* means "safe," and one of the more important ways that one stays safe is by protecting oneself from penetration. They are concerned, in other words, with invulnerability. It should also be clear by now that people of different ranks and followings are safe from penetration in differing degrees, since the protecting layers of peripheries around a given human center become thinner and thinner as we descend the scale of status.

Commoners, who have no entourage of bodyguards to protect them from weapons or insults, are shielded at least by teknonyms, but no one who says their names aloud suffers mabusung. Like nobles, commoners do not indulge themselves in moodiness, and they consider the expression of wrath to be dangerous. Yet they do not cultivate flatness of affect nearly to the extent that high nobles do, with the result that their feelings and views are much more "open" to inspection and assessment.

High nobles with followers are shielded from attacks. Defended by others, they are able to be steady. They also actively cultivate steadiness. Their aim is to be neither defending nor attacking—to be neither "defensive" nor "aggressive" nor a combination thereof, but to be utterly calm. They want to be the still center that holds steady against attacks and expands without effort.

Etiquette is not, as we put it, "mere": it is a contest to the death, metaphorically and sometimes literally. The contest exemplified in etiquette is the same one exemplified in wars and ceremonies. It is a contest for place for, although place is believed to be largely inherited, it is made visible only in its demonstration.

A Wall Someone Else Builds

Protective layerings of people, titles, and flatness of affect shield the sacred navel-centers defined by high nobles. The house follows a similar pattern: an elaborated series of layerings around a center post and center spirit that protects the house's inhabitants. These layerings serve to deflect the hostile missiles from the Other that might otherwise succeed in penetrating.

These layered walls are crucial to a person's safety and status. Yet their existence, as Clifford Geertz points out for Java, seems paradoxical, because they are erected by other people:

> Politeness is something one directs toward others; one surrounds the other with a wall of behavioral (lahir) formality which protects the stability of his inner life feeling, but it is, paradoxically, always a wall someone else builds, at least in part. (Geertz 1960: 255)

The seeming paradox arises not from an internal contradiction in the way that ToLuwu understand the world to be but because of the way that English-speaking Occidentals tend to attribute motives. Translation from one world's "rhetoric of motives" to that of another creates the illusion of paradox. I want to discuss this problem briefly, and then return to the notions of motives and energies that form the analogue of a psychology in Luwu.

The rhetorical device I employed in explicating attacking and shielding was an attribution of intention to the attacker. I tried originally to write the section without attributing intention, but I found it very awkward, for the simple facts about etiquette that I was trying to convey were lost in circumlocutions. The attribution of intention is built into our common-sense psychology and our rhetoric for describing action. We habitually think of individuals as bounded entities, and we think of their sources of energy, their impulses and motives, as originating within themselves, whether inside their physical bodies or their psyches. And so we tend to understand their behavior as an externalized expression of internal energies. Sometimes those energies or impulses are seen as physical/biological, sometimes as conscious and intentional, sometimes as unconscious and unintentional, but their origin is always believed to be internal. We often speak as though utterances are externalized thoughts and as though violence is externalized aggression. The notion of a private psychology locates an impulse in the interior experience of a (bounded) individual, which becomes public when it leaves the mind as speech, the body as emotion or behavior.

These common-sense understandings and the language that almost inevitably casts persons as agents, intentional or unintentional, make it difficult to describe "etiquette" in Luwu without violating its meaning. That one utters respectful titles and holds one's body respectfully is not viewed in Luwu as an expression of one's interiority, as the externalization of an inner impulse. Onlookers do not interpret one's body stance as an expression of one's psychological history or personality characteristics. Body stance and utterances (especially the forms of speech indicating politeness or familiarity) are supposed to reflect the status of the person to whom they are directed.

In a perfect world, a world in which everyone knew their social place and registered it appropriately, the crystalline geometry of high and low statuses would be visible in every interaction, and the world would be still and eventless. Bodies would be transparent registers of relative status—humble to those above, straight and dignified to those below. There would be no challenges, for people would defer to those above them. No one would be dislodged because they would be in their proper places, and their rights would be acknowledged by all. With no challenges, the social world would be without events.

Needless to say, humans are not transparent registers of each others' relative status. Too many things get in the way. For one, there is ignorance: people do not have their precise degrees of status stamped on their foreheads. The social system is not a legal and bureaucratic one, in which people hold social places as sinecures; people must continually negotiate and demonstrate their status. Further, there is self-interest, a tendency to give oneself the benefit of the doubt.

A person who has siri' will not show deference to anyone gratuitously— that is, without first satisfying themselves that the other person is worthy of respect. Only those of very low status, or pitiably lacking in siri', would be polite (deferential) to anyone they met, on the assumption that the unknown person is higher. And so ToLuwu do not consider an initial aggressive rudeness (as we in Euro-America interpret it) to be a fault.

Just as it is not rude to test an unknown person, by the same token it is not considered pushy to resist that testing with dignity. Quite the contrary: what is shameful—obtuse, a flaw, an exhibition of lack of consciousness—is not the initial expansion and testing of another person, but the refusal to retreat and defer in the face of evidence that the other person is worthy of respect. Such a person "has no siri'," no more than a person who retreats too quickly.

The impression that people continually expand into or withdraw from the space occupied by another is actually a rather accurate one. ToLuwu are habitual and sensitive readers of the signs others emit; the reading is so ingrained that it is not conscious. They continually monitor others and adjust their own behavior accordingly. When one shows weakness, the other begins to expand into the opening just revealed; this motion can be read as rudeness or aggressiveness. The mistake would be to imagine that that stance proceeds from bad intentions, or others' bad intentions toward oneself (if one is aggressed against). Stance is impersonal, in a deep sense. One is therefore not justified in being annoyed if people continually expand into one's space. They must expand: if they are too quick to defer to someone unproven, they are exhibiting a lack of siri'. (Even this way of putting it makes it sound too intentional.)

Here is a real contradiction. If both persons in an interaction are adjusting to each other, there will be an endless oscillation, a continual instability. Therefore, in each social interaction, one person is more reactive, the other person is more steady. The test is: Who is the steadiest? Who causes the other to react, while herself remaining impassive and in control?

Assuming for a moment that the person addressed is of higher status, the burden of proof, as it were, is on the higher one. By her[3] stance and demeanor, she evokes, or rather controls, the reactions of the lower person. If the higher one is relaxed, loose, unconscious, silly, then the lower one will react with greater expansiveness and less deference, for the lower one is monitoring the other unconsciously (and sometimes consciously). If the higher one is dignified, steady, and by slight inflections of facial expression and voice shows that she is aware of everything going on and will tolerate no expansion, then the lower one will stay in her (lower) place. Defeat comes from being reactive, from giving up control to the other person, from allowing the other person's stance and demeanor to control one's own. That is part of the meaning of the saying, "If we are defeated in our steadiness as males, our bravery is also defeated." And that is why the Bugis-Makassarese and the Javanese alike constitute their social interactions in such a way that a person evokes the reactions of the people around him. "A central concept in the Javanese traditional view of life is the direct relationship between the state of a person's inner self and his capacity to control the environment," writes Soedjatmoko (quoted in Anderson 1972: 13). One who has control over one's inner and therefore outer or visible self exhibits steadiness, thereby evoking respect and deference; one who has little inner control inspires rudeness and negligence on the part of others.

The impersonality of the reactive tendency to expand when another person shows weakness, thereby inviting lack of deference, remained obscure

---

[3] In this passage I use the feminine pronoun in order to emphasize that the sorts of interactions I describe here characterize the social relations of both sexes.

to me for some time. One reason for my confusion was that I had spoken to the Opu Pa'Bicara and to Andi Anthon about the subject in Indonesian. They had explained that wise leaders stay calm and caution their followers against rash action in the event that the leaders are treated with negligence at a ceremony. Only if the insult was *dengan sengaja* (Ind., "without intention"), they said, should the leader allow himself to acknowledge the discourtesy by demanding an apology. At some point I realized that this Indonesian phrase was getting in the way of my understanding, because intention has nothing to do with it. From fieldnotes:

> Now everyone says, "*Tidak dengan sengaja*," it wasn't deliberate, when someone offends someone else. Opu seems to say this to calm his followers, and follows it by saying that we must not make a disturbance in people's houses. If we are ripakasiri', there are ways for it to be remedied [a public ceremony of apology].
>
> But this "not deliberately" is increasingly seeming to me rather vague. Because what could "deliberately" mean? What counts for being ripakasiri' is being publicly humiliated. No one cares about anyone's deep motives for humiliating them.
>
> The point is, even if someone did not really intentionally humiliate you at a ceremony, nonetheless if it happened then it means that the person did not think you were important enough to be extremely careful of. For instance, it is very unlikely indeed that protocol would be lax for the Datu, and be excused later because it was "unintentional." That would be outrageous and senseless. The point is not whether someone intended anything or not—who cares? In any case one suspects the worst with good reason, because his siri' is opposed to one's own. The point is, he didn't think you important enough to treat with care.
>
> I suggested this thought to Opu and AA, who said, but of course. All this *sengaja* stuff is new, and is said only when speaking Indonesian. It really has nothing to do with anything except people's actions. If someone who offended you is willing to make an apology, then in retrospect it appears unintentional and all right. (Because, Opu said, we have to have pity on people and give them a chance to see that they were mistaken and make it right.) But if they won't apologize, then they wanted a fight, and it was "intentional."

The fact is, humans are fallible. They make errors of judgment all the time about the strength and adamance of the people who are "guests" (by definition ToLaing) at their ceremonies. They press whatever advantage they think they see; if the other person accepts it, the host has won the interaction and a new status quo has been established between them. If the other person resists, and is able to make good his resistance, then the host must retreat and "apologize." "Apology" is a ceremony to prevent bloodshed, when one person has miscalculated the strength of the other and has successfully been called on it. And so a constant a posteriori judgment goes on in everyday life. The person who wins the cockfight of status is the person who ought to have won it. He is the one whose potent presence dominated the weaker one, forcing the weak one to go "kraak" and retreat.

Not unrelated to all this is a strong tendency, in court texts throughout Southeast Asia, to assume that whoever succeeded, say, in winning a kingdom or leading a kapolo, is the one who ought to have succeeded. This stance towards the past is not simply a rationalizing or manipulative rewriting of it by the people who gain power. Even less is it the cynical stance implied in the statement "might makes right," a statement that makes sense as a "cynical" statement only in the context of a secular politics and secular theory of the state. In a sacred politics, the a posteriori judgment makes not a cynical statement but an epistemological one: how can anyone know who should have succeeded, except by seeing who in fact did?

These conceptions imply a psychology, but it is a psychology whose rhetoric and attribution of motives are almost entirely public. If a person was rude to someone who accepted the rudeness or was unable to do anything about it, people attribute it to the weakness of the attacked. This harms the standing of the attacked, who is shown to have been vulnerable to attack. The possibility of being treated familiarly—of being attacked—by people who are unaware of one's status is one of the most salient reasons for high people not to go out into public without a protecting retinue, whose function is both to signal the high person's status and to defend it if necessary. In such a rhetoric and psychology, the person with a status to protect is highly vulnerable, because that person is the one who is seen as responsible for other people's reactions to him (or her).

One might well ask whether ToLuwu do not recognize that the attacker sometimes has a willful desire to disparage the higher person, a desire whose source comes from within himself rather than being evoked by the higher person's blameless presence? The answer is complex. In general, the answer is that the motives of the attacker go unmentioned. Certainly, onlookers never use a language of explanation that legitimizes the rude person on grounds of a private interiority. They do not say, "I wonder why Joe was so obnoxious to Professor Smith. Perhaps he is feeling low because his wife left him [an explanation in terms of the attacker's present psychological state] . . . or maybe he has an unresolved oedipal complex [past psychological history] . . . or he just got up on the wrong side of the bed this morning [inexplicable psychological state] . . . or maybe it was something he ate [a materialist explanation] . . . ," and let it go at that. The attacker is assumed always to be expanding, as it were, into the space created by the chink in another's armored stance. The responsibility for the attack lies with the chink, not within the attacker. Thus people's social places—their standing and ultimately their status—are deeply vulnerable. A person who lets down his or her guard, who loses alert consciousness when confronting other people, in effect invites their attack. The attacker, without intentional malice or forethought of the consequences to the weakness of the person whose presence was weak, expands into the weaker person's social space and "wins" the interaction.

It is considered cowardly always to retreat from possible confrontations. People assume that the habitual retreater is simply impotent, afraid to test his mettle. At the same time, it is a mistake to cultivate associations or put oneself into circumstances that positively invite people to be rude. From fieldnotes:

> It has been my feeling that the Javanese are more defensive in caring for their status, and the Buginese more aggressive. I have been looking around for proofs. WK [an anthropologist who worked in Java] said once that when one of his friends, a young man, got married, WK asked him what was different now. The man said he thinks of his dignity now and doesn't spend time with little children. I wondered if this applied to the Buginese, who seem better at controlling people and less timorous asserting their status aggressively.
>
> I asked X, who was amazed at my ignorance. He said of course little children cannot be controlled, because "*tae pa naisseng bettuang*" [Tae, "They don't yet recognize meaning," that is, behave appropriately, have siri', etc.]. Suppose you spend time with little kids flying kites, he said. Then one day you are with the Camat [Mayor] and you are out on the street, and a little kid comes by and yells, "Hey, hey, X, see you later!"—well, the little child isn't condemned. Rather, it is clear that you lack moso such that little kids feel free to come up to you even when you are with the Camat. Furthermore, since they are so hard to control, if you try to control them you will always be scolding and angry. Buginese men feel they lose their grip on things as well as their moso if they are continually angry and fussing. "It's though our grip on things has disappeared, if we are always fussy/angry. It uses up our energies," he said.

Children are hopelessly unruly, so excessive familiarity with them must be avoided by adults to maintain their dignity. Children cannot be controlled, because "they don't yet know meaning"; adults with siri' do "know meaning," which makes them vulnerable to interaction. In that interaction, one person dominates, controlling the situation and the other person, while the other one reacts. The question is, who will dominate the situation by his presence, forcing the other one to go "kraak!" and, defeated, acknowledge superiority?

Let us return to the "walls" that surround a human center. I began my investigation of etiquette with barriers. Like a house's walls, the titles and followers that surround a high noble form a sort of second skin, a barrier, a protection against invasion. The practical usefulness of these layerings is readily admitted by anyone in Luwu.

Yet this sort of thinking about humans, as for houses, seems backwards to ToLuwu. The question that they have is not whether layers help protect a vital center—clearly they do—but why and how some vital centers, but not others, are able to attract protecting barriers to themselves. Those barriers are human bodyguards, but also include the deferential speech, the titles humbly uttered by those lower. Those "walls, built by someone else," are not expressions of the builders' intentions but are evoked by the centered, steady person. The higher person does not express but elicits the barriers that protect him. That person's power and influence are more analogous to a magnet than to a thrusting weapon.

The diabolical paradox is that in Luwu, the "self" must continually be demonstrated in order to exist. For the same reason, it is constituted by other people. We can take the term "constituted" in a weak sense and a strong sense. In the weak sense, other people constitute one's place, who one is, by making it visible. As the middle-noble follower said to me proudly, "Opu needs us, too. We make *visible* who Opu is." But there is also a strong sense of how the reactions of other people constitute who one is in Luwu: ultimately, there is no other criterion of where a place is—how close it is to the navel-center of the world—than whether it has a periphery, and how big that periphery is.

Chapter Five
The Contest for Place

Although it is conducted at the level of etiquette and implicates the processes we might want to call "psychological," the competition between peers in Luwu is not a private matter but a public activity. It gives form to social life, and the politics of the former states were shaped by it. In this chapter I want to explore some of the consequences for the meaning and conduct of the pre-Independence polities of South Sulawesi by comparing the stance of siri' among several other insular Southeast Asian societies.

Competition as the Effort to Maintain Parity

"Commoners" in Luwu and in other hierarchical polities of South Sulawesi are all peers in status, by definition. They are people who live within societies whose nobles are hierarchically ranked and organized; at the same time, they themselves are not internally ranked according to the nobles' criteria (claims of white blood, titles, or differential social places). To say that these commoners are all status-peers according to nobles' criteria is not to say that they are never competitive with each other, or do not try to differentiate themselves from each other regarding prestige, however prestige may be construed locally. Quite the contrary. In Luwu, I observed the competition between commoners only from a distance, as nobles were the focus of my study. But fortunately we have Chabot's very informative ethnographic account of Makassarese commoners entitled (in translation) *Land, Status, and Sex in South Celebes*. Makassar is the pre-Independence name for the city that was the center of the hierarchical polity of Goa, whose ruler was called a *Karaeng* rather than a Datu. With Luwu and Bone, Goa was one of the major polities of South Sulawesi. (Makassar is now called Ujung Pandang, and it is the capital of the administrative district of South Sulawesi.) Chabot's ethnography, published in 1950, is based on fieldwork done before World War II and Indonesian Independence. At the time of Chabot's observations, the polity of Goa was administered indirectly by the Dutch and still maintained a Karaeng, or ruler. Much of the internal administration of the polity remained intact, including regulation of the use of signs of status by the Karaeng and court. The right to regulate such matters was eliminated, of course, with the advent of independence and "demokrasi."

Commoners in Makassar, Chabot informs us, continually strive (using the ethnographic present for Chabot's book) to outdo each other in terms of standing. I was struck by some of the points Chabot makes about upward striving and about siri' because they resonate with what I had seen in Luwu among peers. This striving is expressed, among other things, in acquiring wealth (land, livestock, and "ornaments," Chabot's term for objects inherited from ancestors, called arajang and mana' in Luwu), in defeating others during fighting or skirmishing, in outdoing them in each personal confrontation, and in adopting outward forms of higher people (Chabot [1950] 1960: 110).

In a different part of the book, Chabot suggests that such striving is prompted by challenge and counter-challenge between peers. He indicates very clearly that challenge and counter-challenge are cast and perceived by Makassarese in terms of affronts to siri'.

Vertical mobility occurs by means of opposition relationships. Men between fifteen and forty years, especially the younger ones among them, must face each other in a perpetual relationship of challenge and outdoing. Each challenge and outdoing demands a reaction. The person who does not react (that is to say, the one who does not participate in what is regarded as important in his culture) has little social standing. The feeling of someone who is outdone is indicated by siri'. Someone is siri' when his social standing is impaired and when another person knows this. As Chabot puts it,

> A man is inclined to regard immediately as outdoing any accidental event at an encounter, or a lucky word on his part, by which he raises himself above the other person, at least in his own eyes. The other, when he hears this, is also siri'.
>
> The reaction may consist of a counter-challenge, a returned insult, by which the original challenger in his turn becomes siri'. It is never possible to determine precisely who "began." The mutual opposition is sometimes explained by an event from the past that is regarded as of great importance, for instance, a murder. But with that the question concerning the origin of the mutual opposition is merely put off.
>
> There exists the possibility that the outdone person will respond by stabbing. The consequence of outdoing can therefore never be foreseen. It remains charged with real danger. Many stabbing brawls in South Celebes are proof of that.
>
> One of the most spectacular challenges is the theft of cattle, horses, or buffalo. Its purpose is, in the first instance, to show one's courage (kaporeanna); only in a few cases are economic motives at the bottom of this. Sometimes a warning is uttered beforehand: "I am coming" (that is to say, "to steal your buffalo"). Stealing cattle is done to find a reason for a brawl. A successful buffalo theft is considered a triumph and at the same time a challenge. ([1950] 1960: 290-91)

Chabot's account describes commoners. Yet everything in his characterization of the dynamic of striving among them seems to me equally apt for characterizing the dynamic between peers at any level, including the highest nobles, in South Sulawesi. Peers strive to outdo or best one another, using whatever medium is accessible: house structure and ornamentation, the size of ceremonies, the magnificent names they give their children, the largeness of their followings, their wealth, their bravery in the face of overwhelming odds, marriage to a person of high standing, appropriating the claim to a title such as Andi (possible only in the uncontrolled city of Ujung Pandang), or whatever.

Even slight success by a peer that excels what that peer had been or done before is perceived as a challenge to one's own dignity and standing. Each success must then be met with a similar success, in effect a counter-challenge. Who "began" is not really at issue, for the competition is intrinsic to being peers. There never was a starting point at which the relationship was stable, without tension.

To fail to take a peer's success as a challenge to oneself, and therefore to make no effort to meet it or best it, indicates that one accepts the other person's superiority. In short, peers construe any excellence or success by another peer as an attack on their siri'. If they did not react to meet that attack, therefore, they would show themselves to be lacking in siri'. A peer of any level must continually challenge and counter-challenge in order to maintain parity, or else be left behind.

Some societies in island Southeast Asia that have no principle of institutionalized hierarchy consist exclusively of status-peers. The Ilongot tribe of Luzon (Philippines), described most fully in the work of R. Rosaldo (1980) and M. Z. Rosaldo (1980), represent such a society. In a striking argument that links local social dynamics to local ways of construing emotions, M. Z. Rosaldo has argued that the Ilongot insist that they are all "the same," all "peers." She suggests that it is the Ilongot preoccupation with maintaining parity among themselves that in fact generates competition among them. When one person does something outstanding, Ilongot say, other Ilongot become envious, and envy stirs *liget* (anger, excitement, energy). When a woman's yam crop is especially large, or when a man takes a head, or when a hunter kills a large amount of game, other Ilongot feel liget stirred within them. They see that someone else is excelling, standing out as better or more accomplished than themselves. They find it intolerable for someone to stand out: "Are we not all Ilongot? Are we not all the same?" they ask. The liget of those who have been superseded prompts them to go out and accomplish great deeds themselves, in order that they remain peers of the one who excelled. " 'Without liget to move our hearts,'

Ilongots have told me, 'there would be no human life.' It is envy, they explain, that stimulates industry and spurs people on to labor . . ." (M. Z. Rosaldo, 1980: 47). Competition and energy are thus generated in the Ilongot effort to restore and maintain parity. Like Luwu peers, Ilongot peers compete fiercely—in order not to be left behind.

Although the dynamic of challenge and counter-challenge in order to maintain parity could be said to characterize the interaction of peers, regardless of who the peers might be (members of a hill tribe in central Luzon, commoners in Makassar, or nobles of similar status in Luwu), the social outcomes of their strivings are rather different. In those societies which have institutionalized rank in some form, the oppositional striving can be said to have a direction, and that direction is "up." The same cannot be said of the Ilongot. In Ilongot, there is virtually no social up or down. As the Ilongot put it, "We are all the same." Only one level of parity exists.

If we picture the inflationary and expansive tendencies of social striving as a sort of soufflé that rises in the oven of challenge, we could say that the pan constituted by Ilongot society is like a cookie sheet: it has no sides. The ingredients for rising are there; in the heat of challenge the soufflé rises magnificently. But with no way to consolidate, reify, or permanently mark its gains, it collapses once again to its former level flatness. Societies with institutionalized ranking systems, by contrast, provide markers of standing that give sides to the pan: a person's rise in standing in such a society attaches itself to some marker and clings to it, never again to fall to its former level.

Again, Chabot provides some very interesting observations on this matter as it pertains to the commoners of Makassar. He describes how commoners in Makassar strive to differentiate themselves from one another. Commoners do not have white blood in differing degrees. They consequently lack claims to what Chabot calls (in Dutch) *stand*, which only the nobility have. (Chabot's *stand* is essentially what I have termed "status" or "social place," *onro*.) From the point of view of nobles looking at their own society, then, commoners in South Sulawesi are all "the same," or, as they sometimes put it in Indonesian, "level" (*rata-rata*). Nobles would regard any differences in degrees of prestige among commoners as trivial. To commoners, however, the differences in prestige among themselves are far from trivial. While commoners cannot compete for "status," they do strive to outdo each other in terms of what Chabot calls (in Dutch) *aanzien*, or "standing."

The differentiation in standing among commoners is brought about through women. The social worth of a woman (which is to say the standing of her family) is measured by the bridewealth given at her marriage. A woman cannot be given less bridewealth than what was given for her mother. Moreover, a woman may not marry a man of lesser standing than herself.

This arrangement constructs a vertical direction and a means of measuring one's rise within it. Thus, Chabot writes, if we imagine Makassarese society as a ladder, women—or rather the bridewealth given for them—are the ladder's rungs. He points out that if female hypogamy were allowed, then the rungs of the ladder would no longer hold. It would be impossible to measure advancement by the offer or receipt of a brideprice of a certain amount. This set of arrangements, in short, provides the sides to the soufflé pan, the marks of advancement to which the upward-striving ingredients can cling and never again fall below. People hope that in the next generation a yet higher mark, a larger brideprice, will be reached.

A little reflection will make it clear that in such a system of measuring standing, it is in the interest of both the bride's family and the groom's family for the bridewealth to be as large as possible. Since the bride's social standing is measured by her bridewealth, her family's interest in a large bridewealth is clear. But recall that female hypogamy is not allowed. The obverse is that male hypergamy is also prohibited: a man may not marry a woman higher than himself.[1] Since the groom is therefore assumed to be at least as high as the bride, and since the measure of the bride's standing is the bridewealth she receives, the groom's standing, too, is measured by the bridewealth.

The Polity Regulated Inflation

This set of circumstances encouraged inflation. The minimum bridewealth was fixed by what was given for the bride's mother, so there could be no falling back, no loss of the gains in standing made in the previous generation. At the same time, it was in both parties' interest to make the bridewealth larger than it was in the previous generation. "It is therefore comprehensible," Chabot writes, "that the *sunrang* [bridewealth] has a tendency to rise" ([1950] 1960: 116).

This tendency to inflation could not help but pose a problem to those people who were higher in standing or status than commoners. Since the lower tended continually to become higher, the bridewealth for common-

---

[1] In fact, the obscurity of people's status and standing was such that social mobility in the form of a man marrying a higher woman was not uncommon. When both families acknowledged the discrepancy, the brideprice was supposed to be twice or triple (depending upon the discrepancy in status) what it would usually be. This form of marriage in Luwu is called *ngalli'dara'*, "to buy blood."

ers could eventually equal that paid for the lowest rank of nobles. Lower nobles, in turn, needed to inflate the bridewealth paid among themselves in order to differentiate themselves from commoners. And so it went, on up through the system. If the top of the system refused to inflate and remained stable, one could imagine everyone eventually reaching parity with the top. That could not be allowed to happen, and was not. As Chabot puts it:

> In his kingdom, the prince is the highest. He, and with him his kinsmen of the same blood, should therefore have the highest sunrang [bridewealth] within that kingdom. As a result he is concerned that the sunrang in his region be clearly established according to rank and status, and known to everyone, so that his subjects will not pay or receive a higher sunrang than he himself. Hence, one repeatedly encounters prescriptions concerning the amount of the sunrang in *lontar* [palm-leaf manuscripts]. Nature, however, seems to be stronger than rules. There always arises, some time after the amount has been officially established, the tendency to surpass the prescribed limits. Rules are only too gladly forgotten. As time goes on, more and more people seem to have paid and received a sunrang that was higher than they were permitted. Consequently, a new sunrang edict must be issued periodically. ([1950] 1960: 116)

Scholarship on Southeast Asia has often and correctly called the ruler of the realm "the fount of status." Not only did the ruler have the most of whatever attributes and items acted as signs of status in the realm, but one of the ruler's functions was to distribute those signs, in the form of titles, favors, official positions, and to generate embodied rank by producing offspring of his own high rank. He was indeed the source and fount of status. But it will be clear from the passages quoted from Chabot that the ruler was not only the fount of status but also its guarantor. Because of the inflationary tendency to which any medium or criterion of status was subject, a tendency ultimately traceable to competition between peers, the ruler had to guarantee that signs of status throughout the system had some meaning. This he did by issuing edicts that fixed the value of signs.

The value of the system of signs as a whole was fixed by establishing signs as a range stretching from "high" to "low." Humans attached themselves to the system of signs by using and displaying signs in a way that corresponded with their alleged degree of white blood: each level of social rank was constituted precisely in the privilege to display and use a certain degree or level of the signs of status. Thus clothing colors, for instance, were ranged from high to low by edict, and only high people were allowed to wear colors designated "high"; house structures and decorations, similarly, were sorted into a hierarchy of possible attributes and elaborations so that houses could be used to signify different degrees of rank (unlike clothing colors, this range is still roughly observed). Bridewealth was measured in quantity of gold, and, as Chabot tells us, the amount and therefore the range of payments was fixed by edict. And, of course, humans not only used signs of status but embodied them, knowing full well that they were and are shedders of signs that will be interpreted by others; humans were themselves signs of status.

Almost any medium through which humans interacted, and thereby signalled what their social place was, entered the system, from the gross divisions visible in the color of clothing or the accoutrements of interaction at ceremonies (such as number of serving plates and place of seating), to the delicate and fluctuating fine-tuning of status relations visible in body stance, gesture, and speech. Few media were neutral in this system of signs.

The system was a perfectly Saussurian one in which the value of a particular content depended entirely on its placement within the whole system. "Meaning" here means purely that a particular sign of status was located below some signs and above others. Because the meaning of signs depended on their placement, their placement within a range had to be fixed and guaranteed (backed by sanctions) if any individual sign were to signify, to make sense, to be meaningful. Hence this sort of system required a stabilizer in two respects. First, the range of signs had to be defined and the place of any particular sign (e.g., the wearing of green clothing, the meaning of three tipe-tipe on a house-front) had to be fixed within it. This could be done by edict and tradition. Second—and this required constant monitoring—the use of signs had to be regulated so that only high people wore "high" clothing colors, were served with a "high" number of plates, put a "high" number of tipe-tipe on their houses, and so forth. Maintaining the separation of signs, both in their range of values and in their use, was necessary if the system of signs was to remain vertical, culminating in the ruler. The presence of the ruler, then, stabilized the system of signs by giving it a ceiling in both theory and practice. The sign "the ruler," who fixed the value of signs and guaranteed their correct usage, gave the system the meaning it had by providing a fixed point to which all other signs referred.

Without the guarantee that the separation would be maintained, vertical ranking in the akkarungeng would have over the course of years ceased to exist, becoming instead a state of level peerdom. The soufflé pan would have no sides and would be indistinguishable from a cookie sheet; the kingdom would begin to look like a hill tribe. . . . Such a collapse of hierarchy in a hierarchical polity would be the collapse of order itself; this specter of chaos that haunts this sort of hierarchy results in the sensibility I mentioned in Chapter One, which insists that everything should be in its place. A hierarchy without a ceiling is more or less what I encountered during fieldwork in 1976—not so much in Luwu, where the presence of the

Opu Pa'Bicara and the absence of much in the way of government offices, business, or other non-agricultural and non-kinship-based sources of wealth and status, made the illusion that we were living in a modified version of certain aspects of the old regime temporarily plausible—but in other areas. People all over South Sulawesi, after all, retain a hierarchical sensibility, and they continue to aspire to achieve the signs of high status from the old regime, such as marrying white blood, having high nobles as protectors, having wealth, and so on. Yet while people still aspire to exhibit and achieve such signs of status, the signs no longer form a system with a definite range and guarantee of their meaningfulness (i.e., placement), because the fount and guarantor of the system of signs, the ruler (of each of the South Sulawesi polities), has been eliminated.

What is incorrectly called "feodalisme" (it was hierarchy, not feudalism) has been replaced by what is just as incorrectly called "demokrasi." The elimination of "feodalisme" has meant the elimination of ceilings on the level of signs of status which people of any given level may aspire to exhibit. In some cases, the elimination of ceilings is relatively harmless. People say that there is an "inflasi Andi" in the cities, an inflation of people who give themselves the title "Andi." Indeed, I don't believe I have ever met a Buginese of Makassarese in Jakarta or the United States who did not introduce himself as "Andi Such-and-Such"; it has become the equivalent of "Mr." or "Mrs.," with an ethnic identity attached. "Datu," similarly, is beginning to be used (but only by very very high nobles) in Ujung Pandang and Bone. Once I received a letter from a woman who had been the ruler of a small kingdom south of Luwu. The return address was "ex-Datu So-and-So," and I thought to myself, "The 'ex' is where it's at!" These days quite a few people can be "Datu," but only real ones can be "ex."

In some cases, the elimination of ceilings results in an inflation so extreme it brings about hardship. In Tana Toraja, the mountainous northern part of South Sulawesi, prestige continues to be measured by the number of buffalo slaughtered at one's funeral. Under the old regime, the local political structure set the number permitted to each social level. Now, tens of buffalo may be slaughtered at funerals, sometimes with ruinous consequences for the children of the deceased.

In other cases, the change to "demokrasi" simply indicates a change in the means by which signs of standing can be acquired, or it means the invention of new forms that demonstrate new sorts of standing. Most obviously and profoundly, it marks the beginnings of a shift to monetization. The impact of this shift can be seen in Ujung Pandang on the occasion of weddings.

A wedding used to be one of the occasions at which a noble's influence and following were exhibited to his superiors (among others), for hundreds of followers gathered to work in the ceremony. The ruler's attention was drawn to someone who was striving upward and succeeded in acquiring and maintaining a large following, a following whose extent was made visible at weddings and other ceremonies. A ruler would be politically very unwise to ignore a person with a large following when the ruler distributed appointments, titles, and honors. People who sought honors from above, then, also had to look down to their inferiors and followers, attending to their needs in order not to alienate and lose them. The fount of honors and prestige was from above, but the groundswell of influence and power on which those honors were predicated (in effect if not in theory) came from below. A following could not, and cannot, be bought.

It is very common now in Ujung Pandang for persons who in former times would have been relatively low nobles and who therefore would not have had many followers, to attain positions of some importance in the present government or military, and/or to be rather rich. How to exhibit one's standing at one's child's wedding without any followers to speak of becomes a problem for these people. Such persons tend to have a small wedding in their homes, announcing to visiting anthropologists that it is *maju* and *moderen* (progressive and modern) to regard weddings as *privadi* (private affairs). This private wedding is then followed by an enormous and expensive "resepsi" in a hired hall with hundreds of guests. (High nobles living in the city and separated from their rural base of followers, whom they have neglected for the last twenty years, experience a similar dilemma, and often adopt the same solution.) A hall can be hired; workers assisting in one's kitchen for a ceremony cannot.

The advent of "demokrasi," then, does not mean that everyone is now equal but rather that no one wants to acknowledge that anyone else is better than themselves. In other words, people (especially in cities) tend to regard everyone they meet as an inferior whose dignity can be encroached upon or, at best, a peer with whom they are in competition. In the absence of very overwhelming evidence to the contrary, they acknowledge no superiors. "Demokrasi" is a removal of layered ceilings.

Each person above oneself acted as a ceiling, a hard object against which one could bump one's head during one's expansion "up" and "out." This fact was well understood by at least some people in Luwu, as this conversation taken from fieldnotes attests:

> I told Opu of my feeling that everyone is continually expanding and going up with their siri', and the only reason it doesn't get out of bounds is that it comes up against the Datu, like bumping into a ceiling. Opu said it was ever so true, and gave this example. It seems that people are offended if someone of their own

status reprimands their children: Who are they to reprimand them, after all? But with people of clearly higher status who are their ToMatoa, they may instruct their child, *"Iari pattette uluta iaté,"* "Here, finally, is the one who may rap our heads."

The Polity Regulated Encroachment

To say that the ruler regulated inflation by being the guarantor against encroachment on the privileges of each level from the level below is to take the perspective of someone above looking down. Another perspective would be to look across at peers. From this point of view, the ruler guaranteed that peers did not encroach upon each other's place. To understand this, and to understand the perspective of the person looking "across" at the deeds of peers, it is necessary to recognize that the ranking system of polities like Luwu or Goa prior to Indonesian Independence was not merely vertical but also hierarchical, in Dumont's sense. In such a system, the rank "above" another also encompasses the one below it; to "rise" is not merely to go "up," but also to expand by incorporating as inferiors the people who are presently one's peers. Rising and expanding are the same act.

In my discussion of siri', I wrote that one's only choice when dealing with peers is to absorb them as inferiors or else be absorbed by them. A person who uses signs of status from the level above himself is trying to absorb his peers as his inferiors. Such an act poses a challenge to those peers, and they will resist it. They regard the expander as no better than themselves. To allow themselves to be absorbed by him into a relationship of inferiority, as though he could become their patron and protector, is out of the question. They will interpret his slight and temporary rise as a challenge.

From this point of view, the ruler's control of the use of the system of signs, such that each level of persons would use them appropriately according to their status, also offered an implicit guarantee that the dignity and worth of persons in each level would be maintained against the aggressive ambitions of their peers. I am certain, as was Chabot, that people of any given level who tried to use the signs of status appropriate to the level above themselves wished less to imitate their superiors than to vanquish their peers.

"Law"

The ruler (as an institution and presence) was the fount of status and its ceiling. As the ceiling of status, the ruler fixed the range and content of its signs. That part was easy, since it was effected by edict and tradition. As the ceiling of status, the ruler was also the ultimate regulator of the use of its signs. That part was more difficult, for it required constant vigilance and ultimately the threat of force. It was also entirely necessary. Without regulation of the use of signs of status, the distinct levels, whose separation constituted a vertical range, would be conflated. Verticality itself, culminating in the ruler, would be obscured. Therefore, controlling the use of signs of status was necessarily one of the primary concerns of the polity's top-center. In a well-run polity, retribution against those trying to use signs of status inappropriate to their level—wearing clothes of an inappropriate color, or giving one's child a name too grand—would have been swift.

How was this system of law constituted? Edicts set the rules specifying the signs that each level of rank was privileged to use. In Luwu, for instance, the ruler was to be served with twelve plates; nobles of the highest rank were to be served with eight plates; those of the next with four; next, two; and finally, one. Such edicts, clearly, can delineate only the most gross differences in rank.

Leaders at each level administered the edicts by checking people at the lower levels over whom the leader, as social center, had authority. The leaders of a following could "reprimand" a follower who seized some privilege beyond his station. When I was in Luwu, I saw several instances that demonstrated how this would have happened in the old regime but now does not.

One incident involved the naming of an infant. One of the Opu Pa'Bicara's followers was a middle-level noble who had married a woman who, many whispered, was hardly a noble at all. His first wife had been lower than himself, but higher (by general consensus) than the present one. The second wife apparently felt herself to be in competition with the first one, and wanted her children not to be viewed as lower than their half-siblings by the first wife. She gave her new baby a name that everyone considered scandalously inappropriate, since it implied a very high status.

It would have been an enormous triumph, a vindication of her assertion of her claims, had her acknowledged high-status elders (the central-core leaders of the kapolo) smiled approvingly when informed of this name, in effect accepting it. Instead, they remained completely impassive, neither approving nor reprimanding. This left the matter in a sort of limbo. One can be sure that, as the child grows up, its peers and its mother's peers will not call it by the name she gave it, for people would choke on uttering an exalted name for a peer. It will probably be called by a nickname, and its exalted name will be ignored by all but its mother, who will always rankle and complain that people don't address her child properly.

I suspect that she would not have dared to test her status in such a way in the old regime. But if she had done so, a messenger would have been sent from the kapolo's high core bearing another name direct from the Opu to replace the one its parents gave it. If the name sent by the Opu were a good one, acknowledging low nobility, it would have been a gesture of both reprimand and incorporation. The woman and her husband would have felt both humbled (for they would know that they were wrong) and grateful (for they could have been dealt with more severely but were not). If the Opu wanted to reprimand them severely, he would have sent the name of a commoner. That would have been humiliating and humbling, for it would have denied the father's status.

The authority and the force that backed the right of the high core of a grouping to reprimand its followers emanated ultimately from the ruler. So, for instance, in the old polity, having a title and post appointed by the ruler was a clear confirmation to his followers and peers of a leader's claimed status. Within the kapolo, the same effect occurred with more minor posts. A leader could (and still does) send title and names to newly married followers (names change upon marriage—see Chapter Six) that would indicate and confirm their status. As one woman said to me, "I know I am truly a Daeng [because] Opu sent me my name." Or the leader could (and still does) entrust a follower with an important function, allow the follower to accompany him on an important trip, and so on. These acts by the higher person continue to validate the status of a person on a lower level, especially with respect to his peers. Within that person's own circle of peers and immediate inferiors (such as junior kinspeople), he could and can speak with authority, for his elder's validation of the follower's status makes visible to his peers who he is.

At the same time, the charters and titles sent from above would be of little use if the person who tried to exert influence, especially in matters like settling disputes or reprimanding, did not have a loyal following of people who would guard fervently his privileges and siri' and right to reprimand people like themselves. Although authority was given from above, the force that backed the reprimand was exerted from below: it consisted of the adamant bodyguard of loyal followers who obeyed their navel-center and executed his orders. These people were precisely the ones who were subject to their navel-center's authority.

In the course of things, not all polities were always well run. Retribution was not always swift. There could not help but be, in systems such as this, many failures of administration. The high center of a political grouping, whether kapolo or akkarungeng, sometimes failed to act quickly enough, with the result that an inflationary encroachment became a fait accompli, more dangerous politically to correct late than to allow to stand. Perhaps a high center wavered uncertainly, or had neglected to bind its followers to it strongly, or lacked the strong backing from the authority in the level above itself that it had presumed. The result could be that a lower leader became strong enough to challenge the higher one. Southeast Asian history is filled with such incidents; indeed, the bulk of political history of indigenous hierarchical Southeast Asia consists of just such events. The status and standing of everyone in the polity was constantly subject to retrospective assessment, depending on how much a person was able to get away with claiming without being reprimanded.

In the large schemes of social regulation, which embraced not only offenses against the use of signs of status but also hundreds of other crimes, status specificity was part and parcel of the codification. The magnitude of a fine depended on the rank of both offender and offended. The fine for a person of the fifth rank (if we say the ruler was of the first rank) offending a peer by stealing his cattle, for instance, was considerably less than if that same person stole cattle from a person of the second rank. Offending a person of higher status was, in short, a greater offense than offending a person of lower status.

In this, as in several other respects, the law of the polities of South Sulawesi strongly resembled the indigenous law of the Ifugao, a hill people of Northern Luzon (Philippines) studied by R. F. Barton ([1919] 1969). The injured party in a large number of offenses, including insult, adultery, and other less touchy matters, could demand compensation or fines from the offenders. The fines were graded by social level. At the time Barton studied them, Ifugao had only two levels: *kadangyan*, a type of wealthy Big Man who obtained the right to be called a kadangyan by performing a series of public feasts; and free persons or commoners. A kadangyan obtaining compensation from another kadangyan demanded, by custom, a greater fine than a free person would from another free person. When a kadangyan injured a free person or vice versa, the fine often was negotiated to be halfway between the fines appropriate to each category.

Ifugao had no hegemonic legal or political authority, but people did keep track of their myriad kin, who acted as a mutual-aid society in times of difficulty. In order to obtain satisfaction for an injury, people gathered together their kin and threatened, through a mediating negotiator, the offender and his or her kin. (Incidentally, the negotiating strength of a poor free person against a rich kadangyan with many kinspeople was his simple desperation, a lack of investment in his own life. Because he cared nought for life, he could threaten to kill, and be believed, even if he knew he would incur a retributive death from his victim's surviving kin.)

The negotiation can be subtle and nearly endless; Barton's book is instructive and vivid in conveying what matters are subject to debate in a case that appears on the surface to be straightforward. Offenses between groupings of kin, who are always mutually suspicious, had to be settled with either fines or violence. The threat of violent retribution by overwhelming numbers of adamant supporters-kin greatly aided the injured party in its quest to obtain satisfaction. But if the feuders preferred blood revenge to compensation, little could be done to prevent it, for no one had hegemonic power—or even pretensions to it.

Like Ifugao "law," the law of Luwu largely consisted of the codification of fines. Like Ifugao law, those fines took status into account. And like Ifugao law, the threat of violence by myriad supporters-kin was a potent argument in obtaining satisfaction, especially between near-peers. But unlike Ifugao kadangyan, Luwu's ruler, like those of other polities we designate as "states" or "chiefdoms," had pretensions, at least, to hegemonic power. The reason that Luwu's system of fines appears at first glance to be analogous to a system of law rather than a guide to controlled feuding was that Luwu's codification and its enforcement had a single point of view, that of the ruler. It was as though one of the feuding parties in Ifugao became larger than the others, commanding more loyal force. The ruler had a modicum of hegemony, always somewhat unstable and subject to erosion. And it is as though this nearly hegemonic force adopted for itself the function of setting the range of fines as well as enforcing them, and made offenses against itself the most serious ones.

In Luwu, a powerful center was one that could mobilize the support and ultimately the force necessary to regulate and control signs of status. Power effected peace, a state in which the ruler was relatively unchallenged in his authority to give value to the system of signs and to regulate their use. Peace meant hegemony over the system of signs.

"Morality"

The dynamic that impelled expansion at each level of status was the competition between peers, which automatically resulted in, among other things, an inflationary tendency. Controlling that tendency was, of course, a considerable concern for the people of the upper levels. As I have mentioned, I share Chabot's opinion that people of a given level who tried to use signs of status appropriate to levels above themselves wished less to imitate their superiors than to vanquish their peers; but appropriating signs of status from above was only one of many alternatives used by peers to challenge each other.

One of the most direct challenges, and therefore one most fraught with danger, concerns relations between the sexes. Chabot points out that "the male striving to rise in social standing is touched at the core through impairment of a female relative" ([1950] 1960: 293). He explains the great importance of maintaining a female relative's honor in this way:

> A woman may not lose any standing. Her position is a fixed point for the men who are constantly outdoing each other. An impairment of her standing immediately calls for the most violent reaction, namely, the death of the challenger. Whoever does not react is "matésiri'" [literally, dead in siri'], that is to say, "socially dead." This is expressed by saying that such a person is no longer "of use," or that he is generally despised. Killing is used because what has happened is felt to be so bad that no other reaction is considered possible.

Although some were more clearly damaging than others, almost any medium of challenge would do. As Chabot points out in a passage I quoted before, anything may be construed as a challenge, from "a lucky word on [the challenger's] part, by which he raises himself above the other person, at least in his own eyes," to the theft of buffalo, which is "considered a triumph and at the same time a challenge" ([1950] 1960: 290-91). The content of a challenge is, in fact, a matter of indifference. The content and occasion of insults constantly shifts. As I pointed out in Chapter Four, the insult of being offended lies in being offended, not so much in the particular means by which the offense was accomplished.

I was at first puzzled in Luwu by the shifting content of what people considered offensive. My original perception—that almost anything, given the correct context, could make someone feel ripakasiri'—proved correct. My puzzlement at the multiplicity of the content of offensive acts was due to several unconscious assumptions I had made about practices or acts that I categorized as analogues of law and morality as I knew them. My assumptions about legality, morality, and etiquette, of course, are derived ultimately, if vaguely, from the scripturalist religious traditions of the Middle East: Judaism, Christianity, and Islam. In these religions, morality is closely associated with a notion of explicit rules, abstracted from particular contexts and universally applicable within the community of believers—a form of "everyone equal before the Law." Moreover, in these religions, a person follows the rules in order to avoid trouble. And so I initially assumed that people in Luwu, too, wished to avoid provoking each others' siri', and that they followed rules as one observes the traffic regulations on Interstate 80: if one wants to avoid a collision, one sticks to the right side of the road. I was doubly mistaken in all this.

First, there are few explicit rules in Luwu's status system, and virtually none that apply to everyone regardless of status. Context is everything: offenses are person-specific and status-specific, not universal. The point of attacking and defending siri' is that people are unequal. Siri' offenses are specific to persons, which is to say, specific to their claimed standings or ranks. After all, challenges are directed at a person's dignity, which in South Sulawesi cannot be disjoined from standing. Since offenses are graded by the relative rank of the people involved, what is an offense to one is not an offense to another. What would be perfectly acceptable between peers in the fifth rank would be a mortal insult if a third rank person did it to someone of the second rank. Similarly, the same act done by the person of the second rank to the one in the fifth rank would be acceptable, even kindly (for instance, to utter the other person's name out loud). All this means that whether an action is offensive or not depends almost purely upon the two parties' assessments of their own standing relative to each other, and their assessments of whether they have a chance, when confronting the other person, of obtaining satisfaction or not. (In this, siri' offenses are parallel in structure to their codification in law, but, of course, what I have described here takes place on a much finer scale than the gross divisions demarcated by law.) The characteristic antagonism between peers comes about because of the obscurity of the difference (in titles, number of followers, etc.) between them. The nearer two people are in standing and status (the more nearly they approach being peers), the less visible are the differences between them; the more likely that each considers himself to be marginally higher than the other; the closer the show of force that either party can mobilize to threaten the other; and the more good reason each has to be suspicious that the other wishes to vanquish him.

The second way in which I was mistaken was in assuming that people want to avoid trouble. On the contrary, the demonstration of masculinity and siri' (as it pertains to men) requires and promotes a relish in aggressive testing, a constant impulse to challenge and risk offending to the furthest extent to which they are capable, without being crushed by the other person's retribution. The question is not whether to challenge, but how much offense one can get away with. Interactions, then, especially between peers, are a constant dance of expansion and retraction. A person begins with a slight challenge—a slightly disrespectful gesture, say, that tests the reaction of the other person. If the other person accepts it, offering no resistance, the first one expands further, escalating the disrespect in increments until it is checked. If, however, the other person's reaction is immediate and firm, showing that not even a slight presumption will be tolerated, the testing gesture disappears. The tester retreats, until another opportunity to strike presents itself. All this challenge and counter-challenge happens so automatically and so subtly that most of it occurs below the level of explicit awareness; it lies in the realm of sensibilities.

"Delicate Sensibilities"

When a person is being attacked, no rules are being broken. It is not one's legal rights that are under attack, but one's self or social dignity. Any attack, however slight, implicates the self. What is at stake in interaction is one's dignity, one's place, one's social worth: to put it concisely, one's siri'.

As I have pointed out before in a variety of ways and contexts, there are no alternatives when confronting peers other than defending oneself from encroachment or expanding aggressively into them. One could say that there are no equals: one person must be superior, one inferior. One could also say that there is little notion of a private psychology as we conceptualize it: since a direct reading of invisible interior worth can be made by observers of outward visible behavior, there can be no withdrawal when one is engaged in social interaction. There is no island of interior "privacy" onto which one can step to rest, out of the swirling stream of social life. There is no dark interior grotto where one can stand sheltered from the burning light of the social day. A person who tries to retreat from competition and challenge is merely a coward, impotent; people do not excuse it by saying things like "still waters run deep." To fail to participate is not to opt for privacy but to announce to the world that one has no siri', that one is socially dead.

In some of the more "level" (as contrasted with "hierarchical") societies of island Southeast Asia, virtually everyone is a peer in status.[2] In such societies, encroachment is a constant theme and feuding a pervasive fact of life, for among peers, authority is hardly granted. When it is—say, in negotiations conducted in order to settle a dispute—it is only by the temporary willingness of the involved parties to submit to a go-between, who will try to arrange fines and compensation as an alternative to killing when a deep offense has been committed. A judgment made without the agreement of both parties could not be enforced.

[2] "Level" societies, like the hierarchical ones of this area, actually have people who are junior or senior to each other as well as peers. In the most level of these societies, the incipient structure of "vertical" difference is the distinction between senior and junior generational layers, which are demarcated in the type of kinship terminology most prevalent in the area. In such societies, elders usually have the privilege of giving advice to their juniors without causing offense to the latter. Their advice need not be followed, and they have no means except public opinion to persuade. The authority of such seniors is weak and unelaborated, when compared with the authority of people in hierarchical societies who are senior in rank (not just by generation).

If encroachment (or its threat) by peers implicates the self-worth and social dignity of each, as it patently does, then local ways of construing the emotions and the "self" cannot be irrelevant to accounts of law and morality. In Luwu, reciprocal encroachment is cast in terms of siri'. Other societies in island Southeast Asia cast experience in other terms, use varying expressions and connotations to describe the nature of social relations, and construe the emotions in locally particular ways. Yet local ways of understanding "feeling" figure prominently in a number of ethnographies whose main subjects are social structure or law. It is striking how many of these societies construe fine feeling, a delicate sensibility, to be an exquisite sensitivity to the feelings of the other person regarding that other person's dignity and standing. Schlegel, for instance, begins *Tiruray Justice* (1970), a book about a hill people of Mindanao, with an explication of *fedew*. Fedew is something like interior feeling, and it can be "hurt" if it is offended. It is offended by another person's disregard of its "standing," *tindig*. Tiruray "justice" is a matter of feuding and fines, retribution for offended fedew. Crucial to Dentan's (1968) description of the negrito Semai, whom he calls "a nonviolent people of Malaya," is an account of the state of *punan*. A person is punan when his or her request is refused; in short, it is a state of (more or less) frustrated desire. The punan person may ask for compensation, or may endure the punan with an "unhappy heart" and avoid the offender. Obversely, it is tabu to *persusah* another, which is to say, to persist in making requests that the other person does not want to grant. The Tausug, an aggressive coastal people of the southern Philippines, have been studied by Thomas Kiefer (1972). Their sensibilities are remarkably like those of the Buginese, but they call their dignity *sipug* rather than siri'. An important feature of their social organization consists of men who form bands of shifting size and personnel whose main function is to feud, defending their sipug or attacking that of others. Hildred Geertz (1961: 111) traces the Javanese child's development of "emotions," which turn out to be names for states of more and more refined sensibilities concerning other people's status.

Part III
Centripetal Structures

In Part II I discussed the meaning and implications of siri', the stance of demonstrating social place that informs Luwu's ethos and its local psychology. In Part III I turn to white blood, the great differentiator, the element that makes vertical relations both possible and (in theory) stable in Luwu. White blood was institutionalized in such a way as to allow those who had it to exhibit and perpetuate it. The exhibition and perpetuation were by no means automatic; they required effort, and Part III is about those efforts.

For a fight to be over before it has begun, the difference in rank between the confronting parties must be highly obvious to both of them—either visible initially or quickly established. Each person must be a walking signpost of his or her status. Before Indonesian Independence, when matters of status were still regulated by the power at the polity's center, the use of virtually all human artifacts was regulated so as to make them function as signs of social place. The construction, materials, and decoration of a person's house; the use of certain fabrics, patterns, and colors; the number and design of dishes at ceremonies; and so on—all were regulated in order to indicate a person's degree of nobility. Those categories were, admittedly, gross ones: the finer negotiations for status happened among near-peers, implicating deference and demeanor (discussed in Chapter Four). But the gross categories had to be maintained if the more subtle ones were to hold their meaning (the subject of Chapter Five). Behind the logic of etiquette and the shape of the state lay the notion of difference in intrinsic worth among humans. Luwu's social universe assumes that all humans are created different, not the same. We can call that difference one of prestige. By a person's "prestige," I mean those attributes which elicit respect and deference from his or her fellows.

Attributes of prestige must be acquired, whether by effort, birth, or a combination of the two. Some of those attributes are transitory: they can be acquired in a person's lifetime, but, because they are not institutionalized, cannot be passed on to the next generation. I will call this sort of prestige "standing." In all societies, even the most level, some people have more standing than others. "Standing" depends to a considerable extent on what we would call a person's "personality" or "character": I am thinking, for instance, of one's stance and inclination to demonstrate siri', an attribute that elicits respect generally and deference in particular sorts of interactions. A person who acquires knowledge of invulnerability practices (magic, use of talismans, and the like) and emerges unscathed from difficult situations could also be said to have acquired prestige. And so on for any valued substance, attitude, accomplishment, or quality that a person is thought to have that elicits respect and deference, even if the deference is limited to particular contexts. Viewed at the most general level, then, to acquire this sort of prestige requires that a person behave in ways that are socially approved and valued and that bring respect in the community. This sort of prestige may be confined to particular contexts, and cannot be transmitted directly to one's children.

Some attributes of prestige are inherited or bestowed. I call this sort of prestige in Luwu "status," "rank," or "place." Because it can be passed between generations, "status" differs from "standing." We call Luwu a "hierarchical" society because certain attributes of prestige can be passed between generations. In Luwu, "place" is institutionalized in "white blood," which by definition can be acquired only by nobles. It is said to be inherited from both parents and its degree of purity constitutes the person's onro, (rank or place). Because it can be passed between generations, white blood has the effect of giving some people—*arung*, nobles—a head start and permanent toe-hold, as it were, in the ladder of prestige.

Viewed over several generations, standing and place continually interact. Those whose places are high, yet who do not attend to their standing, will not themselves lose their inherited places. But their ability to make good (high) marriages for themselves or for their children is impaired, and their followers may fall away to seek more competent protectors, with the likely result that their children's and grandchildren's degree of white blood and political influence will be lower than their own.

The continual process of locating oneself in the range of prestige by differentiating oneself from others is a process that, viewed from a secular perspective outside it, would be called "politics." The subject of Part III is the politics of high and low; since high and low have a center as well as a top, its subject is the politics of the periphery trying to become central and the center trying to maintain itself as such. I discuss these matters in three overlapping arenas: naming, the keeping of genealogies, and marriage.

Chapter Six, "The Potency of Names," discusses the power of names and the logic of naming in a society where names are not merely arbitrary labels and where preserved names can form the basis of a political arsenal. Chapter Seven, "Forgetting Genealogies," reveals the politics of genealogical memory and its importance in the formation and maintenance of groupings. Chapter Eight, "Centripetal Marriage," explicates the logic and shape of endogamous marriage patterns in what I call the "Centrist Archipelago," the marriage strategies that follow from them and finally the contrast of these patterns with the better-known asymmetric alliance patterns of Eastern Indonesia.

Chapter Six
The Potency of Names

Lévi-Strauss has observed that "some societies jealously watch over their names and make them last practically forever, others squander them and destroy them at the end of every individual existence" (1962: 199). The example of Luwu gives us not two societies but two parts of a single society with radically different policies regarding the names of their respective members: the one erases and forgets what the other cherishes and preserves. Teknonymy, the naming system of commoners, has the effect of erasing and forgetting; the naming system of nobles has the effect of recollecting and storing names in genealogies, using them as political weapons and a spiritual resource.

Using a vivid term borrowed from J. A. Barnes, H. Geertz and C. Geertz have argued that teknonymy as practiced by Balinese commoners (a system more elaborate than Luwu's, but similar in structure and in many details) creates "genealogical amnesia" by actively inhibiting genealogical knowledge and systematically suppressing the past. They argue that it "creates, through its progressive suppression of personal names and its regular substitution of what are essentially impersonal status terms, a curtain of genealogical amnesia which steadily descends over each generation in turn" (1964: 94).

Pertinent here is the fact that both Balinese and Luwu commoners practice teknonymy, while genealogies are kept by both Balinese and Luwu nobles. The internal contrast between these two sorts of naming policies suggests that the practices form a system, each part of which creates the other. Each practice has a political meaning that can best be understood within the context created by the other. Each has consequences for the sorts of people that the two together constitute, as well as for the sorts of politics that people in each category are enabled to conduct.

Names are signs of the status and worth of the person in Luwu, but they also help to create that worth. The dialectic between the worthiness of the person and the worthiness of the name he or she carries can be understood only if we realize that names are not arbitrary labels in Luwu. (Needless to say, news of the arbitrariness of the sign has not reached Luwu.) People and objects have not only earthly names but "true names" in heaven (*asseng si-tongeng-tongenna*). Many spells have this form:

> Asseng tongeng-tongemmu rilangi-é . . . *anu*[1] . . .
> mu nonno' rilino-é muriasseng . . . *anu*. . . .
>
> Your true name in the sky . . . *anu*
> you come down to the world and you are called *anu*. . . .

The implication is that the person uttering the spell to the wood, for instance, when a house is built, has power over the wood because he knows its origins. The household in which I lived during my stay in Luwu had bought a new tractor. Several people were hanging around to try it out, but the driver could not make the ignition work. Someone in the group said to him jokingly, "Well, it's clear you don't know its true name in heaven!"

To know a person's name is to know his or her origins, and to know those origins is to have some power over the person. To utter someone's name is to assert that power. Black magic can be practiced, in a pinch, by someone who knows only the name of the intended victim, even without any of the person's leavings. Thus people may utter the unadorned names of their juniors and inferiors, but not the reverse. It is insulting as well as dangerous to oneself to utter the name of a person senior (by age or status) to oneself. A forebear is, by definition, senior to oneself; to utter a forebear's name would automatically make one suffer mabusung, be afflicted with sickness or misfortune. Mabusung is said to be experienced by people who presume above their station, or encroach on the privileges of their superiors. The more elevated in status the forebear was when alive, the more extreme is the fault of pronouncing the deceased person's name.

A baby who is given a name that is too potent for it may die or suffer mabusung; a potent baby given a weak name may similarly sicken and die. One aspect of the suitability of a name and a person has to do with the mesh between them: the parents of a sickly baby may change its name, in hopes that the new name will suit the baby better and it will become healthy. There must be a mesh between the name and the person's intrinsic potency, coded publicly as the person's degree of white blood or rank. Thus it is that commoners' names should be of little consequence, while nobles' names must be magnificent and potent. If names were votes, commoners would be disenfranchised. Commoners are disadvantaged not only by the intrinsic weakness of their names but also by how names are bestowed and used. Thus the naming practices of nobles and commoners

---

[1] *Anu* means "so-and-so," "such-and-such," or merely "umm."

contrast in content and meaning, and, as we shall see, in political consequences.

Teknonymy and Common Names

Villagers are in no great hurry to name their children. Until it is given a name, a little girl may be called "Lai" or "Bece' " and a boy called "Baco' " or "Laso'." Such terms indicate only sex and commoner status. Giving the child its personal name is also of little consequence or ceremony. Anyone may suggest a name, and there is a recent fad of drawing the name by lottery. One baby was said to have "chosen his own," because when the radio was on and the winner of a Quran-reading contest was named, the baby made a noise; so they named him the name of the winner. When the name or names are chosen, usually at least one is Islamic. Sometimes village names commemorate an event: La Upa, "Fortunate Male"; La Sappe, "Male Who Survived"; Indo' Tuo, "Mother of the Live One." Often, too, villager children will be given nicknames, like "Scar" or "Clubfoot." Commoners may be called different names by different people, and one has the impression that their names are given and changed casually.

Villagers practice teknonymy; that is, a person becomes known by the name of his or her oldest child and eventually grandchild. When Lido becomes a father of a child named "Usman," he acquires a teknonym, as does the mother: he becomes "Father of Usman" (*Ambe'Usman*); she, "Mother of Usman" (*Indo'Usman*). The teknonym may be used in either reference or address. Meanwhile, Lido's own mother and father, who until their grandchild's birth had been called by their own child's name (they were called Indo'Lido and Ambe'Lido), now become "Grandparent of Usman" (Nene'Usman). At least, Usman's peers will call Usman's grandparents "Nene'Usman."

People of Lido's generation, who formerly called Lido's mother "Indo'Lido," may now refer to her with additional respect as "Nene'Indo'Lido," which means not "Grandparent of the Mother of Usman," but rather "Grandparent (Mother of Usman)." (An adult without descendants may be called Ua' [uncle or aunt] followed by the name of the oldest child of the person's sibling, or Nene' followed by the name of the oldest grandchild of the person's sibling.)

Villagers often utter the names of their peers in generation and status, unadorned by honorifics. But it is rude to say aloud the name of a person senior to oneself; so as a boy named Lido, for example, grows up and acquires more and more juniors (in age and generation), and as those who are senior in generation die off, few people will utter his unadorned name.

Those who are junior to him in his own generation might call him "Older Sibling" (Daeng); those junior to him in generation might call him "Uncle/Aunt" (Ua'). The same is true of females.

The crucial factor in the use and creation of teknonyms, it will be apparent, is the relative generations of the speaker and the one who is spoken to. The most salient feature of the kinship terminology used in Luwu is that it classifies people into strata of generations. I will be explicating further the uses to which this type of terminology is put, but for the moment it suffices to point out that generational peers call each other by their unadorned personal names when they are children. Those generation peers will eventually call each other "Mother of X" or "Father of Y." People junior to them in generation, however, often add "Ua'" in front of the teknonym, constructing a name that would translate as "Aunt, the Mother of X" or "Uncle, the Father of Y."

All this shifting of names happens only with respect to the firstborn child in each generation, regardless of sex. There is no ceremony to initiate a new teknonym's use—it is a matter of gradual change in the way people address and refer to someone. And, as I have indicated, people in the same generation tend to keep calling their peers by their childhood names or their first teknonyms.

An effect of teknonymy is to shield the adults who practice it from the indignity of having their names uttered allowed. The shielding offered by teknonyms, however, is slight when compared to the protection offered by nobles' titles.

Titles and Potent Names

Social life among nobles is predicated on the ideal of difference rather than parity among people. Before Indonesian Independence, I have mentioned, the use of virtually all human artifacts was regulated by the polity's center in order to constitute them as a system of signs of difference. House shape and material, personal adornment, body stance and demeanor—all were made to speak to the matter of ordered difference.

Among these signs of rank were sets of titles and names in each polity of South Sulawesi. Historically, these sets were complex and inconsistent from polity to polity. (A useful discussion of their obscurity and complexity can be found in Pelras 1971.) Like other artifacts that signalled rank, names and titles were ultimately regulated by and distributed from the center of the polity. One of the highest posts in the old polity was the genealogist, who not only kept track of genealogies but also sent messengers to people who were using names or titles too high for their places, warning them to cease and desist. Names and titles not only indicate rank but have power in themselves, for if someone calls another "Opu," the speaker acknowledges the other's superiority. Thus, potent names and important titles both signal rank and constitute it.

I will refer to the labels of nobles as "title-names." By the "title" portion, I mean the person's "status-title" (in Geertz's term, 1973c), which is shared with his or her full siblings: for instance, one of the highest status-titles in Luwu is *Andi*; if it is applied at all, it is applied to all the full siblings of a set of siblings, regardless of sex or relative age. The title indicates only high prestige, a high degree of white blood; it does not imply the inheritance of an office or an estate. By the "name," I mean that portion of a person's title-name which is specific to that person and is not shared with his or her siblings. Below is a chart of the forms that these title-names take among Luwu nobility. The letters refer to the "name" portion of the title-name.

Unmarried	*Married*
(high end)	
Andi A	Opu B
La C (male), Wé' D (female)	Opu E
La F, Wé' G	Daeng H
(low end)	

The highest married nobles in Luwu at the time I was there had title-names in this form: Andi X Opu Y. Andi X is the title-name given to a very high infant soon after its birth. Opu Y is the title-name given to that person soon after marriage, preferably by someone of higher rank.

My informants said that "Andi" is a higher title in Luwu than "Opu," in that some nobles may not be called "Andi" yet are given the "Opu" title when they are married. The history of the term *Andi* is obscure. It means, literally, "younger sibling." When it came to be used in South Sulawesi is uncertain, though Pelras (1971) suggests it may have been in the late nineteenth century; it does not appear in older texts. In any case, it has now become, in Luwu, the highest title for an unmarried person. The high-noble infant, then, is an "Andi" before it has a personal name.

The personal name given to an Andi is a matter of great import. Like anyone else, a high-noble infant must be intrinsically potent enough to bear the name that it is given; but since potency is, to a large extent, considered to be inherited, such children can bear very potent names. For example, a common form for high-noble names is "Tenri," followed by another word. "Tenri" is an elevated form of language indicating "not, plus impersonal agent." The name Andi Tenri Padang, "Without Peer," "Unequalled," "Incomparable," is reserved for Datu-level nobles, since only they are peerless. Andi Tenri Peppang means "Cannot Be Avoided" or

"Cannot Be Dislodged [from his place]," implying that the person is king of the mountain, his place so secure and unshakeable that he cannot be challenged, much less dislodged. Andi Tenri Leleang, "Not Allowed to Be Viewed," a woman's name, indicates that the bearer is a precious and protected being. Not all noble names begin with "Tenri." One very high name is Andi Cella', "Red," the color of blood and bravery. Its application is confined to nobles of the very highest ranks, a name so elevated that it may be given to an infant only if the name is sent by the ruler. I was told of several high nobles who had been given the name but had soon perished for it was too potent for them. Some names are poetic, like Andi Lelellung, "Floating, Moving Clouds," the implication being that the bearer is very high above and that her social place is not confined to a small territory; she moves freely throughout the world because it is filled with obedient followers rather than challenging peers. Similarly, the Opu Pa'Bicara's married name was Opu Tosinilele, which means "Known Everywhere." High nobles often take noble titles from Java or Bali and make them into personal names, becoming, for instance, Andi Pangerang or Andi Gusti. When I was collecting examples of high-noble names and saw their implications, I suggested to our little discussion group that someone ought to be called "Opu Kamineng Makerre'." This is hard to translate but it is outrageous—something like "The One of Unsurpassed Potency" (in Indonesian, "Opu Paling Sakti," which gives something of the flavor). My informants, high nobles all, laughed heartily at the idea, because the imaginary name captures precisely, but just a tiny bit too overtly, the message behind their elevated and potent names.

Another possible, and very assertive, way to form high noble names is by adding the name of a village or area to "Andi." Nobles in Southeast Asia collect and have influence over people rather than over territory or villages. Thus Andi X does not mean "Andi Whose Territorial Fiefdom Is X," but rather, "Andi, the Noble Protector of the People of X." But since it indicates influence and dominance over the people of a village, a title-name in which the name is a village or area must be bestowed with some caution. During my stay in Luwu it was pointed out that no noble was called Andi Bua'. Bua' is a district inhabited by several competing noble families. To name any child Andi Bua' would indicate a claim to hegemony of influence, and would therefore infuriate the other high-noble cores who also had influence (followers, dependents) in Bua'. One of the Opu Pa'Bicara's children could, of course, have been given the name Andi Senga, since Senga was in effect the family seat, the regional stronghold outside the akkarungeng's center, which was Palopo. But Senga is too small and too securely under that high core's influence to require naming a child to indicate its connection to them. It is more likely that a child would be named for a very large village or area where the high-noble core's influence is strong; the name will serve to connect the area's inhabitants with the high noble. One of the Opu Pa'Bicara's children is named Andi Raja, after the Toraja (*To* [people] plus *raja* [interior or hinterland]). He was named to commemorate, celebrate, and indicate this high-noble core's connection to, acknowledgment of, and willingness to protect Toraja. I was told that historically, such names were useful for people from villages distant from the political center. When such people came to the political center, for the state celebrations or on other business, they would have few kin or acquaintances, perhaps have no place to stay, and would need protection and help. With an Andi named for their area, though, someone in town might say, "Oh, you're from X. There is an Andi X—he must be your Andi," and they could go to their Andi. Such names, then, served as banners under whose aegis far-flung followers could gather.

The most elevated name of this sort was that of the last ruler of Luwu, named Andi Jemma'. The term comes from an Arabic word; my informants in Luwu translated it into Indonesian as *manusia*, which means "human." In at least some estimations, then, the Datu's name meant "the Andi of all humans" . . . a potent name indeed.

Most nobles are not high enough to be called Andi. In that case, the name may be preceded by "La" for males, "Wé " for females, although often these titles are not used. (These, not Andi, are used in the origin-epic *I La Galigo*, even for the very highest nobles.) The personal names of nobles also differentiate them from commoners. Some of the middle-noble names I collected include Daeng Massiga ("Prompt"), implying that the bearer responds quickly when given an order; Daeng Malewa ("Stable," "Unswerving"), implying that the bearer is unswervingly faithful; and Daeng Parenreng ("Wall" or "Barrier"), implying that the bearer protects like a wall. Unlike the names of commoners, which are sometimes nonsense syllables, nicknames, or names that commemorate personal events, these middle-noble names have some dignity in noble eyes; but obviously, their intent is to indicate a connection to people of great potency rather than to assert that the name belongs to a person who is potent himself or herself. Islamic names are also common and popular.

Nobles acquire the second portion of their title-names soon after marriage. All those who were Andi become Opu, thus completing their name: Andi X Opu Y. Middle-level nobles become Daeng, a term that means literally "older sibling." And so the complete form of a man's name might be "La X Daeng Y"; of a woman's, "Wé X Daeng Y." People will sometimes say in rebuke, "What's a two-name person like you doing a thing like that for?" For convenience, I will refer to these title-names (Opu Y or Daeng Y) as "marriage title-names," though that is not an indigenous term.

Everyone hopes that his or her name will be sent by a more elevated personage. The high core of a kapolo sends such names to its followers; the Datu sent such names to the high cores of the largest kapolo in the akkarungeng. A few weeks or even months after the wedding, a messenger appears with a name sent from the more elevated protector of the newlyweds. In this modern chaotic age, there are few controls over the use of titles, especially in cities. People will simply use "Andi" or "Daeng." Having one's name sent from above, by someone in authority, is quite a different matter. As one woman said to me, "I know I'm a Daeng, because Opu sent me my name." If he had not, she would not have dared to use it; but since her Opu sent it, she used it with pride, and the neighbors knew it was valid. In a parallel way, the Opu Pa'Bicara's same-status niece was sent her married name by the widow of the last ruler of Luwu. Thus the font of titles and names, like that of the other signs of status, was either ultimately or immediately the ruler.

TEKNONYMOUS TITLES

An intriguing practice among nobles in Luwu is that of bestowing what I will call here "teknonymous titles." (Again, this is not an indigenous term; there is no special name for the phenomenon.) A person sending a title to one of his or her followers sends the marriage title-name (Opu or Daeng plus an appropriate name). The interest of the high-core donor who sends a name to the follower is, of course, to bind the follower to the core and its same-status descendants, guaranteeing that the future kapolo of the core's same-status descendants will be large. Some of the marriage names in Luwu are constructed as teknonyms of the donor's dependents, a practice that shows a relationship between the donor and the receiver of the title-name. So, for instance, one of the Opu Pa'Bicara's same-status children was named Andi Muchlis (an Islamic name). The Opu Pa'Bicara had sent his child's name to one of his high kapolo members when she married, and she became Opu DaMuchlis. ("Da" is an elevated form, used only in titles, for "mother.") Another example is the title sent to Andi Minneng, a same-status niece of the Opu Pa'Bicara, whose wedding occurred during my stay. A few months after the wedding, Opu Datu (the widow of the last Datu of Luwu) sent a name to Andi Minneng. She sent her the marriage title-name Opu DaTenri Peppang, after one of her grandchildren, Andi Tenri Peppang.

A teknonymous title links the person who receives it to the child of a higher or more central person, but it also indicates the approximate level of the difference in status and generational layer between them. Take the name Saddakati, for instance, a high name meaning "Pure Gold." Some transformations of this name into teknonymous titles follow:

Opu Nene'na [grandparent of] Saddakati, for a person of either sex two generational layers above Saddakati and of about the same rank;

Opu Ambe'na [father of] Saddakati or Opu ToSaddakati, for a male person one generational layer above Saddakati and of about the same rank;

Opu Indo'na [mother of] Saddakati or Opu DaSaddakati, for a female person one generational layer above Saddakati and of about the same rank;

Opu Daeng na [older sibling of] Saddakati, for a person of either sex in the same generational layer as Saddakati and of about the same rank.

According to Andi Anthon, to whom I am indebted for these hypothetical examples, these teknonymous titles will virtually always be given to people who are senior to Saddakati either in generational layer or in absolute age, albeit of similar rank to Saddakati. If a lower noble is bestowed with a teknonymous title formed from Saddakati's name, one who would ordinarily be given the title "Daeng," he or she will be known as Nene'na Saddakati, Ambe'na Saddakati, or Indo'na Saddakati and will not use the title "Daeng." People who are somewhat lower than that, if given a teknonymous title, would become Nene' Saddakati, Ambe' Saddakati, or Indo' Saddakati.

Such teknonymous titles have several effects. They clearly assert the high status of the proud possessor. "Tenri Peppang," for instance, is a very elevated name, and a person who becomes "DaTenri Peppang" cannot be far behind. Moreover, such a title affirms a close relation between the name's sender and its possessor. It is inconceivable, after all, that a donor would send a high-close dependent's name to be used by a follower unless the donor wished to honor the receiver and considered the receiver very trustworthy. Sending the name of one's child or grandchild is a gesture of benevolence and incorporation, an affirmation of closeness. The practice creates an expectation on the part of the teknonymously titled person that he or she is especially close to, and especially bound to serve and make claims on, the person whose name formed the base of the teknonym.

Because these teknonymous titles, though based on a constant name, vary in form to reflect the generational level and rank of the title's recipient (as I indicated with the example of Saddakati), the names of the high core's children and grandchildren, and in fact all the high core's high close relatives of younger generational layers, provide a kind of resource by which the high core can bind its followers to itself with its beneficent distributions of names. In that sense, teknonymous-title bestowal is analogous to marriage: in each case the high core beneficently distributes parts of itself to its followers, binding them to it in loyalty and gratitude. (I call this form of marriage "centrifugal," and explicate it in Chapter Eight.)

TITLES FROM THE RULER

Historically, quite another type of title could be acquired by nobles in Akkarungeng Luwu, but far from all achieved it. Titles that included responsibilities and were attached to arajang, such as the titles of the four main ministers of the inner court (Opu Pa'Bicara, Opu Balairante, etc.), and of the many other ministers of the center (Opu AndeGuru Attoriolong, Opu AndeGuru Pampawaepu, etc.); the regional titles (Opu Ma'Dika Bua', Opu Ma'Dika Ponrang, etc.); and so on, were given for the recipient's lifetime, barring treason or other serious reasons for the ruler's disfavor. Such titles would be relinquished by the receiver (thus made available for bestowal on someone else) if the title-holder were given another title with other arajang and duties. For instance, the Opu Pa'Bicara had been the Opu Ma'Dika Bua' before he was appointed Opu Pa'Bicara, and, when his father died, he would likely have ceased his duties as official spokesperson and taken his father's place as Opu AndeGuru Anakkarueng, the keeper of genealogies.

Such titles are relinquished, but far from forgotten. They were written in palm-leaf manuscripts in the biography, as it were, of the ancestor. The accumulation of more and more magnificent and elevated titles and names attested to the ancestor's potency and high degree of white blood.

DEATH TITLES

When a person dies, one may not utter aloud his or her title-name. For one thing, it is very disrespectful to do so. (It is to observe this respect that I have referred to the man in whose household I lived during my stay as the Opu Pa'Bicara rather than by his marriage title-name.) It also incurs mabusung on the utterer. One may, however, utter the person's death title. Historically, only very high nobles who had been given titles and prerogatives from the ruler would be given death titles as well. Being given a death title is the ultimate achievement, in both senses: it is one's last achievement as well as the highest one attainable. Like other titles, these were and are sent from above, from the ruler. The practice has continued in order to honor the last heroes of the pre-Independence period. The last ruler of Luwu, who died in 1965, and the Opu Pa'Bicara, who died in 1977

shortly after I left South Sulawesi, had been very active in the war for Independence against the Dutch that took place during World War II. The
Indonesian Goverment designates people as National Hero or Regional
Hero and sends, in effect, death titles to them. It also designates the appropriate burial ground for them. Both of these men have been sent death
titles by the Indonesian Goverment.

The Politics of Names: Commoner and Noble Names Contrasted

Commoners practice teknonymy. They begin with a nearly anonymous label meaning "little girl" or "little boy," and eventually acquire a personal
name, which is then replaced with the name of their first child and, later,
their first grandchild. By the time they die, it is very possible that no one
will recall their personal name, and it has not been memorized or written
down. In a profound sense, commoners lose, rather than acquire, names in
the course of their lives. And because commoners do not keep written genealogies, their names ultimately disappear, unremembered and unre-
corded.

Nobles, by contrast, accumulated titles and names in the course of a lifetime when the akkarungeng existed. A noble began life with a potent name
(*asseng*), acquired a second one at marriage, may have been given potent
titles (*pattellareng*) by the ruler, and at death could have been given yet
another title, a death title (Bug. *ganti maté*). Thus it is possible to conceptualize a noble's life course as the acquisition of more and more glorious
names and titles, rather than (as with commoners) their loss. Most crucial,
these names and titles, rather than disappearing at death, were recorded in
writing and became the core of genealogies and a source of spiritual potency for future generations of a noble's descendants.

One of the effects of this contrastive naming system was a difference in
the meaning and potency of persons of different ranks, which still persists.
Names are potent in themselves; the fact that commoners are deprived of
potent names is both a reason for their political impotence (speaking sociologically) and an index of it (speaking from a Luwu point of view).

In their article on teknonymy, the main thrust of which is to explicate a
Balinese (commoner) notion of "time," Geertz and Geertz [1964] also suggest some of the political implications of commoners' "genealogical amnesia." They point out that commoner groupings in Bali remain localized
and relatively small, inhibited from joining with related kin groupings in
other localities by their members' genealogical ignorance of wider linkages.
Balinese gentry, by contrast, do not usually use teknonyms but rather keep
genealogies; and the gentry have large, more enduring, more corporate,

and more geographically far-reaching kin groups (see H. Geertz and C. Geertz 1964, 1975).

In Luwu as well, commoners' genealogical amnesia implies both a structural political disadvantage and a personal lack of power. Commoners, obviously, do not preserve names. To put it another way, they do not keep genealogies, nor do they have other institutionalized means of recollecting and keeping track of their relations. In a society in which followers and protectors tend to be relatives, sometimes quite distant genealogically, a severely constricted knowledge of relations was and remains an acute political disadvantage.

The relation between names and genealogies is a direct one in Luwu. A genealogy consists of names, sometimes elaborated with stories, of forebears, preserved by descendants. In this sense, both commoners and nobles have and keep genealogies; but the genealogy of a commoner is likely to stop at the grandparental generation, while that of a high noble may continue through tens of generations, up to Batara Guru and the founding of Luwu.

With the subject of genealogies we come to a subject wider than naming systems. Genealogies implicate siri', the shape and meaning of knowledge, the meanings of the past, and the shape of society lived as a process rather than recounted as a structure.

Chapter Seven
Forgetting Genealogies

Most humans do not use timepieces or have a notion of cumulative, linear chronological time. But it is probably sufficiently unprejudicial to say that all humans do have ways of thinking about "the past," about the people and the events that occurred before them. I use the terms "the past" and "duration" in preference to "history" and "time" in order to denote, vaguely and neutrally, that which happened prior to the present and the medium in which events occur, without prejudging their structure or their relation to the present.

In any given society, "the past" is given a culturally specific shape and meaning. One of the many ways that humans may think about the structure of the past is through accounts of their ancestors' generations. The classic work that explores the theme of genealogies as analogues of "time" is Evans-Pritchard's "Nuer Time Reckoning" (1939). Nuer time, he argues, is not "chronological" but "structural." He suggests that the Nuer conceptually organize their past by means of patrilineal genealogies, which go back approximately fourteen generations. Nuer genealogies provide the structure of public memory.

One would expect that Nuer genealogies would become progressively longer as more generations of Nuer are born and added. Yet in fact, their genealogies are always about fourteen generations deep. They must therefore be subject to systematic forgetting and merging of ancestors. Evans-Pritchard calls this movement "telescoping," and explains how it structures forgetting within the shape of Nuer remembering. Because of "telescoping," the first apical ancestor of the Nuer always remains equidistant from the present.

Quite a different approach is taken by Hildred and Clifford Geertz in discussing the structure of the past in Bali in their article, "Teknonymy in Bali: Parenthood, Age-Grading, and Genealogical Amnesia" (1964). As I pointed out in Chapter Six, this article is about forgetting the past rather than structuring its shape. The authors argue that the naming system practiced by Balinese commoners actively inhibits genealogical knowledge and systematically suppresses the past, creating "a curtain of genealogical amnesia which steadily descends over each generation in turn" (1964: 94).

204   Part III: Centripetal Structures

Southeast Asians are not generally known for having deep genealogies. People of the so-called "hill tribes" (those societies which are more level than hierarchical, whose economic surpluses are farily small, and which often practice shifting cultivation) almost universally have shallow genealogies, although many have very broad ones. The commoners who existed at the the base of the vast hierarchical structures of the former so-called "Indic States" of the area likewise continue to tend to have restricted knowledge of their forebears. The most notable and consistent exceptions to the general rule of shallow genealogies in island Southeast Asia are the genealogies still kept by the nobles of the hierarchical Indic States. These nobles were—and many continue to be—preoccupied with their own origins. Their purpose in writing (in Indic- and Arabic-derived scripts) seems largely to have been to record the deeds of their noble ancestors and to trace their relations to those forebears. The court texts and chronicles of such societies commonly trace noble origins to the Upper World. At the same time, they fail utterly to mention the origins of commoners, as though commoners had no origins, or their origins were of no consequence, which are much the same thing. At first glance oddly, life confirms myth: nobles, who write or have scribes in their employ, know, and therefore have, origins; commoners, for various reasons, do not.

In Luwu, the preservation of origins through writing is related in complex ways to the accumulation and preservation of names by nobles; the loss of origins or their suppression is related to teknonymy and the loss of names by commoners. Bali's system of naming and genealogy-keeping appears to be in many ways parallel. In other words, Luwu and Bali are each societies in which the two parts of the single society have different naming policies: the high one preserves, the low one forgets. The internal contrast within a single society suggests that the practices form a system. It suggests that the two parts mutually illuminate and create each other. Each has its existence and its raison d'etre within the context formed by the other.[1]

One aspect of the system is clearly political in the sense outlined at the end of Chapter Six: commoner groupings are local and small, for their members are genealogically ignorant of wider links; noble groupings can become large, for, knowing their ancestors, nobles can link themselves with people we call "collaterals," thus forming alliances of relatives called kapolo.

Another implication of this systemic contrast concerns the shape of "time" and the meaning of the "person." Commoners erase their forebears' names and with that erasure lose a certain type of connection with the past.

[1] For more information on this contrast in Bali, see H. Geertz and C. Geertz 1975.

Nobles' relations to their past in this respect give them another sort of advantage over commoners, for they have access to the ancestral potency that is one of the bases of their claim to superiority.

Although not obvious to the purely sociological imagination, these two implications are linked. In fact, each is a way of stating the other. Groupings in Luwu, after all, are formed around potent centers: maintaining oneself as a potent center is the way to attract a following. The terminological mechanics, as it were, in which the followers' relations to the center are cast, are worked out in the terms that, reified through social-science talk, would be given names like "social organization" and "kinship."

The first section of this chapter forms a kind of primer on "kinship" in island Southeast Asia, as a background to my subsequent discussion of the shape of genealogies at different social levels and the political implications of those practices, arguments that relate to the meanings of marriage practices discussed in Chapter Eight. But I am concerned here also with the meanings of knowledge and "time." At first glance, it appears that, while commoners' naming practices erase (or at least do not preserve) the genealogical past, nobles' naming practices and genealogy-keeping preserve a past and constitute it as a sequentially ordered structure—not so unlike the "structural time" of the Nuer. But I will eventually conclude that the preservation of the past by Luwu nobles is neither sequential nor temporal, and that nobles, too, are subject to a sort of genealogical amnesia, albeit one achieved much more elaborately than that of commoners.

Origin Points Moving through Duration

It is extremely common for societies in Malayo-Polynesia to imagine themselves each as having its origin in a unitary "source," root, or point of origin. Some societies or subgroups of the society trace themselves to it genealogically; others postulate it in the distant past, inaccessible; others imagine it to be only a few generations back, relatively close to the present. The ancestral origin is often labeled by a word including the root *pu* or *fu*. *Pu* implies a unitary point in the past (ancestral or residential), a cause, a source, an ancestor, a place of origin.

The unitary ancestral source, moving through duration, divides into generational layers of "siblings." Each layer of siblings is further from the source. The phenomenon of "sinking status," as the cadet lines of "ramages" or "status-lineages" in Polynesia and a similar phenomenon in Bali become separated from the central core, is directly related to this conception.[2] Writing on Polynesia, Shore describes this structure as "the classic Polynesian socio-political structure—the graded ramage, . . . where descent lines are ordered in terms of decreasing genealogical seniority, and thus increasing distance from an original and authentic source of power" (Shore, n.d., 7).

In this scheme of things, age—or better, seniority—is the primary symbolic differentiation between people on a dimension we could call "hierarchical" (as opposed to "complementary"): an image of difference, a criterion of difference, and an organizer of terms indicating difference. Some examples of the symbolic elaboration of "age" in rank and prestige (and sometimes authority) in Malayo-Polynesia are instructive. In much of Polynesia, children of a sibling set are ranked by birth order, and the eldest son of the eldest son is presumed to inherit the title to which all aspire; junior lines of younger brothers form "cadet lines" attached to the main lines, whose center is defined in every generation by the eldest brother. In Eastern Indonesia, "Houses" (often labeled "patrilineages") stand to each other as "older brother" and "younger brother," the former ritually encompassing the latter. In even the most level and unranked societies of the societies of the northern part of insular Southeast Asia in which relations are traced bilaterally, generational layers form the inchoate structures of authority: people in senior generational layers should protect and direct those in junior ones, while junior people should respect and obey senior ones. (Needless to say, these "authority structures," if they can be so dignified, are effective only if people act as they are supposed to, and often they do not.) In the more hierarchical societies of island Southeast Asia, the generational layers are overlaid, but not displaced, by institutionalized structures of inheritable prestige. Terms of respect and titles in these societies often implicate age or ancestors or the "source." For instance, the Buginese term *ToMatoa* and the Javanese *wong tuwā*, literally "old person," can denote also a person who is a generational layer or two senior to the speaker, a person who is respected, a noble person, and a spiritually potent person. Terms of respect denoting or connoting age are used as pervasively in parts of insular Southeast Asia as the term "Big Man" is in New Guinea. Then, too, Opu (note the *pu* root) is a noble title in Luwu, while Ampo (same root) is in Java; cognates of such titles are also very common.

Another way that seniority forms a structural and symbolic means of differentiation is in "kinship" terminology, which (following Maybury-Lewis 1965) I prefer to call "relationship terminology." Relationship ter-

---

[2] This pattern has been elaborated far more generally and strikingly for Polynesia than for insular Southeast Asia; on the former, see Goldman 1970 and Sahlins 1983; on Bali, see H. Geertz and C. Geertz 1975.

minology, of course, has no special status in telling us about either social organization or ideas about relationship: peoples with similar terminologies may organize themselves into groupings that are quite different from each other, and may have very different ideas about the internal connections of categories the terms construct. Yet since terminology provides a verbal-symbolic milieu within which social life takes place, it is worth exploring for the light it can shed on the shape of the thought it helps construct.

Throughout island Southeast Asia, relationship terminologies divide people into generational layers. I find it useful to think of island Southeast Asian societies as falling into two main groupings of variations of relationship terminologies and many other characteristic symbolic forms. One well-known set occurs within the geographic space called "Eastern Indonesia." This set of variations tends to include asymmetric alliance in marriage, and paired dualistic contrasts and complements pervade its symbolic forms. Relationship terminologies in Eastern Indonesia divide people into generational layers, but they also divide them into "Houses." The latter division, coupled with aspects of their marriage practices, gives a "lineal" cast to their terminology that obscures its fundamental relationship with and similarity to the terminologies in the other major grouping of island Southeast Asia. Societies in that other major grouping tend to be located in the swath of islands rimming mainland Southeast Asia, stretching from the Malay peninsula through Borneo, dipping into Java, Sulawesi, the Moluccas, and Mindanao, Luzon, the Visayas, and other Philippine islands. For the sake of simplicity, I will refer to this heretofore unnamed space as the "Centrist Archipelago," since, in contrast to many of the societies of Eastern Indonesia, its social and symbolic forms tend to emphasize centers rather than dualities. Here I am concerned primarily with the Centrist Archipelago, the geographical and conceptual space within which Luwu falls. I have provided a map (Fig. 1) showing the location of these two major variations for the sake of convenience, but I want to insist that these are conceptual spaces more than geographical ones in order to eliminate the need constantly to qualify generalizations and footnote variations. (I exclude Sumatra from discussion because I do not intend the following chapters to be a treatise on comparative social organization. For my purposes, Eastern Indonesia provides the starkest and therefore most enlightening contrast to Luwu and other hierarchical centrist societies of the area.)

In Centrist Archipelago relationship terminologies, Ego and his or her siblings and cousins tend to be classed together. In Murdockian (1949, 1960) terms, these terminologies are often Hawaiian. (Some of these soci-

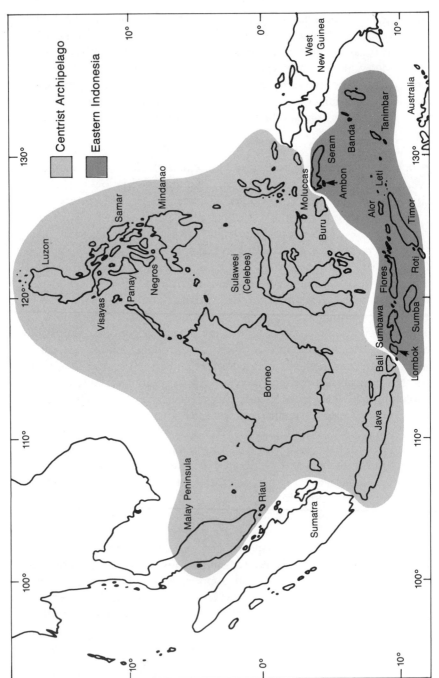

Figure 1. The Centrist Archipelago and Eastern Indonesia

eties use Eskimo terms, in which siblings and cousins are differentiated; but regardless of the terms used, these peoples tend to view cousins as more distant siblings; so, for the sake of simplicity, I will refer to these societies as if all of their terminologies were Hawaiian.) Keesing (1980), writing about a similar Pacific terminology system, labels full siblings "zero-degree siblings," first cousins "first-degree siblings," second cousins "second-degree siblings," and so forth. I have adopted his convenient terms. In this text, by "full siblings" I mean "zero-degree siblings"; the unqualified term "siblings," with or without quotes (which are sometimes added for the sake of clarity), means zero- to nth-degree siblings (ranging from what we call full siblings to distant cousins) who form one generational layer.

This scheme divides the people whom one calls by relationship terms into successive strata of "siblings." A "layer" in the Centrist Archipelago is constituted by a set of siblings. Some are nearer to Ego (zero-degree siblings) and some are further away (first-degree to nth-degree siblings). The layer just above Ego's consists of parents and their siblings from zero to the nth degree. Ego's children and their siblings from zero to the nth degree (people we would call children, nephews and nieces, and the children of Ego's cousins) form the layer junior to Ego's; and so on.

Sibling sets succeed each other through duration as a sort of elementary structure in this part of the world (Fig. 2).[3] This sort of terminology does not even distinguish between lineal forebears and collateral relatives, as some cognatic terminologies do (see Fig. 3), and it contrasts sharply with terminologies that isolate exogamous lineages (a type of social organization well known to Social Anthropology), which distinguish cross-generational "lines" of people from each other (Fig. 4). In the Centrist Archipelago, these layers of "siblings" are the equivalent of known, ordered society itself. Outside the layers of "siblings" (that is, outside the realm of "kin") lies a blank; socially, this blank tends to be occupied by people who are hostile or distant—strangers, non-kin, (in Luwu) ToLaing. The working-out of sibling layers is rather different in Eastern Indonesia. (The contrast between the two is diagrammed very schematically in Fig. 5.) Social groupings there are often called "Houses" in local terms. Terminology there, as in the Centrist Archipelago, is layered by generations within each

---

[3] It is my impression that most languages of island Southeast Asia have words for these layers and that those words would very appropriately be translated "layers"; but anthropologists have on the whole tended to pay more attention to the "cognatic" aspect of these terminologies and have mentioned in passing, but made little of, the layered aspect. The word in Luwu is *peppa* (Bug.) or *paapa* (Tae). One could point out the relation between X and Y, for instance, like this: *Mappammula tellu peppa'labe'-é na makkapolo X sibawa Y* (Bug.), "Three layers ago was the beginning of X and Y's being kapolo."

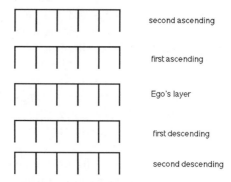

second ascending

first ascending

Ego's layer

first descending

second descending

Figure 2. Layers of "siblings" (adapted
from a drawing made by an Ilongot for
R. Rosaldo [1968])

House. (The "siblings" within an Eastern Indonesian House, however,
consist only of what we call patri-parallel cousins, while in Luwu all four
types of cousins, two cross and two parallel, count as "siblings."[+]) But Eastern Indonesian Houses are exogamous and have terms to refer to people
in other Houses with whom they already have structured affinal relationships. Since people of the same generational layer are supposed to marry
each other there (as is the case throughout most of the Centrist Archipelago), people in one House are well aware of the generational layers of
people in other Houses with which their House has affinal relationships.
    Throughout island Southeast Asia, people of one layer are supposed to
obey, serve, and listen respectfully to the people in the layers senior to their
own. People of senior layers, in turn, are supposed to protect and advise
those of junior layers, looking out for their material and spiritual welfare.
Thus it is that even the most level and unhierarchical societies of island
Southeast Asia have an implicit, albeit unenforceable, authority structure:
people may be undifferentiated by wealth or inherited rank, but they none-

[+] The layers of siblings in Centrist Archipelago societies that trace relations "cognatically"
include all the people we call "cousins," whether cross or parallel (Fig. 5a). Eastern Indonesian
societies, however, sort out all four types into different Houses, and different categories and
terms for these people often vary by the sex of Ego (Fig. 5b). Figure 5 is exceedingly sche-
matic: every House has multiple wife-giving Houses, multiple Houses to which it has given
its sisters, and multiple Houses with which it shares wife-giving Houses. Ego's natal House
(A) siblings consist (in our terms) of full siblings and patrilateral parallel cousins. Ego's matrilateral parallel cousins, although in a different House (B) from the person's own natal
House, are unmarriageable, for each House received women (the two sisters) from the same
House, which stands as wife-giver to each of the receiver Houses. Ego's matrilateral cross-
cousins will be in the natal House (C) of the Ego's mother, the House still occupied by his
or her mother's male "siblings." Ego's patrilateral cross-cousins will be in the House (D) to
which a person's natal House gives and has given its "sisters."

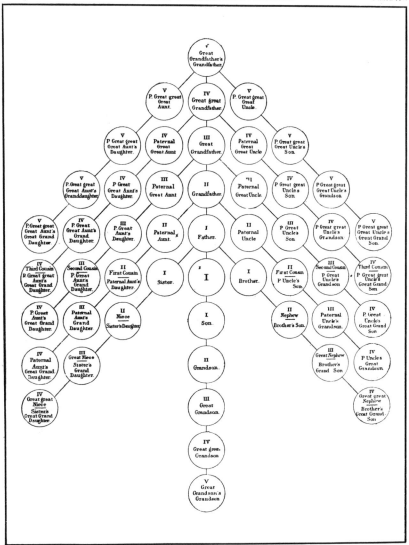

Figure 3. Diagram of consanguinity: English (from Lewis H. Morgan's *Systems of Consanguinity and Affinity* [1871])

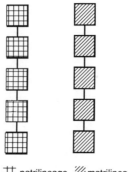

⊞ patrilineage ▨ matrilineage

Figure 4. Unilineal "lines"
of relatives

theless sort themselves into seniors and juniors on the basis of their generational layer. Needless to say, in such societies junior people often ignore their elders with impunity, while senior people may have little stake in protecting their juniors. Still, throughout island Southeast Asia, an understanding of the appropriate relations of seniors and juniors on the basis of generational layer is well understood. Moreover, it cross-cuts or lies behind relationships of respect even in hierarchical societies, where spiritual potency and inherited rank make high people automatically "senior," regardless of their generational layer. In those societies, high people of junior levels are nonetheless supposed to act politely to lower people of senior levels.

The same assumptions tend to inform relations between full siblings, who throughout island Southeast Asia tend to be classified and sometimes named by birth order. Again, younger siblings should listen to and run errands for their older siblings; older siblings should indulge and protect their younger brothers and sisters.

English-speakers are often struck by the fact that "sibling" terms are gender-neutral in much of island Southeast Asia and in parts of Oceania. These languages often have terms translatable as "my same-sex sibling" and "my opposite-sex sibling," a distinction relative to the speaker rather than to an absolute categorization. And when people ask about siblings, they do not say, "How many brothers and sisters do you have?" but, "How many older-siblings and younger-siblings do you have," and they are answered in kind. That brings us to the fact that Polynesians, Micronesians, island Melanesians, and island Southeast Asians speak languages of the Austronesian group, which are fundamentally gender-neutral. (Some local variants may be more gendered than others, as in Eastern Indonesia.) In the

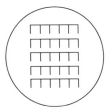

Figure 5a. the "wishfully autonomous"
House(s) of Centrist Archipelago societies.
Outside the layers of relatives lie usually hostile
non-relatives

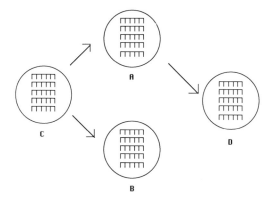

Figure 5b. The multiple Houses of Eastern
Indonesian societies. Arrows indicate the "flow
of women" between Houses with affinal
relations with each other

Figure 5. The Houses of the Centrist Archipelago
and Eastern Indonesia contrasted (circles indicate Houses)

languages of this family with which I am familiar, neither nouns nor pronouns are gendered. (English-speakers often find it hard to follow Indonesians narrating a story in English, because the narrator will call the pro-
tagonist first "he," then "she." The listeners lose track of the story,
imagining that their minds have wandered when they in fact have not.)
The terms for "human" or "person," likewise, are gender-neutral, and must
be marked specially to show gender. I think of this genderless discourse as
forming a flat and neutral surface, from which seniority terms and distinctions protrude like the design of a frieze. They are all the more obvious for
standing out on a smooth and colorless ground.

This brings us to another point, the status of gender in island Southeast Asia as a way of construing difference. Speaking globally, age and sex are usually said to be the "natural" grounds of biological differences between humans that either can be elaborated in a particular social/symbolic structure in order to create a significant difference, or can be suppressed in order to create differences that locally count as insignificant. Some societies (most obviously those of mainland New Guinea and of the Middle East) take the difference between the sexes to be the difference of overwhelming significance—as though sexual difference were the most profound and salient distinction that life offers up for humans to inspect and elaborate. In other societies, among them many of Malayo-Polynesia, age is the difference that codes significant difference of prestige and/or rank.

If seniority signals hierarchical or rank distinction, in Malayo-Polynesia gender tends to signal complementary distinction. My impression is that in Malayo-Polynesia the paradigm and icon of the male-female pair is the brother-sister pair (see, e.g., Huntsman and McLean 1976). (That contrasts with the paradigmatic male-female pair in Euro-America, which seems to me to be husband-wife; we think initially of a sexual relation of non-kin rather than an asexual relation of kin.) Brothers and sisters, in short, code complementary dualism in these Malayo-Polynesian societies that are otherwise predicated on non-complementary distinction; and brothers and sisters indeed form a cross-sex pair bearing a heavy symbolic load throughout Malayo-Polynesia, although its intensity varies. This is a subject I will take up again in Chapter Eight.

Hawaiian terminologies are "cognatic" or "bilateral"; that is, terms for relatives on both the mother's and the father's side are the same. In my view, the "cognatic" aspect of many Oceanic terminology systems has been overemphasized to the neglect of the "layered" aspect, but, of course, it is the combination of these two principles rather than either alone that informs Centrist Archipelago terminology and ways of thinking about relations. Having outlined the principle of "layers," I want now to explore some implications of the "cognatic" shape of relations in the Centrist Archipelago.

"Cognatic" terminology is often seen in the anthropological literature on kinship as being compatible with a "kindred" mode of organizing groupings. A "kindred," more or less by definition, is a grouping or a conception of a grouping of relatives that varies with the point of view of the person who stands as the "Ego." Hence kindreds are said to be "Ego-centered." J. D. Freeman, one of the most astute commentators on cognatic terminology and kindreds, points out, however, that it is probably more useful to think of the Iban (and, I would suggest, other peoples of the

Centrist Archipelago) as having "sibling-centered" kindreds, at least until each sibling marries. Freeman, generalizing about kindreds beyond those of the Iban, puts it thus:

> Strictly speaking no two individuals have precisely the same kindred. However, if the relationships between themselves are excepted, and assuming they have not produced children of their own, the members of the same sibling group do have the same kindred. Looked at in this way, a kindred is seen as radiating out bilaterally from the children of an elementary family to include all those persons to whom relationship can be traced consanguineally through both male and female links. (1960: 71)

A set of full siblings forms a kindred center, a set of allies, a mini-grouping in the understanding of many societies of the Centrist Archipelago. Like many peoples of island Southeast Asia, ToLuwu often describe certain relationships as plants. They say that full siblings have a common "source" or "root" (*apongeng*). They form a "clump" (rapu). Coconut palms, banana trees, and bamboo also grow in rapu. The common root of a clump of stems of these plants is hidden from view, but (ToLuwu point out) it would be a mistake to say that the several stems are different plants: the clump is one plant with several stems. Those stems are siblings. ToLuwu imply that since siblings are really a single entity, they should always act in accord. First-degree siblings (first cousins in our terms) are siblings whose common source or root is two generational layers removed from themselves (i.e., in the grandparental layer); second-degree siblings' common root is three layers removed. In this way, being "close" (macawe) and "far" (mabela) from a common source can be easily measured and discussed.

Because full siblings, who have exactly the same "source" (i.e., parents) in the layer senior to themselves, are regarded as equivalents in whatever is regarded as being passed on from a source to its descendants (in Luwu, white blood; in other societies, other attributes), many peoples of the Centrist Archipelago consider themselves to be as fully related to their parents' or grandparents' full siblings as to their parents or grandparents. This is another way of saying that lineality is in almost no way acknowledged in many of these societies. Forebears tend to be imagined as occurring in layers rather than in lines.

Cognatic relationship systems, even imagined in a moderately linear mode like the one diagrammed by Morgan (Fig. 4), have the effect of greatly multiplying the number of a person's forebears in comparison to purely lineal systems. A person has two parents, four grandparents, eight great-grandparents, etc. In the "Hawaiian" mode of cognatic relations, a person has two parents, but also includes among his or her "forebears" all their full siblings, which could easily be ten people in the layer immediately senior to Ego, and so forth throughout the layers above that; the number of "forebears" quickly becomes astronomical.

Partly as a consequence of the stunning number of forebears a person can legitimately claim to have, it is common throughout the Centrist Archipelago and Oceania (as has often been pointed out) for people to trace themselves not *from* forebears but *to* forebears. In other words, a person does not begin with an idea of descent through a line that eventually results in himself or herself. Rather, surveying what one knows of one's connections to people in senior layers, one traces oneself to the specific and important forebears of one's choice.

Considering this practice, which is common in Southeast Asia, O. W. Wolters makes the useful distinction between "forebears" and "ancestors." He reserves the word "ancestor" for the "men of prowess" (cf. Wolters 1979, 1982) whom people are keen to claim as forebears, however many generational layers back. "Ancestor status," Wolters writes, "had to be earned" (1982: 6).

Spiritual potency or special powers—the capacities that make people into men (and sometimes women) of prowess—are widely held throughout island Southeast Asia to be available to humans of special qualities, fortitude, or luck. This statement is true even of commoners and people in relatively level "hill tribes." Those special people may gain their powers through trances and communion with the spirits, by studying invulnerability techniques, by acquiring potent talismans, or any number of other ways; they may demonstrate their prowess as shamans, orators, warriors, sorcerers, and so forth. But commoners remain commoners instead of becoming nobles, and level societies remain level instead of becoming hierarchical ones, precisely because the potency acquired by particular individuals in those part-societies and societies cannot be conveyed automatically to their children. To put it in Weberian terms, these sorts of social organizations have no way of institutionalizing charisma. As a consequence, people in each generational layer must start anew in their search to acquire and maintain their potency. However charisma is institutionalized, however potency is encoded, commoners have little or no access to its institutionalized forms.

In Luwu, of course, potency is an aspect of white blood. Commoners' blood is all the same, and therefore their rank is all the same. Nobles say that commoners are "level" or "even" or "all the same" from the point of view of social "place" by virtue of their homogeneous and undifferentiated state of "blood." That is not to say that commoners recognize no internal differences among themselves. Commoners in Luwu, in South Sulawesi generally, and probably throughout the hierarchical societies of island Southeast Asia in fact go to some trouble to differentiate themselves from each other in terms of prestige. Nonetheless, they seem "level" to nobles because any increase in prestige or potency they achieve cannot be passed to the next generation in the form of white blood. Their competition is for what, following Chabot ([1950] 1960), I have called "standing" rather than "status" or "place." Social place is inherited, equivalent to white blood, something a person cannot change. Standing is not inherited. The prestige and potency that commoners garner during life is evanescent, vanishing with waning skills or death. Like their names, their standing dies with them. It must be achieved anew, if at all, by their descendants.

I turn now to a discussion of the shape of memory of forebears among commoners, whose ancestors are equally memorable or, as it happens, equally forgettable.

Commoner Genealogies

Commoners are all the same status, measured by level of white blood. The main structural differentiation among commoners is seniority by relative age. Senior generational strata ought to be respected and attended by younger ones; older siblings ought to be consulted and deferred to by younger ones. Kin relations are traced to both parents equally. One might imagine that the genealogies of such people, if they kept them, would ramify in all directions. Their kinship diagrams, spreading out indefinitely, would exemplify "ego-centered cognatic kinship." Each person has two parents, and four grandparents, and eight great-grandparents, and sixteen great-great-grandparents. Keeping track of all forebears and their descendants would be quite a task. Luwu commoners are not faced with that task, however, nor is the anthropologist who studies them, because they have very limited knowledge of who their relatives are. What shape does their memory of ascending generations take, and how does that shape come about?

Let us imagine the female Nene'Usman (Grandparent of Usman), a villager and widow, who has five children and sixteen grandchildren. Four of the five children live in adjoining hamlets; one, a male, who has become a sailor, married in Java and comes back only infrequently to Luwu. His three children and wife are not acquainted with their Sulawesi relatives. (That he married a woman who is not Bugis-Makassarese is itself instructive. South Sulawesi nobles are under considerable pressure to marry someone else of white blood—by definition a Bugis-Makassarese noble—

in order to keep the same level of white blood for their children. Commoners, with no such claims, are not under the same pressure.)

The four nearby children (zero-degree or full siblings) work in each other's ceremonies, lend each other money on occasion, visit and generally interact often. Their own thirteen children (first-degree siblings, what we call first cousins) likewise see quite a bit of each other, and know that "our parents are [full] siblings." As the thirteen children grow up, some marry in other hamlets; their children (second-degree siblings) see each other at hamlet ceremonies, and there is some visiting between their parents. Nonetheless, the second-degree siblings are not very important to each other socially. For one thing, they all have their own zero-degree siblings and first-degree siblings with whom to interact. The others are more "distant." For another, the descendants of Nene'Usman do not have any occasion on which to act as a coherent grouping. Indeed, the most likely occasion on which the descendants will assemble is for Nene'Usman's funeral. That occasion, ironically, is precisely the one at which she, the most senior center and focus of the collection of descendants, disappears. By now all her own full siblings are dead, and her great-grandchildren will never have known them. They called her "great-grandparent," never by her name or her teknonym, and she was not very important to any of them except those in the house she inhabited. After her death, it is prohibited to mention her name, even more than during her life. When the great-grandchildren's parents (themselves first-degree siblings) get together, they say to their children, "Look! That's your 'sibling'! His mother and I are 'siblings!' " (People do not specify the degree of siblingship without a reason to do so.) As the children grow up, they will know that at least some of their [second-degree] siblings are "siblings," but they do not know what degree of siblingship they are. They may say to each other, if the occasion warrants solidarity, "After all, our parents were siblings." But in the absence of a reason and focus for social interaction, and in the absence of a memory node in the form of an apical forebear's name, and in the absence of any driving motivation to keep track of all their siblings of various degrees, they soon lose track of them. Ignorance of forebears may easily imply ignorance of those forebears' descendants, especially of the people we call "collaterals." Commoners' knowledge of ascending generations and of the "spread" of their relations (their siblings of various degrees) is exceedingly restricted.

One may well ask whether the shallowness of memory about ascending generations among Luwu commoners is attributable to the practice of teknonymy. It seems to me that this practice probably does contribute to "genealogical amnesia" in Luwu, in the important respect that people do not have a mnemonic name, a memory node, on which to hang relationships.

If there were a social reason to do so, people could alter their practices or circumvent them, but their memory problem is a social problem and a political problem. Luwu commoners are all "peers," all "level," all undifferentiated with respect to white blood. They live within a very hierarchical society that is in deep ways predicated on the importance of difference. The most important difference lies in spiritual potency, institutionalized among nobles in the notion of white blood. Commoners are all "the same" because red blood is all "the same." Given that context of assumptions, there is little opportunity or reason for commoners to remember one great-grandparent over another, for their blood is all "the same." Forebears are all equally memorable, and equally forgettable.

The exception to commoners' "genealogical amnesia" is instructive. When a low-noble man marries a commoner woman, he may well become a local hamlet leader or village leader, if the village is distant from the residences of nobles higher than himself. Inhabitants of his hamlet and neighboring ones will use the polite form of "yes" when addressing him, saying *iek'* rather than *io'*. They may address him as "Daeng." If he is a tactful and reasonable sort of person, he may become quite influential locally during his lifetime. If he has ties to higher nobles in distant villages and goes to their ceremonies, he is likely to be yet more highly regarded. His name may be recalled locally, a few generations later, as the dignitary of the place, a kind of generalized local ancestor for the entire hamlet or village. It is my impression from several instances like this, however, that villagers would not try to trace specific descent from him.

Commoners' restricted knowledge of kin is, as Marxists say, no accident. In a political system of entourage-groupings in which followers and supporters are largely drawn from relations that are junior by either status or generation, genealogical amnesia has important political implications. Quite simply, a commoner has very few junior relations who can be collected into an entourage. A commoner's "following," as it were, is likely to consist at the most of his or her younger zero-degree siblings and their children. As juniors, they are automatically if marginally inferior, hence suitable to act as followers. But other than the help offered by those few, most likely in matters involving siri', relations between commoner siblings are quite reciprocal, particularly in matters of labor, given and received in preparations for ceremonies and in the rice fields.

Noble Kinship

The presumed existence of white blood among some but not all people in a particular society has several implications for the ways that people regard and recollect their forebears. All forebears among commoners are equal; like the commoners themselves, they are "level" with respect to blood. Nobles' forebears, however, can be very different in their level of white blood and their prestige. Some had more white blood than others. Some received titles and posts from the ruler in the akkarungeng. It is such people who are worthy of being remembered and worthy to be claimed as "ancestors" instead of mere forebears. It is such ancestors whose names become the nodal points in the past to which nobles trace themselves.

I want to discuss two types of genealogical memory among nobles in Luwu. One type occurs among the nobles who are followers, under the protection of a yet higher-level noble. I will speak of them as "middle-level" or "Daeng-level" nobles, although that is not entirely accurate in that everyone is a follower of someone higher. The high ToMatoa who form the high core of a kapolo were themselves followers of the ruler. Only the ruler was subordinate to none. Moreover, some extremely high-level nobles can be "followers" (supportive inferiors) of a close kinsman who is just a few shades above them and who is the ToMatoa of a large following. Nonetheless, the gross outlines of the system will be easier to explicate using the distinction between middle-level and high-level nobles. The second type of genealogical memory I will discuss is that of the very high nobles who lead substantial kapolo in Luwu. The interest in genealogies displayed by these two categories of people (followers and leaders) is rather different, as is their remembrance.

MIDDLE-LEVEL NOBLE GENEALOGIES

In explaining the structure of the kapolo to me, members of the high core did not say that it was constituted of "people" or of "followers," but of rapu. A rapu is a sibling set, a "clump" of people who, like stems of certain plants, grow from a single root. Rapu are socially important because they tend to act as a unit, especially in matters of siri'. Moreover, the siblings of a rapu share a common genealogy. This genealogy is transmitted orally as well as jotted down. I turn first to the shape of Daeng-level genealogies.

The Shape of Genealogies

A Daeng rapu, in keeping its own genealogy, looks up (through ascending generations) and back (through the past) toward the ancestor who represents its connection with its present Opu. Several sorts of forebears are included in a Daeng-level genealogy: those whose blood (and therefore place) influenced that of the rapu keeping the genealogy; those who have distinguished themselves and become eminent, even locally eminent; and those who connect the Daeng rapu to its present Opu.

If, for instance, one of the grandmothers of a middle-level noble rapu was a commoner and one of its grandfathers was a Daeng, the commoner grandmother must be included among its forebears because her level of blood is relevant to its level of blood. At the same time, there is no reason to remember *her* forebears, because her level of blood, being simply red, does not need to be calculated further: the rapu's own level of blood can be calculated adequately by remembering only hers. This means that peripheral vision is limited for middle-level nobles looking back into the past, since anyone whose blood did not influence one's own need not be remembered. For instance, suppose a Daeng-level rapu had an eminent grandfather who had a lower male half-sibling. The half-sibling married a woman lower than himself. Neither the lower half-sibling, nor his wife, nor their issue will be remembered by the Daeng-level rapu, because that blood did not directly influence the rapu's, nor do those relatives serve to connect the rapu more closely to their present Opu.

A forebear who was distinguished as a great warrior or loyal henchman of a high noble may be remembered, though such a person may not necessarily connect one's sibling-set directly to the present Opu. There is, for instance, a function in South Sulawesi called a *sulewatang*, literally, a substitute body or a stand-in. A sulewatang can exist at any level: it is a person who speaks for the higher person, and who should be attended on that count. In the village of Senga, Opu had a sulewatang in the person of a Daeng-level man. The sulewatang's responsibility was to act as the village liason between the Opu and the other kapolo members of the area, to oversee his rice fields and stands of coconut, and to convey official messages, such as when the Opu would arrive or when a particular ceremony would take place. When Opu's niece was married in Palopo, this man travelled between Palopo and Senga constantly, organizing the large influx of people and foodstuffs that were needed for such a large ceremony. This is a job of great responsibility, and the man's grandchildren and grandnieces and grand-nephews will be likely to include him in their genealogies. He will be evidence of their forebears' eminence and loyalty.

Finally, Daeng-level genealogies serve to connect the Daeng rapu with its Opu. The route that connects them may be circuitous: connections are traced through both sexes, and the practice of polygyny by some high nobles guarantees a myriad of relatives. Moreover, people are as likely to trace themselves through the full siblings of their forebears as through their forebears, as I have pointed out. (Since full siblings share the same substance from a common source, those full siblings' children quite justifiably regard themselves as sharing as much substance with their parents' or grandparents' full siblings as they do with their parents or grandparents. Those people are rightly claimed as ancestors should their place and deeds warrant it.)

The shape of middle-level genealogies, which epitomize the Malayo-Polynesian practice of tracing oneself to rather than from an ancestor, can be thought of as a version of what has been called the "famous relative syndrome" in American kinship studies: Americans are aware of the genealogical and affinal path that connects them to their famous relatives, and that kinship knowledge goes far beyond their knowledge of non-famous people of comparable genealogical distance from themselves. People who may be genealogically closer but less important socially or conceptually are simply forgotten. A difference is that the "famous relative," the ancestor of a ToLuwu, will almost necessarily be of higher inherited status, and often of an older generation, than the person who traces the relation.

The Politics of Genealogies

I have mentioned that peripheral vision is limited in this way of tracing genealogies. By that I mean to say that certain sorts of forebears are remembered—those whose blood level influenced one's own, distinguished forebears, and forebears who serve as connecting links to the present Opu—but the descendants of these people are not. As a result, Daeng-level genealogies may easily be deeper than they are broad. To put it another way, they are ancestor-oriented rather than "sibling"-oriented. The depth is greater than the spread. Indeed, Daengs' knowledge of their "siblings" of various degrees may easily be only a little broader than that of commoners'. Daengs certainly know their first-degree siblings, and they may know or know of their second-degree siblings; but they almost certainly do not have accurate knowledge of those siblings' degrees of white blood, their true social place. Unless their Opu informs them, they may well be ignorant of the identity of their third-degree siblings.

The political consequences of limited lateral vision are considerable. A rapu's allies are its juniors by age or social place, but a Daeng-level rapu has very few status-juniors. It may receive political support from its first-degree siblings in a siri' dispute, but the rapu of its second-degree siblings are already too distant in siri' and may be too close in status to act as juniors. (Although Daengs do not usually have certain genealogical information about rapu as distant as second-degree siblings, they inevitably have stories and views about each other, always mutually disparaging of the other's place.)

As is the case among commoners, the narrowness of Daeng-level genealogies is no accident, politically speaking. The middle-level noble rapu's
mode of genealogy-keeping inhibits it from collecting a mass of lower relatives who will look up to it as a leader. Such rapu therefore do not form
an independent power base within the kapolo that could threaten the authority and control of the high core that leads it. I say this is "no accident"
because marriages are arranged not by the middle-level nobles themselves
but by the high core of the kapolo that they follow. The high core has its
own interests to pursue in these arrangements, which I will explicate in
greater detail in Chapter Eight.

The Secrecy of Genealogies

One might ask why middle-level nobles do not share their genealogies and
form large, solidary groupings. The answer is that genealogies reveal status, and status competition is a continual preoccupation of nobles. Genealogies are therefore carefully guarded. The need for secrecy stems from
the double dilemma of challenge and vulnerability. To say something
about one's origins in public, to strangers, is to challenge them. It is to say:
"I am such-and-such: just who are you?" By the same token, if a person's
origins are not very elevated, he or she would prefer to keep them unre-
vealed. As one of the high core said to me, speaking of a very low Daeng,
some of whose forebears were nearly commoners, "Of course she doesn't
remember her forebears! The more she remembers, the more anxious she
feels!"

Even if one's forebears are nobles, one feels uneasy if other people—that
is, one's similar-status peers, with whom one is always in some competition—know one's genealogy in detail. This fear was dramatically described
to me by a middle-level noble, a close henchman of the Opu Pa'Bicara', on
the veranda one afternoon. You never know what evil ToLaing will be up
to, he said; they want to treat you as badly as possible, so you must "know
who you are" or "recognize yourself" (*isseng onromu*, "recognize your
place") so that you know you are superior to them. You think about your
ancestor's names, and you know, "That is who I am." Knowing your
origins, he said, is like having sufficient food provisions for a trip when
you journey afar into the territory of ToLaing. You hope that everything
will be easy, that you won't have to use it—but it is there for an emergency.
But if your enemies know your forebears while you do not know theirs,
they "recognize who you are" while you do not "recognize" them. You are
helpless! They can treat you any way they please!

The man was saying that ToLaing can treat you rudely as though you were nobody, and you will feel unsure of yourself instead of reacting to the insult appropriately. If you know that they know your origins, while you are unaware of theirs, their confidently insulting behavior gives you reason to believe that they have grounds to act towards you in that way; and yet you are far from certain that they are really so much higher than yourself.

Middle-level nobles therefore try to keep their origins firmly fixed in mind, especially regarding how they are connected to their high Opu, when confronting strangers, enemies, and peers. From their high To-Matoa, however, they have no secrets. Their ToMatoa possesses their genealogies and guards their siri', which they have surrendered to his care and protection. As they put it,

> De'nagaga, de'nagaga ucoé-coérekeng . . .
> siri'kumi.

> There is nothing, nothing at all, I follow along for
> . . . just my siri'.

The ToMatoa "recognizes" his followers, knows them for who they are, better than they do themselves.

As a result, lower-noble followers who live in distant places will come to their high Opu to check in and update their genealogies. During my stay in Luwu, a man came from the mountainous neighboring region of Tana Toraja (the land of Toraja). He had not visited for twenty years, due to the enormous civil disruption in the area from the mid-fifties to the mid-sixties. He brought his genealogy, plotted on a notebook pad, to show the Opu Pa'Bicara all the marriages that had taken place and all the children that had been born in the interim. He, in turn, took away the names of the children born to the Opu in the interim and news of their marriages and activities. Having reaffirmed his ties with the Opu, he will return to his village in Tana Toraja, no doubt making much of his visit—how well he was treated, how intimately he became acquainted with the Opu's current household, and the like—thus confirming to other villagers that he is someone who truly is a relative of the Opu's and is of a higher order than his supposed peers.

HIGH-NOBLE GENEALOGIES

High nobles keep written genealogies, which are their own high rapu's sacred texts. The highest noble in the akkarungeng was the Datu, and his genealogy formed part of the akkarungeng's sacred heirlooms. The sacred texts kept by lesser nobles were stored in the upper level of the house, analogous to the attic. The Palopo house of the high nobles in whose family I stayed had no upper level, for Palopo is a town, and houses there are one-story structures built of concrete. There, the texts were kept in an inner room, carefully wrapped, on top of a high cupboard. The family brought them down for me to look at with considerable ceremony. Shades were drawn and doors closed (in order to let possible visitors know they should not intrude), small incense lamps were lit, and prayers were said before the books were unwrapped and opened. They are called lontara', palm-leaf manuscripts, but all those which I saw were in large bound notebooks (written in Buginese script).

Like others of rank, ranging from the ruler down to the lowest noble, high nobles need genealogies to tell them who they are. Unlike middle-level nobles, high nobles do not have a living, breathing ancestor in the form of a ToMatoa who leads and protects them. (Structurally, the Datu was ToMatoa to the whole kingdom, especially to the highest nobles, who were his close "siblings.") And so, unlike middle-level nobles, the highest nobles keep track of their own genealogies in order to "recognize who they are." High nobles who lead large kapolo must, in self-defense against their peers who lead other large kapolo, be aware of their own places, their own genealogies. Without their genealogies, my high-noble informants said, they would feel that they had lost their "grip" or "handle," that which centers them and makes them stable. "Knowing who they are" is their anchor in a sea of aggressive competition and disputing.

Some of the genealogies that I saw in the Opu Pa'Bicara's house were written in Buginese script: so-and-so married so-and-so, and had five children named so-and-so. Others were graphic depictions. In the latter, the male is represented as a circle, his name placed inside it. His wives are represented by half-moons, like disks partially hidden by the sun. Lines move from between the two indicating their children. Any anthropologist who has tried to construct a genealogy for cognatically traced kin, in which there is virtually no principle of exclusion, will sympathize with the difficulty of representing these relations graphically. The lines and bubbles sprawl all over the page.

All high nobles keep genealogies, in writing and diagrams, that connect them as highly as possible to the ancestors of the past. One large chart-genealogy that I saw in the Opu Pa'Bicara's house, however, was exceptional in its thoroughness and scope. It had been prepared some years ago at the request of the head of the local museum, and had been somewhat rationalized by Western convention, so that the top of the page represented the past and the bottom represented later generations moving toward the present. The genealogy was exceptionally large and thorough because it belonged to the Opu Pa'Bicara, whose father had been the polity's Keeper of Genealogies. As a result, the Opu Pa'Bicara's genealogy—which showed him and his forebears inextricably intertwined with the ruler from time immemorial—was also the genealogy of the Datu and the akkarungeng. (This was the rationale for the museum curator's request.) It traced the Datus of Luwu back to Batara Guru, the spirit of the Upper World who with his wife had come to found Luwu long ago.

I examined no other high-noble genealogies in Luwu, although I saw a number from southern Buginese areas. I doubt, though, that other high-noble cores of kapolo in Luwu were able to trace their genealogies to the world's beginning: that privilege was reserved for the ruler. I suspect that, like Daengs tracing themselves to their own Opu, many are able only to connect themselves only as far as is necessary in order to establish a relation to the present ruler. But they undoubtedly go back as far as they can, and that would mean as far as they have lontara' (written records). I think it is fair to say that Buginese do not usually create genealogies from nothing. What cannot be doubted is that everyone would like to have a genealogy that goes to Batara Guru, and that all high nobles keep and guard their genealogies.

Like lower-noble genealogists, the high core of a kapolo must look back and up, pursuing its most direct connections to the highest ancestors possible. At the same time, the kapolo's high core must know the lower-status descendants of its ancestors as well as the ancestors themselves. After all, it is the lower-status descendants of its ancestors and forebears who are its potential followers. And, of course, a good part of the high core's authority depends upon its certain knowledge of its followers' origins.

Genealogies of high nobles who are responsible for an entourage, then, do not have the single-minded focus of middle-level noble genealogies. As little as possible is left out of these accounts, due to the need to trace ancestors and descendants alike. Throughout Southeast Asia, nobles and leaders, "men of prowess" in O. W. Wolters's words, wanted to increase their entourages and dependents. The point of "kinship" in these circumstances is to be as inclusive as possible. And so the shape of the genealogy is a spreading one, not intrinsically limited: it stops only at the borders defined by ignorance, rather than limiting itself through systematic forgetting.

The Politics of Memory

Genealogies have different shapes and extents in Luwu, depending on a person's social position. Commoners' genealogies are shallow and narrow; middle-noble genealogies are deep and narrow; and high-noble genealogies are deep and broad. The contrasting practices of genealogy-keeping specific to each social level imply different political potential.

I have gone to some lengths to show the sociological or structural reasons for commoners' political disadvantage in this chapter and the last, but it is worth noting that ToLuwu understand the contrastive potency of commoners' and nobles' names as an index of the former's weakness rather than as a sociological system. By preserving their forebears' names, nobles maintain their connection to the ancestral past. Nobles' relation to their past in this respect gives them an advantage over commoners, for they have access to the ancestral potency that is one of the bases of their claim to superiority. Names in themselves, and the direct connection that they provide to the descendants who preserve them—quite apart from the specific structures of genealogies—form memory nodes and access points to potency for descendants. This, too, has political significance. Fixing on their ancestor's names, nobles "know/recognize who they are." That in itself gives them confidence when confronting ToLaing. And in states of danger, they are enjoined to think of a potent forebear's name. I heard many stories, for instance, in which the speaker, retelling an incident of great danger, told that he concentrated on thinking of his forebear and heard a voice saying, "Be calm, grandchild. I am here," and survived. The political advantages of having access to ancestral names, then, are obvious.

The Shape of "Time"

What sort of "past" is constituted by the various modes of naming and retaining names at these different social levels? After all, if "genealogical amnesia" can be related to a teknonymous naming system among Luwu commoners, one might ask about its obverse, the shape of genealogical memory, among the nobles of Luwu. The very highest genealogies appear to stretch deep into the past, even to the origins of the world, when Batara Guru came to earth. They seem, at first glance, comparable to the "structural time" of Nuer Genealogies. I want here to add some comments on the shape of the past that is implied in the different modes of reckoning genealogies in Luwu.

For commoners, it would seem, the genealogical past is extremely short. One could suggest, as Hildred and Clifford Geertz have done (1964) regarding the practice of teknonymy in Bali, that the reference point by which the continuity of generations is structured moves continually into the present. The reference point is the newborn child. As more children are born, the past, in the form of parental and grandparental names, is sloughed off and disappears, leaving hardly a trace.

From what I have written so far, it might appear that the past for Luwu nobles contrasts with that of commoners on this count, at least, for it is shaped and structured by their genealogies. The shape of their past might therefore better be likened to Nuer "structural time" than to the past's erasure implicit in the practice of teknonymy among commoners.

On the contrary though, among middle-level nobles, something analogous to commoner "genealogical amnesia" happens. Their title-names and their genealogies are continually being revised in order to refer to the present and even future high core of the kapolo in which they find themselves. The reference point of their genealogies continually moves into the present in two ways: through the revision of their genealogies and through teknonymous titles.

The first of these results from the marriage system and the way of tracing genealogies practiced by middle-level nobles. When a distant (say, fourth-degree) female sibling of the kapolo's high core marries a close (say, first-degree) sibling of the high core, the people in her rapu will reorient their genealogies along with their new closer relation to the high core. Her brothers will no longer have to claim connection to their "famous relative," their living ancestor, by pointing out that they are merely fourth-degree siblings. Instead, they will be brothers-in-law to people very close to the center. Her children will be second-degree siblings (through their father) of the high core itself. Although these children will acknowledge that they are fifth-degree siblings (through their mother) as well, this relation, being distant, is significantly less important. There is no special reason to maintain a memory of that relation, especially a couple of generations down the line. The wise high core arranges marriages among its followers precisely in order to keep rapu of its distant siblings from drifting far from its realm of influence. As a result, the genealogies of middle nobles are revised, shortened, and come to refer to the present high core rather than to a forebear far in the past.

The continual revision of what could be called "structural time" for middle-level nobles is compounded by the way that kapolo are known and by the use of what I have called "teknonymous titles." A kapolo does not have a formal name that identifies it through a number of generations, nor is it located or attached to a piece of named territory that could function as its label. A kapolo is known, if named, by the name of its leader: "kapolona Opu A." When Opu A dies, his name must not be mentioned aloud. A new ToMatoa, meanwhile, is emerging from the younger generation of the high core. The one named Opu B becomes preeminent. Eventually his many followers come to be known, and know themselves, as "kapolona Opu B." The way the kapolo is referred to, then, does not link it to a name that might pinpoint a past period, nor is there a way to attach the grouping conceptually to a set of names that forms a set of continuous generations. The label of the social grouping is constantly being moved into the present of its leader.

The teknonymous titles held by some of the kapolo's members have a similar effect. These title-names refer to the childhood name of persons in the high core who are its junior generation. For instance, the ToMatoa's son Andi C becomes the basis of the names of the followers Opu DaC, Indo'na C, Ambe C, etc. The multiplicity of teknonymous titles based on any or all of the names of high-core junior members allows the senior generation of the high core to rope in and tie to itself far more lower nobles than it would be practical or desirable for the high core to marry or to marry to one of its close-high siblings. Yet the effects of the two practices (roping-in marriage and bestowing teknonymous title-names) are similar: they tie the lower people to the center, and they put the reference point of the naming and genealogical systems into the future, in the junior generational layer of the high core.

These processes, it would seem, create a reference point for the kapolo itself that continually moves into the present, though at a much slower pace and much more elaborately than does the analogous process among commoners. If genealogies among nobles could be said to form a sort of "structural time" in Luwu, it is a structural time whose "structure" is continually being revised and pulled into the present.

The deepest and broadest genealogies, kept by the very highest nobles and the ruler of Luwu, trace present people to Batara Guru and even beyond, into the Upper World. At first glance these, if no others, appear to structure the past into some sort of sequential whole.

As it happens, Buginese accounts of events often meticulously record the same details that contemporary European ones do. That is, the events recounted "really happened" or are plausible in a Western historical epistemology. (Of course, the organization of the indigenous texts and the interpretation of the events they so carefully record are something else again. No one claims that those are written with a historical consciousness or sensibility.) Partly as a result of this fact, historians working in Occidental modes of historical writing can to some extent reconstruct successive generations of rulers and high nobles, and they can use these texts to construct sequential and sometimes chronological frameworks within which to shape narratives about the past (cf. Abidin 1971; Noorduyn 1965; Pelras 1975a).

Nonetheless, however much these records can now be used by present-day historians, the larger motivation for these records was not primarily a historicizing impulse. What motivated the system was not to record or conceptualize the "past" or its shape, nor to record the succession of generations. The way that high nobles preserve ancestral names, as well as their purposes in doing so, ultimately flatten the past and construe it atemporally. The past, in the sense of dead ancestors, is a source of potency, and ancestral names are means of access to it for descendants.

The internal arrangement of genealogies as written documents is not easily apprehended by the reader as a succession through time. Genealogies are not rationalized charts or family trees, in which the shape of the genealogy is itself indicative of the passage of time. Genealogies that document who married whom in South Sulawesi do not have the simple form that is possible in a genealogy in which only one sex is of importance (A begat B, B begat C, and so on). Everyone should be included, and their ancestors, and their descendants, of both sexes. The statuses of these people can be judged partly by their titles and names, and partly by the success and demeanor of their descendants (or vice versa: the status of the ancestors can be surmised by the success or failure of their descendants). And so these written notations of marriages, which try to be comprehensive, are confusing and complex, the more so if they are regarded as documents that ought to be arranged sequentially. The more complete they purport to be, the more spreadingly shapeless, apparently endless, and confusing they cannot help but be.

But the more germane point here is that the aim of preserving the names of ancestors and their marriages is not so much to trace oneself back through duration to the world's beginning, although it would certainly be desirable if one could, but rather meticulously to keep track of what degrees of white blood merged and issued forth what other degrees of white blood, finally resulting in oneself and one's followers and one's rivals. And so these records try less to represent a sequential succession of generations through time than they do to make a complete accounting of the preservation and dilution of white blood's purity. If an image of a past that is structured generationally emerges from a reading of these accounts, it is because parents contribute their white blood to their children, rather than the reverse. But that irreversibility is, as it were, a historical accident. The accounts that high nobles keep of their ancestors and their ancestors' descendants, their own lower-status relatives, provide less a way of structuring the past than they do of understanding and enforcing the status relations of current people.

How are the genealogies generated? During their lifetimes, the senior-generation members of the high core of a kapolo jot down notes to themselves on a variety of subjects: the marriages that they have arranged, and the issue produced; events that have occurred; their thoughts on how to attain a clean soul; and other matters. The descendants of these writers preserve the jottings, and may add information about the titles and accomplishments of the deceased. The manuscripts may be recopied and modified in the course of several generations. They will be stored in the form of lontara', literally palm-leaf manuscripts, but now written and recopied in notebooks in Bugis script.

Lontara' present themselves physically to their reader-owners, the descendants of those who produced them, in much the way that they can be apprehended conceptually: as an assemblage more than as a narrative. Stored as sacred heirlooms or objects inherited from the ancestors (mana'), these jottings are talismans as well as manuscripts. They are a special sort, for in the process of being read/uttered (baca), they put the reader into a state of conscious awareness of the ancestors, and of who he or she is. The medium of this connection is consciousness (paringerreng), a medium that, being impalpable, is the most appropriate one possible for communication between this world and the invisible world of ancestors and spirits.

Genealogies and lontara' are less a way of attributing a structure to the past than they are a resource that can be tapped by descendants, a point of access to the past. And the "past" is less importantly a temporal era than it is a location, the upper world of ultimate sources of the world's potency and fertility, and the ancestral sources through which human descendants are linked to that upper world. And so noble genealogies, which at first glance appear to constitute the structure of the past and to remember its contents as higher and higher levels of spiritual potency are reached, deplete the past of historicity. "The past" means: potency.

Chapter Eight
Centripetal Marriage

In "A Study of Customs Pertaining to Twins in Bali," Jane Belo addresses a puzzling question. When Balinese commoners gave birth to opposite-sex twins (in the 1930s), the parents and twins were banished from the village for a period, their house was dismantled, and a ritual of purification of the village was performed after the untoward event. (Unless noted, by "twins" I mean opposite-sex ones in this chapter.) The birth of twins to high nobles, by contrast, was greeted with joy. The difference between high- and lower-status people in reception of twins rested on the belief "that the twins had had contact amounting to marital intimacy before birth, in the womb of the mother. For some this intimacy was a good and very portentous thing, and the high caste princes and priests claimed that the boy was born like a god, that he brought his wife with him out of the mother's womb" (Belo [1935] 1970: 3). By this logic, commoner twins, far from the gods, were incestuous: "It is incestuous for opposite-sex twins to occupy a womb; but the higher the status, the less abominable the incest, since for the gods incest is proper" (Boon 1977: 138).

Affinal ambition in Luwu and other Indic States like Bali had a center: people wanted, and wanted their children, to marry "in" and "up," toward the center that was ultimately defined by the ruler. Thus marriage in Luwu, like naming and genealogy-keeping, manifested a centripetal urge whose practice gave kinship relations a center. (In the modern absence of a ruler whose presence defined the polity's high center, we would have to call the striving merely "up" rather than "toward the [high] center.") Twin-birth beliefs thus form a condensed icon for whole marriage systems in insular Southeast Asia's Indic States, where high nobles still strive to marry close (at best, first-degree "siblings") while close marriage is abhorred by and formerly was prohibited to lower people. Full-sibling marriage or its compromise act, close-sibling marriage, in short, is a statement about status; among commoners, Clifford Geertz has remarked, "incest" is less a sin than a status mistake. (But then, in this part of the world, a large part of sinning is making status mistakes.)

Ideas about appropriate and inappropriate, desirable and undesirable sorts of marriage do not float in a disinterested vacuum of "beliefs" and

"symbols." Marriage and its most visible celebration, the wedding ceremony, are powerful symbols in the Bugis-Makassarese areas of South Sulawesi precisely because they provide an arena in which the themes that
most preoccupy people are played out publicly, exhibited for all to assess:
the necessity of demonstrating siri', the urge to confirm one's degree of
blood, the fear and distrust of ToLaing, the desire to vanquish ToLaing,
protection or lack of it by superiors, loyalty or lack of it from subordinates.
Unlike cockfights in Bali (cf. C. Geertz 1973a), weddings in South Sulawesi
are the ultimate in "real-life" "deep play": status *can* be lost, gained, or held
steady at a wedding, both in challenges and counter-challenges between
peers and, most important, in the alliances the marriage being celebrated
confirms and the degrees of white blood its issue will embody.

Nor (I am inclined to believe) are ideas about appropriate and inappropriate marriages most usefully regarded as manifestations of alleged cultural universals regarding "the incest tabu." I do not intend to discuss
Luwu promotion of the marriage of closer and closer relatives in the upper
echelons of the hierarchy as a local manifestation of an alleged universal
prohibition, "the incest tabu"; rather, I want to approach centripetal marriage in Luwu from the bottom up, so to speak—within the comparative
context of systems of understandings and practices about relations and social groupings specific to the Centrist Archipelago and against the backdrop of analogous practices in Eastern Indonesia and parts of Oceania. Its
most condensed icon is twin-marriage: twin-marriage, in turn, is a condensed and extreme form of "sibling" marriage; and sibling-marriage is the
most centripetal and center-producing of possible marriages in a politico-
mythical system that postulates and values centers. I want now to discuss
centripetal marriage in Luwu by recasting some of the ways that "social
organization" can be seen in island Southeast Asia, drawing especially on
the arguments made and background sketched in Chapters Three and
Seven.

House Societies

The houses of many Indonesian societies display spectacularly elaborate
structures, often an indication of the ritual and cosmological importance
of these architecturally-defined spaces. Even if the architecture is not ar-
resting, houses tend to be invested with a great deal of meaning (as in
Luwu). But the significance of "houses" is not limited to dwellings as ritual
spaces defined by physical structures: many peoples of insular Southeast
Asia use a word meaning "house" both for a dwelling and for their society's
major type of grouping. "House," for example, is the direct translation of

the indigenous term used in many Eastern Indonesian societies for their wife-giving and wife-taking groupings. (These same entities are also known in the anthropological literature by the less satisfactory, to my mind, "patrilineages.") In other Indonesian societies where the word "house" does not denote a type of social grouping, the structure and meanings of the dwelling often are congruent with local ideas about the polity (as in Luwu).

Lévi-Strauss has recently (1982, 1984) introduced the term "*sociétés à maisons*" to characterize many of the social formations of Indonesia, Polynesia, Melanesia, and the American Pacific Northwest, and the term has been promoted by James Boon (in recent works, explicitly or implicitly; see Boon 1982 and forthcoming). What are *sociétés à maisons*? (I will call them "House societies," ignoring Lévi-Strauss's plural "maisons" but capitalizing the word to distinguish it from a dwelling.) And why do we need yet another term? To understand at a deep level the emergence of this term and why it is useful, it would be necessary to review the history and metaphysics of kinship studies emanating from the English-speaking world, especially from British Social Anthropology, as these models and later others were applied to the Pacific after World War II. I will not do that, but I will review some of this background.

Social Anthropology in its classic form, i.e., the mainly British theory of society that developed primarily in the study of Africa before World War II and in the 1950s, is inconceivable without the idea of the *group*. In the discussion of Indonesian *sociétés à maisons* in *Paroles Données* (1984: 192-99), Lévi-Strauss explains for a French audience the curious foreign term *corporate group* as used by ethnologists of the English language. (He italicizes it, as will I, to show that its meaning is far from transparent.) A main point in Lévi-Strauss's discussion is that *corporate groups* are considered substantive things in themselves that have an existence and perpetuate themselves as though of their own accord and for their own reasons. The idea of the *corporate group*, Lévi-Strauss points out, encountered difficulty accommodating the "cognatic" kinship systems of the Pacific.

A complete history of this encounter would also spell out the relation to the *corporate group* of the importance of descent, the meanings of "kinship" and "kinship terminology," jural rights, structures of roles, and other notions. While not as basic as the *corporate group*, these notions were all entwined in Social Anthropology and historically were seldom disaggregated. Partly as a consequence, Social Anthropologists commonly used to classify societies by "kinship" "type" as though, e.g., "matrilineal societies" were a category in nature. Although that particular practice has fallen into disuse, many anthropologists still write as though "matriliny," for instance, were something substantive and full of content that could be given a non-trivial cross-cultural meaning. In any case, accommodating the cluster of ideas around the *corporate group* (with its usually unstated conceptual baggage of the importance of descent to the formation of groups, the idea that kinship terminology is a distorted reflection of biological reality, etc., etc.) proved to be a strain when it came to Pacific societies, which often trace their "kinship" relations "cognatically" or "bilaterally," where groupings often have vague or permeable boundaries, where recruitment to groupings is often not strictly along genealogical or descent lines, where, indeed, "kinship" (in the sense of a belief in shared body substance) sometimes does not feature in either the formation of groups or the reference of what we call "kinship" terminology. This produced a major debate in Anglo-American anthropological theory in the 1960s and 1970s. Out of this debate came a plethora of neologisms and compromise labels—ambilineal, optative kinship, quasi-groups, non-unilineal, and many more—as well as David Schneider's radical insistence that "kinship" itself is a great conceptual imposition by anthropologists.

Schneider's view is that the study of "kinship," as the subject has been developed in anthropology, assumes that the terms by which people refer to and address the people we deem to be their "kin" and the relations they have with the people we deem to be their "kin" are based on shared body substance, the importance of coitus in producing children, etc. These ideas are our own cultural productions; they need have nothing to do with the logic and passions that the people in question bring to their interactions and to their nomenclature; but we of course think that shared body substance is a fact that cannot be avoided. The study of "kinship" has therefore traditionally had a privileged place in anthropological thought because, unlike other aspects of culture such as economics and religion, it was assumed ultimately to have a real referent, the "bedrock" of biology. Schneider argues that we do not have to believe that religious practices ultimately refer to real spirits and gods to make sense of them; in fact, to do so probably would inhibit our understanding of religious beliefs and practices on their own terms. Similarly, the beliefs, terms, and practices that generally go under the rubric "kinship" can be studied as systems of symbols and meanings without our insisting that they are ultimately grounded in a "real" biological referent. I find Schneider's views very useful, but, in any case, it is probably not an accident that this line of thought came from someone whose first fieldwork was in the Pacific. The view can be read as a sign of the frustration that people who were taught that kinship was a bedrock or "backbone" of society, as Radcliffe-Brown put it, experienced when trying to make such ideas fit Pacific data.

Lévi-Strauss, to continue, insists that the idea of the *corporate group* as the foundation of social order dissolves if we apply it to Indonesia, where groups may be of variable membership and exist for only a short time, and where neither property, nor genealogy, nor residence need form the basis or criterion for the group's existence. But while *corporate groups*, he writes, dissolve under our investigative gaze, marriage alliances emerge, for, "whether in Borneo or in Java, the conjugal couple forms the veritable core of the family" (1984: 194, my translation). Not descent and kinship, then, but alliance is the place to look to understand social formations. (This is of course the classic contrast between British and French anthropology that emerged in the post-World War II kinship debates.)

Unlike the idea of a *corporate group*, Lévi-Strauss cautions us, marriage or alliance is not something substantive but a relation: "We must move from the idea of an *objective substratum* to one of the *objectification of a relation*: the unstable relation of marriage, which, as an institution, the House has the role of immobilizing or fixing" (1984: 195, my translation). Indeed, he writes, just as Marx wrote that the value of exchange is fetished or fixed or objectified in commodities, so, by analogy, the social relations between groupings and persons can be viewed as a "thing" and objectified in the House. The House is a specific institution that deserves a place in anthropological terminology, because it does not exist in filiation, property, or residence as such but rather as a projection of a relation that may manifest itself in any of several forms (1984: 195).

The societies that best exemplify and give credence to Lévi-Strauss's assertions are those of Eastern Indonesia and to some extent Sumatra, and it is no accident that Lévi-Strauss and Dutch writers on this subject before him pay far more attention to societies in these areas than to those in what I call the Centrist Archipelago. The image of the House as the fetishization or objectification or solidification of the relationship of marriage is especially apt, for instance, in Eastern Indonesia, where the House's existence is predicated on its function as a node to mobilize valuables to exchange at marriage. Eastern Indonesia also illustrates the fundamental importance of the conjugal pair as the basis of social organization, for Houses exist in order to exchange, and the excuse for exchange of valuables is people, mainly sisters who leave their brothers' Houses to wed in other Houses and form conjugal pairs. The logic of the system of exchange is predicated on the necessity of marriage between, rather than within, each House.

Can these of Lévi-Strauss's ideas about the House—that it is a reification of exchange relations, and that the marriage alliance and the conjugal pair form the foundation of social order—also be enlighteningly applied to societies of the Centrist Archipelago? I think they can be, but it is not as immediately obvious, because these societies, especially the former Indic States, practice a politics of the center rather than a politics of exchange; this structural twist, in which marriages tend to be in-House in order to consolidate the center, rather than outside the House, which promotes exchange and makes it impossible to consolidate a center, tends to obscure the relevance of alliance theory and marriage as the basis of social order. Moreover, the House in Indic States coincides with the State itself, which gives it a somehow more solid and corporate groupish aspect, even if that is ultimately illusory. The best known of structuralist efforts concerning the Indic States, which are fairly rare, is James Boon's work on Bali (see especially Boon, forthcoming; see also Kemp [1978] on Thailand). My project here is far from fully structuralist, and far from an application of structuralist principles, but I do want to use several of Lévi-Strauss's observations.

I think Lévi-Strauss is very right to reject the *corporate group* as the foundation of social order and right to replace it with marriage alliance in island Southeast Asia. I also think it very sensible to put the conjugal pair at the center of Indonesian social organizations, and to think of the pair's marriage as a short-lived objectification of a marriage alliance, which in the simplest societies may consist of nothing but the two individuals, but which in more complex societies consists of many more people. In the explication of Centrist Archipelago marriage that follows, however, I emphasize the brother-sister pair over the conjugal pair for two reasons. For one, throughout island Southeast Asia, including both the Centrist Archipelago (with the exception of societies where a person is not allowed to marry a relative) and Eastern Indonesia, the spouse is mythically and ritually a substitute for the sibling, from whom one must part because of the "incest tabu." (This is of course Lévi-Strauss's general theory of incest, promoted in other, previous works.) For another, the hierarchical Centrist societies that most concern me are preferentially endogamous, and the brother-sister and husband-wife bonds merely reinforce each other; in some sense it is hard to say which is more the "core" than the other. I want to note here, though, that it is my impression that in societies in the Centrist Archipelago there is a correlation between increasing "level" "flatness" of societies and their emphasis on the conjugal pair over the brother-sister bond, which in them (though not in noble Houses) must loosen or dissolve with marriage.

Another advantage of using the term "House" to characterize island Southeast Asian groupings is that it does not classify the society by "kinship" type. Classifying societies by "kinship type" obscures the very obvious fact that two Indonesian social organizations, only one of which is (for example) "matrilineal," have more in common than two "matrilineal" social organizations, only one of which is Indonesian (assuming the second one is outside Malayo-Polynesia). Lévi-Strauss's way of dismissing "kinship" is to say that the House is a bundle of contradictions if viewed through the lens of "kinship":

> Patrilineal descent and matrilineal descent, filiation and residence, hypergamy and hypogamy, close marriage and distant marriage, heredity and election: all these notions, which usually allow anthropologists to distinguish the various known types of society, are reunited in the House, as if, in the last analysis, the spirit (in the eighteenth-century sense) of this institution expressed an effort to transcend, in all spheres of collective life, theoretically incompatible principles. (1982: 184)

Lévi-Strauss, it is true, retains the "language of kinship and affinity," and sees the House as composed of "theoretically incompatible principles"; but they are incompatible only if we expect to classify societies by consistent "kinship" "types," or if we expect that we can compare "matriliny" cross-culturally and come up with a useful generalization. Some of the "contradictions" disappear if we do not import alien ideas about "kinship" to the data. My way of dealing with the relation of "kinship" to the House in Indonesia is to invoke the ideas of David Schneider where relevant (see my summary of Schneider's views above).[1] In any case, calling Indonesian social formations "Houses" encourages us to see the very strong underlying similarities between the "patrilineal" Eastern Indonesians, the "cognatic"

---

[1] The effort to use "African models" in the Pacific resulted, as I mentioned, in many awkward terms, as well as a great deal of nearly unreadable ethnography on New Guinea for about a decade, in which it was literally impossible to make sense of the accounts of social groupings unless one understood that the ethnographers' real argument was about what these groupings were *not*. The situation was reminiscent of Thomas Kuhn's (1970) account of Ptolemaic astronomy; Kuhn points out that even after Copernicus, the movements of heavenly bodies *could* be described in Ptolemaic terms, but the whole descriptive apparatus, as knowledge grew, became increasingly complex and hedged with qualifications, exceptions, and extra factors. I think, similarly, we are in a state in studies of the Pacific where it is *possible* to describe social organizations in kinship terms, but it becomes increasingly cumbersome and pointless to do so. David Schneider's ideas, which imply that we should take seriously local ideas and terms rather than calling them (for instance) "fictive," "metaphorical," or an "idiom" for something else, offer a way out of some unwieldy ways of conceptualizing and describing social groupings. Nonetheless, I am not quite as relentless as David Schneider in eliminating any vestige of our own belief system in our descriptions. To continue the analogy begun above, even after Copernicus, Ptolemaic description was adequate for some purposes—it remains useful, for instance, for navigators at sea to assume that stars move and the earth stays still. By the same token, when in note 4 of Chapter Seven, above, I described the categories of Houses in Eastern Indonesia into which the people we describe as cross- and parallel cousins fall, I used the word "cousin," which comes out of our views that people can be either lineal or collateral relatives, a view that is alien to Eastern Indonesia. At some points in description, it is simplest to assume that the earth you are standing on stays still, even if in fact the earth is moving and you are on a drifting boat.

Javanese and South Sulawesians, and the "matrilineal" Minangkabau of Sumatra.

In sum, I accept the importance of alliance and exchange, hence of the conjugal pair, and the contradictory nature of "kinship" (if we accept the category) within many especially hierarchical Houses of the area. But other than that, how shall we characterize the island Southeast Asian House? I suggest that Houses in this part of the world are profoundly centered entities, consisting of a center and a serving group. The center is often a stable object, such as a temple, a palace, or a set of regalia. The center is often regarded as the descendant or visible remains of an ancestral "root" or "source," and often is designated with a term containing the syllable *pu* (hence my use below of the Indonesian word *pusaka* for any such objects, although the local terms vary). Because the center does not reproduce or die (it often consists of leavings of the dead, or of objects called "inanimate" in Euro-American cosmology), it lasts through long periods. The center is retained by the serving group, not exchanged or sold. Because it does not enter relations of exchange, it is metaphorically stable or still, even if it is occasionally transported from place to place by its serving group. But it is usually relatively immobile in space.

The serving group, or caretakers, or worship community, of the center consists of humans. Humans do die, and consequently they must recruit more humans to the service group if the central object is to be served in the future. Worship communities may recruit members by adopting them from other Houses or through conquest. An extremely common mode of recruitment to service groupings in island Southeast Asia is to give birth, that is, to recruit members by reproducing them from the bodies of worship-community members. The service grouping may or may not believe that its members share body substance, and the grouping may or may not consider shared body substance an important criterion for worship-community membership. The service grouping forms the periphery around its central objects; because it consists of humans who die and breathe and move around, the periphery is metaphorically and usually literally more mobile than its center. What is central (if I may so put it) to the House in island Southeast Asia—what defines the service grouping as an entity—is not the periphery, the "social group," but the center.

My characterization of the island Southeast Asian House obviously fits the Indic States of the area very well. The only proviso for Indic States would be to insist that to distinguish between persons and objects as I just did is to project our metaphysics onto island Southeast Asia. As I have been at pains to point out, high nobles in Luwu, for instance, are walking, breathing talismans, ambulatory regalia, while arajang and mana', like humans' bodies, are tangible locations for ancestral potency. Those "persons" and "objects" are not so much different in kind as in degree, displaying different proportions of a mix of invisible potency, which is malinrung, and its visible evidence, which is talle'. We can think, then, of Akkarungeng Luwu as an entourage defined and centered by its arajang; the populace formed its serving group, its caretakers (cf. Chapter Three). Of course, Akkarungeng Luwu consisted of many arajang and mana', each of which defined smaller centers with smaller serving groupings, ranging from "region," to "kapolo," to "household."

Indic States with their regalia and temples are obviously centered spaces, but what of more level societies? The example I will use here and later is the Iban of Sarawak (Borneo), in the Centrist Archipelago. Iban live in stem families in *bilek* (individual apartments) in communal longhouses, which are effectively "villages." Because of J. D. Freeman's several lucid accounts of their kinship system in the Social Anthropology mode, the Iban have become the paradigmatic example of a "cognatic" society in the anthropological literature. Yet a reading of Freeman's ethnography *Report on the Iban* (1970), rather than just his articles on kinship, reveals that each bilek family is in fact the caretaking grouping for *padi pun*, the rice-source or rice-spirit, as well as for other pusaka retained by the bilek family. If the bilek family fails to perpetuate itself by giving birth, it adopts a child or children from other bilek, and the adopted child has all the rights and duties of a child recruited by birth. As a social anthropologist writing about "kinship" and believing in it, Freeman casts his accounts as if the bilek family in a Durkheimian (or better, Radcliffe-Brownian) move wishes to perpetuate the group for its own sake. It is just as cogent to insist that the bilek-family, the serving group of various sorts of pusaka, can reproduce itself in a variety of ways to assure a serving group in the future for its pusaka.

One obvious way that any serving group can recruit members and perpetuate itself in the future is by giving birth to them. Birth ideally requires a prior marriage in most of island Southeast Asia, and it is here that Lévi-Strauss's views on alliance are most relevant. Two characteristically different marriage patterns in island Southeast Asia prompted me to divide the area into the Centrist Archipelago and Eastern Indonesia, and to write that the former societies, in which marriage with a relative is allowed, practice a politics of the center, while the latter societies practice a politics of exchange. Centrist societies allow an in-House marriage and subsequent reproduction of persons: that is, the serving group gives itself permission to reproduce itself without seeking outside help. (Among these are the To-Luwu and the Iban, whose tactics I will discuss later at greater lengths.) It is this permission to reproduce itself that prompts James Boon to write in various places that Bali and other hierarchical House societies are wishfully autonomous and complete.

Eastern Indonesian Houses present a somewhat different case, at first glance somewhat more difficult to fit into my notion of the House in Indonesia as a centered social space. Houses there, too, consist of regalia or ancestral objects plus their worship communities or serving groups. But they refuse to allow in-House marriages, thereby initiating the need for spouse exchange with other Houses so that the serving group for the pusaka can be perpetuated.

Eastern Indonesians, for the most part, think that women are the source of life; even though Eastern Indonesians do not deny the role of coitus in reproduction, they downplay the importance of the man's contribution to the child's body substance. Since women are not allowed to reproduce within their natal Houses, they are sent away to other Houses to marry men other than their natal-House "brothers." Valuables (not ancestral pusaka, which stay fixed within the House, but other valuables) are exchanged between the wife-giving and wife-receiving Houses to create marriages.

A woman gives birth, then, to children who "belong" (because of exchanged valuables) to the children's father's House, not to their mother's natal House. The female children, like their mothers before them, must eventually leave their natal-House "brothers" to go to yet another House to marry and reproduce; the male children, like their fathers, remain fixed in their natal House, there eventually to receive other Houses' "sisters" as their brides.

One consequence of this exchange system is that the boys who share a natal House are there by virtue of the fact that exchanges of valuables have been made for their mothers by the House their fathers belong to; similar exchanges had been made in the previous generation for the mothers of the boys' fathers. As a result, these boys and men of different generations share a House. They do not share a common House because of being related by "blood" or body substance; rather, the House may be regarded as a sort of legal relation rather than a relationship based on shared body substance, a point that Hoskins (1984) and McKinnon (1983) make very clear.

The obverse of the above is that one's "blood" relations are not in one's natal House but in one's mother's natal House, currently occupied by her "brothers." That House, not one's own, is one's source of life. A person's mother's "brothers" become his or her local and immediate root, *pu*, or source of life in the preceding generation. People share body substance with others who are outside their natal House. (Schneiderians, therefore, would object to calling Eastern Indonesian House-members "agnates" and the Houses "patrilineages," terms that imply that the foundation of the grouping lies in shared body substance. In Eastern Indonesian thought and practice, it does not, and using the term confuses an analysis.)

Men of Eastern Indonesia, in fact, are part of two worship communities in different respects and on different occasions: one centers at their natal House's pusaka and orients them "inward," "towards the center," and "up"; the other is oriented to their mother's "brothers'" natal House and orients them "sideways," "up," and "back," to their own mother's natal House and back through its mother's brothers' Houses and so on to their ancestral source. This splitting of loyalties in a man's worship community obligations is only one of the splits that gives almost all Eastern Indonesian ritual activity a dualistic cast.

Another thing worth noting in Eastern Indonesia because of the resonances with Centrist Archipelago symbolism is the symbolism of weight and lightness, stability and mobility worked out in this scheme. McKinnon (1983) paints a picture of Tanimbar, one of the more hierarchical societies of Eastern Indonesia, in which noble named Houses are metaphorically dense, immobile, and weighty, while the unnamed and lesser Houses are more mobile (for they disappear and appear) and "lighter." Objects, like people, are divided conceptually into those which are central, immobile, and close to the ancestral center (the House pusaka and *tavu* in Tanimbar), and those which circulate (the valuables that are exchanged, that are effectively in motion). Both, like people, are grounded in ancestral powers. Other items besides Houses and people in other Eastern Indonesian societies may participate in centrist symbolism, but centrist symbolism, imagery, and ritual and social action are as pervasive as dualistic ones there. (This combination of the two prompts Lévi-Strauss [1963] to write that these societies exhibit "concentric dualism.")

Houses in Indonesia, then, consist of two aspects: a center, often consisting of or fixed by an (animate) object, and a grouping of humans that takes care of the center. Houses seek to perpetuate themselves, which requires perpetuating both aspects of themselves. They seek to perpetuate their central ancestral object by caring for it through rituals and seeing that it comes to no danger or harm. They seek to perpetuate their serving grouping primarily, though not usually exclusively, by giving birth to more people. The perpetuation of human groupings by means of giving birth brings us to the subject conventionally known as kinship. In this chapter, I outline some of the strategies used by both Centrist Archipelago and Eastern Indonesian Houses in order to perpetuate themselves by marriage and giving birth. I concentrate, however, on how endogamous Centrist Archipelago societies maintain social centers, partly because those strategies are less explored in anthropological literature than Eastern Indonesian ones, but mainly because my aim here is not so much to interpret all of island Southeast Asian social organizations as it is to use these formations to clarify how Luwu's centrist marriage practices tended to perpetuate the social places of nobles. I turn now to marriage practices and strategies within and around House societies of the Centrist Archipelago, and will return to Eastern Indonesia at this chapter's end.

Nets of Relations

Both Centrist Archipelago and Eastern Indonesian House societies use relationship terminology that divides people into layers of "siblings," as I pointed out in Chapter Seven. The House societies of the Centrist Archipelago that are endogamous could be diagrammed as one big House, "wishfully autonomous," while Eastern Indonesian Houses are multiple (see Fig. 5, p. 213 above). Layers of siblings are themselves articulated by two principles: birth order (within a sibling set), which orders (at least in theory) authority relations between juniors and seniors; and sex, which often codes complementary difference. Intermarrying "siblings" form dense centers of "nets" of relations.

BROTHERS AND SISTERS

Because layers of "siblings" feature so prominently in relationship terminology of this area, it is not surprising that brothers and sisters have a special place in the symbolism and practice of marriage in this area, both in the Centrist Archipelago and in Eastern Indonesia, and, for that matter, in other parts of island Southeast Asia and much of the Pacific.

Some Centrist Archipelago Houses prohibit any degree of "siblings" from marrying (e.g., the Ifugao of northern Luzon, the Semai of the Malay peninsula). Many, however, actively encourage "siblings" (though not full siblings) to marry (e.g., the Iban of Sarawak [Borneo], the nobility of South Sulawesi). Regardless of the degrees of sibling that their prohibition covers (all or some), however, it is extremely common in the Centrist Archipelago (and for that matter throughout Oceania) for societies' founding myths to feature brothers and sisters. The pair sometimes knows itself to be brother-sister, sometimes not; sometimes marries and produces children, sometimes not; sometimes is forced to separate because discovered to be brother-sister, sometimes not. The brother-sister pair, I believe, stands as an icon of primordial unity in many of these societies, in part because they are the issue of a single "source." But what is worth remarking here is that in the Centrist Archipelago the more level societies tell simply of brothers and sisters, while only the most hierarchical ones feature twins.

The brother-sister separation of the Wana, a "level" people of Central Sulawesi, is told like this by their ethnographer, Jane Atkinson:

> Batu-é ngkeo and Lolo ngkambuno, the morning and evening star respectively, were brother and sister. They parted as children, met again as lovers. As she deloused him she discovered a scar on his head and realized they were siblings. When she bore his child, a trough was used to catch her blood lest it fall to earth and cause the sea to flood the land. Their child was cut in half horizontally through the middle. The two halves themselves became small stars. Just as the child could not remain united, so too Batu-é ngkeo and Lolo ngkambuno must be kept apart, lest the state and consequence of incest—known as kabuyu—prevail. (Kabuyu means incessant rains, floods, avalanches). (Atkinson, personal communication, 1986)

In myths of more hierarchical societies of the area, twins, the most dense and concentrated form of siblings, have a special place. Bali is one of them; Luwu is another. The origin myths of both areas begin with twins. In Bali, the gods married their twins; in Luwu, twins separated. In Luwu, it is said that Batara Guru came from the Upper World with his wife Wé Nylittimo' (who was his first-degree sibling from the Lower World) and many relatives and retainers to populate the Middle World and to found Luwu. The couple's grandchildren were twins, Sawerigading and Tenri Abeng, who were separated at birth. Meeting as youths, they fell passionately in love and wanted to marry. This was disallowed. Sawerigading rebuked those who separated him from his twin, pointing out that no one else in Luwu was his "match," his own status; he left Luwu for a distant land to seek his first cousin as his bride, explicitly as a substitute for his twin sister. Tenri Abeng married a dewata (spirit) of the Upper World, ascended to it, and now receives the prayers and supplications of her brother and his descendants.

IBAN AND TOLUWU COMPARED

The Centrist Archipelago societies that allow "siblings" to marry at all have a centripetal impulse. Luwu's centripetal impulse and practice is so complex, however, that I want first to explicate a simpler, more level version as practiced in a far more level society that nonetheless shares many of Luwu's assumptions: the Iban of Sarawak (Borneo).

The pattern of relationships constituted by sibling marriage in each of the Centrist Archipelago societies can be regarded as forming "nets," to use an Iban metaphor. Speaking to J. D. Freeman, their best-known ethnographer, an Iban named Unggat compared their family relations to the making of an Iban casting-net (*jala*), which when first begun "is a very small cone, but as the knotting proceeds and one circle of mesh loops is succeeded by the next, it increases in size until its final circumference is measured not in inches but in fathoms" (Freeman 1970: 68). Iban "nets" of relationship seem to refer to the sibling set in a *bilek* (compartment in a longhouse). Luwu "nets" of relationship, by contrast, refer ultimately to the Datu and thus are effectively ancestor-centered.

These social nets are comparable in these two societies because, although the Iban and ToLuwu are at different ends of a scale measuring wealth and social complexity, they are just a transformation away from each other in their ideas about relationships and marriage practices: Their relationship terminologies arrange people into layers of "siblings," and they prohibit marriage between people of adjacent layers. They allow marriage between people of the same layer. Each society traces relations "cognatically" or "bilaterally," and each describes those relations in terms of plants. ToLuwu and Iban divide the world into two great camps: relatives/allies and non-relatives/untrustworthy others, with a few shades between. Both societies prohibit marriage between zero-degree siblings but allow and even encourage marriage between first-degree siblings (first cousins in our terms). These tendencies result in similarly shaped "nets" of relatives, in which social groupings consist of dense knots of closely-related intermarrying people at the center and more dispersed distantly-related or unrelated people at the borders. But the "nets" in the two societies differ in size and scope.

Both the mechanics and the cultural-political impulses of centripetal marriage in Luwu can be usefully understood within the broader context of the meanings of brothers and sisters in the Centrist Archipelago. I will discuss in some detail the similarities among the Iban and ToLuwu mentioned above in order to make the logic of the system as clear as possible, drawing freely on other examples from the Centrist Archipelago.

Their relationship terminology classifies people into layers of siblings, and they prohibit marriage between people of adjacent layers I pointed out in Chapter Seven that relationship terminology in the Centrist Archipelago divides people into layers of "siblings." In some societies, a person is prohibited

from marrying anyone classed as a "relative." Those which do allow relatives to marry assume that proper marriage partners lie within Ego's own
layer of siblings. Marriage is prohibited between people of adjacent layers.
Typically, cross-generational marriages are allowed outside a certain (locally defined) degree of closeness, after a fine and sometimes a cleansing
ritual, and some societies have formal mechanisms for rearranging terminology and their social relations for such marriages.

Cross-layer marriage is ungrammatical in this sort of system on two
counts: it would confuse both the classification of people and authority
relations. First, how would the couple's child be classified? If placed terminologically in the layer below its senior-layer parent, the child would
become the layer-peer of its junior-layer parent, which is clearly unaccept-
able; but if placed in the layer junior to its junior-layer parent, it would
become terminologically the grandchild of its senior-layer parent. Because
of the generational emphasis of the Centrist Archipelago's relationship terminology, these classification incongruities can be inconvenient (see Freeman 1960: 161 n. 17). Perhaps even more important, respect should be
shown by those of the junior younger layer to those of the senior older
layer. If layers mix and produce children who belong to neither, the authority relations implied by layering become more ambiguous (cf. Atkinson 1977; Boon 1977: 137).

They allow marriage between people of the same layer So far, I have spoken
only of "marriage prohibitions," not of "incest," a term that implies coitus.
The two are different. Some human societies allow people coitus but
not marriage with relatives outside a certain degree of closeness. Others
allow marriage without coitus (such as Nuer ghost-marriage and woman-
woman marriage, or the marriage of nuns to Christ). In the Centrist Archipelago, marriage always implies coitus, though coitus can often be had
without marriage; but it is my impression that the partners who are prohibited for the one are always prohibited for the other.

The presumption is universal (among those who allow marriage with a
relative) in the Centrist Archipelago that a person's spouse should be from
his or her own layer of siblings. How then can we conceptualize and depict
the categories of people who are marriageable and unmarriageable?

First, it is useful to contrast the Centrist Archipelago case with those of
systems of terminology and marriage that are more fundamentally lineal
and exogamous. Such systems enjoin against marrying within the lineage,
while the people of certain other lineages are marriageable. In those cases
we can think of the incest tabu as vertical, spanning the generations of
which one's own lineage consists; conversely, the category of "marriage-

able people" is also vertical, spanning layers of generations in marriageable lineages outside one's own (Fig. 6).

In the Centrist Archipelago, it appears at first glance as if the cross-generational vertical incest tabu of exogamous lineages were turned on its side and inside-out. Horizontal layers of siblings are prohibited to each other (Fig. 7). Here, it is as though the only layer that exists, when it comes to marriage, is Ego's own. That being the case, both marriage and marriage prohibitions must operate horizontally, as it were, over the same range of people, namely, "siblings." As a consequence, Ego's own layer has a double function: it provides Ego's siblings, but it also provides Ego's spouse. In spite of the fact that Figure 6 makes these principles look like transformations of each other, the problem of incest versus marriage in this part of the world is quite unlike that in exogamous unilineal marriage systems. A person's own layer of siblings is like a Möbius strip of marriage, in which one begins with a sibling and returns with a spouse, or vice versa; they are the flip side of each other, but they occupy almost the same space.

Each society traces relations "cognatically" or "bilaterally," and each describes those relations in terms of plants Both Iban and ToLuwu trace their relations almost equally and in much the same way to both parents, i.e., they have "cognatic" or "bilateral" ways of reckoning relationship. These systems have classically been considered "ego-centered," but as I pointed out in

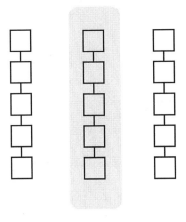

prohibited for marriage

Figure 6. The "incest tabu" in an exogamous lineage system

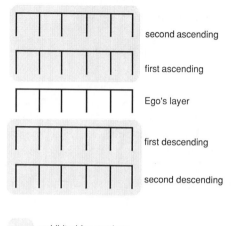

second ascending

first ascending

Ego's layer

first descending

second descending

prohibited for marriage

Figure 7. The "incest tabu" in the Centrist Archipelago

Chapter Seven following Freeman, they could just as well be thought of as "sibling-centered," since siblings, until they marry, have the same net of relations. In the Centrist Archipelago it seems especially appropriate to do so, given the special meaning that siblings have, and given the botanic terms that some of these peoples use in discussing their relationships—as shoots or stems from a common "root" or source.

The Iban, for instance, conceptualize the person as a part of the bilek, the ritual-residential apartment within the longhouse. The bilek is a "House" by Lévi-Strauss's definition and by my modification of the House as a worship community of *pusaka*, inherited precious objects and people. The bilek's pusaka consist of various inherited objects; of the living ances-tor, the bilek's senior member, called "the *pun bilek*—literally the root or foundation of the bilek" (Freeman 1970: 31); and of the bilek's *padi pun*. *Padi* means growing rice, while *pun* is the root or foundation, the source or origin. The padi pun locates the rice spirit, the source of rice, which is served and cared for by bilek members, who store it in a special jar between harvest and the next planting.

Iban cast the image of the person within his or her bilek as a stem grow-ing from a common clump. Freeman outlines a basic Iban understanding of the constitution of the "person":

> According to Iban belief, every person has a *semengat*, or separable soul. This *semengat*, during life, inhabits the body. . . . But in addition to the *semengat*, there is another entity called the *ayu*, which is a kind of secondary soul or soul-

substitute. Everyone has both a *semengat* and an *ayu*, as an old manang, or sha-man, put it: "Our *semengat* and *ayu* share the same breath." . . . But the *ayu* does not reside in the body. It takes the form of a kind of plant—it is usually likened to the bamboo (*buloh*) in appearance—and it is believed to grow on a far off mountain. On the slopes of this vast mountain grow the myriad *ayu* of all the Iban people, and there they are tended by an aged and beneficent supernatural being named Manang Betuah. The *ayu* of each bilek-family are conceived of as growing in a separate and compact clump, and when a child is born a new shoot appears at the base of the clump, just as it does with the bamboo plant itself. The health of the various members of the family—so it is believed—is controlled in a kind of magical symbiosis by the state of growth of their various *ayu*. If, for example, the *ayu* should become overgrown with creepers, the individual whose soul-substitute it is, will become ill; and shamans (*manang*) are frequently com-missioned to visit the *ayu* of sick persons to free them from encumbrances, and generally to tend them. It is the soul of the shaman that carries out this task, while the shaman himself is in a state of trance. (Freeman 1970: 21)

Iban adopt children quite frequently into the bilek-family, for perpetuating the bilek is considered crucial:

> The purpose of the *nusop ayu* ritual, which often accompanies adoption, is the cutting away of the child's *ayu* from the *ayu* clump of his natal group, and the replanting of it with the *ayu* clump of his adoptive bilek-family. The transplant-ing ritual is performed by a shaman, who receives a special fee in return for his services. The child himself is given three articles: a bush-knife . . . , a small jar . . . , and a fathom of cloth. . . . The knife symbolizes the cutting away of the child's *ayu*; the jar (termed in this context, *karong semengat*) is a cask providing magical protection for the soul, or *semengat*, of the child; while the length of cloth forms a covering for the freshly transplanted *ayu* of the child, to shade it and so prevent it becoming shrivelled in the heat of the sun. . . . (Freeman 1970: 22)

A person belongs to only one bilek. Adoption requires the child to leave the natal bilek. The adopted child's rights in the bilek are identical with the rights of a child born to the bilek.

Iban thus do not conceptualize themselves as free-floating individuals, but as shoots or stems growing from a clump composed of other bilek members. Botanic descriptions are prevalent in Eastern Indonesia (cf. Fox 1971b, 1980a). The literature on the Centrist Archipelago does not examine indigenous descriptions of relationships extensively enough to es-tablish that plant images are as pervasive there as they are in Eastern In-donesia. ToLuwu, however, use an image similar to the Iban one, as I have already pointed out. They say that siblings have a common "source" or "root" (apongeng), and like certain other forms of growing plants—coco-nut palms, banana trees, and stands of bamboo—they grow in a "clump" (rapu). Siblings, like stems from a common source, only appear to be sep-arate individuals. They are really offshoots from a common root. First-degree siblings have a common root two generational layers before (i.e., in the grandparental layer); the common root for second-degree siblings is three layers before. When they say that a sibling is far or distant (mabela), they mean that they are both far from a common root.

ToLuwu and Iban divide the world into two great camps: relatives/allies and non-relatives/untrustworthy others Neither the Iban nor ToLuwu have a structured set of terms for non-relatives. There is no category of, say, "people of my mother's brother's lineage, who stand to me as mother's brother in a structured relation even though it is not my own lineage," and the like, as there is in some other types of relation-systems. Aside from "relatives," there is a blank, a void, a formlessness. The category of people who stand in opposition to "relatives" must be, in such a scheme, non-relatives. Relatives tend to be allies and non-relatives tend to be hostile throughout the Centrist Archipelago.

One looks to relatives for material and moral support; clusters of relatives tend to form alliances against non-relatives. Throughout this book, of course, I have emphasized the distinction between kapolo and ToLaing; but analogous distinctions form a pervasive feature of social life in the Centrist Archipelago. From a given sibling set's point of view, the category of "relatives" approximately coincides with the category "Us." (The picture is more complex, of course, as I will discuss soon.)

The emotional intensity and social import of this distinction varies, but not widely, in the Centrist Archipelago. When the opposition between Us and Them as both conceptual categories and social alliances is strongest, social life acquires a rather dualistic cast. In Luwu and South Sulawesi generally, the distinction between kapolo and ToLaing is highly charged emotionally, as it is among the somewhat hierarchical Tausug (Kiefer 1972) of the southern Philippines. It is my impression that in the most level "hill tribe" societies of the Centrist Archipelago, everyday life does not take on the character of a contest between matched antagonists; hence it lacks the pervasively dualistic cast one feels in the most hierarchical of the Centrist Archipelago societies, like Luwu; yet although status-honor (in Weber's sense) is undeveloped in such societies, amour-propre tends to be highly cultivated, and a good part of these people's energies are devoted to feuding, fining, and trying to enforce fines due to offenses. In these societies, Others ("Them") are regarded as uncaring at best, life-threatening at worst. (For some accounts of the meaning of the Other in some hill tribes, see Dentan 1968 on the Semai of the interior of the Malay peninsula; Schlegel 1970, on the Tiruray of Mindanao of the southern Philippines; Barton 1930, 1938, [1919] 1969, on the Ifugao of northern Luzon; R. Rosaldo 1980 on the Ilongot of central Luzon; and Atkinson 1989 on the Wana of central

Sulawesi.) In sum, the distinction between comfortable-helpful-allies-Us and hostile-fearsome-Them itself, as well as some of the emotion of the contrast, is pervasive and perhaps universal in the Centrist Archipelago.

Relations between Us and Them are very commonly imaged as spatial in the Centrist Archipelago. Schematically, relatives and neighbors inhabit safe space, which is "close"; alien or hostile space, inhabited by non-relatives, is more distant. But one has the impression that "far" space is that inhabited by non-relatives; conversely, safe and close space can be converted into alien territory if it is invaded by non-relatives. I have written on safe and hostile space in Luwu in Part I. The situation in central Luzon is similar:

> In the realm of the natural and supernatural, dangers are lodged in the unknown and unseen. In the social realm they lie in the world outside of the kinship network. Both of these pose their opposites—the known environment and the circle of kin—which are realms of safety and security. The unknown geographical realm is less dangerous if one has relatives living in it able to act as companions, at least during the initial stages of a visit. The known environment becomes dangerous if one has no relatives willing to act as supporters, helpers, and guards. (Kaut 1961: 268)

A corollary to the image of distant space as hostile is the symbolic importance of journeying in this part of the world. To leave close, safe, relative- and neighbor-occupied space is conceptualized in most of the Centrist Archipelago as a brave enterprise that tests men's manliness by plunging them into alien hostile territory in which they may come to grief. Spatial relations implicate gender relations: women commonly stay at home, locating the center, for they often are not thought to have "the right stuff" for journeying afar.

The importance of propinquity and intense interaction in creating allies throughout the Centrist Archipelago is related to the spatialization of safety and danger. Neighbors are as important as "kin" in many rituals of unity as well as political alliances in the area, ranging from the *selamatan* of Java, which celebrates harmony and unity and whose participants are neighbors (cf. C. Geertz 1960), to the headhunting alliances among the Ifugao, which involve both kin and hamlet neighbors (cf. Barton 1930, 1938).

Although by most anthropologists they would be called "kin," it is worth remarking that some peoples of the Centrist Archipelago think of the core of Us as predicated on relations that can be created without shared body substance or parturition. The Tagalog of central Luzon, for instance, view their relations as based on *utang na loob* (a debt of the inside or of feeling).[2] Growing up together, siblings are expected to support each other, thus automatically developing utang na loob relations. But they can become alienated from each other if the support is not reciprocal. In such societies, non-kin can become closer social allies than kin. Societies like these sort themselves out into Us versus Them using a high degree of interaction, propinquity, and exchange of favors, goods, and political support.

But then, so do societies like Luwu, where people do believe in the concept of shared body substance among nobles ("white blood"). ToLuwu are quick to assert that harmonious social interaction (*assiwolongpolongeng*) causes solidarity; thus "blood" relations can offend each other and cease to become allies; by the same token, people who live in close proximity must become each other's allies if they are to continue to associate together. Thus servants or visiting anthropologists must conduct themselves as loyal household members.

As a result, relationships in the Centrist Archipelago, even when conceptualized as based partly on shared body substance, must continually be validated socially; furthermore, relationships in that area, even when conceptualized as *not* based on shared body substance, are presumed to evolve primarily from interaction with the people we would ordinarily call "kin." Groupings seem more fluid in central Luzon than in South Sulawesi, but the net effect in either, sociologically speaking, is similar: these societies are characterized by a constant testing of loyalties, with little space for neutral parties, although the borders between Us and Them are permeable.

Understandably, alliances of people (Us) tend to be incorporative, even imperialistic, in this part of the world. Each person tries to increase the number of people who can be counted on for support and to decrease the number of people who might form a hostile opposition. Thus the distinction between Us and Them can be viewed as forming a process of continual expansion and retraction, from any given sibling set's point of view. Since the core of Us is always "kin," the expansionary impulse may take the form of marriage. In that case, an alien Other is captured literally or figuratively in marriage, and converted in the next generational layer into Us.

Since the core of Us tends to be "kin," one would imagine that there are powerful impulses in such societies to keep track of one's relatives. Just as a penny saved is a penny earned, a kinsperson remembered is an ally gained. One way to know an extensive number of kinspeople is by keeping

---

[2] Utang na loob relations are paradigmatically those between parents and children, for parents have given children the gift of life, a gift that makes children forever indebted. This fact creates an optical illusion that "kin" and "allies" (with whom a person feels utang na loob) are categories that coincide perfectly; but that is not actually the case.

long genealogies. Knowing apical forebears far in the past allows recognition of collaterals. The alternative strategy is to keep not long genealogies but shallow and very broad ones. My impression is that these strategies correlate roughly with the society's degree of hierarchy: relatively level egalitarian peoples like the Iban keep shallow broad genealogies, while the elite of more hierarchical societies like Luwu keep deep ones.

Many former headhunters of this archipelago (e.g., the Ifugao of northern Luzon and the Iban of Borneo) seem to make great efforts to remember their relations. Such peoples have relatively flat ranking systems compared to those of the Indic States. People of these level societies form ad hoc alliances among relatives, focused on different leaders for specific tasks: headhunting, revenge, and killing for honor. Knowing their relatives, even very distant ones who may never join them in a warrior-grouping, helps to assure safe passage in alien territory.

The motives for recollecting and tracking large numbers of relatives in hierarchical societies like Bali or South Sulawesi strike me as transformations of those in more level societies of the area. By Luwu definition, for instance, "nobles" have "white blood," ranging in infinite degrees of purity from the Datu (whose blood was pure white), to very high nobles with nearly pure blood, to lesser nobles who formed the entourages of higher ones and whose blood was less pure, to commoners whose blood is merely red. Although all nobles are intrinsically white-blooded in some degree, only some inherit a large entourage of relatives (kapolo), which considerably enhances their standing and prestige. The kapolo's high core keeps genealogies to keep track both of its own forebears and of its forebears' descendants—that is, the high noble core's own siblings to the nth degree, people whose connection to it coupled with their lower (but still noble) status makes them potential followers. By contrast, as already noted, the naming system and genealogy-keeping of Luwu commoners have the opposite effect. As a consequence, high nobles, who are likely to know (thus have) many relatives in far-flung places in the peninsula, have safe passage over a wide territory, whereas commoners who leave their own village immediately find themselves in hostile territory. The family-rich world of a very high noble has few ToLaing, many kapolo; a commoner's world is composed mainly of ToLaing.

Both societies prohibit marriage between zero-degree siblings but allow and even encourage marriage between first-degree siblings "Endogamy" is marrying "in," "exogamy" is marrying "out"—but in and out of what? With lineages, the answer is clear: inside the lineage or outside the lineage. In the Centrist Archipelago, where groupings tend to be defined by their centers rather than at their borders, the answer is not so clear. For the Centrist Archipelago, I use these terms to refer to "inside" Ego's layer of siblings or "outside" Ego's layer of siblings.

Quite a few societies in the Centrist Archipelago prohibit siblings of any degree to marry. For instance, because all "siblings" are prohibited as partners to the the Ifugao of northern Luzon and the Semai of the Malay peninsula, people should marry "out," to strangers, non-Us, potentially hostile Them. "Under this system," Dentan writes of the Semai, "marriage becomes a focus of anxiety." He continues:

> Most marriages must . . . be with *mai* [strangers], that is, with precisely the least trustworthy people around. . . . Not only is a spouse usually *mai* in terms of consanguineal kinship, he or she is doubly *mai* in that he or she is likely to come from a different settlement. The anxiety this situation engenders is reflected in the pattern of residence after marriage. Typically, the newlyweds spend a week or two with the wife's family, then a month or so with the husband's family. They may then return to the wife's settlement for a year or two, and so on at gradually increasing intervals, until they finally settle down once and for all. Even while this shuttling is going on, the couple periodically separate, each person going on week- or month-long visits to his or her consanguineal kinsmen.
>
> There is no explicit rule constraining people to behave this way. The reasons the Semai give for the shuttling and extended visiting are "homesickness" and mistrust of *mai*. A newlywed cut off from consanguineal kinsmen and covillagers feels cut off from meaningful human contacts. For example, one newly married east Semai man living in his wife's house with thirty of her relatives asked me to write a letter begging his elder brother to visit him. "I can't stand it here," he said, "all alone by myself." (Dentan 1968: 73)

This opposition between Us and Them does not form a moiety system in which people inherit the affiliation of one of their parents: parents and children inevitably belong to different sets of allies and enemies among "exogamic" societies there, because the child's birth itself links as "kin" sets of people who were (before its birth) non-kin, and thus reconfigures the borders between the two categories. In kinship theory, we usually think of people of a "cognatic stock" as linked by a common apical forebear to whom they trace themselves. Something like this process happens retroactively in the exogamic societies of the Centrist Archipelago, where the birth of children links people in the generational layers above. Even with the birth of their children, spouses remain non-kin to each other (e.g. Barton 1930: 99), but they are linked by a common kinsperson in the generational layer below themselves. I like to say that affines in such societies are linked by "apical children," a phrase that captures succinctly, even though the image is upside-down, the process I have just described. Thus the process of creating sibling sets that bridge two networks of alliances brings about a slow shifting over time of the boundaries between the Us and

Them to which people in any layer belong. The Us for the people of one sibling set differs from the Us of their respective children's sibling sets, and even more from their grandchildren's.

This exogamy is in a sense imperialistic: expansion into Them is continually being made by Us, for They are converted into Us in and by the next generational layer. But since no stable political center draws boundaries or measures change in Us and Them, nothing consolidates. Us does not become larger, or, if it does, there is no way to tell. Alliances merge and separate in a way that is unpredictable and unique to every sibling set.

"Endogamy" in this part of the world involves marrying within one's layer of siblings. People of the Centrist Archipelago grade siblings in terms of distance. Full siblings are the closest, first-degree siblings are close but more distant, and so forth; thus Iban terms, for example, can be diagrammed as concentric circles. The closest relatives (I will deal only with a person's own generational layer) consist of full siblings, bilek-siblings, and first-degree siblings. *Kaban* are allies, but the implication is that they are kinspeople, as well; the term encompasses approximately second-degree to fifth-degree siblings. (Just as one would not introduce a brother by calling him "my relative," Iban do not use the term *kaban* for close [full-, bilek-, and first-degree] "siblings" [Freeman 1970: 68]; but to simplify explication, I will use the term to mean all known relatives of an Iban.) Beyond the range of kaban, relatives become *juru*; when the ties of relation are even more distant, the people become *suku*; and finally, when no relation is known, they are strangers, *orang bukai* (Freeman 1970: 69). (Few Iban know all their distant kaban, especially the ones who live in distant longhouses.) Since Iban relation-terms construe people as members of generational layers, use of kaban terms is impossible when their respective layers are unknown.

Freeman's Iban informants provided him with striking images of the radial gradation between close and distant *kaban*. They compared their relations to the outward spread of concentric ripples made by a stone dropped in a pond or to an Iban *jala*, a dense and tight cone of mesh loops at the center, but eventually measured in fathoms at its edges. This beautifully apt image of a growing, radiating cone certainly describes the shape of the spread of descendants from an apical sibling-set (the small cone at the center), provided no intermarriage between "siblings" takes place. But Iban prevent loosening, dispersion, and loss of kaban by endogamy: 75 percent of the marriages are between kaban (Freeman 1970: 73).

Iban must not marry their bilek siblings, but first- and second-degree siblings are preferred marriage partners. Continual intermarriage of sib-

lings in successive layers of generations reties and intertwines kaban together once more. Bilek siblings are obliged to separate and marry others.
Their children, first-degree siblings to each other, may marry and produce
another set of zero-degree siblings who must in turn part, but whose respective children may marry each other. In other words, full siblings may
reunite in the persons of their grandchildren in alternating layers; they
need not spread apart, like an Iban casting-net, because the marriage of
their children continually reties them.

   Of course, not everyone marries a first-degree sibling. But because kaban
are preferred to orang bukai as spouses, the three members (for instance)
of a set of full siblings might marry their siblings of the first, second, and
third degree, respectively. Children of the subsequent generational layer
(three sets of full siblings) will be related to each other in several ways: as
first-degree siblings traced through one parent, as third-degree siblings
through another, and so on. Close kaban marriage, in short, effectively re-
knots the net of relations, re-creating a new tightly knit spot of densely-
intertwined close kaban around each person in each succeeding layer of
siblings. This practice prevents the net of kaban from diluting and finally
becoming orang bukai in later generational layers: "The intermarriage of
cousins constantly reinforces the network of cognatic ties linking individual Iban, and kin that might otherwise have become dispersed are brought
together again" (Freeman 1970: 76). Affinal links strengthen existing relationships rather than replace them. Marriage consolidates kaban, with the
effect that the issue of kaban is yet more, closer kaban.

   The Iban are not hierarchical in Dumont's (1970) sense: there is no ritual
encompassment of bilek over bilek. The bilek is the primary House grouping among Iban, and every bilek is an equal center. Iban nets of relations
are bilek-centered (sibling-centered). If depicted graphically or diagram-
matically, they would emerge as multiple centers of knots of close relatives
spread more or less evenly over the whole society.

THE NET OF RELATIONS IN LUWU

House structure in Luwu, unlike that of the Iban, can be cast in terms of a
hierarchically nested set of Houses, each with its own center, its family
mana' inherited from its ancestors or acquired from its patron-nobles.
Higher Houses ritually encompass smaller, lower ones. The most encompassing House, focused on the most encompassing and broadest central
point, was the akkarungeng, the realm itself. Its pusaka were the royal regalia and the ruler himself. The source of the ruler's white blood was the
Upper World of spirits and ancestors, making the Datu a "dewata mallino"

(spirit in worldly form), the only complete being in the realm; everyone else, in lesser and lesser degrees as the hierarchy was descended, was more partial, less complete, lower, and more dependent. This fact was given embodiment, as I mentioned in Chapter Two, by the fact that the ruler's house, alone of all dwellings, had a center or navel-post reaching through all three of its levels, which replicated the levels of the cosmos. Thus persons of higher degrees of white blood ritually encompass persons of lower degrees of white blood, who, when followers of the former, are considered aspects of their person.

Although Iban and ToLuwu share many assumptions about relationships and practices concerning marriage, Luwu nets of relations would look very different from those of the Iban if they could be diagrammed. Luwu nets of relations are Datu-centered ("ancestor-centered"), which is in large part a function of the ways genealogies were kept. Commoners can be imagined as forming the outer circumference of the akkarungeng's net of relations. There on the peripheries of the center, they are relatively isolated from each other and from the center, for their "genealogical amnesia" means their knowledge of forebears and forebears' descendants is extremely limited. Middle-level noble genealogies are narrow but may be deep; they reach in from the mid-periphery towards the center, attaching rapu of middle-level nobles to their relatives near the dense center. High-nobles genealogies are both deep and broad. They stretch in towards the absolute center, towards the Datu and the Datu's spirit ancestors; they stretch out towards each other, their rival-peers who are their noble second- and third-degree siblings of the center; and they stretch out and down to encompass and catch middle-level nobles who form their entourage. The broadest and deepest genealogy in the akkarungeng was the Datu's. It was deep, going back many generations to the descent of Batara Guru. It was also wide, encompassing the genealogies of all the high nobles and their followers. Interestingly but not surprisingly, ToLuwu also use net-like terms to describe the dense intermarrying or interweaving of relatives at the center. They report in Indonesian that they as nobles are *kait-men-kait*, "knotted together" or "tied up." In Buginese, they speak of being *si-tulu'-tellu'*, "braided" at the dense center, and *si-witta-witta*, "loosely woven" a little more distant from the center.

Knowledge of genealogies was secret because knowledge of genealogies was politically powerful and gave access to invisible potency. One of the most important persons of the court was the Opu Ande Guru Anak Karung, Keeper of the Genealogies of the Realm. That title went to a very close relative of the Datu who was himself a ToMatoa of a very large and powerful kapolo, someone as close to being above the fray of status-competition as is possible short of being Datu. The most powerful figure in the realm was the Datu, who had the only complete net of relatives in Luwu. Diagrammed, Luwu relationship nets would form a single large net centered at the Datu.

Centripetal and Centrifugal Marriage in Luwu

Several types of marriage are practiced in Luwu. The marriage of commoners is the simplest. Their use of teknonymy and lack of genealogies limit their knowledge of "siblings" beyond the first degree, and commoners were prohibited to marry first-degree siblings during the akkarungeng's time. Under the Indonesian Republic such marriage is legal, but commoners told me that they feel *ngri* at the thought of marrying a first-degree sibling. *Ngri* is an Indonesian word meaning something like "it is revolting and gives me the shivers." "It would feel just like marrying your full sibling!" they said. Thus commoners can be thought of as marrying outside their own layer of siblings, sometimes by default. They, like Ifugao or Semai, marry "exogamously" to people not known to be kin (there is no way to recover whether they actually are or not). Moreover, commoners' blood is "red." They feel free to mix it with the "red" blood of others—Javanese, Batak, it doesn't matter; such marriages will not dilute their children's blood, because the parents have no white blood to dilute.

Nobles operate under different constraints. Middle-level nobles, followers in a kapolo rather than its leader-core, have their marriages arranged by the high core. The high core wants to ensure that its followers will not marry too close to each other in order to prevent the formation of large rapu of densely interconnected siblings. Such a clump of solidary relatives might challenge the central high core itself. At the same time, the core does not want its followers to marry people outside the kapolo, for the children might be outside the high core's authority. Moreover, the high core cannot arrange such marriages, because the non-kapolo party is outside its authority. The perfect balance from the point of view of the high core is for its followers to marry their third- or fourth-degree siblings, where both parties are under the high core's authority.

Marriage preferences within the high core of a kapolo are even more complex because they are contradictory: they require marriage both away from the center and toward it. Political necessity requires the core of high nobles that leads a kapolo to expand and consolidate its followers by marrying away from the center that the core itself defines; this requires marrying siblings of lower rank and usually of the third or fourth degree. That expansive centrifugal impulse is complemented by a centripetal impulse to conserve rank by marrying towards the center defined by the core itself, or by marrying yet more centrally than the kapolo's core, toward the center defined by the ruler and court. The relevant dimension in this sort of situation is social place, and these marriages can better be described as "isogamic," between people of similar rank, or "anisogamic," between people of different ranks (Lévi-Strauss 1969), rather than as "exogamous" or "endogamous." Many of the politically important marriages in Luwu are anisogamic. That difference in rank, coupled with the degree of siblingship between the bride and groom, are the most salient dimensions that shape marriage patterns there.

The "centrifugal impulse" stems from the political wisdom of the core's marrying "out," away from and lower than the center it defines. Such marriages, which will be between a member of the high core and one of its lower siblings of the third, fourth, or fifth degree, have two aims. One is to generate a periphery of followers. Through such marriages the high core multiplies itself, replicating itself in less perfect form. Those multiple and lesser aspects of itself will be the center's lower-status children, and then grandchildren, and then great-grandchildren as time passes and layers of siblings succeed each other. High-core centrifugal marriages guarantee that the high core's future incarnation (two and three layers below the present) will find itself densely surrounded by lower-status follower-relatives. For instance, the Opu Pa'Bicara had more than a hundred lesser-status first-degree siblings, the fruit of his grandfather's multiple marriages.

The second aim of such centrifugal marriage is to "rope back," as the Opu Pa'Bicara put it, clumps of siblings who have become distant from the central high core. In the absence of sibling-marriage, the distance increases inevitably (as the Iban perceive) in the course of time as successive layers of siblings metaphorically move away from a common center. "Roping back" occurs when a member of the high center of a kapolo marries, say, a lower-status third-degree sibling. If chosen wisely, this sibling will come from a large rapu. The children produced by this marriage will be lower in status than the central core, but higher in status than their other parent. Through these children, the whole rapu of the lower parent will have a much closer relation to the central core. After all, the mother and her full siblings were but third-degree siblings of the high core; her children will be half-siblings[3] to the central core of the next generational layer. In this way, such marriages "rope back" clumps who can be imaged as having drifted from the center. (Of course, the inner core can also "rope back"

---

[3] ToLuwu do not have a term for "half-siblings." They call full and half-siblings "siblings," then add with a significant intonation, "one father, different mothers."

distant rapu by arranging marriages between the more distant lower rapu and its own lower half-siblings and first-degree siblings.) We can conceptualize this centrifugal movement as the center of the net of relations reaching out to its periphery and pulling in siblings from a distance, effectively retying the net to itself. The ultimate political effect of centrifugal marriage is, then, a centripetal gathering of kinspeople around the central high core.

This centrifugal impulse to expand into distant kin is complemented by a counter-impulse to marry centripetally, consolidating the center. High-core centripetal marriages consolidate the core's own clump of kin and perpetuate its degree of white blood in (same-status) children, who will become the high core of the kapolo in the next generational layer.

Thus a dual movement is required by marriage for high nobles. The one, outward and dispersing, dilutes white blood. The other, inward and conservative, preserves and perpetuates white blood. The two contradictory movements are both necessary. They are effected by the unitary high-core center when it divides itself into two aspects, one conserving, one dispersing. Another name for these two aspects is "sister" and "brother."[4]

A sister conserves. She conserves siri' (status-honor) by restrained and dignified behavior. She conserves wealth by carefully monitoring family finances. She conserves family heirlooms and manuscripts, for she is their guardian. She conserves the degree of white blood she and her brother share. Her stewardship of white blood can take three forms.

She can marry a status-peer, preferably a first-degree sibling. It makes cultural sense that women are allowed only one husband, and that he must be at least her peer in status. If that rule is followed, then a woman's children cannot be below her own status nor below that of her brother. This point is made very nicely by Chabot ([1950] 1960) in his pre-Independence study of the Makassarese of South Sulawesi. If we imagine Makassarese social structure as a ladder, he writes, the women are its rungs: they are the fixed points of status by which men know how high they have risen. Understandably, a man's siri' is attacked most directly by an attack upon his sister. Women can be fixed points only if their status is stable; the fixity is attained by requiring monogamy of women and disallowing hypogamy for them. This allows them three options: to marry isogamously (preferably her first-degree sibling), to marry hypergamously, or to not marry.

---

[4] This section on male and female owes a great deal to three articles for inspiration and insight. First among them is Bradd Shore's "Incest Prohibitions and the Logic of Power in Samoa" (1976). For Javanese comparisons, see Anderson's "The Idea of Power in Javanese Culture" (1972), especially for the creativity of male potency; and Ward Keeler's "Speaking of Gender in Java" (forthcoming), for the contrast between the retentive female and the generous male.

The higher the woman, the fewer her potential spouses. Besides being rare, most high men are unsuitable to become her spouse. With the exception of her first-degree male siblings, her other male status-peers (perhaps second-degree or more distant siblings) are likely to form the core of rival kapolos, making such potential marriages fraught with suspicion and difficulties. The hypergamic alternative is desirable but often impossible. The Datu, clearly a desirable spouse, was unlikely to marry such a woman for other reasons. A high-noble man (including the ruler) was allowed to marry only one woman of his own rank or near it. She became his queen consort. A ruler who married an extremely high woman of his own kingdom would be obliged to make her queen consort,[5] thus obviating his chance of marrying his real peer in white blood, the same-status daughter of another ruler.

The third form of blood-stewardship is not to marry at all. Not marrying risks nothing: no affronts to dignity and no dilution of her white blood in her children, however slight, can occur. Because a woman is not allowed to marry polygamously and generally not allowed to marry a man lower than herself, South Sulawesi is strewn with very high noble ladies who are unmarried. A sister who remains unmarried is the perfect retainer of white blood and siri' in every respect; in the higher echelons of social rank, being an unmarried sister is a position of honor (cf. Shore 1976, for a comparison with Samoa). Such a sister may be revered: safe and honored in the house of her eminent brother, regarded as "mother" by her brother's children, honored by their followers as a pure and wise lady, guardian of the family lontara' (sacred palm-leaf manuscripts). That was certainly the position of Opu Senga, the unmarried sister of the Opu Pa'Bicara. A fairly old lady when I met her, she spent her days reading manuscripts and writing in Bugis script, occasionally mediating village squabbles, and often attending followers' ceremonies as an honored delegate of the kapolo core.

A brother, by contrast, disperses in the act of creation. He creates children by dispersing semen. (Although ToLuwu regard themselves as related to both parents, and tend to see semen and mother's milk as parallel substances, still, semen creates, while mother's milk nourishes.) He ought to be generous, dispersing goods and favors with no thought of retention or calculation of utility. To be concerned in any way with conserving wealth

[5] Although it is wrong to think of the ruler as having had one wife and many concubines—all were legitimate, and marriage, like everything else, was graded by rank—nonetheless queen consort was clearly the most honorable position for a wife. A kapolo core of high nobles that was powerful enough to arrange a marriage between one of its sisters and the ruler would certainly not stand for her to be less than the queen consort, and the ruler would as a consequence be unable subsequently to marry a woman of his own rank from another kingdom.

is to be "like a woman": such men "use a cooking-ladle instead of a keris," ToLuwu say. Great procreational abilities are signs of his overflowing potency and creativity. The cultural license for male expansion and self-multiplication is polygyny. Islamic law restricts men to four wives, and now it is enforced. But a few decades ago, high-status, wealthy, and honored men might have tens of them.

All but one of the wives of a high-noble leader of a large kapolo were lower in social place than himself. In Luwu, he married his lower wives before his same-status wife. His marriages with these lower women produced children who would later become the lower-status but elder half-siblings to his same-status but younger children by his final wife. These lower children also were the forebears of the followers (in future generational layers) of his same-status children and grandchildren. These earlier marriages were "centrifugal" in direction.

Only one of a high-noble leader's marriages was centripetal, preferably a marriage to his same-status first-degree sibling who, like the Datu's highest wife, was known as his queen consort. It was likely to be his last: apparently the consort sent all the lower-status wives back to their villages, at least in the modern era. (I was told with some amusement by a man that if an ordinary man married a second wife, as he has a right to do under Islamic law, and his first wife objected, he would rebuke her, saying, "Who do you think you are, a queen consort, that you can raise objections to other women?") Some of the lower wives' children (half-siblings of the consort's own) would continue to live in their father's house, to be reared as the protecting lower-status older siblings of their higher-status younger siblings. Others of the older-lower children would be sent with their mothers back to their villages. There they would be coddled and spoiled in youth, obeyed and respected as they aged, by the women's rapu and the children's own "siblings" of lower status.

Endogamy and Exogamy in the Centrist Archipelago

Spatial relations were signs of social place in the center-oriented hierarchical polities of island Southeast Asia. Throughout such polities, the most "high," "central," and "inner" points of socio-political space coincided in the unitary complex formed by the ruler, the palace, and state regalia. The palace was typically known as the "inside," and court members were "insiders." Marriages were the stuff of political strategy: everyone wanted to marry "up" insofar as it was possible, and, by the same token, to marry "toward the center." Men could not marry the ruler (if the ruler was male, and usually he was), but they could send their sisters or daughters to him as his lesser-status wives. That brother-sister pair can be conceptualized as marrying "toward the center" by means of its female aspect (the sister). By receiving those women as his lesser wives, the ruler was marrying centrifugally.

Thus we can think of the direction of affinal desire by people who are off-center as one that aims inward. I call it an aim rather than a rule because the tendency is difficult to formulate as a rule abstracted from the context of the status of the participants. The high core of a kapolo that effects a roping-back marriage with one of its lower-status third-degree sibling-clumps by means of a marriage between one of the core's male members and his female third-degree sibling is marrying centrifugally; but this woman, in marrying *her* third-degree sibling who is higher than herself, is marrying centripetally. She is marrying more centripetally, in this case, than she would be if she married her own first-degree sibling of her own status. In other words, the relevant center in this sort of society ceases to be the sibling set and becomes the court: it ceases to be Ego and becomes Ancestor.

The discrepancy between the two partners in an anisogamic marriage lessens as both approach the top-inner center, and the marriage becomes more isogamic. From the point of view of preserving the signs of social place (white blood, titles, merit, or whatever else is inherited through two parents and requires coitus), no marriage is as desirable at the top as perfect isogamy, and no partners are as similar as full siblings. Their white blood, their social place, is exactly the same. The tokens and substances of status cannot be diluted by such a marriage.

Close marriage at the top is thus socially "grammatical" in such a society. Moreover, the local ethos supports it. The spectre of the hostile Other, an omnipresent feature of life in many Centrist Archipelago societies, looms especially large in the consciousness of people of high status—not because they are more frightened (if anything, the reverse is true), but because their structural responsibility is to be most conscious and aware of dangers as well as of everything else and to guard against them. The coziness, relaxation, and security of a relationship with someone whose material and status-honor interests are completely merged with one's own and who will therefore always support rather than challenge one—whose siri' one shares—intensifies the closer the parties to the relationship are. The high core's immediate family of same-status members forms an intimate and relaxed grouping for discussions, strategizing, and anecdotes, in radical contrast to the more wary and formal demeanor that is required when others (even lower kapolo members) are present. The coziness and solidarity are especially marked between cross-sex siblings, since full brothers are structurally in competition. The difference in birth order (seniority) was never enough to prevent serious conflict among brothers throughout Malayo-Polynesia; but between sisters and brothers, similarity in rank was mitigated by difference in sex, and that pair could have a complementary relationship. As Valerio Valeri, writing on Hawaii, has put it, the logic of the system implies

> the idea that the relationship of similar beings is positive if their similarity is accompanied by a difference (sex) that makes them complementary and productive (they have children); it is negative if it involves no difference, since this makes them incompatible and therefore mutually destructive. Similarity is in fact always threatening for a hierarchical system predicated on the ultimate dissimilarity, and therefore complementarity, of everybody. But the similarity of people of opposite sex can be neutralized by marriage, since it makes a single entity out of two. [By contrast,] the similarity of people of the same sex [such as full brothers] can be neutralized only if one of them renounces his status or is destroyed. (1985: 168)

The centripetal impulse at the top (the desire to become one with one's opposite-sex siblings) is psychologically powerful in such circumstances. I was struck by a comment made by Andi Anthon, a high noble and one of my best informants, when he visited the United States for several months. After perusing the sorts of magazines and newspapers available at the supermarket in order to improve his English, he observed that American husbands and wives feel they are losing their individuality and their "selves" if they identify completely with their spouse and submerge themselves into the other person, and this feeling of loss of "self" causes Americans to panic and feel they must end the marriage. "With us it's just the opposite," he said. "The more we become one, the calmer[6] we feel."

Even if they are first-degree siblings, husband and wife in Luwu must *become* one. Brother and sister, zero-degree siblings, are *already* one. From material, spiritual, and psychological perspectives, the logical marriage at the top is between full siblings. The fullest, most complete and unitary siblings are opposite-sex twins. Such twins exemplify lack of differentiation, form an icon of unity, in several respects. Like other full siblings, twins occupy a single social "place" measured by white blood, titles, and the like. Moreover, as Boon (forthcoming) has pointed out, cross-sex twins occur at the junction of two scales of difference: the hierarchical difference of seniority and the complementary difference of the sexes. Twins occupy a single age slot, thus conflating the distinction of seniority; and when two

---

[6] The term I translate "calmer" (Ind. *tenang*) carries a much greater weight in Indonesia than in America. It implies a centered calm confidence, a spiritual/psychological stability that is critical to personal dignity and political success—indeed, to sanity in societies like Java or South Sulawesi. The most complete explication of the complex of ideas associated with this complex of notions is Clifford Geertz's *The Religion of Java* (1960).

sexes are born together, they occupy the place that one ordinarily would. The significance of collapsing seniority distinctions can be understood by recalling that seniority forms the metaphorical basis for elaboration of rank and indexes hierarchy within a stratum of siblings (by birth-order) and between strata of siblings. The significance of collapsing a sex distinction can best be appreciated by understanding gender against the backdrop of other insular Southeast Asian societies' conceptions (cf. Atkinson and Errington, forthcoming; and Errington, forthcoming). Suffice it to say that in insular Southeast Asia, brother and sister (male and female) exemplify unity with two aspects rather than, say, two separate energies that are in eternal opposition (as in New Guinea; cf. Strathern, 1987). Thus the twin pair conflates the two principles of distinction (age and sex, hierarchical and complementary difference) on which all social life here is based, making cross-sex twins a "veritable atom of House societies" (Boon, forthcoming) and replicating the primordial unity of the original ancestral source from which the Houses came.

The centripetal impulse and the special place of twins in the founding myths of these hierarchical societies of the Centrist Archipelago and perhaps further afield in Polynesia can best be understood not so much as a distinct "type" of marriage as one extreme on a range that runs from not marrying "siblings" at all to marrying as close as possible. Points on this range can be thought of as something like this:

> the prohibition against marrying any degree of sibling (e.g., East Semai, Ifugao);
> the possibility of marrying a certain degree of siblings, but lack of knowledge of one's siblings beyond the first degree, making marriages "exogamous" by default (e.g., Luwu commoners);
> the allowance of marrying a sibling beyond a certain degree plus the knowledge of one's relatives beyond the prohibited degree (e.g., the Iban, who prefer marriage to a first-, second-, or third-degree sibling);
> the allowance and strong desirability of marrying as close a sibling as possible (e.g., Luwu nobles at the top of a kapolo, who prefer to marry first-degree siblings);
> the impulse to marry one's full sibling or opposite twin, but its disallowance (e.g., Luwu founding myth);
> the desirability and allowance of marrying one's full sibling or opposite-sex twin (e.g., Balinese founding myths);
> the desirability of generating the world out of an unbroken unity, an act that would require no marriage at all.

Unity and Duality

What prevents brothers and sisters from marrying, when both politics and sentiment in the Centrist Archipelago imply the desirability of that union? The obvious answer is "the incest tabu": not a universal one that emanates from human nature, but the local one that people follow. Indeed, an old Luwu woman, discussing these matters with me over tea and cookies, said virtually that. "Sawerigading and Tenri Abeng were not allowed to marry," she said, "and therefore we may not. If they had been permitted, we could, too." Explanation, like the buck, stops here: at the society's mythical charter. But as outsiders, we can press further: Why did Sawerigading and Tenri Abeng have to separate? Or, to phrase the question in a way I can answer, "Why does the separation of Sawerigading and Tenri Abeng make as much mythical sense as their attraction?" To answer requires an excursion into some transformations of unity and dualities in insular Southeast Asia.

Lévi-Strauss (1963) distinguishes the "simple dualism" of moiety systems (typically in New Guinea and the Amazon) from the "concentric dualism" found in Eastern Indonesia. (He does not address the Centrist Archipelago, but in terms of his typology I would say it exhibits "dualistic centrism.") Dualistic and centrist principles rest on each other in both Eastern Indonesia and the Centrist Archipelago, but their valences differ in each place.

The "concentric dualism" of Eastern Indonesia is well known for its dualisms at every level: symbolically, for the distinction between right and left, male and female, heaven and earth, black and white in a variety of media from dwellings to funeral ceremonies; socially, for the distinction between wife-takers and wife-givers; politically, for its diarchies, which split inner, ritual, and dignified authority from outer, instrumental, and active authority; linguistically and ritually, for its use of parallelism in ritual language. (See, e.g., Adams 1969; Cunningham 1964; J. Fox, 1971a, 1973, 1974, 1980; Kuipers, 1986; Traube 1977, 1986; Valeri 1980). At the same time, the societies of Eastern Indonesia postulate, implicitly or expliticly through the arrangement of ritual space, the structure of marriage exchange, and myth, a unitary mythical ancestral center that can no longer be achieved politically or socially. Without a postulated center, hierarchy makes no sense; and these apparently dualistic societies are riddled with hierarchy. Hierarchical difference is coded here, as it is widely in Oceania, as difference in seniority, generational or birth-order precedence. Thus the wife-giver/wife-taker pair encodes the senior-junior generational distinction of mother's brother/sister's son, and "older brother" Houses are ritually superior to their "younger brother" Houses. As James Boon (1986) has pointed out, distinguishing between "right" and "left" requires an outside point from which to have a point of view.[7]

---

[7] Societies exhibiting "simple dualism" (e.g., with moieties "A" and "B") do not tend to

The postulated center, to which differences in hierarchy and the succession of layers of siblings through duration ultimately refer, is an ancestral origin point no longer present socially in this world. For the Mambai of Timor, for instance,

> all houses have their ultimate source in the Lone House on the mountain, where Mother Earth brought forth the first ancestors of humankind. With the subsequent dispersal of the ancestors from the mountain, a process of separation and differentiation is set in motion. Continued over time in successive generations, it results in the multitude of differentiated house groups that make up the present social order. Mambai contrast the unity of the source to the multiplicity of its products. (Traube 1986: 67)

Among the Tanimbarese of the Moluccas, "Ubila'a" names primal unity and undifferentiation, a totalizing god who "is both the wife-giver and the wife-taker to the people of the earth. He-she is the greatest of nobles and the most lowly of thieves. . . . Ubila'a is thus both the representation of a pristine, undifferentiated unity and the source and possibility of its differentiation" (McKinnon 1983: 45). In the condition of primal unity, male and female, sun and moon, earth and sky, exogamous Houses, and other salient differences had not yet been established, or did not have their present significance: brother and sister married each other in Mambai, drank together in Tanimbar, as though they were the same sex.

Unity is shattered by mythical events that herald the institutionalization of differences. Brothers and sisters separate in Mambai:

> The violent separation of the incestuous couple becomes a synecdoche for a new social order based on the obligatory distinction between the marital destinies of brothers and sisters. Women, forbidden to men of their own line, must marry out, and their marital movements create alliances between groups opposed as wife-givers and wife-takers. (Traube 1979: 42)

In Tanimbar:

> Male and female—brother and sister—come to act differently in the world and begin to know how to complement one another. Moreover, it becomes evident that their differences can only be reconciled through the gift of a valuable. (McKinnon 1983: 42)

"Brothers and sisters" within each House separate to marry. The "sisters" move to different Houses to wed other women's "brothers"; their husbands' "sisters," in turn, move to yet other Houses to wed. Thus the "incest tabu," the forced separation of brother from sister, instituionalizes

---

exhibit the dualism that differentially values the closely-matched pair (e.g., "right/left"). When "A" looks to its right, it sees "B"; when it looks to its left, it sees "B." By contrast, the distinction between "wife-givers" and "wife-takers" requires an unstated third term, Ego's own House. Concentric dualistic social forms are predicated on a third element, an unstated center, standing outside the dualities.

the "flow of women" or "exchange of women" from one House to another, in which brothers stay still (remaining in their natal House) while sisters move on to other Houses to marry and procreate. The movement of women is the "flow of life" (J. Fox 1980b).

Although forced asunder, "brother" and "sister" can be reunited two generational layers below themselves in the persons of their cross-sex grandchildren in the event that their own children (whose natal Houses are of course different) marry each other and produce children. Those siblings, in turn, must themselves be parted, and so on through infinity. The marriage of the children of brother and sister thus temporarily creates unity while it maintains the structure of duality:

> To marry a woman from a wife-taking house is to reverse the outward flow and constitutes an "affront against female blood." By the same scheme, marriage between the daughter of a brother and the son of a sister effects the ideal union of male and female blood, a union that symbolically conjoins the brother and sister separated by the incest ban. Mambai understand the socially valued marriage as an oblique or displaced form of the prohibited marriage. They say: "The daughter of a brother and the son of a sister look upon each other as sister and brother." (Traube 1986: 95)

Thus the "preferred marriage" is not a marriage between people standing in a particular genealogical relation to each other, but a union or reunion between Houses. A marriage between members of two Houses that already stand to each other as wife-giver and wife-taker, or as "mother's brother's House" and "sister's son's House," reconfirms the unitary sibling relation between the bride's and groom's respective parents, who are each other's "brother" and "sister," while it nonetheless maintains the overall structure of duality whose existence the separateness of the Houses both ensures and represents.

The Eastern Indonesian system of multiple Houses engaged in exchanging sisters and valuables with each other is predicated on the fact that there are two sexes: without two sexes, there would be no rationale for separation, and therefore none for the exchange of valuables. McKinnon (1983), Traube (1977, 1986), Boon (forthcoming), and of course Lévi-Strauss (1969) have written on the logic of this "incest tabu": the enforced asexuality of "brother" and "sister" within a House generates the entire system of exchange. Brothers and sisters, who jointly become the icon of sexual difference, must be different, and they must be parted, if the world as it is constituted in Eastern Indonesia is to happen as it does. If cross-sex "siblings" within a House were to marry each other, the "flow of women" would reverse itself and all exchange and therefore life would cease, or never could begin.

Thus Eastern Indonesian "brother" and "sister" of a single natal House can never defeat the structure of duality within their own generational layer by marrying each other, the way that the mythical Balinese twins of the origin story did. An in-House marriage is as mythologically horrifying here as it is sociologically impossible. The societies of Eastern Indonesia guarantee the separation of a House's "siblings" by reifying the exchange of women with the exchange of valuable objects: on the occasion of marriage, different sorts of valuables travel in opposite directions, and different sets of relatives' Houses are mobilized for the occasion to assemble and exchange the valuables. Thus the reification of social relations through the exchange of different categories of valuables in each direction makes reversal of the "flow of women" impossible. McKinnon puts it succinctly:

> Were a man to marry [a woman from his House's wife-taker House], the flow of women, life-blood and female valuables would reverse and turn back upon itself. The hierarchical, asymmetric and complementary relation between the two sides would be inverted, or altogether neutralized: the two sides would be simultaneously wife-giver and wife-taker, male and female, superior and inferior to one another. . . . In a system where reciprocity is based upon the perpetuation of asymmetric and hierarchical relations, a symmetric marriage not only denies hierarchy, but also shatters the very possibility of reciprocity. (McKinnon 1983: 231)

Multiple Houses can never marry each other in a reciprocal exchange to create a single all-encompassing and cosmically hegemonic House, a House that would define the center of the world. Significantly, however, a hint of that intent appears in Tanimbar, one of the more hierarchical of Eastern Indonesia societies, and the logic and rationale are consonant with those of the Centrist Archipelago:

> It is significant that considerations of rank form the rationale most often evoked as justification for marrying one's "sister." . . . My sense is that "brother-sister" marriage does not occur simply because there is nobody else around who is sufficiently high rank to constitute one's "match" or "equal." It seems equally true that the very fact of being able to carry off a "brother-sister" marriage and to defy the supernatural sanctions against it establishes those involved as high-ranking. The conflation of the male-female opposition, and the denial of the hierarchical order that is based upon this opposition, place such a marriage between "equals" outside and above hierarchy itself—like Ubila'a, the sun-moon deity in whom male and female remain undifferentiated. (McKinnon 1983: 236)

In Eastern Indonesia, then, unity is postulated but fracture is institutionalized. The social and cosmological route taken by the Centrist Archipelago, by contrast, institutionalized unity but is haunted by duality. Each centrist society there institutionalized its center or centers and strove to make its illusion a reality through its socio-politics of ceremonies and marriage.

I pointed out at some length in Part I that the hierarchical states in the Centrist Archipelago represented themselves to themselves using concentric images with central high points suggesting encompassment and perfect internal unity—mountains, umbrellas, banyan trees, four-sided mandala-like figures—as though there were only One (and that One was the ruler) and no Other, certainly no challenging Other, certainly nothing so opposed as to cause either complementarity or internal division. In Luwu they said of the ruler, *"Mette' tenri bali, makkeda tenri sumpala"* ("He speaks and there is no response, he speaks and there is no contradiction"), thus imaging a perfect lack of reciprocity. In Luwu, entities lesser than the state are also cast in centrist images: men characterized the relations between a respected elder and his entourage as "the pupil and the white of an eye," thus describing a concentric, hierarchical space; ToLuwu often speak of the cure and prevention for various ills as *assituruseng* (Tae, "unity," literally "following-as-one"); they strive to become malebu ("round or spherical," "complete," "perfect") for the sake of spiritual power and health. The hegemonic center—immobile, perfectly unitary through "hierarchical solidarity" (Sahlins 1983), and stable as a mountain—forms the basis of these societies' self-representations.

At the same time, these societies are permeated by dualism, especially the omnipresent distinction between Us and Them. In representations of the state, the challenging Other is suppressed as a scandal, for centers wish to see themselves as undivided, unchallenged and unchallengeable. But in fact centers—those defined by individual human bodies as well as those defined by the state ruler and regalia—were and are continually threatened with de-centering. Wherever there is a center, there is a challenging Outside, a peer-center beyond the borders of each center's influence. It is no accident that in the Centrist Archipelago, the contest between evenly matched peers is one of the most widespread ways of casting experience in narrative, drama, ritual, and conversation. It, too, is a self-representation, a way these societies have of telling themselves what life is like. Contest narratives are the obverse of self-representations as mountains and such. In these narratives, the wishfully immobile center, challenged by a peer, answers the challenge, thus creating a contest. The course of the contest provides the structure of the narratives. The winning center, triumphant, becomes again "the" immobile center—immobile, at least, until another peer challenges. Thus drama has no climax but culminates in a stand-off, as many have pointed out.[8]

[8] On the contest as a representation of status-conflict, see C. Geertz 1973a; on non-climactic patterns of conflict and narrative in Bali, see Bateson [1935] 1972a, [1949] 1972b; on the dynamic homeostasis of "plot," see Becker 1970, 1979; on duality and stability, see Mead 1942.

In the realm of marriage, cross-sex siblings exemplify unchallenged unity. In centrist societies with multiple little centers like the Iban, each bilek is a House and each cross-sex sibling pair is its own center. As among Mambai, Iban full siblings must part because of the "incest tabu." As among Mambai, their children may marry. As among Mambai, the cross-sex sibling pair can thus be re-created two generations below, in the persons of the grandchildren of the original sibling pair who are themselves siblings. Genealogically, much the same movement takes place in the two societies:[9] but the Mambai union takes place within a structure that maintains duality, the Iban within a structure that seeks unity.

In centrist societies of the Centrist Archipelago that strove to achieve a single hegemonic politically encompassing center, such as those in the hierarchical Indic States, the whole society resembled a single House, where full siblings must be parted. But there the closest siblings (twins) were wishfully united at the mythical level; and full siblings of high rank, forced to part by the irksome tabu, sought to marry their closest permitted "sibling" (first-degree) as a substitute for their prohibited closest sibling (zero-degree).

If Eastern Indonesian societies can be thought of as a vast socio-symbolic elaboration of the fact that "brothers" and "sisters," being different, must part, then the Centrist Archipelago societies that allow endogamy can be regarded as a vast socio-symbolic elaboration of the fact that "brothers" and "sisters," being similar, must come together. Within the Centrist Archipelago, full siblings are "the same," stems from a single root. In Luwu, they are distinguished by birth order but not by sex in many respects: in their constitution as persons, in their inheritance, in their status-titles. At some level, it seems to me, the sexual difference between brother and sister has no rightful cosmological place. The existence of two sexes in the Centrist Archipelago—especially in those hierarchical societies there which wished to make themselves into hegemonic and all-encompassing unities—stands as a paradox: it goes against the logic and common sense of the system that humans require two rather than one to generate more humans. Sexual difference is acknowledged, of course, and brother and sister can therefore form a complementary whole; but the complementarity is far weaker than in Eastern Indonesia, and it is denied, rather than elaborated, in the House. The spirit of complementarity in the Centrist Archipelago is almost *faute de mieux*: in the absence of the best—perfect sameness, which

[9] Of course, unlike the Mambai, the Iban man may marry any of his "siblings," whether they are cross or parallel, while in many Eastern Indonesian systems all four types of "siblings" fall into different cateogories of Houses with respect to male Ego, and only one is marriageable.

is total unity, which would require asexual reproduction by a single person—the second-best alternative is complementarity. Thus marriage tended and still tends towards endogamy and centripetality, a movement that collapses difference (between affines and consanguines and ultimately between male and female). The ultimate symbol of this collapse and consolidation is the desirable (albeit prohibited) union between cross-sex twins, two aspects of what is already a unity, folding back once more upon itself to re-create its oneness almost before its duality has taken effect.

The political processes and the cosmo-political problem of Eastern Indonesia and the Centrist Archipelago are therefore the same at one level, different at another. Both begin cosmologically with undivided centers, unitary Houses. But sociologically speaking, Eastern Indonesia begins with a House that has already fractured into multiple Houses, and guarantees for itself that they can never be united into a single House again. The Indic States of the Centrist Archipelago begin with a postulated single House and permit endogamy; their political problem was the danger of the center collapsing in on itself.

Each institutionalizes the "incest tabu" in order to avoid stasis and therefore death, no world happening. But the sorts of world, and the political processes in which they are engaged, are rather different. In Eastern Indonesia, Houses, which are cause, effect, and agents of exchange, would disappear if they could marry themselves. Unity would be reached too quickly, without the detour through exchange, which is equivalent to life in Eastern Indonesia. Thus "brother" and "sister" must part if the multiple-House'd world is to happen.

In centrist societies of the Centrist Archipelago, the "incest tabu" was necessary to avoid further collapse, further unification. These societies were, in the logic set forth here, precariously closer to the death of stasis than are those of Eastern Indonesia. Sawerigading and Tenri Abeng must part, for their parting initiates "outward" movement away from the center. Without the fracture, there could be no striving to mend it. Without the initial centrifugal act, there could be no striving towards the center. There would be no "politics." There would be death, or merely no beginning, which are the same thing.

Perfect unity and perfect stasis for either of these types of insular Southeast Asian societies would mean death. Death is indeed an ideal state, the state of the Ancestor, the state that eradicates difference.

Conclusions

Local Conclusion
Transcending Politics

The Ancestor is immobile, static, potent, without disturbance. The aim of political life, an aim always defeated—by the incest tabu, by human turpitude, by the stance of siri', which all guarantee movement—is to reach perfect stasis, perfect unity. The aim of politics is to transcend politics. The paradox, as I have outlined in many ways already, is that all politics, life, events, are disturbance. Here I want to summarize and recapitulate some insights concerning the shape of "space" in Luwu and other Southeast Asian realms, its centering and de-centering, in order to take political processes one step further, to transcendent emptiness.

Order and the Other

The image of the ruler in the navel of the universe is one of virtual immobility. The image of the orderly polity—in which everyone enacts his or her place and nothing disturbs the realization of that order—is a powerful one in the political and artistic forms (which are the same thing) of the ranked polities of Southeast Asia. One of the most well known of these artistic forms is the Javanese shadow-puppet dramas, called *wayang kulit*. The *lakon* (plays or stories, but literally "steps") begin and end with the image of the rich, fertile, and peaceable Nagara ("kingdom") of (for instance) Nganarta, in which everyone and everything are in their proper places. (Recall that the term for "order" in Javanese is the name for the hierarchical arrangement of people around the ruler.) The lakon that takes place between the beginning and ending image is an enactment or playing out of a disturbance, which is eventually squelched or absorbed by the superior spiritual potency of the court of Nganarta, allowing order once more to be established in the land.

These lakon occur, A. L. Becker has pointed out, in space: the movement of the "steps" is from the orderly court to the outside (the forest, or an enemy kingdom), where conflict and movement, metaphorical and physical, occur; and then back again to the inside, where spiritual potency (for both the audience and the puppet characters) is regained and brought to a higher level by having met and overcome a challenge (cf. Becker 1971,

1979). Becker's point is well taken. But let us now imagine for a moment that the lakon of wayang occur within time rather than within space. After all, there is a narrative structure of sorts within a lakon, and movement from place to place occurs sequentially. First, we will substitute the word "duration" for the word "time," so that we can understand it as a medium in which events can occur rather than as a way of conceptualizing the structure of the past.

If we view the wayang as a depiction of the processes that take place within duration, then we can say that the sequential process it depicts is oscillation. One pole is perfect order, together with its corollary, prosperity and wealth: this is the still place at the lakon's beginning and end. The other pole images its opposite: the challenge, the movement, the disorder and fighting that take place in the lakon's middle sequence, outside the court's center. The events generated by humans and their activities oscillate between those two conditions. Challenge generates disorder; squelching a challenge is equivalent to re-establishing order. There is no "progress," nor any "time" as we conceptualize it: for what are "progress" and "time" except the notion that the world turns into something that it was not, and that human events are following a path whose end is unknown? The analogues of time and human history do not go anywhere in the lakon's depiction (and therefore are not analogues): that is why the lakon must finish where it began, spatially and metaphorically.

In human life, the nearest approximation of the perfect order depicted in dramas and texts was the ceremonial order re-created in the massive state ceremonies. On a smaller scale, cosmological order was and is reproduced within the groupings of leaders and followers called kapolo in Luwu during ceremonies "owned" by the inner core, and on yet smaller scales, in the ceremonies of lower nobles and finally of commoners.

No wonder that the Opu Pa'Bicara and his wife said to me that their ceremonies take place without force or effort, "otomatis." If everything happens "automatically," it means that everyone knows their places and performs the duties associated with it. It means that they enact their places, thus embodying and recreating order publicly. It means that there is no challenge. It means that nothing happens. That is to say, nothing untoward happens; nothing disturbs the order. A perfectly ordered ceremony exhibits dynamic stasis.

Such ceremonies do not depict order iconically, by showing what it is like. They are not mere tableaux vivants, pageants of noisy color. They are political contests. As such they are not representations of "order" but exemplars of it.

The extent of the kapolo, I have pointed out, is made visible on the occasions of ceremonies. The internal organization of the kapolo is predicated upon graduated difference ("hierarchy"). On certain occasions, the high inner core and the least and most peripheral follower are fused together—a fusion made possible precisely because of internal ranking—into a single entity that acts as one in opposition to a rival. Such occasions formerly came about when followers fought together under their ToMatoa during a skirmish or war, or, now as then, when they work together under their ToMatoa's direction for his glory (which is their own) in a ceremony that he "owns." Those occasions are charged with great emotional intensity. People are fused into a single social body, a "one-ness" (*paseddi*). The appropriate emotion that kapolo members should feel is solidarity together against the "guests," the ToLaing, the Other. They must guard their siri', which is the siri' of the entire kapolo.

Ceremonies are always tense, because ToLaing are continually assessing their treatment by the host and other guests in order to judge how much deference the host gives them, especially in relation to other "guests." ToLaing are also closely observing the host's control of his own kapolo members, other guests, and the situation as a whole in order to assess the host's strength or weakness and perhaps discover an opportunity to insist on more deference. The host, in turn, wants to extend as little deference to his rivals, the guests, as possible without being called on it. He also wants to prevent the guests from exhibiting any overt hostility toward each other. Any outbreak of hostility would reflect badly on the host's control of the situation, hence of his claim to potency and deference.

Overt hostility or show of weapons is completely prohibited in the presence of a person higher than oneself. Any outbreak would demonstrate the higher person's weakness, a vulnerability to attack. (That is one reason that lower nobles feel relieved and grateful if their own ToMatoa comes to the ceremonies that they own. The presence of such an elevated personage not only is a sign of favor, but also helps keep everything safe and smooth. For the same reason, very high nobles are honored and pleased if a member of the ruler's immediate family comes to ceremonies they put on.) But even given the status-similarity of host and guests, for a host to be unable to control his own ceremony would demonstrate, if nothing else, that he was too weak to prevent it. It would be humiliating, an indication that the host had incorrectly assessed his own status with respect to a guest, or the statuses of guests with respect to each other, thus offering a guest an opportunity to object in a situation where the host's own political potency was too weak to prevent the objection from occurring. In Luwu, prevention is the greater part of valor: to ensure that no opposition arises is the greatest victory. (To go back to the shadow-puppet theater: in the most secure kingdom, nothing would happen at all. There could be no drama. And there would be no "history," no events.)

My larger point throughout this book has been that fusion into oneness is made possible by the presence of ToLaing; indeed, it occurs because of it. Any given ceremony is preceded and succeeded by ceremonies "owned" by rivals. Its meaning must be understood to be constructed in a context in which reciprocal opposition is one of the motives for living. To converse there must be an Other, or else one is talking to oneself. Similarly, ceremonies in South Sulawesi are demonstrations to the Other, who serves as both audience and rival. Life can hardly be conducted in South Sulawesi without an Other, to whom demonstrating one's "place" motivates what we would call "political" action.

Staying in Place While Moving Around

Space in Luwu is of two types: safe and dangerous. Safe space is safe because it has a protecting center. Dangerous space is space inhabited by ToLaing. A journey into the space defined by ToLaing requires preparation if one is to remain salama', safe/healthy. Before journeying into dangerous space, people examine their own bodies for omens (what side they wake up on, whether their eyes twitch, etc.). On the road, they continue to pay close attention to good and bad omens. It is on a journey that one must be especially alert and on guard, ready for attacks from ToLaing and ready to attack ToLaing at the slightest provocation (the best defense). Still, one must sleep and one cannot be always alert. So, far more than within one's own village, certainly more than within one's own house, people on dangerous journeys take talismans for protection, "an umbrella before it rains," as one man put it.

The fact that journeys are dangerous does not mean that Bugis-Makassarese do not travel. Quite the contrary: they relish the dangers, which test their mettle and which they delight in overcoming. Bugis-Makassarese are known throughout the archipelago as brave and fierce sailors and traders. They travel in groupings that consist of an acknowledged leader and several lower followers. When the journey is made by lower nobles and commoners, it is conceptualized as beginning and ending in their own locality, even if years should elapse between their leaving and returning.

Commoners tend to identify themselves as being of a particular locality: "I am a person of Belopa." When asked about their origins, they do not recount stories of Batara Guru and the founding of Luwu—those are matters too remote, too elevated, and too arcane. Their knowledge, rather, is of the local ancestor and spirits who dwell in nearby hills or mountains visible from their houses. Commoners' place in geography and society is restricted to a single locality, which formerly would have been, at best, in the serving group of a local arajang. When I say that the place of commoners is restricted, I mean it only in one sense: not that they do not travel, which they are famous for doing, but that, when they do travel, they travel into the realm of ToLaing. The space occupied by ToLaing, from the perspective of a commoner or low noble, is enormous. To traverse that dangerous space requires bravery and a quickness in defense and attack, characteristics for which Bugis-Makassarese are also famous.

High nobles, by contrast, are proud not to be identified with a locality. The place they strive for is so high that it is broad, unrestricted to a single locality. The lady who told me she is "like gado-gado, made of all kinds" was telling me that she is of very high status. She was saying that her ancestors were from all over South Sulawesi, which means that her ancestors' lower-status descendants—that is, her own followers-kinspeople—are all over South Sulawesi. The broadness of her family means that she could travel widely and be acknowledged everywhere as a "Puang" or "Arung," a lord. Her place is not restricted to a single village, or even to a single former kingdom: everywhere she goes, she encounters kapolo who defer to her, rather than ToLaing who challenge her. An extreme living example of the breadth of height in status is the young man who is the son of the Datu of Luwu. His maternal grandfather was the Datu of Bone, and his great-grandfather was the Datu of Goa. Luwu, Bone, and Goa—three of the most important of the pre-Independence polities in South Sulawesi—are all, effectively, his place. His social place is so high that it encompasses the entirety of South Sulawesi, which he traverses freely, acknowledged everywhere. To encounter a peer of similar stature (a ToLaing), he would have to leave South Sulawesi to confront other islands' rulers.

A less extreme example of the breadth of height in status would be the career of a high noble who was the center of a large kapolo, members of which would, of course, be widely dispersed throughout the akkarungeng. Such a high noble could imagine his (or her, but more likely his) life's career as the acquisition of increasingly glorious titles. They were marks or signs from the ruler recognizing the noble's extraordinary potency and, not incidentally, his many followers, which, in the epistemology of political knowledge in Luwu, made that potency visible.

A ruler who failed to give a title and arajang appointment (a title and the secondary regalia that located the area) to a high noble with many widely dispersed followers would be courting danger, for two reasons. First, a high noble who was consistently passed over when honors and titles were distributed by the ruler was likely to become disgruntled, the more so if, having myriad followers and being clearly deserving, he was ignored. The noble would, in effect, be "severely disappointed" (Ind. *kacewa*) by the ruler. (Severe disappointment is the step before being ripakasiri'.) A ruler, or anyone else, flirted with disaster if he shamed a person whose status was close to his own and who had a vast number of followers. Further, the point of having a high noble of the center posted to an arajang-realm was to keep order—to prevent petty warring and to mobilize people to come to ceremonies of the center. As I have mentioned in many contexts already, Bugis-Makassarese do not usually take kindly to orders or requests issued from a person whose authority they do not accept with a "willing heart" (*macanning ati*). Their own acknowledged ToMatoa is by far their preferred leader. Thus a ToMatoa acknowledged by many people would be the most efficient appointment, as well as the most politically safe, that a ruler could make to a post.

And so it would happen that a high noble with many widely dispersed followers, who was capable and favored by the ruler, might well move his residence several times in the course of his life, from one local arajang to another (higher) one, finally ending up as a high minister in the polity's center. His physical movement in the course of his life was not a journey from a safe space into a dangerous space and back again, as is the journey of a low-noble trader leaving his village and eventually returning. Rather, it was movement from safe locality to safe locality; the noble was acknowledged as an Opu in each area, endangered in none, always the local political center. Physical movement did not make a journey.

The Empty Center

This way of understanding signs, movement, and the breadth of "place" helps us to understand, I believe, facts that at first seem paradoxical. On the one hand, the ruler was commonly imaged, in Southeast Asia, as the totally unmoving central apex of the world. On the other hand, court texts often recount the ruler's pleasure trips and royal processions around the realm. In fact, many court texts from island Southeast Asia are structured by the enumeration of names of places that the ruler visited.

From the preceding discussion it is evident that when the ruler was travelling around his realm, he may have been moving physically, but he was not changing his place or being dislodged from it. He was moving around *within* his place, which was as broad as the polity itself. The entire akkarungeng was the Datu's place and realm. Moving around within one's own place is not a journey: actually he was staying still, firmly ensconced in his place. In one's own House, where there are no ToLaing, one can relax.

The ruler exhibited the potency of the polity's center in his ability constantly to circumambulate his realm and go on pleasure trips, thereby showing that there were no ToLaing: no challenging peers, but only loyal inferiors. I discussed these matters with the Opu Pa'Bicara and his son during fieldwork, as I was beginning to understand something of the meaning of ToLaing, and they pointed out that it was very obvious to everyone that "higher" is automatically "safer." Lower nobles, commoners, and those of slave descent want to be "close" (macawe) to a high noble, to be in his or her bodyguard or live at the residence. One of the reasons for this centripetal urge is that the higher/more inner a person is, the fewer ToLaing, and therefore the less dangerous it is. In discussing how the ruler's world has no ToLaing, the Opu Pa'Bicara characterized the ruler with these words: "*Mette' tenri bali, makkeda tenri sumpala*." Translated, it means something like "he answers without being answered back, he speaks without being contradicted." To put it abstractly, the ruler was not involved in relations of reciprocity. Within his realm there was no Other to reciprocate. He could speak words (*ada*) but he could not *ewa ada* (converse, speak and be answered back).

To contrast the common human condition with that of the ruler, the Opu Pa'Bicara came up with this saying: "*De'natuo basi-é narekko de'namakki bali*," which means, "Not even [a small and insignificant plant] sprouts if it hasn't an opposite." People strive to excel in order to demonstrate their superiority to their rival-peers: nothing happens without a challenge or a complement. There must be difference for events to happen at all.

The truth is that the ruler did have a *bali*, a reciprocating opposite, in the persons of the other rulers and entourages that constituted the polities that were peers in stature to his own. A ruler of whom it could be said truly with no qualifications that "mette' tenri bali, makkeda tenri sumpala" did not exist. Even if some ruler could have succeeded in unifying all of the polities of South Sulawesi under his own rule, there would have been some larger, different Other—a polity across the sea, for instance. For a ruler not to be answered, not to be contradicted, would mean that he was everything and everyone and everywhere, for there would be no one who was not a part of his extended body, the social body of supporting "trunks" infused and protected by his sumange'. The Other begins where the influence of one's own sumange' wanes, the point at which one can no longer influence or control another. The Other is simply the name for what is left over from oneself.

All this has led me to reflect on the meaning of the Other in the constitution of geopolitical space. When there is no Other, there is no shape. For example, in everyday life, it is clear that people are most on guard, most concentrating, and most, as we say, "centered" when they are about to leave their houses and go into dangerous zones. When they return to their houses or, even better, to the house of a higher-status person who protects them and to whom they are "close," they can relax and allow themselves to become distracted. That luxury is permitted them because they know that they are safe. Similarly, the members of a kapolo are fused into a single entity, made into "one" (paseddi) when the kapolo's high core sponsors a ceremony. The kapolo is fused into a single siri' (maseddi' siri') precisely when the siri' of their leader, which is their own siri', is under duress. It is then that the kapolo's geometrical shape—its center-apex and the range of places surrounding it—is most crucially visible. The kapolo has more "shape," and more visibly orderly shape, on the occasions when ToLaing are there to observe and test it than at any other time. Finally, I would point out that the looseness at the center exhibited by the rulers of these hierarchical Southeast Asian polities on their many pleasure trips was made possible precisely because and when no ToLaing threatened. It is as though the ruler was exhibiting through physical movement the state of relaxed distraction in which one can luxuriate when one is in the safety of one's own House, the opposite pole of the concentrated state of conscious awareness called paringngerreng.

The extreme example of formlessness at the center, which to my mind clinches the thought that social geography is shaped under duress from the challenging Other, is the example of Batara Guru. Batara Guru was said to be the first ruler of Luwu. Although he is dead, people in Luwu insist that they feel the presence of Batara Guru everywhere, all around them, in everything. The world is "full," they say, with Batara Guru. I have the impression that Batara Guru's omnipresence is what makes meditation possible, since the purpose of meditation is to acquire potency. I was conversing about spiritual potency and other such matters several years ago with a Javanese *priyayi* (noble) and a Buginese high noble who were visiting America for several months, and we were discussing the American interest in Buddhism, meditation, and other Asian practices. Both these men had had the experience of finding that it was much harder to get their meditation to jadi (to "take" or to "jell") in America than in Indonesia. They attributed their difficulty to the fact that in America the surrounding world is "empty." Back in Java or in South Sulawesi, they said, they feel the world is "full." In South Sulawesi, "Batara Guru" is another name for the formless potency that is everywhere, the sumange' that infuses the visible world with life and effect and makes it "full."

Batara Guru cannot be located in a particular place. One old lady in Luwu, quite a high noble, was telling me over tea and the inevitable white cookies about how Batara Guru's presence could be felt everywhere. The context of her observations was a discussion of the importance of ancestors and ToMatoa. How much we look to our ToMatoa and our ancestors for protection and comfort, she said, and how disconcerting and discomfitting it is, when we are yearning to hear their voices giving us advice, to wake up one day and find that they have all already died. "We wake up one day and look around and where are they? They are already dead! WE are the ToMatoa!" she said, and people are looking to *us* for comfort and protection. That is why, she said, it is so comforting to visit our ancestors' graves, where we can feel their presence more strongly. But, she said, it is such a shame that Batara Guru has no grave! (She was speaking of Batara Guru as though he had died no more than a couple of generations ago, and as though the lack of a grave were a dreadful oversight that deprived his descendants.) I thought later about her regret, and why a grave for Batara Guru is impossible in the nature of things in Luwu. It would be culturally ungrammatical for Batara Guru to have a grave: it would mean that Batara Guru, or sumange', was confined by being locatable.

Batara Guru is the name for what is most formless and most potent, most invisible and unlocatable. Batara Guru is everywhere, and therefore nowhere: Batara Guru's place is so high that it is place-less, unlocated and unlocatable; he is perfectly one, but perfectly without form. Although it cannot truly be said of any ruler that "*mette' tenri bali, makkeda tenri sumpala*," the statement perfectly describes the condition of Batara Guru. There is no answering Other, for Batara Guru is everything: Batara Guru has no boundary. Batara Guru has no center because there is no edge. There is no empty space. The world is full.

Comparative Conclusion
The Political Geographies of Potency

The central problem raised by this conception of Power, by contrast with the Western tradidion of political theory, is not the exercise of Power but its accumulation.
—Benedict Anderson, "The Idea of Power in Javanese Culture"

"Navel of the world" or "head of state"? These phrases can be regarded as mere figures of speech, mere cultural idioms whose apparent contrast conceals an underlying uniformity in human motivations and political processes. Or they can be regarded, as I have viewed them in this book, as significant points of entrance into vastly different worlds.

As it is conceptualized, pursued, and accumulated in Luwu and the other former Indic States of insular Southeast Asia, potency invents a world in which peripheral matter is oriented around a common central point. The importance of location and placement generally in these areas, as I suggested in Chapter Two, is due to the fact that sumange' or the equivalent accumulates in particular locations. Any location can become imbued with potency, but some areas are intrinsically more able to accumulate and hold it. In the Indic States, of course, potency lay at the center. Mythically, potency descended (in the form of a spirit/ruler and precious regalia) from the Upper World to the Middle World, the level where humans live.

The ruler and regalia's location became by definition the polity's center. These events gave political geography a shape at once centered and vertical. The characteristic movement of potency in these states was *downward*, *out*, and *from a single source*. It created a polity in which humans, who are by definition lower and more peripheral, look upward and inward to the fount of potency.

Thus my explication of "power" in Luwu has been organized spatially, as a kind of sacred political geography: I have moved from stable centers in Part I, to de-centering in Part II, to the structures that tend to hold centers together in Part III.

I turn now to some further observations concerning potency within insular Southeast Asia, beginning with Luwu and the Indic States and then moving to the ways that potency constructs the political geographies of other societies of the area, especially the one I have termed the "Centrist

Archipelago." I make these comments in the interest of expanding an analysis of potency as a system of signs, of power viewed as a cultural system.

Potency is invisible: it is known by its signs. When the potent node is a person, the signs of potency include much wealth and a substantial number of followers. Thus people read the world as a system of signs signifying potency (see Comment on Part I, above). In C. S. Peirce's (1940: 98ff.) terms, "indexical signs" are those bearing an intrinsic connection to the things they signify. Thus heat is an indexical sign of fire, dark clouds an indexical sign of rain. The signs of potency in Luwu are indexical signs to their interpreters: body stance, level of name and title, number of followers, and so on, bear an intrinsic connection to the potency they signify. Because nearly everything was taken as or made into a sign of potency, the signs formerly had to be regulated, restricted, and controlled if the polity was to maintain its central and hierarchical shape.

"Restricted access to potency" could have been the motto of Indic States; it was fundamental to every aspect of their functioning. But since potency is invisible and is known by its signs, it was signs of potency, not potency itself, that could be regulated. The law system, as I described in Chapter Five, was devoted in no small part to this task; insofar as violence enforced the system of law/system of signs (and of course it did, although its use was considered in inverse proportion to the potency that wielded it), it was used by higher against lower in defense of restricted access. Names and titles, as I described in Chapter Eight, were used in such a way as to further disadvantage the disadvantaged and to promote the advantaged. Thus one can reasonably regard the polity, as I did in Chapter Five, as a vast apparatus whose purpose was regulating signs, and the ruler as the ultimate source, ceiling, and regulator of signs.

At base, potency is one, is centralized and unitary, in insular Southeast Asia's Indic States. But potency's unity, as conceptualized in this part of the world, implies duality, because being a center implies having a periphery. Its extended periphery is its audience; it requires a human audience both to signify it and to witness its presence. The audience of followers around a potent leader signifies the leader's potency to the yet wider audience of the world at large. These wider audiences, by orienting themselves around a potent node, bear witness to potency's presence.

The importance of audiences as signifiers of potency may be related to the importance of the performing arts throughout insular Southeast Asia. Dance, trance dance, public curing rites through spirit possession, shadow-puppet theater, public chanting of sacred texts—these are the characteristic and best known of the expressive forms of insular Southeast Asia. The po-

tency of the refined Javanese master-puppeteer (dalang) and of the sha-
man-curer in an isolated hill tribe alike are judged in good measure by the
sizes of the audiences their performances attract. These performances are
spectacles, and can be seen; but, as Mead (1942) pointed out some time
ago, the spectacles are moving ones whose visual figures are often obscured, and they invite the audience's kinesthetic participation at least as
much or more than they draw on the audience's visual capacities. The kinesthetic participation of the audience in these spectacles (something of a
misnomer, we now see) attests to the involvement, literally, of the audience
in the performance: the audience is part of the show, and is expected to be
affected by it. Moreover, sound—e.g., the gamelan musical accompani-
ment and the voices of the characters—not sight, is probably the dominant
sensory mode. This observation is confirmed by the fact that in central Java
the shadow-theater performances by great dalang are broadcast on the radio, and make perfect sense with no alteration, while if the same performances were videotaped without sound for television, say, they would be
utterly incomprehensible. Potency is invisible; it cannot be seen. But it can
be heard, and throughout insular Southeast Asia, sound seems to have a
privileged connection to it.

By the same token, attracting an audience is a political act. This fact is
behind Clifford Geertz's statement (1980: 13) that in nineteenth-century
Bali, power served pomp, rather than (as in the more usual formulations
of Occidental political theory) pomp serving power. Wealth, status, and
influence all were used in the interest of holding ceremonies. Wealth,
which in agriculture-based polities with an excess of land was predicated
largely on having followers who worked the land, was accumulated by potent central leaders, and was expended mainly not on private consumption
but on public ceremonies. Status was pursued as a good in itself, but high
status was also the precondition for having influence and attracting followers (who in turn signified, made visible, a center's status). Influence over
followers confirmed status (by signifying it) and brought wealth, for followers contributed significantly to their center-leader's wealth, particularly
on the occasion of ceremonies, which tested the followers' status along
with their leader's. The system was circular, as any cultural system is. Status
attracted followers, who produced wealth, which was used to hold ceremonies, which confirmed and promoted status, which attracted followers,
who produced wealth, which. . . . But the paradigmatic "political" events,
as I have demonstrated at some length, were ceremonies ("pomp"). These
were not the only such events, but they were the most spectacular and the
most public ones. They were competitions between centers-leaders; they
were demonstrations of potency, which is known by its signs (wealth, fol-

lowers); they were tests of potency, which attracts followers and wider audiences. Audiences are crucial to the demonstration of potency.

In the Indic States, potency was unitary, and its movement was from the center out. But since potency is invisible and generally impalpable, it cannot be perceived as doing anything. It cannot act on its own behalf. Thus it requires an agent who is embodied—visible, palpable, living, moving—to be its spokesperson. A center is helpless without its active sidekick, who is its agent and its connection with its audience. Thus the immobile, dead (hence potent, ancestral) regalia needed the moving, human ruler as its spokesperson and agent in the world. The nearly immobile, potent, but physically helpless ruler needed an Opu Pa'Bicara (a spokesperson) to convey the ruler's wishes. The Opu Pa'Bicara, in turn, was the high center within his own periphery formed by kapolo-followers, and needed his sulewatang (literally "exchanged body," substitute) to carry out his orders. And so on down the line.

ToLuwu express the relation of the two aspects of potency with a saying: "The keris is in the hands of the few, the axe is in the hands of the many." A keris is a sword of particular design, inherited and (formerly) carried only by nobles. It can be used in battle, but its virtue as a weapon lies in its animating spirit and the potency of the one who bears it. Unlike ordinary knives and swords, a keris has a sheath. The sheath shields its keris from the careless glance of the many, but it also protects the impotent many from the stinging moso of the keris. (*Moso*, mentioned in Chapter One, means "sting." Moso is the bite of a snake, the sharpness of a keris, the authority of a noble.) An axe, by contrast, is a crude tool used for practical matters like chopping wood and sago. Appropriately enough, keris were inherited and could not be bought and sold, whereas axes could be made or bought by anyone. Thus keris are non-circulating valuables, metaphorically immobile, like their possessors, whereas axes circulate through barter or money, and hence metaphorically move around, like their possessors. And keris, like their possessors and like impalpable potency, have little practical utility (a keris is useless for chopping wood), while the reverse is true for an axe. So the keris functions metonymically to exemplify noble potency, authority, and immobility, while the axe exemplifies brute force, the material basis of life, activity, practicality, utility, and movement. The contrast reveals the disjunction between what Occidentals call "prestige" or "dignity," and what we call "power": the former is empty and "merely symbolic" in our view, while "power" is active and practical, has a goal, and strives to achieve it. But dignity and "power" are not disjunctive in Luwu: they express the two necessary aspects of unitary potency.

The relations between the sexes, like other relations, can be mapped onto the political geography of potency. A man is more potent than his wife: he is the center of the relation, the encompassing, the unmoving, the more dignified. His wife is his active agent, his spokesperson, his periphery: she attends to practical needs, cooks, looks after children, takes care of money. In both Java and South Sulawesi, women have control over the family finances, and non-noble women are often merchants. Because they are active and control money, from an Occidental point of view they seem powerful and well off, and indeed in many respects they are. But their very "power" and activity reveal their inferior potency, because activity and practicality bear an inverse relation to dignity. Thus, ToLuwu say, a man without a wife is incomplete. He needs a wife to be malebu (Ind. *bulat*), spherical, round, complete, perfect, because dignity *does* nothing, it only *is*. Without a wife, a man is helpless in practical and household matters.

The relation between a sister and brother reverses the mapping of the sexes onto the political geography of potency. In that relation, the sister is the more dignified, status-conserving aspect, emblematic of her brother's honor. The ideal sister for a high-status man is a chaste, unmarried one, who remains a symbol of their joint social place without compromising it with a husband. I mentioned in Chapter Eight that this was the position of Opu Senga, unmarried sister of the Opu Pa'Bicara, the caretaker of the family's heirlooms, herself an heirloom.

Indeed, when it comes to honor, wives (who are substitutes for sisters, as I explained in Chapter Eight) and sisters stand as the dignified aspect of a relation in which men are the defending periphery, both figuratively and (on ceremonial occasions) literally. Thus a woman needs a man, whether husband or brother, in order to be malebu. She is more like a keris than an axe when it comes to honor, and she is helpless to defend herself. She needs a *ToMasiri'*, a guardian of her siri', to accompany her when she leaves the house.

It is therefore impossible to elicit the statement from a Buginese or Makassarese man that women are inferior to men; on the contrary, they insist that they value them highly, as precious creatures to respect. (Other men's sisters at first glance appear to be another matter entirely, since the most effective way to humiliate another man is to make familiar overtures to his sister; but there, too, her value as a victim of excessive familiarity lies precisely with her high value as emblem of his honor.) In discussing the body and house in Chapter Two, I mentioned that women, as practical wives who do the cooking, occupy the area of the house that corresponds to the anal-genital area of the human body. The kitchen is in the back, is often lower than the rest of the house, and from it people descend the back steps in order to take out the garbage or go to the fields to defecate. All this would argue the inferiority of women. Yet at the same time, the unmarried girls of high-noble families used to stay in the most elevated part of the house, the rekeang, the area where the family heirlooms and precious rice were stored—especially when "guests" came to ceremonies held in the front. These two spatial locations of women in the household express the problem they present to their associated men. Women (paradigmatically, sisters) are not inferior to men in Luwu, but they are weaker (more like keris than like axes), and at the same time are dignified precious emblems of honor. This combination makes women a tremendous hazard to their associated men. Like the genital and anal areas of the person, the house's "lower" and "back" area is out of sight and off-limits to other people, especially ToLaing, who literally cannot penetrate into the back area of the house. "Batas Tamu," "off-limits to guests," say hand-lettered signs between the front and back of some houses. (In a society that conceives of invulnerability as hardness and impenetrability, the fact that women are penetrated in the sexual act is probably not without significance. Women's association with the lower-back of the house expresses the precise locus of their vulnerability.) But like heads, women are the emblem of their men's honor; like heads, their place is "high"; like heads, they must not be closely approached; like heads, they can be penetrated by intrusive external elements. Like heads, they are a precious hazard.

How gender is mapped onto potency brings up another matter: the "effeminacy," to European eyes, of the high-status *halus* (refined, potent) men of the insular Indic States. The Javanese hero Arjuna, who appears in shadow theater, is slight of build, soft of voice, with downcast eyes and quiet demeanor. These are precisely the qualities valued in high-status ladies. Yet Arjuna confronts the *rakasasa* (monsters), who reveal themselves to be such by their huge ungainly shapes, their insolently staring, bulging eyes, hideous laughs, and growls and shouts—and Arjuna wins with a flick of the finger. This confrontation, of course, is not between empty dignity and active "power," but between the keris and the axe, between conscious potency and unconscious brute force. The point is not that the high potent noble man is effeminate, but that he and high-noble women are more like the keris than the axe. Gender is mapped onto potency, rather than the reverse.

The unity of potency, I have been suggesting, implies duality, because being a center implies having a periphery; being a keris implies having an axe to serve you. Significantly enough, in some parts of insular Southeast Asia and Polynesia, potency is conceptualized as intrinsically dual. Samoans, for instance, divide the chief function into two aspects of a potent whole, each embodied in a different person: the Sitting Chief (who expresses dignity) and the Talking Chief (who orates and inspires) (see e.g., Shore 1976, 1982). In this respect it seems worth noting that the most important of the four ministers in Luwu was the Opu Pa'Bicara, the Lord Spokesperson; the parallel is exact. As Shore (1976) has shown, the logic of power between men and women shows the same dual structure in Samoa. Duality between the sexes and in nearly everything else, including potency, characterizes Eastern Indonesia. Many of these societies also formerly had two chiefs, one the inner dignified "Mother" Chief, the other the outer active "Father" Chief (both were usually men). The fact that these societies represented potency to themselves as dual, as split into two aspects of nearly (though not quite) equal prestige, itself indexes the fact that in these societies, potency was never fully captured by an entity that could claim symbolic hegemony, as happened in the insular Indic States. (Indeed, these societies institutionalized potency in ways that mitigated the chances or made impossible potency's hegemonic accumulation.) In Luwu and other insular Indic States, potency was more spread out, less compressed; and center and periphery formed an infinite range of gradations.

An analogous analysis could be made of the politics of accumulation of potency in other societies of insular Southeast Asia, for if potency is, as Anderson writes about Java, "that intangible, mysterious, and divine energy which animates the universe . . . ," "manifested in every aspect of the natural world, in stones, trees, clouds, and fire, . . ." then the Indic States were not the only societies in insular Southeast Asia that shared a preoccupation with accumulating it. "This conception of the entire cosmos being suffused by a formless, constantly creative energy," Anderson continues, "provides the basic link between the 'animism' of the Javanese villages, and the high metaphysical pantheism of the urban centers" (Anderson 1972: 7). It also forms a basic link between the former Indic States and the villages on their extreme peripheries, and provides the basis for the politics of many of the so-called hill tribes of the area. Potency in these more level societies and part-societies, of course, necessarily shapes a different political geography.

Like ToLuwu, the people within these more level societies read each other and objects as signs of potency. It is obvious to them that no person or alliance of persons within these societies can claim hegemonic access to potency: no one, in these societies, has a monopoly or near-monopoly on followers and wealth. Of course, some people are able to acquire a little more wealth than others, and some can acquire larger audiences or more clients or allies (as orators, shamans, dispute-settlers, or expedition-leaders), and their prestige within the community increases concomitantly; but these are temporary followers, not permanently attached to their leaders. From the outside, we can point out that the economies of these societies (which generally have very small surpluses) are not conducive to promoting large discrepancies in wealth, nor (in the most level societies) do people have access to the ideas that would justify a cross-generational transfer of status or prestige.[1] Thus their politics of accumulation and of restriction of potency are vastly different from those of the Indic States.

In hill tribes, the collection of potency tends to be open to everyone, and prestige is, as a consequence, "achieved." ("Everyone" includes women, in both Indic States and hill tribes. But, for reasons I have mentioned regarding Indic States and will mention regarding hill tribes, women tend to be less successful collectors of potency.) Individuals may become prominent over the course of their lifetimes, depending on their own luck and skills. But the discrepancy in wealth between richer and poorer in these societies is not enormous, and people in these societies have few institutionalized ways of transferring prestige or potency (like titles or white blood) from one generation to the next.[2]

The source of potency is also different in these more level societies. Since signs of large accumulations of potency are patently lacking within them, people in these smaller societies typically look outside to find and acquire it: to the forest, source of spirit familiars; to the coastal towns on the periphery of Indic States; to the invisible realm of spirits, accessible by trance. The movement of potency into such societies can be conceptualized as *lateral*, moving directionally *from the outside to the inside*, and *from multiple sources* rather than from a single coherent source.

The meaning of physical movement, by the same token, differs between the Indic States and hill tribes. In the Indic States, the theme of stasis figures prominently in the construction of political geography. I mentioned

[1] Wealth in insular Southeast Asian terms is a sign of potency, not a cause; but whether sign or cause, the two imply each other, in either a local Southeast Asian or a secular point of view. From this it does not follow that poor societies are necessarily egalitarian in ideology. Many Eastern Indonesian societies are predicated on an idea of hierarchical difference without having much economic stratification (see Traube 1986). Absence of wealth in insular Southeast Asia means the absence of a way of sustaining large numbers of followers or of holding massive ceremonies. Thus, from a secular historical perspective, it is no accident that the great Indic States of Southeast Asia arose in the fertile wet-rice-growing areas of Java and Bali, and at strategically placed points on the lucrative coasts, where trade could produce large surpluses.

[2] This contrastive characterization applies to Indic States and the simplest, most level of the hill tribes; but insular Southeast Asia includes numerous hill tribes that are somewhat stratified (such as the Toraja of South Sulawesi or the Ifugao of Luzon) and are very much a mixed bag of inherited and achieved status. (So are Indic States, for that matter; what is inherited tends to be the privilege to compete for an office or title rather than the office or title itself.) The function of potency accumulation and cross-generational transfer in these societies is too tangential to my main argument and too complex to explicate here.

in the Comment at the end of Part I that in the Indic States, the center stays still while the periphery moves: their differential movement constructs as well as expresses their relative social places. And in the Local Conclusion, I pointed out that when the ruler physically circumambulated the realm, he nonetheless metaphorically stayed still, for he was moving only within his social place, the realm itself.

The political geography that potency constructs for hill-tribe people is an outward-looking one, in contrast to the inward- and upward-looking politics of Indic States, and the meaning of literal and figurative movement there is consequently different. The prominence of the journey in insular Southeast Asia as a symbolic form and social experience strikes me as related to this configuration of potency. Unlike rulers of Indic States, who figuratively stay still, ordinary men who seek potency in many societies of insular Southeast Asia figuratively and literally travel far. They leave their local settlements and travel into the unknown, seeking wealth and often other things as well (amulets, spirit familiars, invulnerability magic); and then they return home. This looping journey has a special name in many insular Southeast Asian societies, but in Indonesian it is widely known by its Minangkabau name, *merantau*. We could similarly think of the trances of hill-tribe shamans as journeys away from their human settlements into the spirit world, where they collect potency and then return.[3]

Indeed, it is common in these hill tribes for men's feeling of superiority over women to be explained as due to men's ability to move. Let me preface this observation by pointing out that throughout most of insular Southeast Asia, certainly in the part I have termed the "Centrist Archipelago," potency is a sexually neutral energy, and brother and sister are considered the same type of being, aspects or descendants of the same *pu* or ancestral source. People in the Centrist Archipelago tend not to explain the difference between men and women as located directly in their respective anatomies or in the types of potency or energies they can tap, for they tap the same energy (sumange' in Luwu). But men do tend to acquire more potency and prestige than women, and it is striking that among at least several hill tribes they explain the difference between the sexes in terms of

---

[3] This looping movement in fact has a parallel in Indic States as well, although it is not part of the institutionalized accumulation of potency that we can call the "State." Great warriors, rulers, and mystics could leave the center and go meditate in the forest, the way Arjuna, a hero of the Javanese shadow-puppet theater, does in preparation for battle. Signficantly, such practitioners of "high metaphysical pantheism," in Anderson's phrase, *meditated* in the forest rather than going into trance or searching for spirit familiars, so that their methods of acquiring potency outside the realm paralleled their techniques within it. Such journeys to forests or to the mountainous abodes of the gods beyond the institutionalized center of the Indic States are representations or acknowledgments that potency lies outside the ruler, ultimately uncontrollable by human efforts, and ultimately a cosmic rather than human energy.

movement. Among the Ilongot of Luzon, men are said to have "higher hearts"; they are braver and travel far distances, while women stay at home (M. Z. Rosaldo 1980). Among the Wana of Central Sulawesi, being a shaman is the highest position of prestige, and it is an achieved position. Some Wana women become shamans, but very few. Their disadvantage with respect to men in their quest for shamanic potency, which could be seen in terms of the division of labor, can also be indexed in terms of their movement. Men hunt, fish, tap damar, and collect other forest products, activities that take them alone into the forest, the abode of spirit familiars; men travel to the coast to trade and get wealth; men cut down the forest to make new fields. Women, encumbered by children, move more slowly and tend to stay closer to the settlement; when they travel to ceremonies, they go in groups; they work old fields rather than create new. Thus men's movement is characteristically quick, alone, and in realms that contain potency and wealth, while women's movement is characteristically slow, encumbered, in groups, and close to the impotent settlement (cf. Atkinson 1989 and forthcoming). But when Wana women do become shamans, as happens occasionally, they have not broken the rules but beaten the odds, in Atkinson's memorable phrase.

Men travel far to get potency; yet when they return to their settlements, they must become centers. They must attract audiences and followers to show their potency: shamans must have clients, wise old leaders must be brought cases to settle, warriors must collect allies for expeditions, orators must collect neighbors to harangue. Because the source of potency is always elsewhere (in the forest or the coast), not intrinsic to the bodies or beings of the men, the men are only spokespersons for a potency for which they are mere vehicles.[4] Not surprisingly, then, the sort of potency one sees in hill tribes is more active than dignified. The ultra-refined demeanor and quiescence characteristic of Indic States is notoriously (from the point of view of nobles in Indic States) lacking in hill tribes, whose people are characterized as direct, loud, straightforward, and crude by the denizens of Indic States.

Where does that leave the brother-sister and husband-wife pairs? Throughout insular Southeast Asia, including the Indic States, the hill tribes of the Centrist Archipelago, and societies of Eastern Indonesia, founding myths often include a brother and sister who travel together,

---

[4] Nearly the same thing could be said of high nobles in Indic States: there, too, potency is impersonal and non-human, and the person is a vehicle rather than a source. But potency in the form of "white blood" is intrinsic to the noble's body in Luwu, and it is augmented by the noble's conscious awareness. Thus potency, while impersonal, is firmly located in the individual person in a way it is not in more level societies that have little concept of the inheritability of potency.

perhaps commit incest, and who are ultimately separated. Yet brothers and sisters do not seem to carry the heavy symbolic load in hill tribes that they do in Indic States, for reasons that I suggested in Chapter Eight: when little potency can be accumulated or conveyed across generations, the relative importance of marrying "close" is correspondingly less. Siblings are soon replaced by wives, and in hill tribes, the husband-wife pair, it is my impression, is more nearly the icon of the male-female bond than is the brother-sister pair. Sisters and wives stand along with undistinguished men in these level societies as "everyman," the generalized other, the generalized audience, the backdrop against which potent men stand out.

The centeredness of these level settlements is similarly undifferentiated. To my knowledge, peoples of the Centrist Archipelago's hill tribes, like those of Indic States, live within ritual spaces. So, for instance, the Iban long house, analogous to a village, is a space made ritually safe; similarly, the Wana settlement is a ritual space in the sense that people within it can affect others within it by their actions. They urge each other to "unity," "following together," much as people do in Luwu. Similarly, the "unity" can be broken by incest and other transgressions, which can bring cosmic disasters, diseases, and the like on the people within the ritual spaces. In Luwu, ritual/social spaces are hierarchical, and the images ToLuwu use to express unity tend to be concentric: they see the egg as a symbol of perfection, for instance—a bounded space, concentrically differentiated; they say that the ceremonial food *onde-onde*, sticky-rice balls enclosing a palm-sugar center, represents unity and completeness; and lower nobles describe their relation with their ToMatoa as "an iris, a pupil," thus describing a centralized and hierarchical unity. But the ritual space of a very level hill tribe, it is my impression, tends not to be hierarchical or centered. If we imagine a hill tribe's ritual space as an egg, it would be composed of all white, without a yolk. Indeed, how could it have a yolk? The source of potency is outside it, not within it. No location within it has a special status.

General Conclusion
Empowered Signs

Potency is real for the people who have constructed their social worlds around it. It exists; it is neither good nor bad. It stands, in their lives, more like the law of gravity than like the Ten Commandments in Euro-American cosmology. A Euro-American who wants to survive and prosper treats gravity with respect. In a world that operates within the law of gravity, common sense, more than ethics, suggests that stepping off high buildings would be foolish. In the same way, in many parts of Southeast Asia, common sense suggests that it is foolhardy to treat an extremely potent place, human or otherwise, with disrespect. One can suffer ill fortune from courting danger as surely as one suffers from falling off a high building. Living in accordance with the analogue of the law of gravity is both wise and virtuous in such a society. It is foolish to incur ill fortune by being disrespectful to potent people and spirits, but it is also wrong, because it erodes the order of the world, and imperils human access to the potency that, when tapped, brings fertility, health, wealth, and peace. Moral value, then, is predicated on what people think is the structure of the real: people see an intrinsic connection between the way they take things to be and the way they imagine people should act.[1]

Thus, signs may be arbitrary from the perspective of the outsider, but to the people who live them, they do not seem so. *They* think the signs they use and live within reflect reality, that symbols and their referents bear an intrinsic relation to each other. What to Saussure would seem an arbitrary sign, to its users would seem motivated; what to Peirce would be a "symbol" (a sign with an arbitrary relation to its referent) to its users would be, in Peirce's terms, an "indexical sign" (one with an intrinsic relation to its

---

[1] This view of the relation between the real and the moral is basic to much of Clifford Geertz's writing. See especially his article "Religion as a Cultural System" (1973d) and the section of *Islam Observed* (1968) called "The Struggle for the Real." In these Geertzian-Weberian accounts, a conjunction between the real and the moral are seen as characteristic of worlds that are "enchanted," while disenchanted secular folk see a gap between the structure of the real and how they should conduct their lives. But actually, no culture is entirely secular or disenchanted in this sense: all humans seek to ground their moral lives on non-arbitrary grounds, in non-arbitrary metaphors. For a brave modern liberal effort to ground values in "reality," which also addresses the matter explicitly, see Ernest Gellner's *Thought and Change* (1965).

referent). As Bourdieu puts it, "When there is a quasi-perfect correspon-
dence between the objective order and the subjective principles of organization (as in ancient societies) the natural and social world appears as self-
evident" (Bourdieu 1977: 164). And this is how humans, by and large,
would prefer it to be. Few humans seek doubt and skepticism with enthu-
siasm, or feel comfortable in a world where they are made conscious every
moment that signifier and signified are permanently unglued.

But the realities that humans imagine and create are, within the constraints imposed by our embodiment and the physical laws of the universe,
very disparate. Because the nineteenth-century heritage of social science
tends to oppose and contrast material conditions and interpretations of
them as "materialist" and "idealist" respectively, even though a number of
approaches developed in this century (including the one I have been explicating and proposing here) are neither, it is important not to be misunderstood on this matter of constraints and arbitrariness. Culture, a collection
or system of signs that is humanly produced and can be successfully lived
out, is indeed constrained by the material world (our own human embodiment and perceptual apparatus, and the needs produced by our embodiment, and the physical environments in which humans live), and thus is
not entirely arbitrary, not entirely free to "think itself," as Lévi-Strauss so
dramatically phrased it. From one perspective, these constraints are enormous: they begin with the facts that we eat (as Marx put it) and that water
runs downhill, and extend to all the elaborations of those truisms and
truths. But those constraints, while enormous from one perspective, are
negligible from another. The perspective that calls them negligible is this:
that the constraints do not shape or determine a system of signs (to put it
crudely: we cannot predict a culture from its environment, or a people's
concept of the body from the fact that we are embodied beings); they
merely constrain its outer limits. Thus we cannot "read" a culture from its
physical environment, and the superstructure does not reflect perfectly, or
even very well, the material conditions on which it rests. We can say, then,
that by and large, the systems of signs that are constrained by physical
conditions (gravity, the necessity of eating, etc.) nonetheless do not "reflect" them, and for most purposes of cultural analysis have a conventional,
if not actually arbitrary, relation to them. More accurately, they have a
dialectical relation, for each shapes the other.

Realities can be disparate from culture to culture because cultures are
not what they imagine themselves to be, natural entities intrinsically connected to the structure of the cosmos, but rather are systems of signs, systems of representations whose relation to the structure of physical, natural
reality is conventional and relatively arbitrary (again, within the constraints

imposed by physical nature and human embodiment). For the most part, systems of signs are arbitrary, for the simple reason that signs seldom point to relations that really are "indexical" (like the relation of heat to fire or clouds to rain), but to themselves, to cultural facts (e.g. white blood is potent), which have been made to seem real in particular times and places.

Thus the first project of a culture—any culture—is what Roland Barthes calls "mythologizing": to make the merely cultural appear natural, to make what is human and contingent appear to reflect the nature of reality. The first struggle of a system of signs is to promote itself as non-arbitrary, as real, as a reflection of the very structure of the cosmos, and therefore as able to define what is ultimately valuable. Mythologizing takes effort, and perhaps ultimately requires force. As the joke goes: "What is the difference between a language and a dialect?" Answer: "A language is a dialect—with an army and a navy." Any dialect of signs tries to assert that it is not only a language but Language, the voice of reality itself. Ultimately, the dialect of signs makes good its claim to be Language by using an army and a navy, or whatever along those lines it can muster. (In very unstratified societies it may be only the force of public opinion.)

The ultimate arbitrariness of signs, the fact that all "languages" are really dialects with big guns, should not lead us to either of two related false conclusions.

One false conclusion is that, since those signs are ultimately conventional and to that extent "untrue," the people pursuing the things they regard as most valuable cannot, at base, be serious: they must actually be pursuing what the historical and social-scientific imagination regards as real and valuable—wealth and power. I have tried to show, in the preceding pages, that it is far more enlightening to take what is locally regarded as real and valuable as the lynchpin of the political process, a stance that provides a way of construing privilege and competition that allows them to be reconciled with a study of meaning. Studying the polity of Luwu as though it were a huge device for accumulating potency and restricting access to it (rather than, say, as an oppressive structure to exploit the poor, or as an irrational frame in which to pursue advantage) in the end illuminates more about the meanings, the occasions, and therefore the substance of exploitation, wealth, status, advantage, goals, calculation, and the like, than would an analysis that bypasses local ideas as self-deception, bad faith, the masses' opiate, or irrational beliefs and values.

The second, related false conclusion is this: that although *their* systems of signs are arbitrary, our own are not. This is the stance that says, in effect: *they* are superstitious and possibly irrational, pursuing the acquisition of large tubers, white blood, or whatever; *we* see clearly what the structure of the universe is, which allows us to speak with "objectivity" about theirs.

Some of the most talented de-mythologizers of the dominant systems of signs backed by force in Euro-America are, not surprisingly, semiotic Marxists (usually French). That is because the dominant system of signs and the forces that mythologize it and make it real in Euro-America are intimately entwined with capitalism, and semiotic Marxists, standing where they do, see clearly both the arbitrariness of the signs and the forces that make them socially real.

One such writer is Pierre Bourdieu, whose notions of "habitus," "symbolic capital," and "symbolic violence" take us a long way towards a reconciliation between materialist and cultural understandings of social processes, for he does not privilege the material over the meaningful or symbolic, or vice versa. One of his arguments is against what he calls "economism," a stance taken by many materialists and Marxists. He rebukes "economism" for dividing the world into rational calculating economies (those with a money economy) and irrational non-calculating economies (those preoccupied with, e.g., honor and ceremonies of redistribution), condemning them for "naively idyllic representations of pre-capitalist societies (or the 'cultural' sphere of capitalist societies)" (Bourdieu 1977: 177). So far, so good. Moreover, Bourdieu wants to insist that the participants in non-money societies are far from being "disinterested" (as he claims a naive and romantic "economism" would have it), that the elite of the honor and redistribution systems of "pre-capitalist formations" try to remain on top. Again, so far, so good. But his solution for closing the gap between "us" and "them," capitalists and pre-capitalists, in order to escape the "ethnocentrism" of "economism," is to extend economism's metaphor:

> The only way to escape from the ethnocentric naiveties of economism, without falling into populist exaltation of the generous naivety of earlier forms of society, is to carry out in full what economism does only partially, and to extend economic calculation to all the goods, material and symbolic, without distinction, that present themselves as rare and worthy of being sought after in a particular social formation—which may be "fair words" or smiles, handshakes or shrugs, compliments or attention, challenges or insults, honour or honours, powers or pleasures, gossip or scientific information, distinction or distinctions, etc. (Bourdieu 1977: 178)

In short, to avoid suggesting that some people are irrational because they do not maximize, he insists that everyone is ultimately a rational maximizer; and rational, for Bourdieu, means "calculating," "calculating advantage." For him, people in "pre-capitalist" formations accumulate "symbolic capital" and perform "symbolic violence," but these activities are as economically rational as the accumulation of economic capital, taking place as they do in societies where "the accumulation of symbolic capital [is] the only recognized, legitimate form of accumulation" (Bourdieu 1977: 180). His stance in these passages is actually the tautological Utilitarianism I outlined in the Introduction. Thus Bourdieu trades one ethnocentrism for another.

Closing the gap between the observer and the observed, the "us" of monetized economies and the "them" of pre- or non-money economies, by putting both into the same universe of discourse is an admirable project, and it is worth noting in Bourdieu's own work how far this tautological Utilitarian stance, which does not prejudge what is real or valuable, can take us. But seeing "them" as just like "us," calculators, is not the only way to close the gap between us. It is not the only way to "escape the ethnocentric naiveties of economism" while steering clear of romanticism and "populist exaltation" of non-money economies.

A different way to close the gap does not claim that "they," at base, are just like "us," but recognizes that *we* are much like *them*. We, like them, are socially formed; we, like them, live within systems of signs and dominant metaphors that are ultimately conventional; we, like them, live in social worlds that seem real to us because they have been made real by the powers that be; we, like them, can engage in conversation with people of vastly different worlds, but cannot view them "objectively," from stances outside what our respective cultures allow us to do; we, like them, continually interpret and translate what they say into terms we understand, which, like the terms (signs, metaphors, figures of speech) they use, are ultimately cultural products. This way of closing the gap does not promote the use of alien metaphors (such as the metaphor of calculation for all forms of thought, psychological and material investment, and modes of understanding and living in the world) to be imposed or projected onto alien thought processes and social processes, as though a metaphor produced by "us" had a privileged relation to the real.

At the same time, to recognize that the people who live within a system of signs take them to be non-arbitrary, and to ground one's analysis on that fact, is not the same as taking a believer's stance. It is very difficult to write a sociology of religion if one is a believer, and it would be very difficult to write an account of white blood and siri' if one were involved in acquiring and defending them. Or rather, one could, but the account would look less like this book and more like Buginese lontara'. As modes of knowledge, history and social science require a secular stance towards their objects of study. By "secular" I mean something like "disbelieving" or "disen-

chanted." Anthropology, in requiring its practitioners to participate-ob-
serve, has elevated to the state of "method" the Occidental human condition: it requires its practitioners to be believers and disbelievers
simultaneously, or at least alternately. One must live with the tension intrinsic to the condition of seeing systems of signs as real for the people to
whom they are real (and have been made real culturally, for one can kill or
die for siri', whether or not white blood is ultimately an arbitrary, nay illusory sign), while knowing that those signs are arbitrary for oneself—and
one must know that one is, like them, the denizen of a system of signs that
is also arbitrary, but has been made real in a particular time and place. The
world is all that is the case; the system of signs is what is.

Because mythologizing takes effort, often including the use of force; and
because mythologizing defines what is valuable as a by-product of what it
defines as real, and institutionalizes it as something that humans can aspire
to attain—because of these, mythologizing can be studied as a political
process.

A quick survey of human societies reveals that what can be institutionalized as real and valuable varies wildly: value is certainly not limited by
considerations of utility or palpability. Sacred rocks, Kula valuables, enemies' preserved heads, piebald cattle, crumbling ancient books in languages no one can understand, stocks and bonds, white blood, ancestral
bones, overgrown tubers too big to carry—anything that one can think of,
and many that one would not, can be institutionalized as valuable. Sometimes these valuables are reified as objects, in which case they may be cir-
culated or stationary, each with different effects in the constitution of society's shape; sometimes what is most valuable is viewed as an impalpable
substance, exhibited in a person's aptitudes and demeanor but unable to be
stored or exchanged.

When acquired and used in socially approved ways, valuables bring prestige. Some societies make a point of not restricting access to the items or
qualities that bring prestige. Those societies are relatively "level" (as opposed to "hierarchical"), partly because they may work hard at keeping
everyone "the same." They may prohibit the acquisition of too much prestige by individuals through accusations of sorcery, or they may have social
mechanisms and an ethos whose express purpose is to discourage anyone
from standing out in prestige or in acquiring more valuables than everyone
else. I have often referred to the Ilongot of Luzon as an exemplar of one
such society, as explicated by M. Z. Rosaldo (1980); societies like this are
adamant about being composed of "peers," people who are all "the same."

In other societies, competition may be fierce and overt and may allow a social scale of differentiation in prestige. So, for instance, Big Men in New Guinea spend their lives acquiring and distributing valuables whose distribution makes them into "big" men. They hold in contempt the "rubbish men" who do not work hard enough or manage well enough to succeed at what their society values. But culturally specific mechanisms ensure that no Big Man can defeat his rivals permanently, and they limit the transfer of prestige to his heirs. Would-be heirs begin their political lives with the same resources as others of their own generation, and must strive on their own to make themselves "big." The continual collapsing of structures of differentiation in prestige due to the fact that they are personal networks rather than structures of offices makes these societies appear "egalitarian" when viewed from the outside. But in fact, as Bateson pointed out long ago (Bateson [1935] 1972a), their structure is asymmetrical but reciprocal. Their ethos and politicking are very different from those of the adamantly "level" societies of the sort sketched above.

Stratified and hierarchical societies have excited considerably more interest on the part of political analysts than have relatively level ones even though the latter need as much explaining as the former, probably because it is in the analysis of non-level societies that something emerges that is recognizable to the historical and social-scientific imagination as politics, exploitation, and domination. We call a society "stratified" or "hierarchical" when it restricts access to what it values most highly to a small proportion of its members, and when it supplies them with the means to convey the valuables (or the right of access to them) across generations. To study the politics of these societies, we must ask as usual: What does the society take to be real and valuable? How does it construct itself so as to *make* real what it takes to be real? What categories of people have access to what is valued? How is it conveyed across generations? Who controls the access? How is that control enforced?

An account of ambition and competition, of restriction and coercion, can be "cultural" in that goals and ambitions are taken on their own terms, rather than as though they stand as tokens or cover-ups for the acquisition of "real" wealth, status, and power. Values and valuables that to the analyst are worthless, or invisible, or immaterial (as many would put it, "symbolic" rather than "real"), inspire as much ambition, or more, than do the acquisition of wealth or the exercise of power. Access to those valuables may be controlled with as much force or more than is access to the items the analyst believes are worth having. What compels the highest and deepest emotions or the most sustained ambitions and vicious competition in one society may be regarded as the merest superstition in a second, or as perverse and disgusting in a third. Because something is useless or is coded as superstition in one society does not mean that it cannot form the lynchpin of the real and the valued in another. Around it, social life may be organized, ambitions directed, and sensibilities formed.

Human sensibilities are no less local than the goals and contexts that shape them. The psychology (broadly defined) and political strategy of a Big Man seeking shells is different from that of a Buddhist monk in Burma seeking merit and from that of a stockbroker in New York seeking profit. The actors in a political process exhibit not a universal human nature but a local one, with local emotions and local ambitions. Humans and the goals they seek have an intrinsic connection for the simple reason that, like text and context, valuables and the sorts of human natures that seek them shape each other. Political activity, no less than art, requires and constructs the sensibilities that can comprehend it.

Epilogue

Wealth . . . status . . . power. What counts as wealth, the perquisites of status, the pleasures and responsibilities of power, are as locally construed as the most arcane and poetic religious text. And they are, as well, locally pursued: what prompts the sensibilities fostered in a particular society to find them desirable, how their attainment is interpreted and is evaluated by people at large, are as culturally invented and socially maintained as the items we label "myths." The forms of aggression and ambition are cultural artifacts, not raw emotions; they are prompted, are channelled, and retreat, on cultural cues. For how can a world's inhabitants act and react, except in the terms given them?

Culture is circular, but not unchanging. Probably the most radical changes in a system of signs are made when circumstances change in fundamental ways and humans, who inevitably interpret, are forced to make new sense of new circumstances.

Prior to World War II and Indonesian Independence, the structure of the akkarungeng was maintained in Luwu under Dutch rule. It was not like the nineteenth century, for under the Dutch, boundaries were drawn between the warring polities of South Sulawesi, slave-raiding and slave-trading were suppressed, and other changes were made. But rulers and high nobles maintained both authority and the legitimate force to uphold the restricted access to potent signs on which the vertical, centered polity rested.

Indonesian Independence removed legitimate force from the polities of South Sulawesi, transferring it to Jakarta. The akkarungeng and other such polities of South Sulawesi were dismantled, becoming districts in the new republic. Since General Suharto replaced General Sukarno as the president of Indonesia in the mid-1960s, the national agenda has shifted in ways that encourage the monetization of everyday life and make available new opportunities to make money. General Suharto has encouraged the exploitation of natural resources, especially oil and timber; in South Sulawesi, tourism, especially to Tana Toraja, has grown at an astronomical rate since the mid-1970s. This new wealth is used sometimes for consumption, but a good deal of it is used for rather traditional activities—bridewealth, funerals. People formerly of low status and relative poverty are now wealthy, and no ruler issues edicts on how many water buffaloes they can sacrifice at funerals. As a result, funeral displays in Tana Toraja have become yet more spectacular, and sometimes have the effect of impoverishing the newly wealthy, as nothing prevents, indeed everything encourages, their using all their wealth for ceremonies (cf. Volkman 1984, 1985; Crystal 1977). As James Boon (1979) has commented about Bali, "Reenchantment is taking place before disenchantment has made much headway."

Fundamentalist versions of Islam that seek to promote an Islamic state and, especially, that locate potency in the "clean souls" of religious believers, regardless of their inheritance of white blood, have made some progress in South Sulawesi. White blood and marrying white blood continue to be matters of great prestige. But since it is becoming far more unusual to have multiple wives, a wealthy and high-status man tends to choose a woman with the purest white blood available to him for his single wife. Monogamous marriages and sources of wealth outside a family following effectively shift social relations from hierarchy to stratified class relations: the different levels of white blood become isolated from each other both as families and in function.

South Sulawesians continue to strive to differentiate themselves from each other on the basis of prestige, but there is no coherent hierarchy of prestige, and no ceiling on the systems of signs. As the opportunities to gain vast quantities of money arise, and as ideas promoting the pursuit of money as distinct from or in opposition to social relations become more and more prominent (and they will be, since they are promoted as part of "development" and "modernization"), then the circularity of the relations between having status, having followers, having wealth, and holding ceremonies breaks down. The material and symbolic terms in which people are conscious and pursue their lives change. Social evolutionist nineteenth-century thinkers were wrong to imagine that the rest of the world is moving of its own accord, with its own internal dynamic, towards "us," towards the constructions that Europe mythologizes, makes real. But it is true that when a dialect comes on the scene with bigger guns than any other dialect has ever had before, it becomes the language of the day, and other dialects accommodate themselves to it.

Once I was speaking with the Opu Pa'Bicara about kesaktian, the Indonesian term for what I have been calling "potency." I was surprised when he asserted that it no longer exists in the world.

"The era of akkarungeng and datu is over," he said. "Now is the era of 'demokrasi' and the rakyat [the people, the many]. Kesaktian has disappeared from the world."

"But Opu," I objected, "there are still people with clean souls. There are still things that are makerre'. How can you say kesaktian has utterly disappeared?"

"If a pail of water is carried," he answered, "the water moves. If it is set down, the water continues to move, but only briefly. Its energy is used up. Gone. Vanished."

Glossary

ABUSUNGENG (Bug.) The nominal form of *mabusung*

AKKARUNGENG Polity or "kingdom," from the root *arung*, lord or noble

ALMARHUM (Arabic) "The respected deceased"

ARAJANG Royal "regalia" or "ornaments"; the inherited objects from royal ancestors that, with the ruler and residence, defined the center of the realm. Only state
regalia were called *arajang*; personal inherited objects are called *mana'*. See
mana' and *pusaka*

ASEDDINGENG Fright resulting in diminished consciousness, presumed to result
from the loosening of the bond of sumange' with the body

ATA Slave or humble servant

BACA To read; to interpret; to interpret and then gossip about what one has seen;
to utter out loud. *Baca-baca* is to say spells

BATANG See *watang*

BEMO A small passenger van that runs between villages or towns

BERTAPA (Ind.) To do ascetic exercises, such as not sleeping or eating

DATU Ruler. This word (or its cognate *ratu*) is used throughout the Austronesian-
speaking world to mean a ruler or leader. In Luwu, only the ruler was known as
the datu; in Buginese polities to the south, the children of the ruler could also be
addressed and known as "Datu Such-and-Such"

DEWATA Spirit of the Upper or Lower World

GADO-GADO (Jav. and Ind.) A Javanese dish, eaten widely throughout Indonesia,
consisting of a variety of lightly-cooked vegetables with a peanut sauce.

GAMELAN (Jav. and Ind.) An ensemble of mainly percussion instruments used
throughout Java

JIN An invisible spirit, usually one that causes trouble

KABUSUNGANG (Tae) The nominal form of *mabusung*

KAPOLO Often translated as *pamili* ("family") in contrast to *ToLaing*, a kapolo may
contain a few people or an enormous number of followers. The core of a kapolo
consists of the most prominent member's siblings and other close relatives, especially of lower status than himself or herself

KASALLA' The affliction a person incurs by offending the order of the cosmos, particularly by offending the dignity of a person or thing whose social place is lower and less potent than one's own. For instance, a woman who had killed a cat in a rage with a kitchen knife because it kept stealing food later went crazy. She was said to suffer kasalla'

KESAKTIAN The nominalized form of *sakti*

KONSENTRASI (Ind.) Borrowed from "concentration," the more refined and arcane Buginese term is *appaseweng* ("oneness"), from *sewe* ("one")

LONTARA' (Ind. and used in many local languages) A palm-leaf manuscript. For many years Buginese lontara' have been written on paper

MA- (prefix) The stative prefix to a predicate, meaning "in a state of such-and-such'; e.g., a *ToMatoa* is a person (*to*) in a state of being (*ma*) old (*toa*); or "masiri'i!" he or she (final *i*) is in a state of being (ma) embarassed or ashamed (siri'). Its use is often parallel with the Indonesian prefix *ber-*

MABUSUNG The state of being afflicted on account of getting out of place, that is, offending the order of the cosmos, particularly by offending a person or thing whose social place is higher or more potent than one's own. See *kasalla'*

MACANNING ATI A "sweet liver"; a willing heart. A leader should not force his followers to obey using force or its threat; if people obey someone because they want to follow a superior being, rather than because the leader tries to force obedience with harsh words, force, or its threat, they are obeying with a *macanning ati*

MAKERRE' (Ind. *keramat*) Potent and dangerous

MALEBU (Ind. *bulat*) Round; spherical; complete; perfect. People strive to be malebu through being at one with themselves, and a man must have a wife to be complete

MALINRUNG To disappear or to be of the invisible realm of potent spirits, rather than merely *talle'*, tangible and impotent

MANA' Inherited objects from the ancestors, usually family possessions rather than *arajang*

MOSO The sting of a snake; the potent "bite" of authority of a noble leader

ONRO Place, whether spatial or social. For example, *naisseng onrona* means "He or she knows his place"; *Iga monro?* means "Where does he or she dwell?"

PA- (prefix to "verb" root) Prefix that usually forms a causative, as in *pakasiri'* ("to cause someone to be shamed") and *pakurrusumange'* ("to cause someone's sumange' to return"). Its use in Tae and Buginese often parallels the Indonesian prefix *memper-*

PADDISSENGENG "Knowledge," especially the spells stored in the chest. It is the nominalized form of the root *isseng*, "to recognize," which is also the "verb" in *isseng onro*, "to know one's (social) place"

PAKASIRI' To shame. See *siri'*

PAKURRUSUMANGE' A ceremony done to cause the sumange' to return to some-one who, through excessive movement or through fright, has experienced some loss of sumange'

PARINGNGERRENG Consciousness; awareness; memory

POSIK Center or navel, as in *pinposik*, the center-post of the house. See *pusat* and *pu*

PU syllable that appears in Austronesian languages in words meaning "source," "root," "owner," "base"

PUANG Lord or noble; see *pu*

PUSAKA A Javanese word, now part of Indonesian as well, meaning "royal regalia and objects inherited from the ancestors"; overlaps with both *arajang* and *mana'* in South Sulawesi languages. See *pu*

PUSAT (Ind.) Center or navel. See *posik* and *pu*

RAJA (Ind.) Ruler. See *datu*

RAPU A "clump" or "stand" of stems growing from a common root or source, said of coconut trees, banana trees, and human siblings. A kapolo is composed of numerous rapu

RIPAKASIRI' To be shamed. See *siri'*

SAKTI (Ind. and Jav.) Derived from the Sanskrit *shakti*. People throughout Indo-nesia are said to be *sakti* or to have *kesaktian* if they are fearsome but gentle, exhibiting great spiritual potency. In Indonesian, people are usually said to be *sakti* while things are said to be *keramat*; in South Sulawesi, the term *makerre'* is used for both

SALAMA' (salamat) Safe; secure; healthy; well

SANDO' (Tae; or sanro', Bug.) A curer or midwife

SIRI' Honor; shame; *amour propre*; human dignity, which distinguishes humans from animals

SUMANGE' Life-energy; potency; "soul"

TALLE' Tangible and visible, hence less potent than the intangible and invisible realm of spirits, which is *malinrung*

TAU Person. When combined with a modifier, the word is pronounced "toh," as in *ToLuwu, ToLaing*, etc.

TOLAING Stranger; non-kinsperson; other person or people. See *tau*

TOLUWU Person or people of Luwu. See *tau*

TOMASIRI' A man who guards a woman's honor, usually his sister's or first cousin's, by accompanying her. See *tau* and *siri'*

TOMATOA Respected elder(s). See *ma-* and *tau*

TORAJA A person or people from the mountainous district to the west of Luwu called Tana Toraja.

WATANG Trunk of a tree or of a human body

WAYANG KULIT (Ind. and Jav.) The shadow-puppet drama of Central Java

References

Abidin, Andi Zainal. 1971. "Notes on the Lontara' as Historical Sources." Translated by the Editors. *Indonesia* 12: 159-72.

――. 1974. "The I La Galigo Epic Cycle of South Celebes and its Diffusion." *Indonesia* 17: 161-69.

Adams, M. J. 1969. *System and Meaning in East Sumba Textile Design: A Study in Traditional Indonesian Art*. Cultural Report 16. New Haven: Yale University Southeast Asia Studies.

Andaya, Leonard Y. 1975a. *The Kingdom of Johor, 1511-1729*. Kuala Lumpur: Oxford University Press.

――. 1975b. "The Nature of Kingship in Bone." In *Pre-Colonial State Systems in Southeast Asia*, edited by Anthony Reid and Lance Castles, pp. 115-25. Monographs of the Malaysian Branch of the Royal Asiatic Society, no. 6 Kuala Lumpur: Council of the Malaysian Branch of the Royal Asiatic Society of Great Britain.

――. 1981. *The Heritage of Arung Palakka: A History of South Sulawesi (Celebes) in the Seventeenth Century*. The Hague: Martinus Nijhoff.

Anderson, Benedict. 1972. "The Idea of Power in Javanese Culture." In *Culture and Politics in Indonesia*, edited by Clare Holt, Benedict Anderson, and James Siegel, pp. 1-69. Ithaca: Cornell University Press.

――. 1983. *Imagined Communities: Reflections on the Origin and Spread of Nationalism*. London: Verso Editions and NLB.

Atkinson, Jane. 1977. "Opting for the Worst: Inappropriate Marriage among the Wana of Central Sulawesi." Paper presented to the American Anthropological Association annual meeting, Houston.

――. 1989. *The Art and Politics of Wana Shamanship*. Berkeley: University of California Press.

――. Forthcoming. "How Gender Makes a Difference in Wana Society." In *The Paradox of Gender: Essays on Power and Difference in Island Southeast Asia*, edited by Jane Atkinson and Shelly Errington.

――, and Shelly Errington, eds. Forthcoming. *The Paradox of Gender: Essays on Power and Difference in Island Southeast Asia*.

Auerbach, Erich. [1946] 1953. *Mimesis: The Representation of Reality in Western Literature*. Translated by Willard R. Trains. Princeton: Princeton University Press. (First published in Berne, Switzerland, by A. Francke Letd. Co.)

Barthes, Roland. 1972. *Mythologies*. Selected and translated from the French by Annette Lavers. 1st American edition. New York: Hill and Wang.

Barton, R. F. [1919] 1969. *Ifugao Law*. Berkeley: University of California Press. [First published by University of California Publications in American Archeology and Ethnology, vol. 15, no. 1.]

――. 1930. *The Half-Way Sun: Life among the Headhunters of the Philippines*. New York: Brewer & Warren, Inc.

Barton, R. F. 1938. *Philippine Pagans: The Autobiographies of Three Ifugaos*. London: George Routledge & Sons.

Bastin, John. 1964. "Problems of Personality in the Reinterpretation of Modern Malayan History." In *Malayan and Indonesian Studies*, edited by John Bastin and R. Roolvink, pp. 141-55. Oxford: Clarendon Press.

Bateson, Gregory. [1935] 1972a. "Culture Contact and Schizmogenesis." In *Steps to an Ecology of Mind*, pp. 61-72. New York: Ballantine Books. (First published in *Man*, article 199, vol. 25.)

———. [1949] 1972b. "Bali: The Value System of a Steady State." In *Steps to an Ecology of Mind*, pp. 107-127. New York: Ballantine Books. (First published in *Social Structure: Studies Presented to A. R. Radcliffe-Brown*, edited by Meyer Fortes [Oxford: Clarendon Press].)

Becker, A. L. 1971. "Journey through the Night: Notes on Burmese Traditional Theatre." *The Drama Review* 15 (3): 83-87.

———. 1979. "Text-Building, Epistemology and Aesthetics in Javenese Shadow Theater." In *The Imagination of Reality*, edited by A. L. Becker and Aram Yengoyan, pp. 211-43. Norwood, N.J.: Ablex Publishing Company.

Belo, Jane. [1935] 1970. "A Study of Customs Pertaining to Twins in Bali," In *Traditional Balinese Culture*, edited by Jane Belo, pp. 3-56. New York: Columbia University Press. (First published in *Tijdschrift voor Indische Taal-, Land-, en Volkenkunde* 75, no. 4: 483-549.)

Bigalke, T. 1983. "Dynamics of the Torajan Slave Trade in South Sulawesi." In *Slavery, Bondage and Dependency in Southeast Asia*, edited by Anthony Reid, pp. 341-63. St. Lucia: University of Queensland Press.

Boon, James. 1977. *The Anthropological Romance of Bali, 1597-1972: Dynamic Perspectives in Marriage and Caste, Politics and Religion*. Cambridge: Cambridge University Press.

———. 1978. "The Shift to Meaning." *American Ethnologist* 5 (2): 361-67.

———. 1979. "Balinese Temple Politics and the Religious Revitalization of Caste Ideals." In *The Imagination of Reality*, edited by A. L. Becker and Aram Yengoyan, pp. 271-90. Norwood, N.J.: Ablex Publishing Company.

———. 1982. Review of *The Flow of Life: Essays on Eastern Indonesia*, edited by James Fox. *American Anthropologist*, 84(1): 218-20.

———. 1986. "Symbols, Sylphs, and Siwa: Allegorical Machineries in the Taxonomy of Balinese Culture." In *The Anthropology of Experience*, edited by Edward Bruner and Victor Turner, pp. 239-60. Urbana: University of Illinois Press.

———. Forthcoming. "Balinese Twins Times Two: Gender, Birth-Order and 'Household' in Indonesia and Indo-Europe." In *The Paradox of Gender: Essays on Power and Difference in Island Southeast Asia*, edited by Jane Atkinson and Shelly Errington.

Bourdieu, Pierre. 1977. *Outline of a Theory of Practice*. Translated by Richard Nice. New York: Cambridge University Press.

———. 1984. *Distinction: A Social Critique of the Judgment of Taste*. Cambridge, Mass.: Harvard University Press.

Brenneis, Donald Lawrence, and Fred P. Myer, eds. 1984. *Dangerous Words: Language and Politics in the Pacific*. New York: New York University Press.

Chabot, Hendrik. Th. [1950] 1960. *Land, Status and Sex in South Celebes*. Translated by Richard Downs. New Haven: Human Relations Area Files. (Originally published as *Verwantschap, Stand en Sexe in Zuid-Celebes*. Groningen-Djakarta: J. B. Wolters.)

Crick, Bernard. 1959. *The American Science of Politics: Origins and Conditions*. Berkeley: University of California Press.

Crystal, Eric. 1977. "Tourism in Toraja." In *Hosts and Guests: The Anthropology of Tourism*, edited by Valene Smith, pp. 109-126. Philadelphia: University of Pennsylvania Press.

Cunningham, Clark. 1964. "Order in the Atoni House." *Bijdragen tot de Taal-, Land- en Volkenkunde* 120: 34-68.

Dentan, Robert Knox. 1968. *The Semai: A Nonviolent People of Malaya*. Fieldwork edition. New York: Holt, Reinhart and Winston.

Douglas, Mary. 1966. *Purity and Danger*. London: Routledge and Kegan Paul.

Dumont, Louis. 1965. "The Modern Conception of the Individual: Notes on Its Genesis and That of Concomitant Institutions." *Contributions to Indian Sociology* 8: 13-61.

———. 1970. *Homo Hierarchicus: The Caste System and Its Implications*. Translated by Mark Sainsbury, Louis Dumont, and Basia Gulati. Complete revised English edition. Chicago: University of Chicago Press.

———. 1971. "Religion, Politics and Society in the Individualistic Universe." *Proceedings of the Royal Anthropological Institute* for 1970, pp. 31-41.

Errington, Shelly. 1975a. "A Disengagement: Notes on the Structure of Narrative in Hikayat Hang Tuah." *Proceedings of the Conference on Indonesian Literature*, Madison, Wisconsin, pp. 2-13.

———. 1975b. "A Study of Genre: Form and Meaning the Malay Hikayat Hang Tuah." Ph.D. disseration, Cornell University.

———. 1979a. "The Cosmic House of the Buginese." *Asia* 1, no. 5: 8-14.

———. 1979b. "Some Comments on Style in the Meanings of the Past." *Journal of Asian Studies* 38 (2): 231-44.

———. 1983a. "Embodied Sumange' in Luwu." *Journal of Asian Studies* 42 (3): 545-70.

———. 1983b. "The Place of Regalia in Luwu." In *Centers, Symbols, and Hierarchies: Essays on the Classical States of Southeast Asia*, edited by Lorraine Gesick, pp. 194-241. New Haven: Yale University Southeast Asia Monographs no. 26.

———. 1987. "Incentuous Twins and the House Societies of Island Southeast Asia." *Cultural Anthropology* 2 (4): 403-444.

———. Forthcoming. "Power and Difference: An Overview of Island Southeast Asia." In *The Paradox of Gender: Essays on Power and Difference in Island Southeast Asia.*, edited by Jane Atkinson and Shelly Errington.

Evans-Pritchard, E. E. 1939. "Nuer Time Reckoning." *Africa* 12: 189-216.

———. 1940. "Introduction." In *African Political Systems*, edited by Meyer Fortes and E. E. Evans-Pritchard, pp. 1-23. London: published for the International African Institute by Oxford University Press.

Favret-Saada, Jeanne. 1980. *Deadly Words: Witchcraft in the Bocage*. Translated by Catherine Cullen. New York: Cambridge University Press.

Fox, James. 1971a. "Semantic Parallelism in Rotinese Ritual Language." *Bijdragen tot de Taal-, Land- en Volkenkunde* 127: 215-55.

———. 1971b. "Sister's Child as Plant: Metaphors in an Idiom of Consanguinity." In *Rethinking Kinship and Marriage*, edited by Rodney Needham, pp. 219-52. Association of Social Anthropologists Monograph no. 11. London: Tavistock Publications.

———. 1973. "On Bad Death and the Left Hand." In *Right and Left: Essays on Dual Symbolic Classification*, edited by Rodney Needham, pp. 342-68. Chicago: University of Chicago Press.

Fox, James. 1974. "Our Ancestors Spoke in Pairs: Rotinese Views of Language, Dialect, and Code." In *Explorations in the Ethnography of Speaking*, edited by R. Bauman and J. Sherzer, pp. 65-85. London: Cambridge University Press.

———. 1980a. "Introduction." In *The Flow of Life: Essays on Eastern Indonesia*, edited by James Fox, pp. 1-18. Cambridge, Mass.: Harvard University Press.

———, ed. 1980b. *The Flow of Life: Essays on Eastern Indonesia*. Cambridge, Mass.: Harvard University Press.

Freeman, J. D. 1960. "The Iban of Western Borneo." In *Social Structure in Southeast Asia*, edited by G. P. Murdock, pp. 65-87. Chicago: Quadrangle Books.

———. 1970. *Report on the Iban*. London School of Economics Monographs on Social Anthropology no. 41. New York: Humanities Press Inc.

Geertz, Clifford. 1960. *The Religion of Java*. Chicago: University of Chicago Press.

———. 1968. *Island Observed: Religion and Development in Morocco and Indonesia*. New Haven: Yale University Press.

———. 1973a. "Deep Play: Notes on the Balinese Cockfight." In *The Interpretation of Cultures*, pp. 412-53. New York: Basic Books.

———. 1973b. "Ethos, World View, and the Analysis of Sacred Symbols." In *The Interpretation of Cultures*, pp. 126-41. New York: Basic Books.

———. 1973c. "Person, Time, and Conduct in Bali." In *The Interpretation of Cultures*, pp. 360-411. New York: Basic Books.

———. 1973d. "Religion as a Cultural System." In *The Interpretation of Cultures*, pp. 87-125. New York: Basic Books.

———. 1980. *Negara: The Theater State in Nineteenth-Century Bali*. Princeton: Princeton University Press.

———. 1984. "Anti-Anti-Relativism." *American Anthropologist* 86 (2): 263-78.

Geertz, HIldred. 1961. *The Javanese Family: A Study of Kinship and Socialization*. Glencoe, Ill.: The Free Press.

Geertz, Hildred, and Clifford Geertz. 1964. "Teknonymy in Bali: Parenthood, Age-Grading, and Genealogical Amnesia." *Journal of the Royal Anthropological Institute* 94: 94-108.

———. 1975. *Kinship in Bali*. Chicago: University of Chicago Press.

Gellner, Ernest. 1965. *Thought and Change*. London: Weidenfeld and Nicholson.

———. 1983. *Nations and Nationalism*. Oxford: Basil Blackwell.

Goffman, Erving. 1959. *The Presentation of Self in Everyday Life*. Garden City, N.Y.: Doubleday.

Goldman, Irving. 1970. *Ancient Polynesian Society*. Chicago: University of Chicago Press.

Goodenough, Ward H. 1955. "A Problem in Malayo-Polynesian Social Organization." *American Anthropologist* 57: 71-83.

Gullick, J. M. 1958. *Indigenous Political Systems of Western Malaya*. London School of Economics Monographs in Social Anthropology no. 17. London: Athlone.

Hamonic, Gilbert. 1975. "Travestissement et Bisexualite chez les 'Bissu' du Pays Bugis." *Archipel* 10: 121-34.

———. 1987. *Le Langage Des Dieux: Cultes et Pourvoirs Pre-Islamiques en Pays Bugis, Celebes-Sud, Indonesie*. Paris: Edition du Centre National de la Recherche Scientifique.

Hanks, Lucien M. 1962. "Merit and Power in the Thai Social Order." *American Anthropologist* 64: 1247-61.

———. 1975. "The Thai Social Order as Entourage and Circle." In *Change and*

Persistence in Thai Society, edited by William Skinner and Thomas Kirsch, pp. 197-219. Ithaca: Cornell University Press.

————. 1977. "The Corporation and the Entourage: A Comparison of Thai and American Social Organization." In *Friends, Followers, and Factions: A Reader in Political Clientelism*, edited by Steffen W. Schmidt, et al., pp. 161-66. Berkeley: University of California Press.

Harvey, Barbara Sillars. 1974. "Tradition, Islam, and Rebellion: South Sulawesi 1950-1965." Ph.D. dissertation, Cornell University.

Heine-Geldern, Robert. 1956. *Conceptions of State and Kingship in Southeast Asia.* Southeast Asia Program Data Paper no. 18. Ithaca: Cornell Southeast Asia Program.

Hertz, Robert. [1909] 1973. "The Pre-eminence of the Right Hand: A Study in Religious Polarity." Translated by Rodney Needham. In *Right and Left: Essays on Dual Symbolic Classification*, edited by Rodney Needham, pp. 3-31. Chicago: University of Chicago Press. (Originally published as "La Pre-eminence de La Main Droite: Etude sur la Polarite Religieuse," *Revue Philosophique* 68: 553-80.)

Hirschman, Albert O. 1977. *The Passions and the Interests: The Political Arguments for Capitalism before Its Triumph.* Princeton: Princeton Univeristy Press.

Hoskins, Janet. 1984. "Spirit Worship and Feasting in Kodi, West Sumba: Paths to Riches and Renown." Ph.D. dissertation, Harvard University.

————. Forthcoming. "Doubling Deities, Descent, and Personhood: An Exploration of Kodi Gender Categories." In *The Paradox of Gender: Essays on Power and Difference in Island Southeast Asia*, edited by Jane Atkinson and Shelly Errington.

Huntsman, Judith, and Mervyn McLean, eds. 1976. *Incest Prohibitions in Polynesia and Micronesia.* Special issue of *The Journal of the Polynesian Society* 85, no. 2.

Josselin deJong, P. E. de. 1951. *Minangkabau and Negri Sembilan.* Leiden: E. Ydo.

Kaut, Charles. 1961. "Utang na Loob: A System of Contractual Obligations among Tagalogs." *Southwestern Journal of Anthropology* 17: 256-72.

Keeler, Ward. 1987. *Javanese Shadow Plays, Javanese Selves.* Princeton: Princeton University Press.

————. Forthcoming. "Speaking of Gender in Java." In *The Paradox of Gender: Essays on Power and Difference in Island Southeast Asia*, edited by Jane Atkinson and Shelly Errington.

Keesing, Roger M. 1980. "The Uses of Kinship: Kwaio, Solomon Islands." In *The Versatility of Kinship*, edited by Linda S. Cordell and Stephen Beckerman, pp. 29-44. New York: Academic Press.

Kemp, Jeremy. 1978. "Cognatic Descent and the Generation of Social Stratification in Southeast Asia." *Bijdragen tot de Taal-, Land-, en Volkenkunde* 134 (1): 63-83.

Kern, Rudolf A. 1939. *Catalogus van de Boegineesche, tot den I La Galigo-cyclus behoorende handschriften der Leidsche Universiteits-bibliotheek. alsmede van die in andere Europeesche bibliotheken.* Leiden University Library.

Keyes, Charles, ed. 1983. "Peasant Strategies in Asian Societies: Moral and Rational Economic Approaches—A Symposium." *Journal of Asian Studies* 42 (4): 753-868.

Kiefer, Thomas M. 1972. *The Tausug: Violence and Law in a Philippine Moslem Society.* New York: Holt, Reinhart and Winston.

King, Victor T. 1978. "The Maloh." In *Essays on Borneo Societies*, edited by Victor T.

316 References

King, pp. 193-214. Hull Monographs on Southeast Asia no. 7. Oxford: Published for the University of Hull by Oxford University Press.

Kuhn, Thomas. 1970. *The Structure of Scientific Revolutions*. 2nd ed. Chicago: University of Chicago Press.

Kuipers, Joel. 1986. "Talking about Troubles—Gender Differences in Weyewa Speech Use." *American Ethnologist* 13 (3): 448-62.

Lande, Carl H. 1977. "Networks and Groups in Southeast Asia: Some Observations on the Group Theory of Politics." In *Friends, Followers, and Factions: A Reader in Political Clientelism*, edited by Steffen W. Schmidt, et al., pp. 75-99. Berkeley: University of California Press.

Lévi-Strauss, Claude. 1962. *The Savage Mind (La Pensee Sauvage)*. London: Weidenfeld and Nicholson.

———. 1963. "Do Dual Organizations Exist?" In *Structural Anthropology*, translated by Claire Jacobson and Brooke Grundfest Schoepf, pp. 132-63. New York: Basic Books.

———. 1969. *The Elementary Structures of Kinship*. Translated by H. H. Bell, J. R. von Sturmer, and R. Needham. Boston: Beacon Press.

———. 1982. *The Way of the Masks*. Translated by Sylvia Modelski. Seattle: University of Washington Press.

———. 1984. *Paroles Données*. Paris: Plon.

McKinnon, Susan Mary. 1983. "Hierarchy, Alliance, and Exchange in the Tanimbar Islands." Ph.D. dissertation, University of Chicago.

Maybury-Lewis, David. 1965. "Durkheim on Relationship Terminology." *Journal for the Scientific Study of Religion* 4: 253-60.

Mead, Margaret. 1942. "Balinese Character." In *Balinese Character: A Photographic Analysis*, by Margaret Mead and Gregory Bateson. New York: New York Academy of Sciences Publications.

Millar, Susan. 1983. "Gender in Bugis Society." *American Ethnologist* 10 (3): 477-93.

Moertono, Soemarsaid. 1968. *State and Statecraft in Old Java: A Study of the Later Mataram Period, 16th to 19th Century*. Modern Indonesia Project Monograph Series. Ithaca: Cornell University Southeast Asia Program.

Morgan, Lewis Henry. 1871. *Systems of Consanguinity and Affinity of the Human Family*. Smithsonian Contributions to Knowledge no. 17. Washington, D.C.: Smithsonian Institution.

Murdock, G. P. 1949. *Social Structure*, New York: Macmillan.

———. 1960. "Cognatic Forms of Social Organizations." In *Social Structure in Southeast Asia*, edited by G.P. Murdock. Chicago: Quadrangle Books.

Needham, Rodney, ed. 1973. *Right and Left: Essays on Dual Symbolic Classification*. Chicago: University of Chicago Press.

Noorduyn, J. 1965. "Origins of South Celebes Historical Writing." In *An Introduction to Indonesian Historiography*, edited by Soejatmoko, et al., pp. 137-55. Ithaca: Cornell University Press.

Peirce, C. S. 1940. *The Philosophy of Peirce: Selected Writings*. Edited by Justus Buchler. London: Routledge and Kegan Paul.

Pelly, Usman. 1977 "Symbolic Aspects of the Bugis ship and Shipbuilding." *Journal of the Steward Anthropological Society* 8, no. 2: 87-106.

Pelras, Christian. 1971. "Hierarchie et Pouvoir Traditionnels en pays Wadjo' (Celebes)." *Archipel* 1: 169-91 and 2: 197-223.

———. 1974. " 'Herbe Divine': Le Riz Chez les Bugis (Indonesie)." *Etudes Rurales* 53-56: 357-74.

———. 1975a. "Introduction a la litterature bugis." *Archiel* 10: 239-67.

———. 1975b. "La Maison Bugis: Formes, Structures et Fonctions." *Asie Sud-Est et Monde Insulien* 6 (2): 61-99.

———. 1983. "Le Pantheon des Ancien Bugis Vu a Travers les Textes de La Galigo." *Archipel* 29: 107-135.

Popkin, Samuel L. 1979. *The Rational Peasant: The Political Economy of Rural Society in Vietnam*. Berkeley: University of California Press.

Provencher, Ronald. 1979. "Orality as a Pattern of Symbolism in Malay Psychiatry." In *The Imagination of Reality: Essays on Southeast Asian Coherence Systems*, edited by A. L. Becker and Aram Yengoyan, pp. 43-53. Norwood, N.J.: Ablex Publishing Company.

Rabibhadana, Akin. 1969. *The Organization of Thai Society in the Early Bangkok Period, 1782-1873*. Data Paper no. 74. Ithaca: Cornell University Southeast Asia Program Data Papers.

Reid, Anthony, ed. 1983. *Slavery, Bondage, and Dependency in Southeast Asia*. With the assistance of Jennifer Brewster. St. Lucia and New York: University of Queensland Press.

Robinson, Kathryn M. 1986. *The Stepchildren of Progress: The Political Economy of Development in an Indonesian Mining Town*. Albany: State University of New York Press.

Rosaldo, Michelle Z. 1980. *Knowledge and Passion*. New York: Cambridge University Press.

Rosaldo, Renato. 1968. "Ilongot Kin Terms: A Bilateral System of Northern Luzon, Philippines" In *Proceedings of the VIIIth International Congress of Anthropological and Ethnological Sciences*, vol. 2, pp. 81-84. Tokyo: Science Council of Japan.

———. 1980. *Ilongot Headhunting, 1883-1974: A Study in Society and History*. Stanford: Stanford University Press.

Sahlins, Marshall. 1983. "Other Times, Other Customs: The Anthropology of History." *American Anthropologist* 85 (3): 517-44.

Schlegel, Stuart. 1970. *Tiruray Justice: Traditional Tiruray Law and Morality*. Berkeley: University of California Press.

Schneider, David. 1964. "The Nature of Kinship." *Man* 64: 180-81.

———. 1965. "Kinship and Biology." In *Aspects of the Analysis of Family Structure*, edited by A. J. Coale et al., pp. 83-101. Princeton: Princeton University Press.

———. 1968. *American Kinship: A Cultural Account* Englewood Cliffs, N.J.: Prentice-Hall. (2d ed. with a new chapter, Chicago: University of Chicago Press, 1980.)

———. 1969. "Kinship, Nationality and Religion." In *Forms of Symbolic Action*, edited by Victor Turner, pp. 116-25. Proceedings of the 1969 Annual Meeting of the American Ethnological Society.

———. 1972. "What Is Kinship All About?" In *Kinship Studies in the Morgan Centennial Year*, edited by P. Reining, pp. 32-63. Washington, D.C.: Anthropological Society of Washington.

Schrieke, B. 1957. *Indonesian Sociological Studies: Selected Writings of B. Schrieke, Part Two: Ruler and Realm in Early Java*. The Hague: W. Van Hoeve Ltd.

Scott, James C. 1976. *The Moral Economy of the Peasant: Rebellion and Subsistence in Southeast Asia*. New Haven: Yale University Press.

———. 1977. "Patron-Client Politics and Political Change in Southeast Asia." In *Friends, Followers, and Factions: A Reader in Political Clientelism*, edited by

Steffen W. Schmidt, et al., pp. 123-146. Berkeley: University of California Press.

Shore, Bradd. 1976. "Incest Prohibitions and the Logic of Power in Samoa." In *Incest Prohibitions in Polynesia and Micronesia*, edited by Judith Huntsman and Mervyn McLean. Special issue of the *Journal of the Polynesian Society* 85 (2): 275-96.

——. 1981. "Sexuality and Gender in Samoa: Conceptions and Missed Conceptions." In *Sexual Meanings: The Cultural Construction of Gender and Sexuality*, edited by Sherry Ortner and Harriet Whitehead, pp. 192-215. New York: Cambridge University Press.

——. 1982. *Sala'ilua: A Samoan Mystery*. New York: Columbia University Press.

——. N.D. "Polynesian World View: a Synthesis." Manuscript.

Siegel, James T. 1969. *The Rope of God*. Berkeley: University of California Press.

——. 1979. *Shadow and Sound: The Historical Thought of Sumatran People*. Chicago: University of Chicago Press.

Sopher, David. 1965. *The Sea Nomads: A Study Based on the Literature of the Maritime Boat People of Southeast Asia*. Singapore: Lim Bian Han, Government Printer.

Spiro, Melford E. 1968. "Factionalism and Politics in Village Burma." In *Local-Level Politics*, edited by Marc Swartz, pp. 401-421. Chicago: Aldine.

Strathern, Marilyn, ed. 1987. *Dealing with Inequality: Analysing Gender Relations in Melanesia and Beyond*. Cambridge: Cambridge University Press.

Sutherland, Heather. 1983. "Slavery and the Slave Trade in South Sulawesi, 1660s-1800s." In *Slavery, Bondage and Dependency in Southeast Asia*, edited by Anthony Reid with the assistance of Jennifer Brewster, pp. 263-85. St. Lucia and New York: University of Queensland Press.

Tambiah, S. J. 1976. *World Conqueror and World Renouncer*. Cambridge: Cambridge University Press.

Traube, Elizabeth. 1977. "Ritual Exchange among the Mambai of East Timor: Gifts of Life and Death." Ph.D. dissertation, Harvard University.

——. 1979. "Incest and Mythology." *Berkshire Review* 14: 37-53.

——. 1986. *Cosmology and Social Life*. Chicago: University of Chicago Press.

Trilling, Lionel. 1972. *Sincerity and Authenticity*. Cambridge, Mass.: Harvard University Press.

Valeri, Valerio. 1980. "Notes on the Meaning of Marriage Prestations among the Huaulu of Seram." In *The Flow of Life: Essays on Eastern Indonesia*, edited by James Fox, pp. 178-92. Cambridge, Mass.: Harvard University Press.

——. 1985. *Kingship and Sacrifice: Ritual and Society in Ancient Hawaii*. Translated by Paula Wissing. Chicago: University of Chicago Press.

Volkman, Toby. 1984. "Great Performances: Toraja Cultural Identity in the 1970's." *American Ethnologist* 11(1): 152-69.

——. 1985. *Feasts of Honor: Ritual and Change in the Toraja Highlands*. Urbana: University of Illinois Press.

Watt, Ian. 1957. *The Rise of the Novel*. Berkeley: University of California Press.

Wolters, O. W. 1970. *The Fall of Srivijaya in Malay History*. Ithaca: Cornell University Press.

——. 1979. "Khmer 'Hinduism' in the Seventh Century." In *Early Southeast Asia: Essays in Archeology, History, and Historical Geography*, edited by R. B. Smith and W. Watson, pp. 427-42. New York: Oxford University Press.

——. 1982. *History, Culture, and Region in Southeast Asian Perspectives*. Singapore: Institute of Southeast Asian Studies.

Index

Names of societies in Southeast Asia and names of authors are included only if more than passing reference is made to them in the text.

siri' (*cont.*)
    peers, 169–74; ethos of, contrasted with
    legal ethos, 158–60; first mentioned, 17;
    intentionality irrelevant, 163–65; motive of
    Kahar Rebellion, 21; as purity of motive,
    21; sayings about, 146, 152, 224; "spend-
    ing," 158. *See also* contest; legal-bureau-
    cratic structure; *ripakasiri'*
slaves (*ata*), 96, 98–99, 99n
sound. *See* ritual substances
space: placement of objects in, 63; safe and
    dangerous, 56, 250–53, 278–80; shape of in
    Indic States, 65; shape of in "level" socie-
    ties, 290–94; spatial organization of con-
    sciousness in island Southeast Asia, 13. *See
    also* centers; directions
standing, contrasted with status, 189–90, 217
status. *See* place; standing; white blood
stillness. *See* movement; unity
substances, ritual. *See* ritual substances
Sulawesi, South, 14; Kahar Muzakar Rebel-
    lion, 16–17; economy, ethnic groups, lan-
    guages, and religions of, 15–20
sumange': accumulated in specific places, 66;
    ceremony to gather (*pakkurrusumange'*),
    53; concentrated at navel, 51; losing and
    gaining, 51–57; mutual absorption of, 58–
    59; and ranking, 57; and person, 122
Sutherland, H., 98, 98n

Tae, first mentioned, 15. *See also* Sulawesi,
    South
talle', defined, 46
Tanimbar, 267–69
teknonymy, 193–94. *See also* naming, names,
    and titles

territory, meaning of in Indic States, 108–17
"time": as oscillation, 276–78; the shape of
    in genealogies, 227–31; structural, 203–6;
    within a *hikayat*, 11
titles. *See* naming, names, and titles
ToLaing: defined, 56; as peers and guests, 71,
    114. *See also kapolo, ripakasiri'*
ToMalebbi', 96, 98
ToMatoa: defined, 118; as owner of house,
    67–69. *See also kapolo*
Toraja, first mentioned, 15. *See also* Sulawesi,
    South
ToSama, 96, 98
Traube, E., 91, 267, 268
tribute, 116
twins, 232–33. *See also* siblings

unity. *See* centers, dualism and dualities; in-
    ner and outer; meditation; *pu*; twins
utilitarianism, 5–9, 298–99

Valeri, V., 264

water. *See* ritual substances
wayang kulit (shadow puppet theater), 46,
    275
wealth, relation to influence, 109–10
whispers. *See* ritual substances
white blood, mentioned and defined, 19, 23,
    51
Wolters, O. W., 28, 105, 108, 216
women: control household finances, 288;
    distracted by child-care, 156; groupings of
    at ceremonies, 159; like heads a precious
    hazard, 288–89; as rungs in status-ladder,
    183, 260, 288–89. *See also* gender

Andi Pangerang Opu Tosinilele (Opu Pa'Bicara)

Opu Senga

Opu Senga at leisure. The high-noble front porch is used as an informal space for negotiations, chatting, weaving small baskets, crocheting, de-lousing hair on a lazy afternoon, and the like

The house includes a front space for guests. On ceremonial occasions when many guests come, the area is extended by building a temporary platform for guests at the front of the house

A new mother has her first bath outside the house, seven days after the birth of her child, assisted by a *sando'*

In comparison to the spectacular structures in other parts of Indonesia, Luwu houses look plain and utilitarian, suggesting nothing more than the convenience of a roof over one's head

Nenek Baso' sits on the secondary structure's front stairway

Andi Muchlis Pangerang (Andi Anthon)